P9-CRD-279

THE MODERN LIBRARY
OF THE WORLD'S BEST BOOKS

For
my daughter Carmela
With Love
Your dad
Joseph Bellet

THE LIFE OF JESUS

The publishers will be pleased to send, upon request, an illustrated folder setting forth the purpose and scope of THE MODERN LIBRARY, *and listing each volume in the series. Every reader of books will find titles he has been looking for, handsomely printed, in unabridged editions, and at an unusually low price.*

THE
LIFE
OF
JESUS

BY

ERNEST RENAN

INTRODUCTION BY

JOHN HAYNES HOLMES

MODERN LIBRARY · NEW YORK

Random House IS THE PUBLISHER OF

THE MODERN LIBRARY

BENNETT A. CERF · DONALD S. KLOPFER · ROBERT K. HAAS

Manufactured in the United States of America

By H. Wolff

TO THE PURE SOUL OF
MY SISTER HENRIETTE
Who Died at Byblus on the 24th of September, 1861

———

Dost thou recall, from the bosom of God where thou reposest, those long days at Ghazir, in which, alone with thee, I wrote these pages, inspired by the places we had visited together? Silent at my side, thou didst read and copy each sheet as soon as I had written it, whilst the sea, the villages, the ravines, and the mountains, were spread at our feet. When the overwhelming light had given place to the innumerable army of stars, thy shrewd and subtle questions, thy discreet doubts, led me back to the sublime object of our common thoughts. One day thou didst tell me that thou wouldst love this book—first, because it had been composed with thee, and also because it pleased thee. Though at times thou didst fear for it the narrow judgments of the frivolous, yet wert thou ever persuaded that all truly religious souls would ultimately take pleasure in it. In the midst of these sweet meditations, the Angel of Death struck us both with his wing: the sleep of fever seized us at the same time— I awoke alone! . . . Thou sleepest now in the land of Adonis, near the holy Byblus and the sacred stream where the women of the ancient mysteries came to mingle their tears. Reveal to me, O good genius, to me whom thou lovedst, those truths which conquer death, deprive it of terror, and make it almost beloved.

PREFACE

In presenting an English version of the celebrated work of M. Renan, the translator is aware of the difficulty of adequately rendering a work so admirable for its style and beauty of composition. It is not an easy task to reproduce the terseness and eloquence which characterize the original. Whatever its success in these respects may be, no pains have been spared to give the author's meaning. The translation has been revised by highly competent persons; but although great care has been taken in this respect, it is possible that a few errors may still have escaped notice.

The great problem of the present age is to preserve the religious spirit, whilst getting rid of the superstitions and absurdities that deform it, and which are alike opposed to science and common sense. The works of Mr. F. W. Newman and of Bishop Colenso, and the "Essays and Reviews," are rendering great service in this direction. The work of M. Renan will contribute to this object; and, if its utility may be measured by the storm which it has created amongst the *obscurantists* in France, and the heartiness with which they have condemned it, its merits in this respect must be very great. It needs only to be added, that whilst warmly sympathizing with the earnest spirit which pervades the book, the translator by no means wishes to be identified with all the opinions therein expressed.

December 8, 1863.

CONTENTS

CONTENTS.

CONTENTS.

CONTENTS

CHAPTER XIX

Instinctive, Tropistic and Pleasure-and-Pain Actions 283

CHAPTER XX

Organization Inheritance 327

CHAPTER XXI

The Inheritance of Acquired Characters 303

CHAPTER XXII

The Phenomena of Regeneration ....

CHAPTER XXIII

The Mode of Inheritance ....

CHAPTER XXIV

Protective Coloration in Nature ....

CHAPTER XXV

Death of Individuals ....

CHAPTER XXVI

Rejuvenation and Natural Death ....

CHAPTER XXVII

The Problem of Longevity ....

CHAPTER XXVIII

Recent Changes in the World of Science 384

INTRODUCTION

"ERNEST RENAN'S *Vie de Jésus*," said the late Joseph Henry Allen, famous scholar and church historian, "is the one great literary monument of a century of New Testament criticism." This tribute to the immortal Frenchman's masterpiece was paid in 1895, just thirty-two years after its publication in 1863. Now that another thirty-two years have passed away, the tribute is seen to be inadequate. Renan's *Life of Jesus* is something more than a great monument of New Testament criticism. As we look back upon the nineteenth century as a definite period of history, we see that this book was one of the world-shaking books of a world-shaking epoch. It ranks with Darwin's *Origin of Species* and Marx's *Das Kapital* as a work which changed forever the currents of the world's thought and life.

In its own day, the *Life of Jesus* was a sensation of the first order. It brought down upon its author's devoted head such a whirlwind of rage and calumny as few men have ever endured, and fewer still survived. "Jew sprung from the blood of Judas Iscariot" was by no means the worst of the insults he received. The loss of his professorship in the Collège de France was only one of the penalties he suffered. "At the same time, and by the same token," says Renan's most recent biographer, Dr. Lewis Freeman Mott, "he became one of the most celebrated men of the world.

Henceforth not a word he uttered was spoken un-
heard."

From the first hour of its publication, the *Life of
Jesus* sold like a Waverly Novel. Its success was "immediate and immense," unprecedented for a scholarly
work on a religious subject. Like Macauley's *History
of England,* it lay on every library table, and was the
subject of universal discussion. New editions of 5,000
copies each were exhausted in eight or ten days. Two
months after the book's appearance, Renan writes his
friend, Bersot, that "in this last period, the sale, far
from slowing up, even goes faster." By November,
five months after its initial publication, eleven editions, 60,000 copies, had been exhausted. Already
there were German, Italian and Dutch translations of
the book, and an English translation was on the way.
A new and still wider circulation was opened up in
March, 1864, when Renan published, under the simple
title, *Jesus,* a cheap edition for the poor—"the true
disciples of Jesus," as he called them. Offered at one
franc 25 centimes the copy, this edition enjoyed an
enormous sale. In 1876, the work was thoroughly
revised, and incorporated in the author's *Origines du
Christianisme* as Volume I of a series which was completed in 1881 by Volume VII on the reign of Marcus
Aurelius.

Since this date, innumerable editions of the *Life*
have appeared in France and other countries. The
furor, of course, has long since died away. The book
is today only one of a great host of biographies of the
Nazarene, many of which have superceded it in scholarship, as others have surpassed it in radical opinion.
But two full generations after its original appearance,
Renan's volume is read more widely than any of its

successors, and stands as the one sure standard by what these others are judged. Whatever the errors and inadequacies revealed by later extensions of knowledge, and "whatever the various schools may think of it," says Dr. Mott, "it is still a living book." The passing of time, that is today, has only served to establish Renan's *Life of Jesus* as the classic work upon the subject.

In recalling this amazing chapter of literary history, it may be well to consider some of the influences which were at work in the making of such a record.

(1)—Conspicuous is the fact that Renan's book was the first *biography* of Jesus, in the modern historical and literary sense of that word. From the time of Paul, down through all the centuries of Christian history, Jesus was regarded as the Messiah, the Son of God, the Divine Redeemer—that is, as a being apart, not in history but above history. All the writing about him, therefore, was theological, not scientific. The Christ was exalted that men might praise him, not studied and interpreted that men might know him. He was a revelation, like the Bible, to be accepted on penalty of outlawry in this world and damnation in the next. Not till Strauss wrote his stupendous *Leben Jesus,* was the spell upon the Nazarene broken. But the German studied the documents rather than the person, and presented not a man but a myth.

To Renan was left the opportunity and the task of writing about Jesus as a figure of history, and thus of producing a biography in the form and spirit of Voltaire's biography of Charles XII, or Southey's biography of Nelson. Renan set to work, in other words, to study and describe the Nazarene in exactly the same way in which he would have set to work to study and describe any other famous leader of humanity. He treated Jesus as other biographers had treated other great and famous men. Jesus, to him, was not divine, but human; he was not a being without time and place, but a Jew, born in Palestine, in the reign of Augustus. The Gospels were not scriptures, but documents, historical sources; "If the Gospels are like other books," wrote Renan, in the Preface to the thirteenth edition of the *Life,* "I am right in treating them in the same manner as the student of Greek, Arabian, or Hindu lore treats its legendary documents which he studies. Criticism knows no infallible texts; its first principle is to admit the possibility of error in the text which it examines." In the same way, Renan discarded every last vestige of the miraculous; "miracles," he wrote, "are things which never happen," and therefore, things which Jesus never did.

The result of such an attitude, now ordinary enough, but in the middle of the last century extraordinary beyond words to describe, was a life of Jesus which was human, natural, strictly critical, throughout. In this sense, it was something strange, unprecedented. When this book came out with its simple, yet devastating statement, "Jésus naquit á Nazareth, petite ville de Galilée. . . . Il sortit des rangs du peuple. Son père, Joseph, et sa mère, Marie, etaient des gens de mediocre condition" (Jesus was born at Nazareth, a small town of Galilee. . . . He sprang from the ranks of the people. His father, Joseph, and his mother, Mary, were of humble station), the world simply gasped in astonishment and horror. In two sentences there disappeared the lovely Bethlehem story, the dogma of the Virgin Birth, the whole theology of the incarnation and the atonement. And the remainder of the book kept pace with its beginning! Here was the story of a Jewish young man who lived, preached, suffered, made mistakes as well as performed brave deeds, said foolish as well as wise things, did no wonders beyond the wonders of the valiant soul, and at last died, was buried, and remained in the grave. This was a story never written before. It discovered a new phenomenon—the Jesus of History! And it shook the world like an earthquake.

(2)—It is this fact which explains the sensation created by Renan's book. But the sensation is only part of the story. What stirred the public with excitement and the church with anger, stirred as well the amazement and admiration of students. For here was a work of profound learning, a production worthy of one of the half-dozen greatest scholars of the nineteenth century.

It is not always remembered how supreme a figure was Renan among the scholars of his time—among the scholars, indeed, of all time. Master of a brilliant style, his achievements in the field of literature have tended to obscure, if not to hide altogether, his imperishable achievements in the field of learning. The great historian, Mommsen, saw the point when he declared, with some heat, that Renan was a true scholar, "in spite of the beauty of his style"! Certainly, Renan's life was a triumphant record of scholarly labors.

Abandoning the priesthood at the age of twenty-two, he pursued his studies at the University, the School of Oriental Languages, and the Collège de France, and in four years attracted marked attention by winning prizes contributing extensively to period·· icals, and publishing his first book, *Avenir de la Science*

(*The Future of Science*). In 1849, he was sent by the Ministry of Education, and under instructions from the Academy of Inscriptions and Belles-Lettres, on a mission to investigate the libraries of Italy and report on their manuscript collections, particularly the Syrian and Arabic. On his return in 1851, he received an appointment as *attaché* in the department of manuscripts at the Bibliothéque Nationale, began writing for the *Revue des deu Mondes,* took his degree of Docteur-és-lettres, and was elected to the Council of the Societé Asiatique. The next few years were crowded with exhaustive studies, and voluminous writings in magazines both lay and learned. In 1856 he was elected to the Academy of Inscription and Belles-Lettres. In 1859 appeared his *Essais de morale et de critique,* and a translation of the Book of Job. In 1860, after publishing a translation of the Song of Songs, he accepted a mission to excavate Phoenician remains in Syria, under the inspiration of which he wrote the first draft of his *Life of Jesus* at Ghazir. On his return to Paris he was appointed professor of Hebrew, Chaldean and Syrian languages in the Collège de France by imperial decree dated January 11, 1862, an honor which he was destined to lose the following year when his *Life of Jesus* was published. After a second oriental trip in 1864-65, there followed years of exhausting work, first, on his *Origins of Christianity,* and secondly, on his *History of the People of Israel,* two of the supreme productions of nineteenth century scholarship. Master of many languages, ancient and modern, erudite in the lore of ages and places, expert in the technique of investigation and interpretation, imbued with the ideal as well as the methods of modern science, a man simple, sincere, courageous, "a saint, even if judged by the teachings of the Galilean Lake," Renan ranks, alike in spirit and in achievement, with men like Darwin and Pasteur as one of the immortals.

It was learning of this profound and extensive type which Renan brought to the writing of his *Life of Jesus*. More than any other man who has ever written upon the subject, with the possible exception of Nathaniel Schmidt, he was master of all the varied and complex material of language, history, tradition, *locale*, which went into the making of his work. The *Life* has often been condemned as imaginative. So it is— a masterpiece of the creative imagination! "If in writing the life of Jesus," said Renan, in his famous Preface, "one should confine himself to setting forth those matters which are certain, he must limit himself to a few lines . . . the texts give no certainty . . . we must strive to divine what they conceal, without being ever quite certain of having found it." But such imagination is the imagination of the archeologist who constructs a city from broken stones, of the paleontologist who conceives an extinct animal from scattered bones and teeth. Whatever conjecture entered into Renan's work was backed by a wealth of learning controlled by a fearless and faithful mind. It is this which gives to the *Life of Jesus* an authority which has endured unshaken to this day.

(3)—But not yet have we explained the popularity of the book. This rested neither upon the sensational character of its conclusions, nor upon the authoritative nature of its learning, but upon its rare artistic qualities. We have spoken of Renan's literary style. This was unparalleled in the France of the nineteenth century for beauty, as the style of Voltaire was unparalleled in the France of the eighteenth century for clarity. The French are nearly always good writers; their greatest authors are the master stylists of the world; and of these Ernest Renan stands among the first. Put every other virtue aside, and his *Life of Jesus* is immortal simply as a piece of literature. If its conclusions were discredited, and its scholarship outgrown, we should still read it, as we read the *Republic* of Plato, for its perfection as a work of art. The loveliness of the Palestinian countryside, seen with Renan's own eyes and painted in upon the canvas with a brush of extraordinary skill—the color and bustle of the scene in Israel where Jesus lived—the ineffable charm of the brave young man who called his disciples and proclaimed the Kingdom—the pathos and passion of his experiences among his people—the unforgettable scenes of the last journey and the last week—these, as Renan presents them, are an eternal part of the literature of the world. They are among the things which man will not let die. The *Life,* be it said, does not rest alone upon such pages, as its main contribution is certainly not to be found in them. But these are what caught and held the multitude of readers who seized the volume when it came from the press, and it is what makes it now, when its pioneering work is done, a supremely "living book." Today, as not yesterday, we can get our information elsewhere, and get it more fully and accurately. But nowhere else can we read the immortal story in such magic phrases as those with which it has been clothed by Renan. Like a painting of Raphael, it must endure forever in the wonder and affection of mankind.

Sainte-Beuve, leading critic of his day, recognized and acclaimed this fact. Pointing out that the *Life,* addressed to the public, had reached its address, he said, "To be historian and story teller from this new point of view, (Renan) had to begin by being above all a diviner, a poet drawing inspiration from the spirit of times and places, and painter able to read the lines of the horizon, the least vestiges left on the slopes of the hills, and skilled in evoking the genius of the re-gion and the landscape. He has thus succeeded in pro-ducing a work of art even more than a history, and this presupposes on the part of the author a union, till now almost unique, of superior qualities, reflective, delicate, and brilliant."

It is this combination of qualities which makes Renan's *Life of Jesus* the most famous and enduring work upon the subject ever written. If we were to estimate its supreme contribution to mankind, it would be its effect in clearing the way for a scientific and historical approach to the study of the Nazarene and of Christianity. Strauss undoubtedly broke the ground here, but Renan as undoubtedly drove the plough and planted the first seed. "You won for us," said Sainte-Beuve, "the right of discussion in this matter, hitherto forbidden." Since the publication of the *Life,* the study of New Testament times has been on a new basis, of fact instead of fiction, of truth instead of tradition. This whole field, hitherto set apart as a field of magic and miracle, has been reclaimed to his-tory and the normal life of man. The multiplying biographies of Jesus, never so numerous nor so free as in our time, are as so many memorials to the mas-ter. And his own work, as this latest edition so elo-quently certifies, still reigns among them!

JOHN HAYNES HOLMES.

NEW YORK, May, 1927

AUTHOR'S INTRODUCTION,

In Which the Sources of This History Are Principally Treated

A HISTORY of the "Origin of Christianity" ought to embrace all the obscure, and, if one might so speak, subterranean periods which extend from the first beginnings of this religion up to the moment when its existence became a public fact, notorious and evident to the eyes of all. Such a history would consist of four books. The first, which I now present to the public, treats of the particular fact which has served as the starting-point of the new religion, and is entirely filled by the sublime person of the Founder. The second would treat of the apostles and their immediate disciples, or rather, of the revolutions which religious thought underwent in the first two generations of Christianity. I would close this about the year 100, at the time when the last friends of Jesus were dead, and when all the books of the New Testament were fixed almost in the forms in which we now read them. The third would exhibit the state of Christianity under the Antonines. We should see it develop itself slowly, and sustain an almost permanent war against the empire, which had just reached the highest degree of administrative perfection, and, governed by philosophers, combated in the new-born sect a secret and theocratic society which obstinately denied and incessantly undermined it. This book would cover the entire period of the second century. Lastly, the fourth book would show the decisive progress which Christianity made from the time of the Syrian emperors. We should see the learned system of the Antonines crumble, the decadence of the ancient civilization become irrevocable, Christianity profit from its ruin, Syria conquer the whole West, and Jesus, in company with the gods and the deified sages of Asia, take possession of a society for which philosophy and a purely civil government no longer sufficed. It was then that the religious ideas of the races grouped around the Mediterranean became profoundly modified; that the Eastern religions everywhere took precedence; that the Christian Church, having become very numerous, totally forgot its dreams of a millennium, broke its last ties with Judaism, and entered completely into the Greek and Roman world. The contests and the literary labors of the third century, which were carried on without concealment, would be described only in their general features. I would relate still more briefly the persecutions at the commencement of the fourth century, the last effort of the empire to return to its former principles, which denied to religious association any place in the State. Lastly, I would only foreshadow the change of policy which, under Constantine, reversed the position, and made of the most free and spontaneous religious movement an official worship, subject to the State, and persecutor in its turn.

I know not whether I shall have sufficient life and strength to complete a plan so vast. I shall be satisfied if, after having written the *Life of Jesus,* I am permitted to relate, as I understand it, the history of the apostles, the state of the Christian conscience during the weeks which followed the death of Jesus, the formation of the cycle of legends concerning the resurrection, the first acts of the Church of Jerusalem, the life of Saint Paul, the crisis of the time of Nero, the appearance of the Apocalypse, the fall of Jerusalem, the foundation of the Hebrew-Christian sects of Batanea, the compilation of the Gospels, and the rise of the great schools of Asia Minor originated by John. Every- thing pales by the side of that marvellous first century. By a peculiarity rare in history, we see much better what passed in the Christian world from the year 50 to the year 75, than from the year 100 to the year 150.

The plan followed in this history has prevented the introduction into the text of long critical dissertations upon controverted points. A continuous system of notes enables the reader to verify from the authorities all the statements of the text. These notes are strictly limited to quotations from the primary sources; that is to say, the original passages upon which each assertion or conjecture rests. I know that for persons little ac- customed to studies of this kind many other explana- tions would have been necessary. But it is not my practice to do over again what has been already done well. To cite only books written in French, those who will consult the following excellent writings[1] will there find explained a number of points upon which I have been obliged to be very brief:

Etudes Critiques sur l'Evangile de saint Matthieu, par M. Al- bert Réville, pasteur de l'église Wallonne de Rotterdam.[2]

Histoire de la Théologie Chrétienne au Siècle Apostolique, par M. Reuss, professeur à la Faculté de Théologie et au Séminaire Protestant de Strasbourg.[3]

[1] While this work was in the press, a book has appeared which I do not hesitate to add to this list, although I have not read it with the attention it deserves—*Les Evangiles,* par M. Gustave d'Eichthal. Première Partie: *Examen Critique et Comparatif des Trois Premiers Evangiles.* Paris, Hachette, 1863.

[2] Leyde, Noothoven van Goor, 1862. Paris, Cherbuliez. A work crowned by the Society of The Hague for the defence of the Christian religion.

[3] Strasbourg, Treuttel and Wurtz. 2nd edition. 1860. Paris, Cherbuliez.

*Des Doctrines Religieuses des Juifs pendant les Deux Siècles
Antérieurs à l'Ere Chrétienne,* par M. Michel Nicolas, professeur
à la Faculté de Théologie Protestante de Montauban.[1]

Vie de Jésus, par le Dr. Strauss; traduite par M. Littré, Mem-
bre de l'Institut.[2]

Revue de Théologie et de Philosophie Chrétienne, publiée sous
la direction de M. Colani, de 1850 à 1857.—*Nouvelle Revue de
Théologie,* faisant suite à la precédénte depuis 1858.[3]

The criticism of the details of the Gospel texts especially, has been done by Strauss in a manner which
leaves little to be desired. Although Strauss may be
mistaken in his theory of the compilation of the Gospels;[4] and although his book has, in my opinion, the
fault of taking up the theological ground too much,
and the historical ground too little,[5] it will be necessary, in order to understand the motives which have
guided me amidst a crowd of minutiæ, to study the
always judicious, though sometimes rather subtle argument, of the book, so well translated by my learned
friend, M. Littré.

I do not believe I have neglected any source of information as to ancient evidences. Without speaking
of a crowd of other scattered data, there remain, respecting Jesus, and the time in which he lived, five
great collections of writings — 1st, The Gospels, and

[1] Paris, Michel Lévy frères, 1860.

[2] Paris, Ladrange. 2nd edition, 1856.

[3] Strasbourg, Treuttel and Wurtz. Paris, Cherbuliez.

[4] The great results obtained on this point have only been acquired since the first edition of Strauss's work. The learned
critic has, besides, done justice to them with much candor in his
after editions.

[5] It is scarcely necessary to repeat that not a word in Strauss's
work justifies the strange and absurd calumny by which it has
been attempted to bring into disrepute with superficial persons,
a work so agreeable, accurate, thoughtful, and conscientious,
though spoiled in its general parts by an exclusive system. Not
only has Strauss never denied the existence of Jesus, but each page
of his book implies this existence. The truth is, Strauss supposes
the individual character of Jesus less distinct for us than it perhaps
is in reality.

the writings of the New Testament in general; 2d, The compositions called the "Apocrypha of the Old Testament;" 3d, The works of Philo; 4th, Those of Josephus; 5th, The Talmud. The writings of Philo have the priceless advantage of showing us the thoughts which, in the time of Jesus, fermented in minds occupied with great religious questions. Philo lived, it is true, in quite a different province of Judaism to Jesus, but, like him, he was very free from the littlenesses which reigned at Jerusalem; Philo is truly the elder brother of Jesus. He was sixty-two years old when the Prophet of Nazareth was at the height of his activity, and he survived him at least ten years. What a pity that the chances of life did not conduct him into Galilee! What would he not have taught us!

Josephus, writing specially for pagans, is not so candid. His short notices of Jesus, of John the Baptist, of Judas the Gaulonite, are dry and colorless. We feel that he seeks to present these movements, so profoundly Jewish in character and spirit, under a form which would be intelligible to Greeks and Romans. I believe the passage respecting Jesus[1] to be authentic. It is perfectly in the style of Josephus, and if this historian has made mention of Jesus, it is thus that he must have spoken of him. We feel only that a Christian hand has retouched the passage, has added a few words— without which it would almost have been blasphemous[2] —has perhaps retrenched or modified some expressions.[3] It must be recollected that the literary fortune of Josephus was made by the Christians, who adopted his writings as essential documents of their sacred his-

---

[1] *Ant.*, XVIII. iii. 3.   [2] "If it be lawful to call him a man."
[3] In place of χριστὸς οὗτος ἦν, he certainly had these χριστὸς οὗτος ἐλέγετο.—Cf. *Ant.*, XX. ix. 1.

tory. They made, probably in the second century, an edition corrected according to Christian ideas.[1] At all events, that which constitutes the immense interest of Josephus on the subject which occupies us, is the clear light which he throws upon the period. Thanks to him, Herod, Herodias, Antipas, Philip, Annas, Caiaphas, and Pilate are personages whom we can touch with the finger, and whom we see living before us with a striking reality.

The Apocryphal books of the Old Testament, especially the Jewish part of the Sibylline verses, and the Book of Enoch, together with the Book of Daniel, which is also really an Apocrypha, have a primary importance in the history of the development of the Messianic theories, and for the understanding of the conceptions of Jesus respecting the kingdom of God. The Book of Enoch especially, which was much read at the time of Jesus,[2] gives us the key to the expression "Son of Man," and to the ideas attached to it. The ages of these different books, thanks to the labors of Alexander, Ewald, Dillmann, and Reuss, is now beyond doubt. Every one is agreed in placing the compilation of the most important of them in the second and first centuries before Jesus Christ. The date of the Book of Daniel is still more certain. The character of the two languages in which it is written, the use of Greek words, the clear, precise, dated announcement of events, which reach even to the time of Antiochus Epiphanes, the incorrect descriptions of Ancient Babylonia, there

---

[1] Eusebius (*Hist. Eccl.*, i. 11. and *Demonstr. Evang.*, iii. 5) cites the passage respecting Jesus as we now read it in Josephus. Origen (*Contra Celsus,* i. 47 ; ii. 13) and Eusebius (*Hist. Eccl.*, ii. 23) cite another Christian interpolation, which is not found in any of the manuscripts of Josephus which have come down to us.

[2] Iude Epist. 14.

given, the general tone of the book, which in no respect recalls the writings of the captivity, but, on the contrary, responds, by a crowd of analogies, to the beliefs, the manners, the turn of imagination of the time of the Seleucidæ; the Apocalyptic form of the visions, the place of the book in the Hebrew canon, out of the series of the prophets, the omission of Daniel in the panegyrics of Chapter xlix. of Ecclesiasticus, in which his position is all but indicated, and many other proofs which have been deduced a hundred times, do not permit of a doubt that the Book of Daniel was but the fruit of the great excitement produced among the Jews by the persecution of Antiochus. It is not in the old prophetical literature that we must class this book, but rather at the head of Apocalyptic literature, as the first model of a kind of composition, after which come the various Sibylline poems, the Book of Enoch, the Apocalypse of John, the Ascension of Isaiah, and the Fourth Book of Esdras.

In the history of the origin of Christianity, the Talmud has hitherto been too much neglected. I think with M. Geiger, that the true notion of the circumstances which surrounded the development of Jesus must be sought in this strange compilation, in which so much precious information is mixed with the most insignificant scholasticism. The Christian and the Jewish theology having in the main followed two parallel ways, the history of the one cannot well be understood without the history of the other. Innumerable important details in the Gospels find, moreover, their commentary in the Talmud. The vast Latin collections of Lightfoot, Schœttgen, Buxtorf, and Otho contained already a mass of information on this point. I have imposed on myself the task of verifying in the original all the citations which I have admitted, without a single exception. The assistance which has been given me for this part of my task by a learned Israelite, M. Neubauer, well versed in Talmudic literature, has enabled me to go further, and to clear up the most intricate parts of my subject by new researches. The distinction of epochs is here most important, the compilation of the Talmud extending from the year 200 to about the year 500. We have brought to it as much discernment as is possible in the actual state of these studies. Dates so recent will excite some fears among persons habituated to accord value to a document only for the period in which it was written. But such scruples would here be out of place. The teaching of the Jews from the Asmonean epoch down to the second century was principally oral. We must not judge of this state of intelligence by the habits of an age of much writing. The Vedas, and the ancient Arabian poems, have been preserved for ages from memory, and yet these compositions present a very distinct and delicate form. In the Talmud, on the contrary, the form has no value. Let us add that before the *Mishnah* of Judas the Saint, which has caused all others to be forgotten, there were attempts at compilation, the commencement of which is probably much earlier than is commonly supposed. The style of the Talmud is that of loose notes; the collectors did no more probably than classify under certain titles the enormous mass of writings which had been accumulating in the different schools for generations.

It remains for us to speak of the documents which, presenting themselves as biographies of the Founder of Christianity, must naturally hold the first place in a *Life of Jesus*. A complete treatise upon the compila-

tion of the Gospels would be a work of itself. Thanks
to the excellent researches of which this question has
been the object during thirty years, a problem which
was formerly judged insurmountable has obtained a
solution which, though it leaves room for many uncertainties, fully suffices for the necessities of history.
We shall have occasion to return to this in our Second
Book, the composition of the Gospels having been one
of the most important facts for the future of Christianity in the second half of the first century.   We will
touch here only a single aspect of the subject, that
which is indispensable to the completeness of our narrative.   Leaving aside all which belongs to the por-
traiture of the apostolic times, we will inquire only in
what degree the data furnished by the Gospels may be
employed in a history formed according to rational
principles.[1]

That the Gospels are in part legendary, is evident,
since they are full of miracles and of the supernatural;
but legends have not all the same value.   No one
doubts the principal features of the life of Francis
d'Assisi, although we meet the supernatural at every
step.   No one, on the other hand, accords credit to the
Life of Apollonius of Tyana, because it was written
long after the time of the hero, and purely as a
romance.   At what time, by what hands, under what
circumstances, have the Gospels been compiled?   This
is the primary question upon which depends the opinion to be formed of their credibility.

Each of the four Gospels bears at its head the name

---

[1]Persons who wish to read more ample explanations, may consult, in addition to the work of M. Réville, previously cited, the
writings of Reuss and Scherer in the *Revue de Théologie,* vol. x.,
xi., xv.; new series, ii., iii., iv.; and that of Nicolas in the *Revue
Germanique,* Sept. and Dec., 1862; April and June, 1863.

of a personage, known either in the apostolic history, or in the Gospel history itself. These four personages are not strictly given us as the authors. The formulæ "according to Matthew," "according to Mark," "according to Luke," "according to John," do not imply that, in the most ancient opinion, these recitals were written from beginning to end by Matthew, Mark, Luke, and John,[1] they merely signify that these were the traditions proceeding from each of these apostles, and claiming their authority. It is clear that, if these titles are exact, the Gospels, without ceasing to be in part legendary, are of great value, since they enable us to go back to the half century which followed the death of Jesus, and in two instances, even to the eye-witnesses of his actions.

Firstly, as to Luke, doubt is scarcely possible. The Gospel of Luke is a regular composition, founded on anterior documents.[2] It is the work of a man who selects, prunes, and combines. The author of this Gospel is certainly the same as that of the Acts of the Apostles.[3] Now, the author of the Acts is a companion of St. Paul,[4] a title which applies to Luke exactly.[5] I know that more than one objection may be raised against this reasoning; but one thing, at least, is beyond doubt, namely, that the author of the third Gospel and of the Acts was a man of the second apostolic generation, and that is sufficient for our object. The date of this Gospel can moreover be determined

---

[1] In the same manner we say, "The Gospel according to the Hebrews," "The Gospel according to the Egyptians."

[2] Luke i. 1-4.   [3] Acts i. 1. Compare Luke i. 1-4.

[4] From xvi. 10, the author represents himself as eye-witness.

[5] 2 Tim. iv. 11; Philemon 24; Col. iv. 14. The name of *Lucas* (contraction of *Lucanus*) being very rare, we need not fear one of those homonyms which cause so many perplexities in questions of criticism relative to the New Testament.

with much precision by considerations drawn from the
book itself. The twenty-first chapter of Luke, insep-
arable from the rest of the work, was certainly written
after the siege of Jerusalem, and but a short time after.[1]
We are here, then, upon solid ground; for we are concerned with a work written entirely by the same hand,
and of the most perfect unity.

The Gospels of Matthew and Mark have not nearly
the same stamp of individuality. They are impersonal
compositions, in which the author totally disappears.
A proper name written at the head of works of this
kind does not amount to much. But if the Gospel of
Luke is dated, those of Matthew and Mark are dated
also; for it is certain that the third Gospel is posterior
to the first two and exhibits the character of a much
more advanced compilation. We have, besides, on this
point, an excellent testimony from a writer of the first
half of the second century—namely, Papias, bishop of
Hierapolis, a grave man, a man of traditions, who was
all his life seeking to collect whatever could be known
of the person of Jesus.[2] After having declared that on
such matters he preferred oral tradition to books,
Papias mentions two writings on the acts and words of
Christ: First, a writing of Mark, the interpreter of the
apostle Peter, written briefly, incomplete, and not arranged in chronological order, including narratives and
discourses, ($\lambda\epsilon\chi\theta\acute{\epsilon}\nu\tau\alpha\ \mathring{\eta}\ \pi\rho\alpha\chi\theta\acute{\epsilon}\nu\tau\alpha$,) composed from
the information and recollections of the apostle Peter;
second, a collection of sentences ($\lambda\acute{o}\gamma\iota\alpha$) written in

[1] Verses 9, 20, 24, 28, 32. Comp. xxii. 36.
[2] In Eusebius, *Hist. Eccl.*, iii. 39. No doubt whatever can be
raised as to the authenticity of this passage. Eusebius, in fact, far
from exaggerating the authority of Papias, is embarrassed at his
simple ingenuousness, at his gross millenarianism, and solves the
difficulty by treating him as a man of little mind. Comp. Irenæus.
Adv. Hær., iii. 1.

Hebrew[1] by Matthew, "and which each one has translated as he could." It is certain that these two descriptions answer pretty well to the general physiognomy
of the two books now called "Gospel according to Matthew," "Gospel according to Mark"—the first characterized by its long discourses; the second, above all, by
anecdote—much more exact than the first upon small
facts, brief even to dryness, containing few discourses,
and indifferently composed. That these two works,
such as we now read them, are absolutely similar to
those read by Papias, cannot be sustained: Firstly, because the writings of Matthew were to Papias solely
discourses in Hebrew, of which there were in circulation very varying translations; and, secondly, because
the writings of Mark and Matthew were to him profoundly distinct, written without any knowledge of
each other, and, as it seems, in different languages.
Now, in the present state of the texts, the "Gospel according to Matthew" and the "Gospel according to
Mark" present parallel parts so long and so perfectly
identical, that it must be supposed, either that the final
compiler of the first had the second under his eyes, or
vice versa, or that both copied from the same prototype.
That which appears the most likely, is, that we have not
the entirely original compilations of either Matthew or
Mark; but that our first two Gospels are versions in
which the attempt is made to fill up the gaps of the one
text by the other. Every one wished, in fact, to possess a complete copy. He who had in his copy only
discourses, wished to have narratives, and *vice versa.*
It is thus that "the Gospel according to Matthew" is
found to have included almost all the anecdotes of
Mark, and that "the Gospel according to Mark" now

[1] That is to say, in the Semitic dialect.

contains numerous features which come from the *Logia* of Matthew. Every one, besides, drew largely on the Gospel tradition then current. This tradition was so far from having been exhausted by the Gospels, that the Acts of the Apostles and the most ancient Fathers quote many words of Jesus which appear authentic, and are not found in the Gospels we possess.

It matters little for our present object to push this delicate analysis further, and to endeavor to reconstruct in some manner, on the one hand, the original *Logia* of Matthew, and, on the other, the primitive narrative such as it left the pen of Mark. The *Logia* are doubtless represented by the great discourses of Jesus which fill a considerable part of the first Gospel. These discourses form, in fact, when detached from the rest, a sufficiently complete whole. As to the narratives of the first and second Gospels, they seem to have for basis a common document, of which the text reappears sometimes in the one and sometimes in the other, and of which the second Gospel, such as we read it to-day, is but a slightly modified reproduction. In other words, the scheme of the *Life of Jesus,* in the synoptics, rests upon two original documents—first, the discourses of Jesus collected by Matthew; second, the collection of anecdotes and personal reminiscences which Mark wrote from the recollections of Peter. We may say that we have these two documents still, mixed with accounts from another source, in the two first Gospels, which bear, not without reason, the name of the "Gospel *according* to Matthew" and of the "Gospel *according* to Mark."

What is indubitable, in any case, is, that very early the discourses of Jesus were written in the Aramean language, and very early also his remarkable actions were

recorded. These were not texts defined and fixed dog-
matically. Besides the Gospels which have come to us,
there were a number of others professing to represent
the tradition of eye-witnesses.[1] Little importance
was attached to these writings, and the preservers, such
as Papias, greatly preferred oral tradition.[2] As men
still believed that the world was nearly at an end, they
cared little to compose books for the future; it was
sufficient merely to preserve in their hearts a lively
image of him whom they hoped soon to see again in the
clouds. Hence the little authority which the Gospel
texts enjoyed during one hundred and fifty years.
There was no scruple in inserting additions, in vari-
ously combining them, and in completing some by
others. The poor man who has but one book wishes
that it may contain all that is dear to his heart. These
little books were lent, each one transcribed in the mar-
gin of his copy the words, and the parables he found
elsewhere, which touched him.[3] The most beautiful
thing in the world has thus proceeded from an obscure
and purely popular elaboration. No compilation was
of absolute value. Justin, who often appeals to that
which he calls "The Memoirs of the Apostles,"[4] had
under his notice Gospel documents in a state very different from that in which we possess them. At all
events, he never cares to quote them textually. The
Gospel quotations in the pseudo-Clementinian writings,

[1] Luke i. 1, 2; Origen, *Hom. in Luc.* 1 init.; St. Jerome, *Comment.
in Matt.*, prol.
[2] Papias, in Eusebius, *H. E.*, iii. 39. Comp. Irenæus, *Adv. Hær.*,
III. ii. and iii.
[3] It is thus that the beautiful narrative in John viii. 1-11 has always floated, without finding a fixed place in the framework of
the received Gospels.
[4] Τὰ ἀπομνημονεύματα τῶν ἀποστόλων, ἃ καλεῖται
εὐαγγέλια. Justin, *Apol.* i, 33, 66, 67; *Dial. cum Tryph.*, 10,
100-107.

of Ebionite origin, present the same character. The spirit was everything; the letter was nothing. It was when tradition became weakened, in the second half of the second century, that the texts bearing the names of the apostles took a decisive authority and obtained the force of law.

Who does not see the value of documents thus composed of the tender remembrances, and simple narratives, of the first two Christian generations, still full of the strong impression which the illustrious Founder had produced, and which seemed long to survive him? Let us add, that the Gospels in question seem to proceed from that branch of the Christian family which stood nearest to Jesus. The last work of compilation, at least of the text which bears the name of Matthew, appears to have been done in one of the countries situated at the northeast of Palestine, such as Gaulonitis, Auranitis, Batanea, where many Christians took refuge at the time of the Roman war, where were found relatives of Jesus[1] even in the second century, and where the first Galilean tendency was longer preserved than in other parts.

So far we have only spoken of the three Gospels named the synoptics. There remains a fourth, that which bears the name of John. Concerning this one, doubts have a much better foundation, and the question is further from solution. Papias—who was connected with the school of John, and who, if not one of his auditors, as Irenæus thinks, associated with his immediate disciples, among others, Aristion, and the one called *Presbyteros Joannes*—says not a word of a *Life of Jesus,* written by John, although he had zealously collected the oral narratives of both Aristion and *Pres-*

[1] Julius Africanus, in Eusebius, *Hist. Eccl.,* i. 7.

byteros Joannes. If any such mention had been found in his work, Eusebius, who points out everything therein that can contribute to the literary history of the apostolic age, would doubtless have mentioned it.

The intrinsic difficulties drawn from the perusal of the fourth Gospel itself are not less strong. How is it that, side by side with narration so precise, and so evidently that of an eye-witness, we find discourses so totally different from those of Matthew? How is it that, connected with a general plan of the life of Jesus, which appears much more satisfactory and exact than that of the synoptics, these singular passages occur in which we are sensible of a dogmatic interest peculiar to the compiler, of ideas foreign to Jesus, and sometimes of indications which place us on our guard against the good faith of the narrator? Lastly, how is it that, united with views the most pure, the most just, the most truly evangelical, we find these blemishes which we would fain regard as the interpolations of an ardent sectarian? Is it indeed John, son of Zebedee, brother of James (of whom there is not a single mention made in the fourth Gospel), who is able to write in Greek these lessons of abstract metaphysics to which neither the synoptics nor the Talmud offer any analogy? All this is of great importance; and for myself, I dare not be sure that the fourth Gospel has been entirely written by the pen of a Galilean fisherman. But that, as a whole, this Gospel may have originated toward the end of the first century, from the great school of Asia Minor, which was connected with John, that it represents to us a version of the life of the Master, worthy of high esteem, and often to be preferred, is demonstrated, in a manner which leaves us nothing to be desired, both by exterior evidences and by examination of the document itself.

And, firstly, no one doubts that, toward the year 150, the fourth Gospel did exist, and was attributed to John. Explicit texts from St. Justin,[1] from Athenagorus,[2] from Tatian,[3] from Theophilus of Antioch,[4] from Irenæus,[5] show that thenceforth this Gospel mixed in every controversy, and served as corner-stone for the development of the faith. Irenæus is explicit; now, Irenæus came from the school of John, and between him and the apostle there was only Polycarp. The part played by this Gospel in Gnosticism, and especially in the system of Valentinus,[6] in Montanism,[7] and in the quarrel of the Quartodecimans,[8] is not less decisive. The school of John was the most influential one during the second century; and it is only by regarding the origin of the Gospel as coincident with the rise of the school, that the existence of the latter can be understood at all. Let us add that the first epistle attributed to St. John is certainly by the same author as the fourth Gospel;[9] now, this epistle is recognized as from John by Polycarp,[10] Papias,[11] and Irenæus.[12]

But it is, above all, the perusal of the work itself which is calculated to give this impression. The au-

---

[1] *Apol.*, i. 32, 61 ; *Dial. cum Tryph.*, 88.

[2] *Legatio pro Christ*, 10.

[3] *Adv. Græc.*, 5, 7 ; Cf. Eusebius, *H. E.*, iv. 29 ; Theodoret, *Hæretic. Fabul.*, i. 20.   [4] *Ad Autolycum*, ii. 22.

[5] *Adv. Hær.*, II. xxii. 5, III. I. Cf. Eus., *H. E.*, v. 8.

[6] Irenæus, *Adv. Hær.*, I. iii., 6 ; III., xi. 7 ; St. Hippolytus, *Philosophumena* VI., ii., 29, and following.

[7] Irenæus, *Adv. Hær.*, III. xi, 9.   [8] Eusebius, *Hist. Eccl.*, v. 24.

[9] 1 John, i, 3, 5. The two writings present the most complete identity of style, the same peculiarities, the same favorite expressions.

[10] *Epist. ad Philipp.*, 7.

[11] In Eusebius, *Hist. Eccl.*, III. 39.

[12] *Adv. Hær.*, III. xvi. 5, 8 ; Cf. Eusebius, *Hist. Eccl.*, v. 8.

thor always speaks as an eye-witness; he wishes to pass for the apostle John. If, then, this work is not really by the apostle, we must admit a fraud of which the author convicts himself. Now, although the ideas of the time respecting literary honesty differed essentially from ours, there is no example in the apostolic world of a falsehood of this kind. Besides, not only does the author wish to pass for the apostle John, but we see clearly that he writes in the interest of this apostle. On each page he betrays the desire to fortify his authority, to show that he has been the favorite of Jesus;[1] that in all the solemn circumstances (at the Lord's supper, at Calvary, at the tomb) he held the first place. His relations on the whole fraternal, although not excluding a certain rivalry with Peter;[2] his hatred, on the contrary, of Judas,[3] a hatred probably anterior to the betrayal, seems to pierce through here and there. We are tempted to believe that John, in his old age, having read the Gospel narratives, on the one hand, remarked their various inaccuracies,[4] on the other, was hurt at seeing that there was not accorded to him a sufficiently high place in the history of Christ; that then he commenced to dictate a number of things which he knew better than the rest, with the intention of showing that in many instances, in which only Peter was spoken of, he had figured with him and even before him.[5] Already during the life of Jesus, these trifling

[1] John xiii. 23, xix. 26, xx. 2, xxi. 7, 20.
[2] John xviii. 15-16, xx. 2-6, xxi. 15-19. Comp. i, 35, 40, 41.
[3] John vi. 65, xii. 6, xiii. 21, and following.
[4] The manner in which Aristion and *Presbyteros Joannes* expressed themselves on the Gospel of Mark before Papias (Eusebius, *H. E.*, iii. 39) implies, in effect, a friendly criticism, or, more properly, a sort of excuse, indicating that John's disciples had better information on the same subject.
[5] Compare John xviii. 15, and following, with Matthew xxvi. 58; John xx. 2 to 6, with Mark xvi. 7. See also John xiii. 24, 25.

sentiments of jealousy had been manifested between the sons of Zebedee and the other disciples. After the death of James, his brother, John remained sole inheritor of the intimate remembrances of which these two apostles, by the common consent, were the depositaries. Hence his perpetual desire to recall that he is the last surviving eye-witness,[1] and the pleasure which he takes in relating circumstances which he alone could know. Hence, too, so many minute details which seem like the commentaries of an annotator—"it was the sixth hour;" "it was night;" "the servant's name was Malchus;" "they had made a fire of coals, for it was cold;" "the coat was without seam." Hence, lastly, the disorder of the compilation, the irregularity of the narration, the disjointedness of the first chapters, all so many inexplicable features on the supposition that this Gospel was but a theological thesis, without historic value, and which, on the contrary, are perfectly intelligible, if, in conformity with tradition, we see in them the remembrances of an old man, sometimes of remarkable freshness, sometimes having undergone strange modifications.

A primary distinction, indeed, ought to be made in the Gospel of John. On the one side, this Gospel presents us with a rough draft of the life of Jesus, which differs considerably from that of the synoptics. On the other, it puts into the mouth of Jesus discourses of which the tone, the style, the treatment, and the doctrines have nothing in common with the *Logia* given us by the synoptics. In this second respect, the difference is such that we must make choice in a decisive manner. If Jesus spoke as Matthew represents, he

---

[1] Chap. i. 14, xix. 35, xxi, 24, and following. Compare the First Epistle of St. John, chap. i. 3, 5.

could not have spoken as John relates. Between these
two authorities no critic has ever hesitated, or can ever
hesitate. Far removed from the simple, disinterested,
impersonal tone of the synoptics, the Gospel of John
shows incessantly the pre-occupation of the apologist
—the mental reservation of the sectarian, the desire to
prove a thesis, and to convince adversaries.[1] It was
not by pretentious tirades, heavy, badly written, and
appealing little to the moral sense, that Jesus founded
his divine work. If even Papias had not taught us
that Matthew wrote the sayings of Jesus in their original tongue, the natural, ineffable truth, the charm beyond comparison of the discourses in the synoptics,
their profoundly Hebraistic idiom, the analogies which
they present with the sayings of the Jewish doctors of
the period, their perfect harmony with the natural phenomena of Galilee—all these characteristics, compared
with the obscure Gnosticism, with the distorted metaphysics, which fill the discourses of John, would speak
loudly enough. This by no means implies that there
are not in the discourses of John some admirable
gleams, some traits which truly come from Jesus.[2]
But the mystic tone of these discourses does not corre-
spond at all to the character of the eloquence of Jesus,
such as we picture it according to the synoptics. A
new spirit has breathed; Gnosticism has already commenced; the Galilean era of the kingdom of God is
finished; the hope of the near advent of Christ is more

---

[1]See, for example, chaps. ix. and xi. Notice especially, the effect which such passages as John xix. 35, xx. 31, xxi. 20-23, 24, 25,
produce, when we recall the absence of all comments which distinguishes the synoptics.

[2]For example, chap. iv. 1, and following, xv. 12, and following.
Many words remembered by John are found in the synoptics
(chap. xii. 16, xv. 20).

distant; we enter on the barrenness of metaphysics, into the darkness of abstract dogma. The spirit of Jesus is not there, and, if the son of Zebedee has truly traced these pages, he had certainly, in writing them, quite forgotten the Lake of Gennesareth, and the charming discourses which he had heard upon its shores.

One circumstance, moreover, which strongly proves that the discourses given us by the fourth Gospel are not historical, but compositions intended to cover with the authority of Jesus certain doctrines dear to the compiler, is their perfect harmony with the intellectual state of Asia Minor at the time when they were written. Asia Minor was then the theatre of a strange movement of syncretical philosophy; all the germs of Gnosticism existed there already. John appears to have drunk deeply from these strange springs. It may be that, after the crisis of the year 68 (the date of the Apocalypse) and of the year 70 (the destruction of Jerusalem), the old apostle, with an ardent and plastic spirit, disabused of the belief in a near appearance of the Son of Man in the clouds, may have inclined toward the ideas that he found around him, of which several agreed sufficiently well with certain Christian doctrines. In attributing these new ideas to Jesus, he only followed a very natural tendency. Our remembrances are transformed with our circumstances; the ideal of a person that we have known changes as we change.[1] Considering Jesus as the incarnation of truth, John could not fail to attribute to him that which he had come to consider as the truth.

[1] It was thus that Napoleon became a liberal in the remembrances of his companions in exile, when these, after their return, found themselves thrown in the midst of the political society of the time.

If we must speak candidly, we will add that probably John himself had little share in this; that the
change was made around him rather than by him. One
is sometimes tempted to believe that precious notes,
coming from the apostle, have been employed by his
disciples in a very different sense from the primitive
Gospel spirit. In fact, certain portions of the fourth
Gospel have been added later; such is the entire
twenty-first chapter,[1] in which the author seems to
wish to render homage to the apostle Peter after his
death, and to reply to the objections which would be
drawn, or already had been drawn, from the death of
John himself, (ver. 21-23.) Many other places bear
the trace of erasures and corrections.[2] It is impossible
at this distance to understand these singular problems,
and without doubt many surprises would be in store
for us, if we were permitted to penetrate the secrets of
that mysterious school of Ephesus, which, more than
once, appears to have delighted in obscure paths. But
there is a decisive test. Every one who sets himself to
write the Life of Jesus without any predetermined theory as to the relative value of the Gospels, letting himself be guided solely by the sentiment of the subject,
will be led in numerous instances to prefer the narration of John to that of the synoptics. The last months
of the life of Jesus especially are explained by John
alone; a number of the features of the passion, unintelligible in the synoptics,[3] resume both probability and
possibility in the narrative of the fourth Gospel. On
the contrary, I dare defy any one to compose a Life of

[1] The verses, chap. xx. 30, 31, evidently form the original conclusion.

[2] Chap. vi. 2, 22, vii. 22.

[3] For example, that which concerns the announcement of the
betrayal by Judas.

Jesus with any meaning, from the discourses which John attributes to him. This manner of incessantly preaching and demonstrating himself, this perpetual argumentation, this stage-effect devoid of simplicity, these long arguments after each miracle, these stiff and awkward discourses, the tone of which is so often false and unequal,[1] would not be tolerated by a man of taste compared with the delightful sentences of the synoptics. There are here evidently artificial portions,[2] which represent to us the sermons of Jesus, as the dialogues of Plato render us the conversations of Socrates. They are, so to speak, the variations of a musician improvising on a given theme. The theme is not without some authenticity; but in the execution, the imagination of the artist has given itself full scope. We are sensible of the factitious mode of procedure, of rhetoric, of gloss.[3] Let us add that the vocabulary of Jesus cannot be recognized in the portions of which we speak. The expression, "kingdom of God," which was so familiar to the Master,[4] occurs there but once.[5] On the other hand, the style of the discourses attributed to Jesus by the fourth Gospel, presents the most complete analogy with that of the Epistles of St. John; we see that in writing the discourses, the author followed not his recollections, but rather the somewhat monotonous movement of his own thought. Quite a new mystical language is introduced, a language of which the synoptics had not the least idea ("world," "truth," "life," "light," "darkness," etc.). If Jesus had ever

[1] See, for example, chaps. ii. 25, iii. 32, 33, and the long disputes of chapters vii., viii., and ix.

[2] We feel often that the author seeks pretexts for introducing certain discourses (chaps. iii., v., viii., xiii., and following).

[3] For example, chap. xvii.

[4] Besides the synoptics, the Acts, the Epistles of St. Paul, and the Apocalypse, confirm it.   [5] John iii. 3, 5.

spoken in this style, which has nothing of Hebrew, nothing Jewish, nothing Talmudic in it, how, if I may thus express myself, is it that but a single one of his hearers should have so well kept the secret?

Literary history offers, besides, another example, which presents the greatest analogy with the historic phenomenon we have just described, and serves to explain it. Socrates, who, like Jesus, never wrote, is known to us by two of his disciples, Xenophon and Plato; the first corresponding to the synoptics in his clear, transparent, impersonal compilation; the second recalling the author of the fourth Gospel, by his vigorous individuality. In order to describe the Socratic teaching, should we follow the "dialogues" of Plato, or the "discourses" of Xenophon? Doubt, in this respect, is not possible; every one chooses the "discourses," and not the "dialogues." Does Plato, however, teach us nothing about Socrates? Would it be good criticism, in writing the biography of the latter, to neglect the "dialogues"? Who would venture to maintain this? The analogy, moreover, is not complete, and the difference is in favor of the fourth Gospel. The author of this Gospel is, in fact, the better biographer; as if Plato, who, whilst attributing to his master fictitious discourses, had known important matters about his life, which Xenophon ignored entirely.

Without pronouncing upon the material question as to what hand has written the fourth Gospel, and whilst inclined to believe that the discourses, at least, are not from the son of Zebedee, we admit still, that it is indeed "the Gospel according to John," in the same sense that the first and second Gospels are the Gospels "according to Matthew," and "according to Mark." The historical sketch of the fourth Gospel is the Life of

Jesus, such as it was known in the school of John; it is the recital which Aristion and *Presbyteros Joannes* made to Papias, without telling him that it was written, or rather attaching no importance to this point. I must add, that, in my opinion, this school was better acquainted with the exterior circumstances of the life of the Founder than the group whose remembrances constituted the synoptics. It had, especially upon the sojourns of Jesus at Jerusalem, data which the others did not possess. The disciples of this school treated Mark as an indifferent biographer, and devised a system to explain his omissions.[1] Certain passages of Luke, where there is, as it were, an echo of the traditions of John,[2] prove also that these traditions were not entirely unknown to the rest of the Christian family.

These explanations will suffice, I think, to show, in the course of my narrative, the motives which have determined me to give the preference to this or that of the four guides whom we have for the *Life of Jesus.* On the whole, I admit as authentic the four canonical Gospels. All, in my opinion, date from the first century, and the authors are, generally speaking, those to whom they are attributed; but their historic value is very diverse. Matthew evidently merits an unlimited confidence as to the discourses; they are the *Logia,* the identical notes taken from a clear and lively remem-

[1] Papias, *loc. cit.*
[2] For example, the pardon of the adulteress; the knowledge which Luke has of the family of Bethany; his type of the character of Martha responding to the διηχόνει of John (chap. xii. 2): the incident of the woman who wiped the feet of Jesus with her hair; an obscure notion of the travels of Jesus to Jerusalem; the idea that in his passion he was seen by three witnesses; the opinion of the author that some disciples were present at the crucifixion; the knowledge which he has of the part played by Annas in aiding Caiaphas; the appearance of the angel in the agony (comp. John xii. 28, 29).

brance of the teachings of Jesus. A kind of splendor
at once mild and terrible—a divine strength, if we may
so speak, emphasizes these words, detaches them from
the context, and renders them easily distinguishable.
The person who imposes upon himself the task of making a continuous narrative from the gospel history,
possesses, in this respect, an excellent touchstone. The
real words of Jesus disclose themselves; as soon as we
touch them in this chaos of traditions of varied authenticity, we feel them vibrate; they betray themselves
spontaneously, and shine out of the narrative with unequaled brilliancy.

The narrative portions grouped in the first Gospel
around this primitive nucleus have not the same authority. There are many not well defined legends
which have proceeded from the zeal of the second
Christian generation.[1] The Gospel of Mark is much
firmer, more precise, containing fewer subsequent additions. He is the one of the three synoptics who has
remained the most primitive, the most original, the
one to whom the fewest after-elements have been
added. In Mark, the facts are related with a clearness
for which we seek in vain amongst the other evangelists. He likes to report certain words of Jesus in
Syro-Chaldean.[2] He is full of minute observations,
coming doubtless from an eye-witness. There is nothing to prevent our agreeing with Papias in regarding
this eye-witness, who evidently had followed Jesus,
who had loved him and observed him very closely, and
who had preserved a lively image of him, as the apostle
Peter himself.

[1] Chaps. i., ii., especially. See also chap. xxvii. 3, 19, 51, 53. 60,
xxviii. 2, and following, in comparing Mark.
[2] Chap. v. 41, vii. 34, xv. 34. Matthew only presents this peculiarity once (chap. xxvii. 46).

As to the work of Luke, its historical value is sensibly weaker. It is a document which comes to us second-hand. The narrative is more mature. The words of Jesus are there, more deliberate, more sententious. Some sentences are distorted and exaggerated.[1] Writing outside of Palestine, and certainly after the siege of Jerusalem,[2] the author indicates the places with less exactitude than the other two synoptics; he has an erroneous idea of the temple, which he represents as an oratory where people went to pay their devotions.[3] He subdues some details in order to make the different narratives agree;[4] he softens the passages which had become embarrassing on account of a more exalted idea of the divinity of Christ;[5] he exaggerates the marvellous;[6] commits errors in chronology;[7] omits Hebraistic comments;[8] quotes no word of Jesus in this language, and gives to all the localities their Greek names. We feel we have to do with a compiler—with a man who has not himself seen the witnesses, but who labors at the texts and wrests their sense to make them agree. Luke had probably under his eyes the biographical collection of Mark, and the *Logia* of Matthew. But he treats them with much freedom; sometimes he fuses two anecdotes or two parables in one;[9] sometimes he divides one in order to make two.[10] He

[1] Chap. xiv. 26. The rules of the apostolate (chap. x.) have there a peculiar character of exaltation.
[2] Chap. xix. 41, 43, 44, xxi. 9, 20, xxiii. 29.
[3] Chap. ii. 37, xviii. 10, and following, xxiv. 53.
[4] For example, chap. iv. 16.
[5] Chap. iii. 23. He omits Matt. xxiv. 36.
[6] Chap. iv. 14, xxii. 43, 44.
[7] For example, in that which concerns Quirinius, Lysanias, Theudas.
[8] Compare Luke i. 31 with Matt. i. 21.
[9] For example, chap. xix. 12-27.
[10] Thus, of the repast at Bethany he gives two narratives, chap vii. 36-48, and x. 38-42.

interprets the documents according to his own idea; he
has not the absolute impassibility of Matthew and
Mark. We might affirm certain things of his individual tastes and tendencies; he is a very exact devotee;[1] he insists that Jesus had performed all the Jewish
rites,[2] he is a warm Ebionite and democrat, that is to
say, much opposed to property, and persuaded that the
triumph of the poor is approaching;[3] he likes especially all the anecdotes showing prominently the conversion of sinners—the exaltation of the humble;[4] he
often modifies the ancient traditions in order to give
them this meaning;[5] he admits into his first pages the
legends about the infancy of Jesus, related with the
long amplifications, the spiritual songs, and the con-
ventional proceedings which form the essential features
of the Apocryphal Gospels. Finally, he has in the
narrative of the last hours of Jesus some circumstances
full of tender feeling, and certain words of Jesus of
delightful beauty,[6] which are not found in more authentic accounts, and in which we detect the presence
of legend. Luke probably borrowed them from a
more recent collection, in which the principal aim was
to excite sentiments of piety.

A great reserve was naturally enforced in presence

---

[1] Chap. xxiii. 56.

[2] Chap. ii. 21, 22, 39, 41, 42. This is an Ebionitish feature. **Cf.**
Philosophumena VII. vi. 34.

[3] The parable of the rich man and Lazarus. Compare chap. vi.
20, and following, 24, and following, xii. 13, and following, xvi.
entirely, xxii. 35. *Acts* ii. 44, 45, v. 1, and following.

[4] The woman who anoints his feet, Zaccheus, the penitent thief,
the parable of the Pharisee and the publican, and the prodigal son.

[5] For example, Mary of Bethany is represented by him as a sinner who becomes converted.

[6] Jesus weeping over Jerusalem, the bloody sweat, the meeting
of the holy women, the penitent thief, &c. The speech to the
women of Jerusalem (xxiii. 28, 29) could scarcely have been conceived except after the siege of the year 70.

of a document of this nature. It would have been as uncritical to neglect it as to employ it without discernment. Luke has had under his eyes originals which we no longer possess. He is less an evangelist than a biographer of Jesus, a "harmonizer," a corrector after the manner of Marcion and Tatian. But he is a biographer of the first century, a divine artist, who, independently of the information which he has drawn from more ancient sources, shows us the character of the Founder with a happiness of treatment, with a uniform inspiration, and a distinctness which the other two synoptics do not possess. In the perusal of his Gospel there is the greatest charm; for to the incomparable beauty of the foundation, common to them all, he adds a degree of skill in composition which singularly augments the effect of the portrait, without seriously injuring its truthfulness.

On the whole, we may say that the synoptical compilation has passed through three stages: First, the original documentary state ($\lambda\acute{o}\gamma\iota\alpha$) of Matthew, $\lambda\epsilon\chi\theta\acute{\epsilon}\nu\tau\iota$ $\ddot{\eta}$ $\pi\rho\alpha\chi\theta\acute{\epsilon}\nu\tau\alpha$ of Mark), primary compilations which no longer exist; second, the state of simple mixture, in which the original documents are amalgamated without any effort at composition, without there appearing any personal bias of the authors (the existing Gospels of Matthew and Mark); third, the state of combination or of intentional and deliberate compiling, in which we are sensible of an attempt to reconcile the different versions (Gospel of Luke). The Gospel of John, as we have said, forms a composition of another order, and is entirely distinct.

It will be remarked that I have made no use of the Apocryphal Gospels. These compositions ought not in any manner to be put upon the same footing as the

canonical Gospels. They are insipid and puerile amplifications, having the canonical Gospels for their
basis, and adding nothing thereto of any value. On
the other hand, I have been very attentive to collect the
shreds preserved by the Fathers of the Church, of the
ancient Gospels which formerly existed parallel with
the canonical Gospels, and which are now lost—such
as the Gospel according to the Hebrews, the Gospel
according to the Egyptians, the Gospels styled those of
Justin, Marcion, and Tatian. The first two are principally important because they were written in Aramean, like the *Logia* of Matthew, and appear to constitute one version of the Gospel of this apostle, and
because they were the Gospel of the *Ebionim*—that is,
of those small Christian sects of Batanea who preserved the use of Syro-Chaldean, and who appear in
some respects to have followed the course marked out
by Jesus. But it must be confessed that in the state
in which they have come to us, these Gospels are inferior, as critical authorities, to the compilation of
Matthew's Gospel which we now possess.

It will now be seen, I think, what kind of historical
value I attribute to the Gospels. They are neither
biographies after the manner of Suetonius, nor fictitious legends in the style of Philostratus; they are
legendary biographies. I should willingly compare
them with the Legends of the Saints, the Lives of Plotinus, Proclus, Isidore, and other writings of the same
kind, in which historical truth and the desire to present
models of virtue are combined in various degrees.
Inexactitude, which is one of the features of all popular
compositions, is there particularly felt. Let us suppose that ten or twelve years ago three or four old
soldiers of the Empire had each undertaken to write

the life of Napoleon from memory. It is clear that their narratives would contain numerous errors, and great discordances. One of them would place Wagram before Marengo; another would write without hesitation that Napoleon drove the government of Robespierre from the Tuileries; a third would omit expeditions of the highest importance. But one thing would certainly result with a great degree of truthfulness from these simple recitals, and that is the character of the hero, the impression which he made around him. In this sense such popular narratives would be worth more than a formal and official history. We may say as much of the Gospels. Solely attentive to bring out strongly the excellency of the Master, his miracles, his teaching, the evangelists display entire indifference to everything that is not of the very spirit of Jesus. The contradictions respecting time, place, and persons were regarded as insignificant; for the higher the degree of inspiration attributed to the words of Jesus, the less was granted to the compilers themselves. The latter regarded themselves as simple scribes, and cared but for one thing—to omit nothing they knew.[1]

Unquestionably certain preconceived ideas associated themselves with such recollections. Several narratives, especially in Luke, are invented in order to bring out more vividly certain traits of the character of Jesus. This character itself constantly underwent alteration. Jesus would be a phenomenon unparalleled in history if, with the part which he played, he had not early become idealized. The legends respecting Alexander were invented before the generation of his companions in arms became extinct; those respecting St. Francis d'Assisi began in his lifetime. A rapid meta-

[1] See the passage from Papias, before cited.

morphosis operated in the same manner in the twenty or thirty years which followed the death of Jesus, and imposed upon his biography the peculiarities of an ideal legend. Death adds perfection to the most perfect man; it frees him from all defect in the eyes of those who have loved him. With the wish to paint the Master, there was also the desire to explain him. Many anecdotes were conceived to prove that in him the prophecies regarded as Messianic had had their accomplishment. But this procedure, of which we must not deny the importance, would not suffice to explain everything. No Jewish work of the time gives a series of prophecies exactly declaring what the Messiah should accomplish. Many Messianic allusions quoted by the evangelists are so subtle, so indirect, that one cannot believe they all responded to a generally admitted doctrine. Sometimes they reasoned thus: "The Messiah ought to do such a thing; now Jesus is the Messiah; therefore Jesus has done such a thing." At other times, by an inverse process, it was said: "Such a thing has happened to Jesus; now Jesus is the Messiah; therefore such a thing was to happen to the Messiah."[1] Too simple explanations are always false when analyzing those profound creations of popular sentiment which baffle all systems by their fullness and infinite variety. It is scarcely necessary to say that, with such documents, in order to present only what is indisputable, we must limit ourselves to general features. In almost all ancient histories, even in those which are much less legendary than these, details open up innumerable doubts. When we have two accounts of the same fact, it is extremely rare that the two accounts agree. Is not this a reason for anticipating

[1] See, for example, John xix. 23-24.

many difficulties when we have but one? We may say that amongst the anecdotes, the discourses, the celebrated sayings which have been given us by the historians, there is not one strictly authentic. Were there stenographers to fix these fleeting words? Was there an analyst always present to note the gestures, the manners, the sentiments of the actors? Let any one endeavor to get at the truth as to the way in which such or such contemporary fact has happened; he will not succeed. Two accounts of the same event given by different eye-witnesses differ essentially. Must we, therefore, reject all the coloring of the narratives, and limit ourselves to the bare facts only? That would be to suppress history. Certainly, I think that if we except certain short and almost mnemonic axioms, none of the discourses reported by Matthew are textual; even our stenographic reports are scarcely so. I freely admit that the admirable account of the Passion contains many trifling inaccuracies. Would it, however, be writing the history of Jesus to omit those sermons which give to us in such a vivid manner the character of his discourses, and to limit ourselves to saying, with Josephus and Tacitus, "that he was put to death by the order of Pilate at the instigation of the priests"? That would be, in my opinion, a kind of inexactitude worse than that to which we are exposed in admitting the details supplied by the texts. These details are not true to the letter, but they are true with a superior truth, they are more true than the naked truth, in the sense that they are truth rendered expressive and articulate—truth idealized.

I beg those who think that I have placed an exaggerated confidence in narratives in great part legendary, to take note of the observation I have just made.

To what would the life of Alexander be reduced if it were confined to that which is materially certain? Even partly erroneous traditions contain a portion of truth which history cannot neglect. No one has blamed M. Sprenger for having, in writing the life of Mahomet, made much of the *hadith* or oral traditions concerning the prophet, and for often having attributed to his hero words which are only known through this source. Yet the traditions respecting Mahomet are not superior in historical value to the discourses and narratives which compose the Gospels. They were written between the year 50 and the year 140 of the Hegira. When the history of the Jewish schools in the ages which immediately preceded and followed the birth of Christianity shall be written, no one will make any scruple of attributing to Hillel, Shammai, Gamaliel the maxims ascribed to them by the *Mishnah* and the *Gemara,* although these great compilations were writ-ten many hundreds of years after the time of the doc-tors in question.

As to those who believe, on the contrary, that history should consist of a simple reproduction of the docu-ments which have come down to us, I beg to observe that such a course is not allowable. The four principal documents are in flagrant contradiction one with an-other. Josephus rectifies them sometimes. It is nec-essary to make a selection. To assert that an event cannot take place in two ways at once, or in an impos-sible manner, is not to impose an *à priori* philosophy upon history. The historian ought not to conclude that a fact is false because he possesses several versions of it, or because credulity has mixed with them much that is fabulous. He ought in such a case to be very cautious—to examine the texts, and to proceed carefully by induction. There is one class of narratives especially, to which this principle must necessarily be applied. Such are narratives of supernatural events. To seek to explain these, or to reduce them to legends, is not to mutilate facts in the name of theory; it is to make the observation of facts our groundwork. None of the miracles with which the old histories are filled took place under scientific conditions. Observation, which has never once been falsified, teaches us that miracles never happen but in times and countries in which they are believed, and before persons disposed to believe them. No miracle ever occurred in the pres- ence of men capable of testing its miraculous character. Neither common people nor men of the world are able to do this. It requires great precautions and long habits of scientific research. In our days have we not seen almost all respectable people dupes of the grossest frauds or of puerile illusions? Marvellous facts, at- tested by the whole population of small towns, have, thanks to a severer scrutiny, been exploded.[1] If it is proved that no contemporary miracle will bear inquiry, is it not probable that the miracles of the past, which have all been performed in popular gatherings, would equally present their share of illusion, if it were pos- sible to criticise them in detail?

It is not, then, in the name of this or that philosophy, but in the name of universal experience, that we banish miracle from history. We do not say, "Miracles are impossible." We say, "Up to this time a miracle has never been proved." If to-morrow a thaumaturgus present himself with credentials sufficiently important to be discussed, and announce himself as able, say, to

[1] See the *Gazette des Tribunaux*, 10th Sept. and 11th Nov., 1851, 28th May, 1857.

raise the dead, what would be done? A commission, composed of physiologists, physicists, chemists, persons accustomed to historical criticism, would be named. This commission would choose a corpse, would assure itself that the death was real, would select the room in which the experiment should be made, would arrange the whole system of precautions, so as to leave no chance of doubt. If, under such conditions, the resurrection were effected, a probability almost equal to certainty would be established. As, however, it ought to be possible always to repeat an experiment—to do over again what has been done once; and as, in the order of miracle, there can be no question of ease or difficulty, the thaumaturgus would be invited to reproduce his marvellous act under other circumstances, upon other corpses, in another place. If the miracle succeeded each time, two things would be proved: First, that supernatural events happen in the world; second, that the power of producing them belongs, or is delegated to, certain persons. But who does not see that no miracle ever took place under these conditions? but that always hitherto the thaumaturgus has chosen the subject of the experiment, chosen the spot, chosen the public; that, besides, the people themselves—most commonly in consequence of the invincible want to see something divine in great events and great men—create the marvellous legends afterward? Until a new order of things prevails, we shall maintain then this principle of historical criticism—that a supernatural account cannot be admitted as such, that it always implies credulity or imposture, that the duty of the historian is to explain it, and seek to ascertain what share of truth or of error it may conceal.

Such are the rules which have been followed in the

composition of this work. To the perusal of locumentary evidences I have been able to add an important source of information—the sight of the places where the events occurred. The scientific mission, having for its object the exploration of ancient Phœnicia, which I directed in 1860 and 1861,[1] led me to reside on the frontiers of Galilee and to travel there frequently. I have traversed, in all directions, the country of the Gospels; I have visited Jerusalem, Hebron, and Samaria; scarcely any important locality of the history of Jesus has escaped me. All this history, which at a distance seems to float in the clouds of an unreal world, thus took a form, a solidity, which astonished me. The striking agreement of the texts with the places, the marvellous harmony of the Gospel ideal with the country which served it as a framework, were like a revelation to me. I had before my eyes a fifth Gospel, torn, but still legible, and henceforward, through the recitals of Matthew and Mark, in place of an abstract being, whose existence might have been doubted, I saw living and moving an admirable human figure. During the summer, having to go up to Ghazir, in Lebanon, to take a little repose, I fixed, in rapid sketches, the image which had appeared to me, and from them resulted this history. When a cruel bereavement hastened my departure, I had but a few pages to write. In this manner the book has been composed almost entirely near the very places where Jesus was born, and where his character was developed. Since my return, I have labored unceasingly to verify and check in detail the rough sketch which I had written in haste in a Maronite cabin, with five or six volumes around me.

[1] The work which will contain the results of this mission is in the press.

Many will regret, perhaps, the biographical form which my work has thus taken. When I first conceived the idea of a history of the origin of Christianity, what I wished to write was, in fact, a history of doctrines, in which men and their actions would have hardly had a place. Jesus would scarcely have been named; I should have endeavored to show how the ideas which have grown under his name took root and covered the world. But I have learned since that history is not a simple game of abstractions; that men are more than doctrines. It was not a certain theory on justification and redemption which brought about the Reformation; it was Luther and Calvin. Parseeism, Hellenism, Judaism might have been able to have combined under every form; the doctrines of the Resurrection and of the Word might have developed themselves during ages without producing this grand, unique, and fruitful fact, called Christianity. This fact is the work of Jesus, of St. Paul, of St. John. To write the history of Jesus, of St. Paul, of St. John is to write the history of the origin of Christianity. The anterior movements belong to our subject only in so far as they serve to throw light upon these extraordinary men, who naturally could not have existed without connection with that which preceded them.

In such an effort to make the great souls of the past live again, some share of divination and conjecture must be permitted. A great life is an organic whole which cannot be rendered by the simple agglomeration of small facts. It requires a profound sentiment to embrace them all, moulding them into perfect unity. The method of art in a similar subject is a good guide; the exquisite tact of a Goethe would know how to apply it. The essential condition of the creations of art is, that they shall form a living system of which all the parts are mutually dependent and related.

In histories such as this, the great test that we have got the truth is, to have succeeded in combining the texts in such a manner that they shall constitute a logical, probable narrative, harmonious throughout. The secret laws of life, of the progression of organic products, of the melting of minute distinctions, ought to be consulted at each moment; for what is required to be reproduced is not the material circumstance, which it is impossible to verify, but the very soul of history; what must be sought is not the petty certainty about trifles, it is the correctness of the general sentiment, the truthfulness of the coloring. Each trait which departs from the rules of classic narration ought to warn us to be careful; for the fact which has to be related has been living, natural, and harmonious. If we do not succeed in rendering it such by the recital, it is surely because we have not succeeded in seeing it aright. Suppose that, in restoring the Minerva of Phidias according to the texts, we produced a dry, jarring, artificial whole; what must we conclude? Simply that the texts want an appreciative interpretation; that we must study them quietly until they dovetail and furnish a whole in which all the parts are happily blended. Should we then be sure of having a perfect reproduction of the Greek statue? No; but at least we should not have the caricature of it; we should have the general spirit of the work—one of the forms in which it could have existed.

This idea of a living organism we have not hesitated to take as our guide in the general arrangement of the narrative. The perusal of the Gospels would suffice to prove that the compilers, although having a very

true plan of the *Life of Jesus* in their minds, have not
been guided by very exact chronological data; Papias,
besides, expressly teaches this.[1]   The expressions: "At
this time . . . after that . . . then . . and it came
to pass . . .," etc., are the simple transitions intended
to connect different narratives with each other. To
leave all the information furnished by the Gospels in
the disorder in which tradition supplies it, would only
be to write the history of Jesus as the history of a celebrated man would be written, by giving pell-mell the
letters and anecdotes of his youth, his old age, and of
his maturity.   The Koran, which presents to us, in
the loosest manner, fragments of the different epochs
in the life of Mahomet, has yielded its secret to an ingenious criticism; the chronological order in which the
fragments were composed has been discovered so as to
leave little room for doubt.   Such a rearrangement is
much more difficult in the case of the Gospels, the
public life of Jesus having been shorter and less eventful than the life of the founder of Islamism.   Meanwhile, the attempt to find a guiding thread through this
labyrinth ought not to be taxed with gratuitous subtlety.   There is no great abuse of hypothesis in supposing that a founder of a new religion commences by attaching himself to the moral aphorisms already in circulation in his time, and to the practices which are in
vogue; that, when riper, and in full possession of his
idea, he delights in a kind of calm and poetical eloquence, remote from all controversy, sweet and free as
pure feeling; that he warms by degrees, becomes animated by opposition, and finishes by polemics and
strong invectives.   Such are the periods which may
plainly be distinguished in the Koran.   The order

[1] *Loc. cit.*

adopted with an extremely fine tact by the synoptics, supposes an analogous progress. If Matthew be attentively read, we shall find in the distribution of the discourses, a gradation perfectly analogous to that which we have just indicated. The reserved turns of expression of which we make use in unfolding the progress of the ideas of Jesus will also be observed. The reader may, if he likes, see in the divisions adopted in doing this, only the indispensable breaks for the methodical exposition of a profound, complicated thought.

If the love of a subject can help one to understand it, it will also, I hope, be recognized that I have not been wanting in this condition. To write the history of a religion, it is necessary, firstly, to have believed it (otherwise we should not be able to understand how it has charmed and satisfied the human conscience) ; in the second place, to believe it no longer in an absolute manner, for absolute faith is incompatible with sincere history. But love is possible without faith. To abstain from attaching one's self to any of the forms which captivate the adoration of men, is not to deprive ourselves of the enjoyment of that which is good and beautiful in them. No transitory appearance exhausts the Divinity ; God was revealed before Jesus—God will reveal Himself after him. Profoundly unequal, and so much the more Divine, as they are grander and more spontaneous, the manifestations of God hidden in the depths of the human conscience are all of the same order. Jesus cannot belong solely to those who call themselves his disciples. He is the common honor of all who share a common humanity. His glory does not consist in being relegated out of history ; we render him a truer worship in showing that all history is incomprehensible without him.

LIFE OF JESUS

CHAPTER I.

PLACE OF JESUS IN THE HISTORY OF THE WORLD.

THE great event of the History of the world is the revolution by which the noblest portions of humanity have passed from the ancient religions, comprised under the vague name of Paganism, to a religion founded on the Divine Unity, the Trinity, and the Incarnation of the Son of God. It has taken nearly a thousand years to accomplish this conversion. The new religion had itself taken at least three hundred years in its formation. But the origin of the revolution in question with which we have to do is a fact which took place under the reigns of Augustus and Tiberius. At that time there lived a superior personage, who, by his bold originality, and by the love which he was able to inspire, became the object and fixed the starting-point of the future faith of humanity.

As soon as man became distinguished from the animal, he became religious; that is to say, he saw in Nature something beyond the phenomena, and for himself something beyond death. This sentiment, during some thousands of years, became corrupted in the strangest manner. In many races it did not pass beyond the belief in sorcerers, under the gross form in

which we still find it in certain parts of Oceania.
Among some, the religious sentiment degenerated into
the shameful scenes of butchery which form the character of the ancient religion of Mexico.   Amongst
others, especially in Africa, it became pure Fetichism,
that is, the adoration of a material object, to which
were attributed supernatural powers.   Like the instinct of love, which at times elevates the most vulgar
man above himself, yet sometimes becomes perverted
and ferocious, so this divine faculty of religion during
a long period seems only to be a cancer which must be
extirpated from the human race, a cause of errors and
crimes which the wise ought to endeavor to suppress.

The brilliant civilizations which were developed
from a very remote antiquity in China, in Babylonia,
and in Egypt, caused a certain progress to be made in
religion.   China arrived very early at a sort of mediocre good sense, which prevented great extravagances.
She neither knew the advantages nor the abuses of the
religious spirit.   At all events, she had not in this way
any influence in directing the great current of humanity.   The religions of Babylonia and Syria were never
freed from a substratum of strange sensuality; these
religions remained, until their extinction in the fourth
and fifth centuries of our era, schools of immorality, in
which at intervals glimpses of the divine world were
obtained by a sort of poetic intuition.   Egypt, notwithstanding an apparent kind of Fetichism, had very early
metaphysical dogmas and a lofty symbolism.   But
doubtless these interpretations of a refined theology
were not primitive.   Man has never, in the possession
of a clear idea, amused himself by clothing it in symbols: it is oftener after long reflections, and from the
impossibility felt by the human mind of resigning itself

to the absurd, that we seek ideas under the ancient mystic images whose meaning is lost. Moreover, it is not from Egypt that the faith of humanity has come. The elements which, in the religion of a Christian, passing through a thousand transformations, came from Egypt and Syria, are exterior forms of little consequence, or dross of which the most purified worships always retain some portion. The grand defect of the religions of which we speak was their essentially superstitious character. They only threw into the world millions of amulets and charms. No great moral thought could proceed from races oppressed by a secular despotism, and accustomed to institutions which precluded the exercise of individual liberty.

The poetry of the soul—faith, liberty, virtue, devotion—made their appearance in the world with the two great races which, in one sense, have made humanity, viz., the Indo-European and the Semitic races. The first religious intuitions of the Indo-European race were essentially naturalistic. But it was a profound and moral naturalism, a loving embrace of Nature by man, a delicious poetry, full of the sentiment of the Infinite—the principle, in fine, of all that which the Germanic and Celtic genius, of that which a Shakespeare and a Goethe should express in later times. It was neither theology nor moral philosophy—it was a state of melancholy, it was tenderness, it was imagination; it was, more than all, earnestness, the essential condition of morals and religion. The faith of humanity, however, could not come from thence, because these ancient forms of worships had great difficulty in detaching themselves from Polytheism, and could not attain to a very clear symbol. Brahminism has only survived to the present day by virtue of the astonishing faculty of conservation which India seems to possess. Buddhism failed in all its approaches toward the West. Druidism remained a form exclusively national, and without universal capacity. The Greek attempts at reform, Orpheism, the Mysteries, did not suffice to give a solid aliment to the soul. Persia alone succeeded in making a dogmatic religion, almost Monotheistic, and skilfully organized; but it is very possible that this organization itself was but an imitation, or borrowed. At all events, Persia has not converted the world; she herself, on the contrary, was converted when she saw the flag of the Divine unity as proclaimed by Mohammedanism appear on her frontiers.

It is the Semitic race[1] which has the glory of having made the religion of humanity. Far beyond the confines of history, resting under his tent, free from the taint of a corrupted world, the Bedouin patriarch prepared the faith of mankind. A strong antipathy against the voluptuous worships of Syria, a grand simplicity of ritual, the complete absence of temples, and the idol reduced to insignificant *theraphim,* constituted his superiority. Among all the tribes of the nomadic Semites, that of the Beni-Israel was already chosen for immense destinies. Ancient relations with Egypt, whence perhaps resulted some purely material ingredients, did but augment their repulsion to idolatry. A "Law" or *Thora,* very anciently written on tables of stone, and which they attributed to their great liberator Moses, had become the code of Monotheism, and

---

[1] I remind the reader that this word means here simply the people who speak or have spoken one of the languages called Semitic. Such a designation is entirely defective; but it is one of those words, like "Gothic architecture," "Arabian numerals," which we must preserve to be understood, even after we have demonstrated the error that they imply.

contained, as compared with the institutions of Egypt
and Chaldea, powerful germs of social equality and
morality. A chest or portable ark, having staples on
each side to admit of bearing poles, constituted all their
religious *matériel;* there were collected the sacred objects of the nation, its relics, its souvenirs, and, lastly,
the "book,"[1] the journal of the tribe, always open, but
which was written in with great discretion. The family charged with bearing the ark and watching over the
portable archives, being near the book and having the
control of it, very soon became important. From
hence, however, the institution which was to control
the future did not come. The Hebrew priest did not
differ much from the other priests of antiquity. The
character which essentially distinguishes Israel among
theocratic peoples is, that its priesthood has always
been subordinated to individual inspiration. Besides
its priests, each wandering tribe had its *nabi* or prophet,
a sort of living oracle who was consulted for the solution of obscure questions supposed to require a high
degree of clairvoyance. The *nabis* of Israel, organized in groups or schools, had great influence. Defenders of the ancient democratic spirit, enemies of the
rich, opposed to all political organization, and to whatsoever might draw Israel into the paths of other nations, they were the true authors of the religious pre-
eminence of the Jewish people. Very early they announced unlimited hopes, and when the people, in part
the victims of their impolitic counsels, had been
crushed by the Assyrian power, they proclaimed that a
kingdom without bounds was reserved for them, that
one day Jerusalem would be the capital of the whole
world, and the human race become Jews. Jerusalem

[1] Sam. x. 25.

and its temples appeared to them as a city placed on the summit of a mountain, toward which all people should turn, as an oracle whence the universal law should proceed, as the centre of an ideal kingdom, in which the human race, set at rest by Israel, should find again the joys of Eden.[1]

Mystical utterances already made themselves heard, tending to exalt the martyrdom and celebrate the power of the "Man of Sorrows." Respecting one of those sublime sufferers, who, like Jeremiah, stained the streets of Jerusalem with their blood, one of the inspired wrote a song upon the sufferings and triumph of the "servant of God," in which all the prophetic force of the genius of Israel seemed concentrated.[2] "For he shall grow up before him as a tender plant, and as a root out of a dry ground: he hath no form nor comeliness. He is despised and rejected of men; and we hid, as it were, our faces from him; he was despised, and we esteemed him not. Surely he hath borne our griefs, and carried our sorrows; yet we did esteem him stricken, smitten of God, and afflicted. But he was wounded for our transgressions, he was bruised for our iniquities: the chastisement of our peace was upon him; and with his stripes we are healed. All we like sheep have gone astray; we have turned every one to his own way; and the Lord hath laid on him the iniquity of us all. He was oppressed, and he was afflicted, yet he opened not his mouth: he is brought as a lamb to the slaughter, and as a sheep before her shearers is dumb, so he openeth not his mouth. And he

[1] Isa. ii. 1-4, and especially chaps. xl., and following, lx., and following; Micah iv. 1, and following. It must be recollected that the second part of the book of Isaiah, beginning at chap. xl., is not by Isaiah.
[2] Isa. lii. 13, and following, and liii. entirely.

made his grave with the wicked. When thou shalt make his soul an offering for sin, he shall see his seed, he shall prolong his days, and the pleasure of the Lord shall prosper in his hand."

Important modifications were made at the same time in the *Thora*. New texts, pretending to represent the true law of Moses, such as Deuteronomy, were produced, and inaugurated in reality a very different spirit from that of the old nomads. A marked fanaticism was the dominant feature of this spirit. Furious believers unceasingly instigated violence against all who wandered from the worship of Jehovah—they succeeded in establishing a code of blood, making death the penalty for religious faults. Piety brings, almost always, singular contradictions of vehemence and mildness. This zeal, unknown to the coarser simplicity of the time of the Judges, inspired tones of moving prophecy and tender unction, which the world had never heard till then. A strong tendency toward social questions already made itself felt; Utopias, dreams of a perfect society, took a place in the code. The Pentateuch, a mixture of patriarchal morality and ardent devotion, primitive intuitions and pious subtleties, like those which filled the souls of Hezekiah, of Josiah, and of Jeremiah, was thus fixed in the form in which we now see it, and became for ages the absolute rule of the national mind.

This great book once created, the history of the Jewish people unfolded itself with an irresistible force. The great empires which followed each other in Western Asia, in destroying its hope of a terrestrial kingdom, threw it into religious dreams, which it cherished with a kind of sombre passion. Caring little for the national dynasty or political independence, it accepted all governments which permitted it to practise freely its worship and follow its usages. Israel will henceforward have no other guidance than that of its religious enthusiasts, no other enemies than those of the Divine unity, no other country than its Law.

And this Law, it must be remarked, was entirely social and moral. It was the work of men penetrated with a high ideal of the present life, and believing that they had found the best means of realizing it. The conviction of all was, that the *Thora*, well observed, could not fail to give perfect felicity. This *Thora* has nothing in common with the Greek or Roman "Laws," which, occupying themselves with scarcely anything but abstract right, entered little into questions of private happiness and morality. We feel beforehand that the results which will proceed from it will be of a social, and not a political order, that the work at which this people labors is a kingdom of God, not a civil republic; a universal institution, not a nationality or a country.

Notwithstanding numerous failures, Israel admirably sustained this vocation. A series of pious men, Ezra, Nehemiah, Onias, the Maccabees, consumed with zeal for the Law, succeeded each other in the defense of the ancient institutions. The idea that Israel was a holy people, a tribe chosen by God and bound to Him by covenant, took deeper and firmer root. An immense expectation filled their souls. All Indo-European antiquity had placed paradise in the beginning; all its poets had wept a vanished golden age. Israel placed the age of gold in the future. The perennial poesy of religious souls, the Psalms, blossomed from this exalted piety, with their divine and melancholy harmony. Israel became truly and specially the people of God, while around it the pagan religions were more and more reduced, in Persia and Babylonia, to an official charlatanism, in Egypt and Syria to a gross idolatry, and in the Greek and Roman world to mere parade. That which the Christian martyrs did in the first centuries of our era, that which the victims of persecuting orthodoxy have done, even in the bosom of Christianity, up to our time, the Jews did during the two centuries which preceded the Christian era. They were a living protest against superstition and religious materialism. An extraordinary movement of ideas, ending in the most opposite results, made of them, at this epoch, the most striking and original people in the world. Their dispersion along all the coast of the Mediterranean, and the use of the Greek language, which they adopted when out of Palestine, prepared the way for a propagandism, of which ancient societies, divided into small nationalities, had never offered a single example.

Up to the time of the Maccabees, Judaism, in spite of its persistence in announcing that it would one day be the religion of the human race, had had the characteristic of all the other worships of antiquity, it was a worship of the family and the tribe. The Israelite thought, indeed, that his worship was the best, and spoke with contempt of strange gods; but he believed also that the religion of the true God was made for himself alone. Only when a man entered into the Jewish family did he embrace the worship of Jehovah.[1] No Israelite cared to convert the stranger to a worship which was the patrimony of the sons of Abraham. The development of the pietistic spirit, after Ezra and Nehemiah, led to a much firmer and more logical con-

[1] Ruth i. 16.

ception.   Judaism became the true religion in a more
absolute manner; to all who wished, the right of entering it was given;[1] soon it became a work of piety to
bring into it the greatest number possible.[2]   Doubtless
the refined sentiment which elevated John the Baptist,
Jesus, and St. Paul above the petty ideas of race, did
not yet exist; for, by a strange contradiction, these con-
verts were little respected and were treated with disdain.[3]   But the idea of a sovereign religion, the idea
that there was something in the world superior to country, to blood, to laws—the idea which makes apostles
and martyrs—was founded.   Profound pity for the
pagans, however brilliant might be their worldly fortune, was henceforth the feeling of every Jew.[4]   By a
cycle of legends destined to furnish models of immov-
able firmness, such as the histories of Daniel and his
companions, the mother of the Maccabees and her
seven sons,[5] the romance of the race-course of Alexandria[6]—the guides of the people sought above all to
inculcate the idea, that virtue consists in a fanatical attachment to fixed religious institutions.

The persecutions of Antiochus Epiphanes made this
idea a passion, almost a frenzy.   It was something
very analogous to that which happened under Nero,

[1] Esther ix. 27.

[2] Matt. xxiii. 15; Josephus, *Vita*, 23; *B. J.*, II. xvii. 10, VII. iii. 3;
Ant., xx. ii. 4; Horat., Sat. I., iv., 143; Juv., xiv. 96, and following;
Tacitus, *Ann.*, II. 85; *Hist.*, v. 5; Dion Cassius, xxxvii, 17.

[3] Mishnah, *Shebiit*, x. 9; Talmud of Babylon, *Niddah*, fol. 13 *b;*
Iebamoth, 47 *b, Kiddushim*, 70 *b;* Midrash, *Jalkut Ruth*, fol.
163 *d.*

[4] Apocryphal letter of Baruch, in Fabricius, Cod. *pseud. v. t.*, ii.,
147, and following.

[5] 11. Book of Maccabees, ch. vii. and the *De Maccabæis*, attributed to Josephus. Cf. Epistle to the Hebrews xi. 33, and following.

[6] III. Book (Apocr.) of Maccabees: Rufin, Suppl. ad Jos., *Contra
Apionem*, ii. 5.

two hundred and thirty years later. Rage and despair threw the believers into the world of visions and dreams. The first apocalypse, "The Book of Daniel," appeared. It was like a revival of prophecy, but under a very different form from the ancient one, and with a much larger idea of the destinies of the world. The Book of Daniel gave, in a manner, the last expression to the Messianic hopes. The Messiah was no longer a king, after the manner of David and Solomon, a theocratic and Mosaic Cyrus; he was a "Son of man" appearing in the clouds[1]—a supernatural being, invested with human form, charged to rule the world, and to preside over the golden age. Perhaps the *Sosiosh* of Persia, the great prophet who was to come, charged with preparing the reign of Ormuzd, gave some features to this new ideal.[2] The unknown author of the Book of Daniel had, in any case, a decisive influence on the religious event which was about to transform the world. He supplied the *mise-en-scène*, and the technical terms of the new belief in the Messiah; and we might apply to him what Jesus said of John the Baptist: Before him, the prophets; after him, the kingdom of God.

It must not, however, be supposed that this profoundly religious and soul-stirring movement had particular dogmas for its primary impulse, as was the case in all the conflicts which have disturbed the bosom of Christianity. The Jew of this epoch was as little theological as possible. He did not speculate upon the

[1] Chap. vii. 13, and following.

[2] *Vendidad,* chap. xix. 18, 19; *Minokhired,* a passage published in the *"Zeitschrift der deutschen morgenländischen Gesellschaft,"* chap. i. 263; *Boundehesch,* chap. xxxi. The want of certain chronology for the Zend and Pehlvis texts leaves much doubt hovering over the relations between the Jewish and Persian beliefs.

essence of the Divinity; the beliefs about angels, about the destinies of man, about the Divine personality, of which the first germs might already be perceived, were quite optional—they were meditations, to which each one surrendered himself according to the turn of his mind, but of which a great number of men had never heard. They were the most orthodox even, who did not share in these particular imaginations, and who adhered to the simplicity of the Mosaic law. No dogmatic power analogous to that which orthodox Christianity has given to the Church then existed. It was only at the beginning of the third century, when Christianity had fallen into the hands of reasoning races, mad with dialectics and metaphysics, that that fever for definitions commenced which made the history of the Church but the history of one immense controversy. There were disputes also among the Jews — excited schools brought opposite solutions to almost all the questions which were agitated; but in these contests, of which the Talmud has preserved the principal details, there is not a single word of speculative theology. To observe and maintain the law, because the law was just, and because, when well observed, it gave happiness—such was Judaism. No *credo,* no theoretical symbol. One of the disciples of the boldest Arabian philosophy, Moses Maimonides, was able to become the oracle of the synagogue, because he was well versed in the canonical law.

The reigns of the last Asmoneans, and that of Herod, saw the excitement grow still stronger. They were filled by an uninterrupted series of religious movements. In the degree that power became secularized, and passed into the hands of unbelievers, the Jewish people lived less and less for the earth, and became more and more absorbed by the strange fermentation which was operating in their midst. The world, distracted by other spectacles, had little knowledge of that which passed in this forgotten corner of the East. The minds abreast of their age were, however, better informed. The tender and clear-sighted Virgil seems to answer, as by a secret echo, to the second Isaiah. The birth of a child throws him into dreams of a universal palingenesis.[1] These dreams were of every-day occurrence, and shaped into a kind of literature which was designated Sibylline. The quite recent formation of the empire exalted the imagination; the great era of peace on which it entered, and that impression of melancholy sensibility which the mind experiences after long periods of revolution, gave birth on all sides to unlimited hopes.

In Judea expectation was at its height. Holy persons—among whom may be named the aged Simeon, who, legend tells us, held Jesus in his arms; Anna, daughter of Phanuel, regarded as a prophetess[2]— passed their life about the temple, fasting, and praying, that it might please God not to take them from the world without having seen the fulfillment of the hopes of Israel. They felt a powerful presentiment; they were sensible of the approach of something unknown.

This confused mixture of clear views and dreams, this alternation of deceptions and hopes, these ceaseless aspirations, driven back by an odious reality, found at last their interpretation in the incomparable man, to

[1] Egl. iv. The *Cumæum carmen* (v. 4) was a sort of Sibylline apocalypse, borrowed from the philosophy of history familiar to the East. See Servius on this verse, and *Carmina Sibyllina*, iii. 97-817; cf. Tac., *Hist.*, v. 13.
[2] Luke ii. 25, and following.

whom the universal conscience has decreed the title of Son of God, and that with justice, since he has advanced religion as no other has done, or probably ever will be able to do.

CHAPTER II.

INFANCY AND YOUTH OF JESUS—HIS FIRST
IMPRESSIONS.

JESUS was born at Nazareth,[1] a small town of Galilee, which before his time had no celebrity.[2] All his life he was designated by the name of "the Nazarene,"[3] and it is only by a rather embarrassed and round-about way,[4] that, in the legends respecting him,

[1] Matt. xiii 54, and following; Mark vi. 1, and following; John i. 45-46.

[2] It is neither named in the writings of the Old Testament, nor in Josephus, nor in the Talmud.

[3] Mark i. 24; Luke xviii. 37; John xix, 19; Acts ii. 22, iii. 6. Hence the name of *Nazarenes* for a long time applied to Christians, and which still designates them in all Mohammedan countries.

[4] The census effected by Quirinus, to which legend attributes the journey from Bethlehem, is at least ten years later than the year in which, according to Luke and Matthew, Jesus was born. The two evangelists in effect make Jesus to be born under the reign of Herod (Matt. ii. 1, 19, 22; Luke i. 5). Now, the census of Quirinus did not take place until after the deposition of Archelaus, *i.e.*, ten years after the death of Herod, the 37th year from the era of Actium (Josephus, *Ant.*, XVII. xiii. 5, XVIII. i. 1, ii. 1). The inscription by which it was formerly pretended to establish that Quirinus had levied two censuses is recognized as false (see Orelli, *Inscr. Lat.*, No. 623, and the supplement of Henzen in this number; Borghesi, *Fastes Consulaires* [yet unpublished], in the year 742). The census in any case would only be applied to the parts reduced to Roman provinces, and not to the tetrarchies. The texts by which it is sought to prove that some of the operations for statistics and tribute commanded by Augustus ought to extend to the dominion of the Herods, either do not mean what they have been made to say, or are from Christian authors who have borrowed this statement from the Gospel of Luke. That which proves, besides, that the journey of the family of Jesus to Bethlehem is not historical, is the motive attributed to it. Jesus was not of the family of David (see Chap. XV.), and if he had been, we should still not imagine that his parents should have been forced, for an operation purely registrative and financial, to come to enrol themselves in the place whence their ancestors had pro-

he is made to be born at Bethlehem. We shall see
later[1] the motive for this supposition, and how it was
the necessary consequence of the Messianic character
attributed to Jesus.[2] The precise date of his birth is
unknown. It took place under the reign of Augustus,
about the Roman year 750, probably some years before
the year 1 of that era which all civilized people date
from the day on which he was born.[3]

The name of *Jesus,* which was given him, is an alteration from *Joshua.* It was a very common name; but
afterward mysteries, and an allusion to his character of
Saviour, were naturally sought for in it.[4] Perhaps he,
like all mystics, exalted himself in this respect. It is
thus that more than one great vocation in history has
been caused by a name given to a child without pre-
meditation. Ardent natures never bring themselves to
see aught of chance in what concerns them. God has

ceeded a thousand years before. In imposing such an obligation,
the Roman authority would have sanctioned pretensions threaten-
ing her safety.

[1] Chap. XIV.

[2] Matt. ii. 1, and following; Luke ii. 1, and following. The omission of this narrative in Mark, and the two parallel passages,
Matt. xiii. 54, and Mark vi. 1, where Nazareth figures as the
"country" of Jesus, prove that such a legend was absent from the
primitive text which has furnished the rough draft of the present
Gospels of Matthew and Mark. It was to meet oft-repeated objections that there were added to the beginning of the Gospel of
Matthew reservations, the contradiction of which with the rest of
the text was not so flagrant, that it was felt necessary to correct
the passages which had at first been written from quite another
point of view. Luke, on the contrary (chap. iv. 16), writing more
carefully, has employed, in order to be consistent, a more softened
expression. As to John, he knows nothing of the journey to
Bethlehem; for him, Jesus is merely "of Nazareth" or "Galilean,"
in two circumstances in which it would have been of the highest
importance to recall his birth at Bethlehem (chap. i. 45, 46, vi.
41, 42).

[3] It is known that the calculation which serves as basis of the
common era was made in the sixth century by *Dionysius the Less.*
This calculation implies certain purely hypothetical data.

[4] Matt. i. 21; Luke i. 31.

regulated everything for them, and they see a sign of the supreme will in the most insignificant circumstances.

The population of Galilee was very mixed as the very name of the country[1] indicated. This province counted amongst its inhabitants, in the time of Jesus, many who were not Jews (Phœnicians, Syrians, Arabs, and even Greeks).[2] The conversions to Judaism were not rare in these mixed countries. It is therefore impossible to raise here any question of race, and to seek to ascertain what blood flowed in the veins of him who has contributed most to efface the distinction of blood in humanity.

He proceeded from the ranks of the people.[3] His father, Joseph, and his mother, Mary, were people in humble circumstances, artisans living by their labor,[4] in the state so common in the East, which is neither ease nor poverty. The extreme simplicity of life in such countries, by dispensing with the need of comfort, renders the privileges of wealth almost useless, and makes every one voluntarily poor. On the other hand, the total want of taste for art, and for that which contributes to the elegance of material life, gives a naked aspect to the house of him who otherwise wants for nothing. Apart from something sordid and repulsive which Islamism bears everywhere with it, the town of Nazareth, in the time of Jesus, did not perhaps much differ from what it is to-day.[5] We see the streets

[1] *Gelil haggoyim*, "Circle of the Gentiles."
[2] Strabo, XVI. ii. 35; Jos., *Vita*, 12.
[3] We shall explain later (Chap. XIV.) the origin of the genealogies intended to connect him with the race of David. The Ebionites suppressed them (Epiph., *Adv. Hær.*, xxx. 14).
[4] Matt. xiii. 55; Mark vi. 3; John vi. 42.
[5] The rough aspect of the ruins which cover Palestine proves that the towns which were not constructed in the Roman manner

where he played when a child, in the stony paths or little crossways which separate the dwellings. The house of Joseph doubtless much resembled those poor shops, lighted by the door, serving at once for shop, kitchen, and bedroom, having for furniture a mat, some cushions on the ground, one or two clay pots, and a painted chest.

The family, whether it proceeded from one or many marriages, was rather numerous. Jesus had brothers and sisters,[1] of whom he seems to have been the eldest.[2] All have remained obscure, for it appears that the four personages who were named as his brothers, and among whom one, at least—James—had acquired great importance in the earliest years of the development of Christianity, were his cousins-german. Mary, in fact, had a sister also named Mary,[3] who married a certain Alpheus or Cleophas (these two names appear to designate the same person[4]), and was the mother of several sons who played a considerable part among the first disciples of Jesus. These cousins-german who adhered to the young Master, while his own brothers opposed him,[5] took the title of "brothers of the Lord."[6]

were very badly built. As to the form of the houses, it is, in Syria, so simple and so imperiously regulated by the climate, that it can scarcely ever have changed.

[1] Matt. xii. 46, and following, xiii. 55, and following; Mark iii. 31, and following, vi. 3; Luke viii. 19, and following; John ii. 12, vii. 3, 5, 10; *Acts* i. 14.

[2] Matt. i. 25.

[3] That these two sisters should bear the same name is a singular fact. There is probably some error arising from the habit of giving the name of Mary indiscriminately to Galilean women.

[4] They are not etymologically identical. $A\lambda\phi\alpha\hat{\iota}o\varsigma$ is the transcription of the Syro-Chaldean name Halphaï; $K\lambda\omega\pi\tilde{\alpha}\varsigma$ or $K\lambda\varepsilon\acute{o}\pi\alpha\varsigma$ is a shortened form of $K\lambda\varepsilon\acute{o}\pi\alpha\tau\rho o\varsigma$. But there might have been an artificial substitution of one for the other, just as Joseph was called "Hegissippus," the Eliakim "Alcimus," &c.

[5] John vii. 3, and following.

[6] In fact, the four personages who are named (Matt. xiii. 55,

The real brothers of Jesus, like their mother, became important only after his death.[1] Even then they do not appear to have equaled in importance their cousins, whose conversion had been more spontaneous, and whose character seems to have had more originality. Their names were so little known, that when the evangelist put in the mouth of the men of Nazareth the enumeration of the brothers according to natural relationship, the names of the sons of Cleophas first presented themselves to him.

His sisters were married at Nazareth,[2] and he spent the first years of his youth there. Nazareth was a small town in a hollow, opening broadly at the summit of the group of mountains which close the plain of Esdraelon on the north. The population is now from three to four thousand, and it can never have varied much.[3] The cold there is sharp in winter, and the

Mark vi. 3) as sons of Mary, mother of Jesus, Jacob, Joseph or Joses, Simon, and Jude, are found again a little later as sons of Mary and Cleophas. (Matt. xxvii. 56; Mark xv. 40; *Gal.* i. 19; *Epist. James* i. 1; *Epist. Jude* 1; Euseb., *Chron.* ad ann. R. DCCCX.; *Hist. Eccl.*, iii. 11, 32; *Constit. Apost.*, vii. 46.) The hypothesis we offer alone removes the immense difficulty which is found in supposing two sisters having each three or four sons bearing the same names, and in admitting that James and Simon, the first two bishops of Jerusalem, designated as brothers of the Lord, may have been real brothers of Jesus, who had begun by being hostile to him and then were converted. The evangelist, hearing these four sons of Cleophas called "brothers of the Lord," has placed by mistake their names in the passage *Matt.* xiii. 5 = *Mark* vi. 3, instead of the names of the real brothers, which have always remained obscure. In this matter we may explain how the character of the personages called "brothers of the Lord," of James, for instance, is so different from that of the real brothers of Jesus as they are seen delineated in John vii. 2, and following. The expression "brother of the Lord" evidently constituted, in the primitive Church, a kind of order similar to that of the apostles. See especially 1 *Cor.* ix. 5.

[1] *Acts* i. 14. [2] Mark vi. 3.

[3] According to Josephus (*B. J.*, III. iii. 2), the smallest town of Galilee had more than five thousand inhabitants. This is probably an exaggeration.

climate very healthy. The town, like all the small Jewish towns at this period, was a heap of huts built without style, and would exhibit that harsh and poor aspect which villages in Semitic countries now present. The houses, it seems, did not differ much from those cubes of stone, without exterior or interior elegance, which still cover the richest parts of the Lebanon, and which, surrounded with vines and fig-trees, are still very agreeable. The environs, moreover, are charming; and no place in the world was so well adapted for dreams of perfect happiness. Even in our times Nazareth is still a delightful abode, the only place, perhaps, in Palestine in which the mind feels itself relieved from the burden which oppresses it in this unequaled desolation. The people are amiable and cheerful; the gardens fresh and green. Anthony the Martyr, at the end of the sixth century, drew an enchanting picture of the fertility of the environs, which he compared to paradise.[1] Some valleys on the western side fully justify his description. The fountain, where formerly the life and gaiety of the little town were concentrated, is destroyed; its broken channels contain now only a muddy stream. But the beauty of the women who meet there in the evening—that beauty which was remarked even in the sixth century, and which was looked upon as a gift of the Virgin Mary[2]—is still most strikingly preserved. It is the Syrian type in all its languid grace. No doubt Mary was there almost every day, and took her place with her jar on her shoulder in the file of her companions who have remained unknown. Anthony the Martyr remarks that the Jewish women, generally disdainful to Christians, were

[1] *Itiner.*, § 5.
[2] Ant. Martyr, *Itiner.*, § 5.

here full of affability. Even now religious animosity is weaker at Nazareth than elsewhere.

The horizon from the town is limited. But if we ascend a little the plateau, swept by a perpetual breeze, which overlooks the highest houses, the prospect is splendid. On the west are seen the fine outlines of Carmel, terminated by an abrupt point which seems to plunge into the sea. Before us are spread out the double summit which towers above Megiddo; the mountains of the country of Shechem, with their holy places of the patriarchal age; the hills of Gilboa, the small, picturesque group to which are attached the graceful or terrible recollections of Shunem and of Endor; and Tabor, with its beautiful rounded form, which antiquity compared to a bosom. Through a depression between the mountains of Shunem and Tabor are seen the valley of the Jordan and the high plains of Peræa, which form a continuous line from the eastern side. On the north, the mountains of Safed, in inclining toward the sea conceal St. Jean d'Acre, but permit the Gulf of Khaïfa to be distinguished. Such was the horizon of Jesus. This enchanted circle, cradle of the kingdom of God, was for years his world. Even in his later life he departed but little beyond the familiar limits of his childhood. For yonder, northward, a glimpse is caught, almost on the flank of Hermon, of Cæsarea-Philippi, his furthest point of advance into the Gentile world; and here southward, the more sombre aspect of these Samaritan hills foreshadows the dreariness of Judea beyond, parched as by a scorching wind of desolation and death.

If the world, remaining Christian, but attaining to a better idea of the esteem in which the origin of its religion should be held, should ever wish to replace by authentic holy places the mean and apocryphal sanctuaries to which the piety of dark ages attached itself, it is upon this height of Nazareth that it will rebuild its temple. There, at the birthplace of Christianity, and in the centre of the actions of its Founder, the great church ought to be raised in which all Christians may worship. There, also, on this spot where sleep Joseph, the carpenter, and thousands of forgotten Nazarenes who never passed beyond the horizon of their valley, would be a better station than any in the world beside for the philosopher to contemplate the course of human affairs, to console himself for their uncertainty, and to reassure himself as to the Divine end which the world pursues through countless falterings, and in spite of the universal vanity.

CHAPTER III.

EDUCATION OF JESUS.

THIS aspect of Nature, at once smiling and grand, was the whole education of Jesus. He learned to read and to write,[1] doubtless, according to the Eastern method, which consisted in putting in the hands of the child a book, which he repeated in cadence with his little comrades, until he knew it by heart.[2] It is doubtful, however, if he understood the Hebrew writings in their original tongue. His biographers make him quote them according to the translations in the Aramean tongue;[3] his principles of exegesis, as far as we can judge of them by those of his disciples, much resembled those which were then in vogue, and which form the spirit of the *Targums* and the *Midrashim*.[4]

The schoolmaster in the small Jewish towns was the *hazzan,* or reader in the synagogues.[5] Jesus frequented little the higher schools of the scribes or *sopherim* (Nazareth had perhaps none of them), and he had none of those titles which confer, in the eyes of the vulgar, the privileges of knowledge.[6] It would, nevertheless, be a great error to imagine that Jesus was what we call ignorant. Scholastic education among us draws a profound distinction, in respect of personal worth, between those who have received and those who have been deprived of it. It was not so in the East,

[1] John viii. 6.   [2] *Testam. of the Twelve Patriarchs,* Levi. 6.
[3] Matt. xxvii. 46; Mark xv. 34.
[4] Jewish translations and commentaries of the Talmudic epoch.
[5] Mishnah, *Shabbath,* i. 3.
[6] Matt. xiii. 54, and following; John vii. 15.

nor, in general, in the good old times. The state of ignorance in which, among us, owing to our isolated and entirely individual life, those remain who have not passed through the schools, was unknown in those societies where moral culture, and especially the general spirit of the age, was transmitted by the perpetual intercourse of man with man. The Arab, who has never had a teacher, is often, nevertheless, a very superior man; for the tent is a kind of school always open, where, from the contact of well-educated men, there is produced a great intellectual and even literary movement. The refinement of manners and the acuteness of the intellect have, in the East, nothing in common with what we call education. It is the men from the schools, on the contrary, who are considered badly trained and pedantic. In this social state, ignorance, which, among us, condemns a man to an inferior rank, is the condition of great things and of great originality.

It is not probable that Jesus knew Greek. This language was very little spread in Judea beyond the classes who participated in the government, and the towns inhabited by pagans, like Cæsarea.[1] The real mother tongue of Jesus was the Syrian dialect mixed with Hebrew, which was then spoken in Palestine.[2]

[1] Mishnah, *Shekalim*, iii. 2; Talmud of Jerusalem, *Megilla*, halaca xi.; *Sota*, vii. 1; Talmud of Babylon, *Baba Kama*, 83 *a; Megilla*, 8 *b*, and following.

[2] Matthew xxvii. 46; Mark iii. 17, v. 41, vii. 34, xiv. 36, xv. 34. The expression ἡ πάτριος φωνή in the writers of the time, always designates the Semitic dialect, which was spoken in Palestine (11. Macc. vii. 21, 27, xii. 37; *Acts* xxi. 37, 40, xxii. 2, xxvi. 14; Josephus, *Ant.*, XVIII., vi., 10, xx. sub fin; *B. J.*, proœm 1; v. vi., 3, V. ix 2, VI. ii. 1; *Against Appian*, I. 9; *De Macc.*, 12, 16). We shall show, later, that some of the documents which served as the basis for the synoptic Gospels were written in this Semitic dialect. It was the same with many of the Apocrypha (IV. Book of Macc. xvi. ad calcem, &c.). In fine, the sects issuing directly from the first Galilean movement (Nazarenes, *Ebionim*, &c.), which

Still less probably had he any knowledge of Greek culture. This culture was proscribed by the doctors of Palestine, who included in the same malediction "he who rears swine, and he who teaches his son Greek science."[1] At all events it had not penetrated into little towns like Nazareth. Notwithstanding the anathema of the doctors, some Jews, it is true, had already embraced the Hellenic culture. Without speaking of the Jewish school of Egypt, in which the attempts to amalgamate Hellenism and Judaism had been in operation nearly two hundred years, a Jew—Nicholas of Damascus—had become, even at this time, one of the most distinguished men, one of the best informed, and one of the most respected of his age. Josephus was destined soon to furnish another example of a Jew completely Grecianized. But Nicholas was only a Jew in blood. Josephus declares that he himself was an exception among his contemporaries;[2] and the whole schismatic school of Egypt was detached to such a degree from Jerusalem that we do not find the least allusion to it either in the Talmud or in Jewish tradition. Certain it is that Greek was very little studied at Jerusalem, that Greek studies were considered as dangerous, and even servile, that they were regarded, at the best, as a mere womanly accomplishment.[3] The study of the Law was the only one accounted liberal and worthy of a thoughtful man.[4] Questioned as to

continued a long time in Batanea and Hauran, spoke a Semitic dialect, Eusebius, *De Situ et Nomin Loc. Hebr.*, at the word Χωβά; Epiph., *Adv. Hœr.*, xxix. 7, 9, xxx. 3; St. Jerome, *in Matt.* xii. 13; *Dial. adv. Pelag.*, iii. 2).

[1] Mishnah, *Sanhedrim*, xi. 1; Talmud of Babylon, *Baba Kama*, 82 *b* and 83 *a; Sota*, 49 *a* and *b; Menachoth*, 64 *b;* comp. II. Macc. iv. 10, and following.

[2] Jos.. *Ant.* xx. xi., 2.

[3] Talmud of Jerusalem, *Peah*, i. 1.

[4] Jos., *Ant.*, loc. cit.; Orig., *Contra Celsum*, ii. 34.

the time when it would be proper to teach children
"Greek wisdom," a learned rabbi had answered, "At
the time when it is neither day nor night; since it is
written of the Law, Thou shalt study it day and
night."[1]

Neither directly nor indirectly, then, did any element
of Greek culture reach Jesus. He knew nothing beyond Judaism; his mind preserved that free innocence
which an extended and varied culture always weakens.
In the very bosom of Judaism he remained a stranger
to many efforts often parallel to his own. On the one
hand, the asceticism of the Essenes or the Therapeutæ;[2] on the other, the fine efforts of religious philosophy put forth by the Jewish school of Alexandria, and
of which Philo, his contemporary, was the ingenious
interpreter, were unknown to him. The frequent resemblances which we find between him and Philo, those
excellent maxims about the love of God, charity, rest in
God,[3] which are like an echo between the Gospel and
the writings of the illustrious Alexandrian thinker,
proceed from the common tendencies which the wants
of the time inspired in all elevated minds.

Happily for him, he was also ignorant of the strange
scholasticism which was taught at Jerusalem, and
which was soon to constitute the Talmud. If some
Pharisees had already brought it into Galilee, he did
not associate with them, and when, later, he encountered this silly casuistry, it only inspired him with disgust. We may suppose, however, that the principles

[1] Talmud of Jerusalem, *Peah,* i. 1; Talmud of Babylon, *Menachoth,* 99 *b.*

[2] The *Therapeutæ* of Philo are a branch of the Essenes. Their
name appears to be but a Greek translation of that of the *Essenes*
(Εσσαῖοι, asaya, "doctors"). Cf. Philo, *De Vita Contempl.,* init.

[3] See especially the treatises *Quis Rerum Divinarum Hæres sit*
and *De Philanthropia* of Philo.

of Hillel were not unknown to him.   Hillel, fifty years before him, had given utterance to aphorisms very analogous to his own.   By his poverty, so meekly endured, by the sweetness of his character, by his opposition to priests and hypocrites, Hillel was the true master of Jesus,[1] if indeed it may be permitted to speak of a master in connection with so high an originality as his.

The perusal of the books of the Old Testament made much impression upon him.   The canon of the holy books was composed of two principal parts—the Law, that is to say, the Pentateuch, and the Prophets, such as we now possess them.   An extensive allegorical exegesis was applied to all these books; and it was sought to draw from them something that was not in them, but which responded to the aspirations of the age.   The Law, which represented not the ancient laws of the country, but Utopias, the factitious laws and pious frauds of the time of the pietistic kings, had become, since the nation had ceased to govern itself, an inexhaustible theme of subtle interpretations.   As to the Prophets and the Psalms, the popular persuasion was that almost all the somewhat mysterious traits that were in these books had reference to the Messiah, and it was sought to find there the type of him who should realize the hopes of the nation.   Jesus participated in the taste which every one had for these allegorical interpretations.   But the true poetry of the Bible, which escaped the puerile exegetists of Jerusalem, was fully revealed to his grand genius.   The Law does not appear to have had much charm for him; he thought

[1] *Pirké Aboth,* chap. i. and ii.; Talm. of Jerus., *Pesachim,* vi. 1; Talm. of Bab., *Pesachim,* 66 *a; Shabbath,* 30 *b* and 31 *a; Joma,* 35 *b.*

that he could do something better. But the religious lyrics of the Psalms were in marvellous accordance with his poetic soul; they were, all his life, his food and sustenance. The prophets—Isaiah in particular, and his successor in the record of the time of the captivity[1] —with their brilliant dreams of the future, their impetuous eloquence, and their invectives mingled with enchanting pictures, were his true teachers. He read also, no doubt, many apocryphal works—*i. e.*, writings somewhat modern, the authors of which, for the sake of an authority only granted to very ancient writings, had clothed themselves with the names of prophets and patriarchs. One of these books especially struck him, namely, the Book of Daniel. This book, composed by an enthusiastic Jew of the time of Antiochus Epiphanes, under the name of an ancient sage,[1] was the *résumé* of the spirit of those later times. Its author, a true creator of the philosophy of history, had for the first time dared to see in the march of the world and the succession of empires, only a purpose subordinate to the destinies of the Jewish people. Jesus was early penetrated by these high hopes. Perhaps, also, he had read the books of Enoch, then revered equally with the holy books,[2] and the other writings of the same class, which kept up so much excitement in the popular

---

[1]The legend of Daniel existed as early as the seventh century B.C. (Ezekiel xiv. 14 and following, xxviii. 3). It was for the necessities of the legend that he was made to live at the time of the Babylonian captivity.

[2]*Epist. Jude,* 14 and following; 2 Peter ii. 4, 11; *Testam. of the Twelve Patriarchs,* Simeon. 5; Levi, 14, 16; Judah, 18; Zab., 3; Dan, 5; Naphtali, 4. The "Book of Enoch" still forms an integral part of the Ethiopian Bible. Such as we know it from the Ethiopian version, it is composed of pieces of different dates, of which the most ancient are from the year 130 to 150 B.C. Some of these pieces have an analogy with the discourses of Jesus. Compare chaps. xcvi.-xcix. with Luke vi. 24, and following.

imagination. The advent of the Messiah, with his glories and his terrors—the nations falling down one after another, the cataclysm of heaven and earth—were the familiar food of his imagination; and, as these revolutions were reputed near, and a great number of persons sought to calculate the time when they should happen, the supernatural state of things into which such visions transport us, appeared to him from the first perfectly natural and simple.

That he had no knowledge of the general state of the world is apparent from each feature of his most authentic discourses. The earth appeared to him still divided into kingdoms warring with one another; he seemed to ignore the "Roman peace," and the new state of society which its age inaugurated. He had no precise idea of the Roman power; the name of "Cæsar" alone reached him. He saw building, in Galilee or its environs, Tiberias, Julias, Diocæsarea, Cæsarea, gorgeous works of the Herods, who sought, by these magnificent structures, to prove their admiration for Roman civilization, and their devotion toward the members of the family of Augustus, structures whose names, by a caprice of fate, now serve, though strangely altered, to designate miserable hamlets of Bedouins. He also probably saw Sebaste, a work of Herod the Great, a showy city, whose ruins would lead to the belief that it had been carried there ready made, like a machine which had only to be put up in its place. This ostentatious piece of architecture arrived in Judea by cargoes; these hundreds of columns, all of the same diameter, the ornament of some insipid *"Rue de Rivoli,"* these were what he called "the kingdoms of the world and all their glory." But this luxury of power, this administrative and official art, displeased him. What he loved were his Galilean villages, confused mixtures of huts, of nests and holes cut in the rocks, of wells, of tombs, of fig-trees, and of olives. He always clung close to Nature. The courts of kings appeared to him as places where men wear fine clothes. The charming impossibilities with which his parables abound, when he brings kings and the mighty ones on the stage,[1] prove that he never conceived of aristocratic society but as a young villager who sees the world through the prism of his simplicity.

Still less was he acquainted with the new idea, created by Grecian science, which was the basis of all philosophy, and which modern science has greatly confirmed, to wit, the exclusion of capricious gods, to whom the simple belief of ancient ages attributed the government of the universe. Almost a century before him, Lucretius had expressed, in an admirable manner, the unchangeableness of the general system of Nature. The negation of miracle—the idea that everything in the world happens by laws in which the personal intervention of superior beings has no share—was universally admitted in the great schools of all the countries which had accepted Grecian science. Perhaps even Babylon and Persia were not strangers to it. Jesus knew nothing of this progress. Although born at a time when the principle of positive science was already proclaimed, he lived entirely in the supernatural. Never, perhaps, had the Jews been more possessed with the thirst for the marvellous. Philo, who lived in a great intellectual centre, and who had received a very complete education, possessed only a chimerical and inferior knowledge of science.

Jesus, on this point, differed in no respect from his

[1] See, for example, Matt. xxii. 2, and following.

companions. He believed in the devil, whom he regarded as a kind of evil genius,[1] and he imagined, like all the world, that nervous maladies were produced by demons who possessed the patient and agitated him. The marvellous was not the exceptional for him; it was his normal state. The notion of the supernatural, with its impossibilities, is coincident with the birth of experimental science. The man who is strange to all ideas of physical laws, who believes that by praying he can change the path of the clouds, arrest disease, and even death, finds nothing extraordinary in miracle, inasmuch as the entire course of things is to him the result of the free will of the Divinity. This intellectual state was constantly that of Jesus. But in his great soul such a belief produced effects quite opposed to those produced on the vulgar. Among the latter, the belief in the special action of God led to a foolish credulity, and the deceptions of charlatans. With him it led to a profound idea of the familiar relations of man with God, and an exaggerated belief in the power of man—beautiful errors, which were the secret of his power; for if they were the means of one day showing his deficiencies in the eyes of the physicist and the chemist, they gave him a power over his own age of which no individual had been possessed before his time, or has been since.

His distinctive character very early revealed itself. Legend delights to show him even from his infancy in revolt against paternal authority, and departing from the common way to fulfill his vocation.[2] It is certain, at least, that he cared little for the relations of kinship.

---

[1] Matt. vi. 13.

[2] Luke ii. 42 and following. The Apocryphal Gospels are full of similar histories carried to the grotesque.

His family do not seem to have loved him,[1] and at times he seems to have been hard toward them.[2] Jesus, like all men exclusively preoccupied by an idea, came to think little of the ties of blood. The bond of thought is the only one that natures of this kind recognize "Behold my mother and my brethren," said he, in extending his hand toward his disciples; "he who does the will of my Father, he is my brother and my sister." The simple people did not understand the matter thus, and one day a woman passing near him cried out, "Blessed is the womb that bare thee, and the paps which gave thee suck!" But he said, "Yea, rather blessed are they that hear the word of God, and keep it."[3] Soon, in his bold revolt against nature, he went still further, and we shall see him trampling under foot everything that is human, blood, love, and country, and only keeping soul and heart for the idea which presented itself to him as the absolute form of goodness and truth.

[1] Matt. xiii. 57; Mark vi. 4; John vii. 3, and following.
[2] Matt. xii. 48; Mark iii. 33; Luke viii. 21; John ii. 4; Gospel according to the Hebrews, in St. Jerome, *Dial. adv. Pelag.,* iii. 2.
[3] Luke xi. 27, and following.

CHAPTER IV.

THE ORDER OF THOUGHT WHICH SURROUNDED THE DEVELOPMENT OF JESUS.

As the cooled earth no longer permits us to understand the phenomena of primitive creation, because the fire which penetrated it is extinct, so deliberate explanations have always appeared somewhat insufficient, when applying our timid methods of induction to the revolutions of the creative epochs which have decided the fate of humanity. Jesus lived at one of those times when the game of public life is freely played, and when the stake of human activity is increased a hundredfold. Every great part, then, entails death; for such movements suppose liberty and an absence of preventive measures, which could not exist without a terrible alternative. In these days, man risks little and gains little. In heroic periods of human activity, man risked all and gained all. The good and the wicked, or at least those who believe themselves and are believed to be such, form opposite armies. The apotheosis is reached by the scaffold; characters have distinctive features, which engrave them as eternal types in the memory of men. Except in the French Revolution, no historical centre was as suitable as that in which Jesus was formed, to develop those hidden forces which humanity holds as in reserve, and which are not seen except in days of excitement and peril.

If the government of the world were a speculative problem, and the greatest philosopher were the man

best fitted to tell his fellows what they ought to believe,
it would be from calmness and reflection that those
great moral and dogmatic truths called religions would
proceed.   But it is not so.   If we except Cakya-Mouni,
the great religious founders have not been meta-
physicians.   Buddhism itself, whose origin is in pure
thought, has conquered one-half of Asia by motives
wholly political and moral.   As to the Semitic religions, they are as little philosophical as possible.
Moses and Mahomet were not men of speculation; they
were men of action.   It was in proposing action to
their fellow-countrymen, and to their contemporaries,
that they governed humanity.   Jesus, in like manner,
was not a theologian, or a philosopher, having a more
or less well-composed system.   In order to be a disciple of Jesus, it was not necessary to sign any formu-
lary, or to pronounce any confession of faith; one thing
only was necessary—to be attached to him, to love him.
He never disputed about God, for he felt Him directly
in himself.   The rock of metaphysical subtleties,
against which Christianity broke from the third century, was in nowise created by the Founder.   Jesus had
neither dogma nor system, but a fixed personal resolution, which, exceeding in intensity every other created
will, directs to this hour the destinies of humanity.

The Jewish people had the advantage, from the captivity of Babylon up to the Middle Ages, of being in a
state of the greatest tension.   This is why the interpreters of the spirit of the nation during this long period
seemed to write under the action of an intense fever,
which placed them constantly either above or below
reason, rarely in its middle path.   Never did man seize
the problem of the future and of his destiny with a
more desperate courage, more determined to go to ex-

tremes.   Not separating the lot of humanity from that
of their little race, the Jewish thinkers were the first
who sought for a general theory of the progress of our
species.   Greece, always confined within itself, and
solely attentive to petty quarrels, has had admirable
historians; but before the Roman epoch, it would be in
vain to seek in her a general system of the philosoph;
of history, embracing all humanity.   The Jew, on the
contrary, thanks to a kind of prophetic sense which
renders the Semite at times marvellously apt to see the
great lines of the future, has made history enter into
religion.   Perhaps he owes a little of this spirit to
Persia.   Persia, from an ancient period, conceived the
history of the world as a series of evolutions, over each
of which a prophet presided.   Each prophet had his
hazar, or reign of a thousand years (chiliasm), and
from these successive ages, analogous to the Avatär of
India, is composed the course of events which prepared
the reign of Ormuzd.   At the end of the time when the
cycle of chiliasms shall be exhausted, the complete
paradise will come.   Men then will live happy; the
earth will be as one plain; there will be only one language, one law, and one government for all.   But this
advent will be preceded by terrible calamities.   Dahak
(the Satan of Persia) will break his chains and fall
upon the world.   Two prophets will come to console
mankind, and to prepare the great advent.[1]   These
ideas ran through the world, and penetrated even to
Rome, where they inspired a cycle of prophetic poems,
of which the fundamental ideas were the division of the
history of humanity into periods, the succession of the

---

[1] *Yaçna,* xiii. 24; Theopompus, in Plut., *De Iside et Osiride,* sec.
47; *Minokhired,* a passage published in the *Zeitschrift der deutschen morgenländischen Gesellschaft,* i., p. 263.

gods corresponding to these periods—a complete renovation of the world, and the final advent of a golden
age.[1] The book of Daniel, the book of Enoch, and
certain parts of the Sibylline books,[2] are the Jewish
expression of the same theory. These thoughts were
certainly far from being shared by all; they were only
embraced at first by a few persons of lively imagination, who were inclined toward strange doctrines. The
dry and narrow author of the book of Esther never
thought of the rest of the world except to despise it,
and to wish it evil.[3] The disabused epicurean who
wrote Ecclesiastes, thought so little of the future, that
he considered it even useless to labor for his children;
in the eyes of this egotistical celibate, the highest stroke
of wisdom was to use his fortune for his own enjoyment.[4] But the great achievements of a people are
generally wrought by the minority. Notwithstanding
all their enormous defects, hard, egotistical, scoffing,
cruel, narrow, subtle, and sophistical, the Jewish people
are the authors of the finest movement of disinterested
enthusiasm which history records. Opposition always
makes the glory of a country. The greatest men of a
nation are those whom it puts to death. Socrates was
the glory of the Athenians, who would not suffer him
to live amongst them. Spinoza was the greatest Jew
of modern times, and the synagogue expelled him with
ignominy. Jesus was the glory of the people of Israel,
who crucified him.

A gigantic dream haunted for centuries the Jewish

[1] Virg., Ecl. iv.; Servius, at v. 4 of this Eclogue; Nigidius quoted
by Servius, at v. 10.
[2] Book iii., 97-817.
[3] Esther vi. 13, vii. 10, viii. 7, 11-17, ix. 1-22; and in the apocryphal parts, ix. 10, 11, xiv. 13, and following, xvi. 20, 24.
[4] Eccl. i. 11, ii. 16, 18-24, iii. 19-22, iv. 8, 15, 16, v. 17, 18, vi. 3, 6,
viii. 15, ix. 9, 10.

people, constantly renewing its youth in its decrepitude.
A stranger to the theory of individual recompense,
which Greece diffused under the name of the immortality of the soul, Judea concentrated all its power of love
and desire upon the national future. She thought she
possessed divine promises of a boundless future; and
as the bitter reality, from the ninth century before our
era, gave more and more the dominion of the world to
physical force, and brutally crushed these aspirations,
she took refuge in the union of the most impossible
ideas, and attempted the strangest gyrations. Before
the captivity, when all the earthly hopes of the nation
had become weakened by the separation of the northern
tribes, they dreamt of the restoration of the house of
David, the reconciliation of the two divisions of the
people, and the triumph of theocracy and the worship
of Jehovah over idolatry. At the epoch of the captivity, a poet, full of harmony, saw the splendor of a
future Jerusalem, of which the peoples and the distant
isles should be tributaries, under colors so charming,
that one might say a glimpse of the visions of Jesus
had reached him at a distance of six centuries.[1]

The victory of Cyrus seemed at one time to realize
all that had been hoped. The grave disciples of the
Avesta and the adorers of Jehovah believed themselves
brothers. Persia had begun by banishing the multiple
dévas, and by transforming them into demons (*divs*),
to draw from the old Arian imaginations (essentially
naturalistic) a species of Monotheism. The prophetic
tone of many of the teachings of Iran had much analogy with certain compositions of Hosea and Isaiah.
Israel reposed under the Achemenidae,[2] and under

---

[1] Isaiah lx., &c.   [2] The whole book of Esther breathes a great
attachment to this dynasty.

Xerxes (Ahasuerus) made itself feared by the Iranians themselves. But the triumphal and often cruel entry of Greek and Roman civilization into Asia, threw it back upon its dreams. More than ever it invoked the Messiah as judge and avenger of the people. A complete renovation, a revolution which should shake the world to its very foundation, was necessary in order to satisfy the enormous thirst of vengeance excited in it by the sense of its superiority, and by the sight of its humiliation.[1]

If Israel had possessed the spiritualistic doctrine, which divides man in two parts—the body and the soul —and finds it quite natural that while the body decays, the soul should survive, this paroxysm of rage and of energetic protestation would have had no existence. But such a doctrine, proceeding from the Grecian philosophy, was not in the traditions of the Jewish mind. The ancient Hebrew writings contain no trace of future rewards or punishments. Whilst the idea of the solidarity of the tribe existed, it was natural that a strict retribution according to individual merits should not be thought of. So much the worse for the pious man who happened to live in an epoch of impiety; he suffered, like the rest, the public misfortunes consequent on the general irreligion. This doctrine, bequeathed by the sages of the patriarchal era, constantly produced unsustainable contradictions. Already at the time of Job it was much shaken; the old men of Teman who professed it were considered behind the age, and the young Elihu, who intervened in order to combat them, dared to utter as his first word this essentially revolutionary sentiment, "Great men are not always wise;

[1] Apocryphal letter of Baruch, in Fabricius, *Cod. pseud., V.T.,* ii. p. 147, and following.

neither do the aged understand judgment."[1] With the complications which had taken place in the world since the time of Alexander, the old Temanite and Mosaic principle became still more intolerable.[2] Never had Israel been more faithful to the Law, and yet it was subjected to the atrocious persecution of Antiochus. Only a declaimer, accustomed to repeat old phrases denuded of meaning, would dare to assert that these evils proceeded from the unfaithfulness of the people.[3] What! these victims who died for their faith, these heroic Maccabees, this mother with her seven sons, will Jehovah forget them eternally? Will he abandon them to the corruption of the grave?[4] Worldly and incredulous Sadduceeism might possibly not recoil before such a consequence, and a consummate sage, like Antigonus of Soco,[5] might indeed maintain that we must not practise virtue like a slave in expectation of a recompense, that we must be virtuous without hope. But the mass of the people could not be contented with that. Some, attaching themselves to the principle of philosophical immortality, imagined the righteous living in the memory of God, glorious forever in the remembrance of men, and judging the wicked who had persecuted them.[6] "They live in the sight of God; . . . they

[1] Job xxxiii. 9.
[2] It is nevertheless remarkable that Jesus, son of Sirach, adheres to it strictly (chap. xvii. 26-28, xxii. 10, 11, xxx. 4, and following, xli. 1, 2, xliv. 9). The author of the book of *Wisdom* holds quite opposite opinions (iv. 1, Greek text).
[3] Esth. xiv. 6, 7 (apocr.); the apocryphal Epistle of Baruch (Fabricius, *Cod. pseud., V.T.*, ii. p. 147, and following).
[4] 2 *Macc.* vii.
[5] *Perké Aboth.*, i. 3.
[6] *Wisdom* ii.-vi.; *De Rationis Imperio*, attributed to Josephus, 8, 13, 16, 18. Still we must remark that the author of this last treatise estimates the motive of personal recompense in a secondary degree. The primary impulse of martyrs is the pure love of the Law, the advantage which their death will procure to the

are known of God."[1]   That was their reward.   Others,
especially the Pharisees, had recourse to the doctrine of
the resurrection.[2]   The righteous will live again in
order to participate in the Messianic reign.   They will
live again in the flesh, and for a world of which they
will be the kings and the judges; they will be present at
the triumph of their ideas and at the humiliation of
their enemies.

We find among the ancient people of Israel only very
indecisive traces of this fundamental dogma.   The
Sadducee, who did not believe it, was in reality faithful
to the old Jewish doctrine; it was the Pharisee, the
believer in the resurrection, who was the innovator.
But in religion it is always the zealous sect which inno-
vates, which progresses, and which has influence.   Besides this, the resurrection, an idea totally different
from that of the immortality of the soul, proceeded
very naturally from the anterior doctrines and from the
position of the people.   Perhaps Persia also furnished
some of its elements.[3]   In any case, combining with
the belief in the Messiah, and with the doctrine of a
speedy renewal of all things, it formed those apocalyptic theories which, without being articles of faith (the
orthodox Sanhedrim of Jerusalem does not seem to
have adopted them), pervaded all imaginations, and
produced an extreme fermentation from one end of the
Jewish world to the other.   The total absence of dogmatic rigor caused very contradictory notions to be

people, and the glory which will attach to their name. Comp.
Wisdom iv. 1, and following; *Eccl.* xliv., and following; Jos.,
B. J., II. viii. 10, III. viii. 5.
    [1]*Wisdom,* iv. 1; *De Rat. Imp.,* 16, 18.
    [2]2 *Macc.,* vii. 9, 14, xii. 43, 44.
    [3]Theopompus, in *Diog. Laert.,* Prœm, 9. *Boundehesch,* xxxi.
The traces of the doctrine of the resurrection in the Avesta are
very doubtful.

admitted at one time, even upon so primary a point Sometimes the righteous were to await the resurrection;[1] sometimes they were to be received at the moment of death into Abraham's bosom;[2] sometimes the resurrection was to be general;[3] sometimes it was to be reserved only for the faithful;[4] sometimes it supposed a renewed earth and a new Jerusalem; sometimes it implied a previous annihilation of the universe.

Jesus, as soon as he began to think, entered into the burning atmosphere which was created in Palestine by the ideas we have just stated. These ideas were taught in no school; but they were in the very air, and his soul was early penetrated by them. Our hesitations and our doubts never reached him. On this summit of the mountain of Nazareth, where no man can sit to-day without an uneasy, though it may be a frivolous, feeling about his destiny, Jesus sat often untroubled by a doubt. Free from selfishness — that source of our troubles, which makes us seek with eagerness a reward for virtue beyond the tomb—he thought only of his work, of his race, and of humanity. Those mountains, that sea. that azure sky, those high plains in the horizon, were for him not the melancholy vision of a soul which interrogates Nature upon her fate, but the certain symbol, the transparent shadow, of an invisible world, and of a new heaven.

He never attached much importance to the political events of his time, and he probably knew little about them. The court of the Herods formed a world so different to his, that he doubtless knew it only by name. Herod the Great died about the year in which Jesus was born, leaving imperishable remembrances—monu-

---

[1]John xi. 24.   [3]Luke xvi. 22.   Cf. *De Rationis Imp.*, 13, 16, 18.
[2]Dan. xii. 2.   [4]2 *Macc.* vii. 14.

ments which must compel the most malevolent posterity to associate his name with that of Solomon; nevertheless, his work was incomplete, and could not be continued. Profanely ambitious, and lost in a maze of
religious controversies, this astute Idumean had the
advantage which coolness and judgment, stripped of
morality, give over passionate fanatics. But his idea
of a secular kingdom of Israel, even if it had not been
an anachronism in the state of the world in which it
was conceived, would inevitably have miscarried, like
the similar project which Solomon formed, owing to
the difficulties proceeding from the character of the
nation. His three sons were only lieutenants of the
Romans, analogous to the rajahs of India under the
English dominion. Antipater, or Antipas, tetrarch of
Galilee and of Peræa, of whom Jesus was a subject all
his life, was an idle and useless prince,[1] a favorite and
flatterer of Tiberius,[2] and too often misled by the bad
influence of his second wife, Herodias.[3] Philip,
tetrarch of Gaulonitis and Batanea, into whose dominions Jesus made frequent journeys, was a much better
sovereign.[4] As to Archelaus, ethnarch of Jerusalem,
Jesus could not know him, for he was about ten years
old when this man, who was weak and without character, though sometimes violent, was deposed by Augustus.[5] The last trace of self-government was thus lost
to Jerusalem. United to Samaria and Idumea, Judea
formed a kind of dependency of the province of Syria,
in which the senator Publius Sulpicius Quirinus, well
known as consul,[6] was the imperial legate. A series of

---

[1]Jos., *Ant.*, VIII. v. 1, vii. 1 and 2; Luke iii. 19.
[2]Ibid., XVIII. ii. 3, iv. 5, v. 1.   [3]Ibid., XVIII. vii. 2.
[4]Ibid., XVIII. iv. 6.   [5]Ibid., XVII. xii. 2; and *B. J.*, II. vii. 3.
[6]Orelli, *Inscr. Lat.*, No. 3693; Henzen, *Suppl.*, No. 7041; *Fasti
prænestini,* on the 6th of March, and on the 28th of April (in the

Roman procurators, subordinate in important matters
to the imperial legate of Syria—Coponius, Marcus
Ambivius, Annius Rufus, Valerius Gratus, and lastly
(in the twenty-sixth year of our era), Pontius Pilate[1]
—followed each other, and were constantly occupied in
extinguishing the volcano which was seething beneath
their feet.

Continual seditions, excited by the zealots of Mosaism, did not cease, in fact, to agitate Jerusalem during
all this time.[2] The death of the seditious was certain;
but death, when the integrity of the Law was in question, was sought with avidity. To overturn the
Roman eagle, to destroy the works of art raised by the
Herods, in which the Mosaic regulations were not
always respected[3]—to rise up against the votive escutcheons put up by the procurators, the inscriptions of
which appeared tainted with idolatry[4]—were perpetual
temptations to fanatics, who had reached that degree
of exaltation which removes all care for life. Judas,
son of Sariphea, Matthias, son of Margaloth, two very
celebrated doctors of the law, formed against the established order a boldly aggressive party, which continued
after their execution.[5] The Samaritans were agitated
by movements of a similar nature.[6] The Law had
never counted a greater number of impassioned disciples than at this time, when he already lived who, by

Corpus Inscr. Lat., i. 314, 317) ; Borghesi, *Fastes Consulaires*
(yet unedited), in the year 742; R. Bergmann, *De Inscr. Lat. ad.*
P. S. Quirinium, ut videtur, referenda (Berlin, 1851). Cf. Tac.,
Ann., ii. 30, iii. 48; Strabo, XII. vi. 5.

[1] Jos., *Ant.,* l. XVIII.
[2] Ibid., the books XVI. and XVIII. entirely, and *B. J.,* books I.
and II.
[3] Jos., *Ant.,* XV. x. 4. Compare Book of Enoch, xcvii. 13, 14.
[4] Philo, *Leg. ad Caium,* § 38.
[5] Jos., *Ant.,* XVII. vi. 2, and following ; *B. J.,* I. xxxiii. 3, and following.   [6] Jos., *Ant.,* XVIII. iv. 1, and following.

the full authority of his genius and of his great soul, was about to abrogate it. The "Zelotes" (Kenaïm), or "Sicarii," pious assassins, who imposed on themselves the task of killing whoever in their estimation broke the Law, began to appear.[1]   Representatives of a totally different spirit, the Thaumaturges, considered as in some sort divine, obtained credence in consequence of the imperious want which the age experienced for the supernatural and the divine.[2]

A movement which had much more influence upon Jesus was that of Judas the Gaulonite, or Galilean. Of all the exactions to which the country newly conquered by Rome was subjected, the census was the most unpopular.[3]   This measure, which always astonishes people unaccustomed to the requirements of great central administrations, was particularly odious to the Jews.   We see that already, under David, a numbering of the people provoked violent recriminations, and the menaces of the prophets.[4]   The census, in fact, was the basis of taxation; now taxation, to a pure theocracy, was almost an impiety.   God being the sole Master whom man ought to recognize, to pay tithe to a secular sovereign was, in a manner, to put him in the place of God.   Completely ignorant of the idea of the State, the Jewish theocracy only acted up to its logical induction —the negation of civil society and of all government. The money of the public treasury was accounted stolen money.[5]   The census ordered by Quirinus (in the year

[1] Mishnah, *Sanhedrim,* ix. 6; John xvi. 2; Jos., *B. J.,* book ɪᴠ., and following.
[2] *Acts* viii. 9.   Verse 11 leads us to suppose that Simon the magician was already famous in the time of Jesus.
[3] Discourse of Claudius at Lyons, Tab. ii. sub fin.   De Boisseau, *Inscr. Ant. de Lyon,* p. 136.
[4] 2 Sam. xxiv.
[5] Talmud of Babylon. *Baba Kama.* 113 *a;* ˢ𝐾abbath. 33 *b.*

6 of the Christian era) powerfully reawakened these ideas, and caused a great fermentation. An insurrection broke out in the northern provinces. One Judas, of the town of Gamala, upon the eastern shore of the Lake of Tiberias, and a Pharisee named Sadoc, by denying the lawfulness of the tax, created a numerous party, which soon broke out in open revolt.[1] The fundamental maxims of this party were — that they ought to call no man "master," this title belonging to God alone; and that liberty was better than life. Judas had, doubtless, many other principles, which Josephus, always careful not to compromise his co-religionists, designedly suppresses; for it is impossible to understand how, for so simple an idea, the Jewish historian should give him a place among the philosophers of his nation, and should regard him as the founder of a fourth school, equal to those of the Pharisees, the Sadducees, and the Essenes. Judas was evidently the chief of a Galilean sect, deeply imbued with the Messianic idea, and which became a political movement. The procurator, Coponius, crushed the sedition of the Gaulonite; but the school remained, and preserved its chiefs. Under the leadership of Menahem, son of the founder, and of a certain Eleazar, his relative, we find them again very active in the last contests of the Jews against the Romans.[2] Perhaps Jesus saw this Judas, whose idea of the Jewish revolution was so different from his own; at all events, he knew his school, and it was probably to avoid his error that he pronounced the axiom upon the penny of Cæsar. Jesus, more wise,

[1] Jos., *Ant.*, xviii. i. 1 and 6; *B. J.*, ii. viii. 1; *Acts* v. 37. Previous to Judas the Gaulonite, the *Acts* place another agitator, Theudas; but this is an anachronism, the movement of Theudas took place in the year 44 of the Christian era (Jos., *Ant.*, xx. v. 1).

[2] Jos., *B. J.*, ii. xvii. 8, and following.

and far removed from all sedition, profited by the fault of his predecessor, and dreamed of another kingdom and another deliverance.

Galilee was thus an immense furnace wherein the most diverse elements were seething.[1] An extraordinary contempt of life, or, more properly speaking, a kind of longing for death,[2] was the consequence of these agitations. Experience counts for nothing in these great fanatical movements. Algeria, at the commencement of the French occupation, saw arise, each spring, inspired men, who declared themselves invulnerable, and sent by God to drive away the infidels; the following year their death was forgotten, and their successors found no less credence. The Roman power, very stern on the one hand, yet little disposed to meddle, permitted a good deal of liberty. Those great, brutal despotisms, terrible in repression, were not so suspicious as powers which have a faith to defend. They allowed everything up to the point when they thought it necessary to be severe. It is not recorded that Jesus was even once interfered with by the civil power, in his wandering career. Such freedom, and, above all, the happiness which Galilee enjoyed in being much less confined in the bonds of Pharisaic pedantry, gave to this district a real superiority over Jerusalem. The revolution, or, in other words, the belief in the Messiah, caused here a general fermentation. Men deemed themselves on the eve of the great renovation; the Scriptures, tortured into divers meanings, fostered the most colossal hopes. In each line of the simple

---

[1] Luke xiii. 1. The Galilean movement of Judas, son of Hezekiah, does not appear to have been of a religious character; perhaps, however, its character has been misrepresented by Josephus (*Ant.*, XVII. x. 5).

[2] Jos., *Ant.*, XVI. vi. 2, 3; XVIII. i. 1.

writings of the Old Testament they saw the assurance, and, in a manner, the programme of the future reign, which was to bring peace to the righteous, and to seal forever the work of God.

From all time, this division into two parties, opposed in interest and spirit, had been for the Hebrew nation a principle which contributed to their moral growth. Every nation called to high destinies ought to be a little world in itself, including opposite poles. Greece presented, at a few leagues' distance from each other, Sparta and Athens—to a superficial observer, the two antipodes; but, in reality, rival sisters, necessary to one another. It was the same with Judea. Less brilliant in one sense than the development of Jerusalem, that of the North was on the whole much more fertile; the greatest achievements of the Jewish people have always proceeded thence. A complete absence of the love of Nature, bordering upon something dry, narrow, and ferocious, has stamped all the works purely Hierosoly-mite with a degree of grandeur, though sad, arid, and repulsive. With its solemn doctors, its insipid canon-ists, its hypocritical and atrabilious devotees, Jerusalem has not conquered humanity. The North has given to the world the simple Shunammite, the humble Canaan-ite, the impassioned Magdalene, the good foster-father Joseph, and the Virgin Mary. The North alone has made Christianity; Jerusalem, on the contrary, is the true home of that obstinate Judaism which, founded by the Pharisees, and fixed by the Talmud, has tra-versed the Middle Ages, and come down to us.

A beautiful external nature tended to produce a much less austere spirit—a spirit less sharply monothe-istic, if I may use the expression, which imprinted a charming and idyllic character on all the dreams of

Galilee. The saddest country in the world is perhaps
the region round about Jerusalem. Galilee, on the contrary, was a very green, shady, smiling district, the
true home of the Song of Songs, and the songs of the
well-beloved.[1] During the two months of March and
April, the country forms a carpet of flowers of an incomparable variety of colors. The animals are small,
and extremely gentle—delicate and lively turtle-doves,
blue-birds so light that they rest on a blade of grass
without bending it, crested larks which venture almost
under the feet of the traveller, little river tortoises with
mild and lively eyes, storks with grave and modest
mien, which, laying aside all timidity, allow man to
come quite near them, and seem almost to invite his
approach. In no country in the world do the mountains spread themselves out with more harmony, or
inspire higher thoughts. Jesus seems to have had a
peculiar love for them. The most important acts of
his divine career took place upon the mountains. It
was there that he was the most inspired;[2] it was there
that he held secret communion with the ancient
prophets; and it was there that his disciples witnessed
his transfiguration.[3]

This beautiful country has now become sad and

[1] Jos., *B. J.*, III. iii. I. The horrible state to which the country
is reduced, especially near Lake Tiberias, ought not to deceive us
These countries, now scorched, were formerly terrestrial para-
dises. The baths of Tiberias, which are now a frightful abode,
were formerly the most beautiful places in Galilee (Jos., *Ant.*,
XVIII. ii, 3.) Josephus (*Bell. Jud.*, III. x. 8) extols the beautiful
trees of the plain of Gennesareth, where there is no longer a
single one. Anthony the Martyr, about the year 600, consequently
fifty years before the Mussulman invasion, still found Galilee
covered with delightful plantations, and compares its fertility to
that of Egypt (*Itin.*, § 5).

[2] Matt. v. I, xiv. 23; Luke vi. 12.

[3] Matt. xvii. 1, and following; Mark ix. I, and following; Luke
ix. 28, and following.

gloomy through the ever-impoverishing influence of Islamism. But still everything which man cannot destroy breathes an air of freedom, mildness, and tenderness, and at the time of Jesus it overflowed with happiness and prosperity. The Galileans were considered energetic, brave, and laborious.[1] If we except Tiberias, built by Antipas in honor of Tiberius (about the year 15), in the Roman style,[2] Galilee had no large towns. The country was, nevertheless, well peopled, covered with small towns and large villages, and cultivated in all parts with skill.[3] From the ruins which remain of its ancient splendor, we can trace an agricultural people, no way gifted in art, caring little for luxury, indifferent to the beauties of form and exclusively idealistic. The country abounded in fresh streams and in fruits; the large farms were shaded with vines and fig-trees; the gardens were filled with trees bearing apples, walnuts, and pomegranates.[4] The wine was excellent, if we may judge by that which the Jews still obtain at Safed, and they drank much of it.[5] This contented and easily satisfied life was not like the gross materialism of our peasantry, the coarse pleasures of agricultural Normandy, or the heavy mirth of the Flemish. It spiritualized itself in ethereal dreams—in a kind of poetic mysticism, blending heaven and earth.

[1] Jos., *B. J.*, III. iii. 2.
[2] Jos., *Ant.*, XVIII. ii. 2; *B. J.*, II. ix. 1; *Vita*, 12, 13, 64.
[3] Jos., *B. J.*, III. iii. 2.
[4] We may judge of this by some enclosures in the neighborhood of Nazareth. Cf. Song of Solomon ii. 3, 5, 13, iv. 13, vi. 6, 10, vii. 8, 12, viii. 2, 5; Anton. Martyr, *l. c.* The aspect of the great farms is still well preserved in the south of the country of Tyre (ancient tribe of Asher). Traces of the ancient Palestinian agriculture, with its troughs, threshing-floors, wine-presses, mills, &c., cut in the rock, are found at every step.
[5] Matt. ix. 17, xi. 19; Mark ii. 22; Luke v. 37, vii. 34; John ii. 3, and following.

Leave the austere Baptist in his desert of Judea to preach penitence, to inveigh without ceasing, and to live on locusts in the company of jackals. Why should the companions of the bridegroom fast while the bridegroom is with them? Joy will be a part of the kingdom of God. Is she not the daughter of the humble in heart, of the men of good will?

The whole history of infant Christianity has become in this manner a delightful pastoral. A Messiah at the marriage festival—the courtezan and the good Zaccheus called to his feasts—the founders of the kingdom of heaven like a bridal procession; that is what Galilee has boldly offered, and what the world has accepted. Greece has drawn pictures of human life by sculpture and by charming poetry, but always without backgrounds or distant receding perspectives. In Galilee were wanting the marble, the practiced workmen, the exquisite and refined language. But Galilee has created the most sublime ideal for the popular imagination; for behind its idyl moves the fate of humanity, and the light which illumines its picture is the sun of the kingdom of God.

Jesus lived and grew amidst these enchanting scenes. From his infancy, he went almost annually to the feast at Jerusalem.[1] The pilgrimage was a sweet solemnity for the provincial Jews. Entire series of psalms were consecrated to celebrate the happiness of thus journeying in family companionship[2] during several days in the spring across the hills and valleys, each one having in prospect the splendors of Jerusalem, the solemnities of the sacred courts, and the joy of brethren dwelling together in unity.[3] The route which Jesus ordinarily

[1] Luke ii 41.   [2] Luke ii. 42-44.   [3] See especially Ps. lxxxiv., cxxii., cxxxiii. (Vulg., lxxxiii., cxxi., cxxxii).

took in these journeys was that which is followed to this day through Ginæa and Shechem.[1] From Shechem to Jerusalem the journey is very tiresome. But the neighborhood of the old sanctuaries of Shiloh and Bethel, near which the travellers pass, keeps their interest alive. *Ain-el-Haramie*,[2] the last halting-place, is a charming and melancholy spot, and few impressions equal that experienced on encamping there for the night. The valley is narrow and sombre, and a dark stream issues from the rocks, full of tombs, which form its banks. It is, I think, the "valley of tears," or of dropping waters, which is described as one of the stations on the way in the delightful Eighty-fourth Psalm,[3] and which became the emblem of life for the sad and sweet mysticism of the Middle Ages. Early the next day they would be at Jerusalem; such an expectation even now sustains the caravan, rendering the night short and slumber light.

These journeys, in which the assembled nation exchanged its ideas, and which were almost always centres of great agitation, placed Jesus in contact with the mind of his countrymen, and no doubt inspired him whilst still young with a lively antipathy for the defects of the official representatives of Judaism. It is supposed that very early the desert had great influence on his development, and that he made long stays there.[4] But the God he found in the desert was not his God. It was rather the God of Job, severe and terrible, ac-

---

[1] Luke ix. 51-53, xvii. 11; John iv. 4; Jos., *Ant.*, xx. vi. 1; *B. J.*, II. xii. 3; *Vita*, 52. Often, however, the pilgrims came by Peræa, in order to avoid Samaria, where they incurred dangers; Matt. xix. 1; Mark x. 1.

[2] According to Josephus (*Vita*, 52) it was three days' journey. But the stage from Shechem to Jerusalem was generally divided into two.

[3] lxxxiii. according to the Vulgate. v 7.   [4] Luke iv. 42, v. 16.

countable to no one.   Sometimes Satan came to tempt
him.   He returned, then, into his beloved Galilee, and
found again his heavenly Father in the midst of the
green hills and the clear fountains—and among the
crowds of women and children, who, with joyous soul
and the song of angels in their hearts, awaited the salvation of Israel.

CHAPTER V.

THE FIRST SAYINGS OF JESUS—HIS IDEAS OF A DIVINE FATHER AND OF A PURE RELIGION—FIRST DISCIPLES.

JOSEPH died before his son had taken any public part. Mary remained, in a manner, the head of the family, and this explains why her son, when it was wished to distinguish him from others of the same name, was most frequently called the "son of Mary."[1] It seems that having, by the death of her husband, been left friendless at Nazareth, she withdrew to Cana,[2] from which she may have come originally. Cana[3] was a little town at from two to two and a half hours' journey from Nazareth, at the foot of the mountains which bound the plain of Asochis on the north.[4] The prospect, less grand than at Nazareth, extends over all the plain, and is bounded in the most picturesque manner by the mountains of Nazareth and the hills of Sepphoris. Jesus appears to have resided some time in this place. Here he probably passed a part of his youth, and here his greatness first revealed itself.[5]

He followed the trade of his father, which was that

---

[1] This is the expression of Mark vi. 3; cf. Matt. xiii. 55. Mark did not know Joseph. John and Luke, on the contrary, prefer the expression "son of Joseph." Luke iii. 23, iv. 22; John i, 45, iv. 42.

[2] John ii. 1, iv. 46. John alone is informed on this point.

[3] I admit, as probable, the idea which identifies Cana of Galilee with *Kana ei Djélil.* We may, nevertheless, attach value to the arguments for *Kefr Kenna,* a place an hour or an hour and a half's journey N.N.E. of Nazareth.

[4] Now *El-Buttauf.*

[5] John ii. 11, iv. 46. One or two disciples were of Cana, John xxi. 2; Matt. x. 4; Mark iii. 18.

of a carpenter.[1] This was not in any degree humiliating or grievous. The Jewish customs required that a man devoted to intellectual work should learn a trade. The most celebrated doctors did so;[2] thus St. Paul, whose education had been so carefully tended, was a tent-maker.[3] Jesus never married. All his power of love centred upon that which he regarded as his celestial vocation. The extremely delicate feeling toward women, which we remark in him, was not separated from the exclusive devotion which he had for his mission. Like Francis d'Assisi and Francis de Sales, he treated as sisters the women who were loved of the same work as himself; he had his St. Clare, his Frances de Chantal. It is, however, probable that these loved him more than the work; he was, no doubt, more beloved than loving. Thus, as often happens in very elevated natures, tenderness of the heart was transformed in him into an infinite sweetness, a vague poetry, and a universal charm. His relations, free and intimate, but of an entirely moral kind, with women of doubtful character, are also explained by the passion which attached him to the glory of his Father, and which made him jealously anxious for all beautiful creatures who could contribute to it.[4]

What was the progress of the ideas of Jesus during this obscure period of his life? Through what meditations did he enter upon the prophetic career? We have no information on these points, his history having come to us in scattered narratives, without exact chronology. But the development of character is every-

---

[1] Mark vi. 3; Justin, *Dial. cum Tryph.*, 88.
[2] For example, "Rabbi Johanan, the shoemaker, Rabbi Isaac, the Blacksmith."   [3] *Acts* xviii. 3.
[4] Luke vii. 37, and following; John iv. 7, and following; viii. 3, and following.

where the same; and there is no doubt that the growth
of so powerful individuality as that of Jesus obeyed
very rigorous laws. A high conception of the Divinity—which he did not owe to Judaism, and which
seems to have been in all its parts the creation of his
great mind—was in a manner the source of all his
power. It is essential here that we put aside the ideas
familiar to us, and the discussions in which little minds
exhaust themselves. In order properly to understand
the precise character of the piety of Jesus, we must forget all that is placed between the gospel and ourselves.
Deism and Pantheism have become the two poles of
theology. The paltry discussions of scholasticism, the
dryness of spirit of Descartes, the deep-rooted irreligion of the eighteenth century, by lessening God, and
by limiting Him, in a manner, by the exclusion of
everything which is not His very self, have stifled in
the breast of modern rationalism all fertile ideas of the
Divinity. If God, in fact, is a personal being outside
of us, he who believes himself to have peculiar relations
with God is a "visionary," and as the physical and
physiological sciences have shown us that all supernatural visions are illusions, the logical Deist finds it
impossible to understand the great beliefs of the past.
Pantheism, on the other hand, in suppressing the
Divine personality, is as far as it can be from the living
God of the ancient religions. Were the men who have
best comprehended God — Cakya-Mouni, Plato, St.
Paul, St. Francis d'Assisi, and St. Augustine (at
some periods of his fluctuating life)—Deists or Pan-
theists? Such a question has no meaning. The physical and metaphysical proofs of the existence of God
were quite indifferent to them. They felt the Divine
within themselves. We must place Jesus in the first

rank of this great family of the true sons of God. Jesus had no visions; God did not speak to him as to one outside of Himself; God was in him; he felt himself with God, and he drew from his heart all he said of his Father. He lived in the bosom of God by constant communication with Him; he saw Him not, but he understood Him, without need of the thunder and the burning bush of Moses, of the revealing tempest of Job, of the oracle of the old Greek sages, of the familiar genius of Socrates, or of the angel Gabriel of Mahomet. The imagination and the hallucination of a St. Theresa, for example, are useless here. The intoxication of the Soufi proclaiming himself identical with God is also quite another thing. Jesus never once gave utterance to the sacrilegious idea that he was God. He believed himself to be in direct communion with God; he believed himself to be the Son of God. The highest consciousness of God which has existed in the bosom of humanity was that of Jesus.

We understand, on the other hand, how Jesus, starting with such a disposition of spirit, could never be a speculative philosopher like Cakya-Mouni. Nothing is further from scholastic theology than the Gospel.[1] The speculations of the Greek fathers on the Divine essence proceed from an entirely different spirit. God, conceived simply as Father, was all the theology of Jesus. And this was not with him a theoretical principle, a doctrine more or less proved, which he sought to inculcate in others. He did not argue with his dis-

---

[1] The discourses which the fourth Gospel attributes to Jesus contain some germs of theology. But these discourses being in absolute contradiction with those of the synoptical Gospels, which represent, without any doubt, the primitive *Logia*, ought to count simply as documents of apostolic history, and not as elements of the life of Jesus.

ciples;[1] he demanded from them no effort of attention.
He did not preach his opinions; he preached himself.
Very great and very disinterested minds often present,
associated with much elevation, that character of perpetual attention to themselves, and extreme personal
susceptibility, which, in general, is peculiar to women.[2]
Their conviction that God is in them, and occupies
Himself perpetually with them, is so strong, that
they have no fear of obtruding themselves upon others;
our reserve, and our respect for the opinion of others,
which is a part of our weakness, could not belong to
them. This exaltation of self is not egotism; for such
men, possessed by their idea, give their lives freely, in
order to seal their work; it is the identification of self
with the object it has embraced, carried to its utmost
limit. It is regarded as vain-glory by those who see in
the new teaching only the personal phantasy of the
founder; but it is the finger of God to those who see the
result. The fool stands side by side here with the
inspired man, only the fool never succeeds. It has not
yet been given to insanity to influence seriously the
progress of humanity.

Doubtless, Jesus did not attain at first this high
affirmation of himself. But it is probable that, from
the first, he regarded his relationship with God as that
of a son with his father. This was his great act of
originality; in this he had nothing in common with his
race.[3] Neither the Jew nor the Mussulman has understood this delightful theology of love. The God of

---

[1] See Matt. ix. 9, and other analogous accounts.
[2] See, for example, John xxi, 15, and following.
[3] The great soul of Philo is in sympathy here, as on so many
other points, with that of Jesus. *De Confus. Ling.*, § 14; *De Migr.
Abr.*, § 1; *De Somniis*, ii., § 41; *De Agric. Noë*, § 12; *De Muta-
tione Nominum*, § 4. But Philo is scarcely a Jew in spirit.

Jesus is not that tyrannical master who kills us, damns us, or saves us, according to His pleasure. The God of Jesus is our Father. We hear Him in listening to the gentle inspiration which cries within us, "Abba, Father."[1] The God of Jesus is not the partial despot who has chosen Israel for His people, and specially protects them. He is the God of humanity. Jesus was not a patriot, like the Maccabees; or a theocrat, like Judas the Gaulonite. Boldly raising himself above the prejudices of his nation, he established the universal fatherhood of God. The Gaulonite maintained that we should die rather than give to another than God the name of "Master;" Jesus left this name to any one who liked to take it, and reserved for God a dearer name. Whilst he accorded to the powerful of the earth, who were to him representatives of force, a respect full of irony, he proclaimed the supreme consolation—the recourse to the Father which each one has in heaven—and the true kingdom of God, which each one bears in his heart.

This name of "kingdom of God," or "kingdom of heaven,"[2] was the favorite term of Jesus to express the revolution which he brought into the world.[3] Like almost all the Messianic terms, it came from the book of Daniel. According to the author of this extraordinary book, the four profane empires, destined to fall, were to be succeeded by a fifth empire, that of the saints, which should last forever.[4] This reign of God

[1] Galatians iv. 6.

[2] The word "heaven" in the rabbinical language of that time is synonymous with the name of "God," which they avoided pronouncing. Compare Matt. xxi. 25; Luke xv. 18, xx. 4.

[3] This expression occurs on each page of the synoptical Gospels, the Acts of the Apostles, and St. Paul. If it only appears once in John (iii. 3, 5), it is because the discourses related in the fourth Gospel are far from representing the true words of Jesus.

[4] Dan. ii. 44, vii. 13, 14. 22. 27.

upon earth naturally led to the most diverse interpretations. To Jewish theology, the "kingdom of God" is most frequently only Judaism itself—the true religion, the monotheistic worship, piety.[1] In the later periods of his life, Jesus believed that this reign would be realized in a material form by a sudden renovation of the world. But doubtless this was not his first idea.[2] The admirable moral which he draws from the idea of God as Father, is not that of enthusiasts who believe the world is near its end, and who prepare themselves by asceticism for a chimerical catastrophe; it is that of men who have lived, and still would live. "The kingdom of God is within you," said he to those who sought with subtlety for external signs.[3] The realistic conception of the Divine advent was but a cloud, a transient error, which his death has made us forget. The Jesus who founded the true kingdom of God, the kingdom of the meek and the humble, was the Jesus of early life[4]—of those chaste and pure days when the voice of his Father re-echoed within him in clearer tones. It was then for some months, perhaps a year, that God truly dwelt upon the earth. The voice of the young carpenter suddenly acquired an extraordinary sweetness. An infinite charm was exhaled from his person, and those who had seen him up to that time no longer recognized him.[5] He had not yet any disciples,

[1] Mishnah, *Berakoth*, ii. 1, 3; Talmud of Jerusalem, *Berakoth*, ii. 2; *Kiddushin*, i. 2; Talm. of Bab., *Berakoth*, 15 *a; Mekilta*, 42 *b; Siphra*, 170 *b*. The expression appears often in the *Medrashim*.

[2] Matt. vi. 33, xii. 28, xix. 12; Mark xii. 34; Luke xii. 31.

[3] Luke xvii. 20, 21.

[4] The grand theory of the revelation of the Son of Man is in fact reserved, in the synoptics, for the chapters which precede the narrative of the Passion. The first discourses, especially in Matthew, are entirely moral.

[5] Matt. xiii. 54 and following; Mark vi. 2 and following; John v. 43.

and the group which gathered around him was neither a sect nor a school; but a common spirit, a sweet and penetrating influence was felt.   His amiable character, accompanied doubtless by one of those lovely faces[1] which sometimes appear in the Jewish race, threw around him a fascination from which no one in the midst of these kindly and simple populations could escape.

Paradise would, in fact, have been brought to earth if the ideas of the young Master had not far transcended the level of ordinary goodness beyond which it has not been found possible to raise the human race. The brotherhood of men, as sons of God, and the moral consequences which result therefrom, were deduced with exquisite feeling.   Like all the rabbis of the time, Jesus was little inclined toward consecutive reasonings, and clothed his doctrine in concise aphorisms, and in an expressive form, at times enigmatical and strange.[2] Some of these maxims come from the books of the Old Testament.   Others were the thoughts of more modern sages, especially those of Antigonus of Soco, Jesus, son of Sirach, and Hillel, which had reached him, not from learned study, but as oft-repeated proverbs.   The synagogue was rich in very happily expressed sentences, which formed a kind of current proverbial literature.[3]   Jesus adopted almost all this oral teaching, but imbued it with a superior spirit.[4]   Exceeding the

[1]The tradition of the plainness of Jesus (Justin, *Dial. cum Tryph.*, 85, 88, 100) springs from a desire to see realized in him a pretended Messianic trait (Isa. liii. 2).

[2]The *Logia* of St. Matthew joins several of these axioms together, to form lengthened discourses.   But the fragmentary form makes itself felt notwithstanding.

[3]The sentences of the Jewish doctors of the time are collected in the little book entitled, *Pirké Aboth*.

[4]The comparisons will be made afterward as they present themselves.   It has been sometimes supposed that—the compilation of

duties laid down by the Law and the elders, he demanded perfection. All the virtues of humility—forgiveness, charity, abnegation, and self-denial—virtues which with good reason have been called Christian, if we mean by that that they have been truly preached by Christ, were in this first teaching, though undeveloped. As to justice, he was content with repeating the well-known axiom—"Whatsoever ye would that men should do to you, do ye even so to them."[1] But this old, though somewhat selfish wisdom, did not satisfy him. He went to excess, and said—"Whosoever shall smite thee on thy right cheek, turn to him the other also. And if any man will sue thee at the law, and take away thy coat, let him have thy cloak also."[2] "If thy right eye offend thee, pluck it out, and cast it from thee."[3] "Love your enemies, do good to them that hate you, pray for them that persecute you."[4] "Judge not, that ye be not judged."[5] "Forgive, and ye shall be forgiven."[6] "Be ye therefore merciful as your Father also is merciful."[7] "It is more blessed to give than to receive."[8] "Who-

the Talmud being later than that of the Gospels—parts may have been borrowed by the Jewish compilers from the Christian morality. But this is inadmissible—a wall of separation existed between the Church and the Synagogue. The Christian and Jewish literature had scarcely any influence on one another before the thirteenth century.

[1] Matt. vii. 12; Luke vi. 31. This axiom is in the book of *Tobit*, iv. 16. Hillel used it habitually (Talm. of Bab., *Shabbath*, 31 *a*), and declared, like Jesus, that it was the sum of the Law.

[2] Matt. v. 39, and following; Luke vi. 29. Compare Jeremiah, *Lamentations* iii. 30.

[3] Matt. v. 29, 30, xviii. 9; Mark ix. 46.

[4] Matt. v. 44; Luke vi. 27. Compare Talmud of Babylon, *Shabbath*, 88 *b*; *Joma*, 23 *a*.

[5] Matt. vii. 1; Luke vi. 37. Compare Talmud of Babylon, *Kethuboth*, 105 *b*.

[6] Luke vi. 37. Compare *Lev.* xix. 18; *Prov.* xx. 22; *Ecclesiasticus* xxviii. 1, and following.

[7] Luke vi. 36; Siphré, 51 *b* (Sultzbach, 1802).

[8] A saying related in *Acts* xx. 35.

soever shall exalt himself shall be abased; and he that
shall humble himself shall be exalted."[1]

Upon alms, pity, good works, kindness, peaceful-
ness, and complete disinterestedness of heart, he had
little to add to the doctrine of the synagogue.[2] But he
placed upon them an emphasis full of unction, which
made the old maxims appear new. Morality is not
composed of more or less well-expressed principles.
The poetry which makes the precept loved, is more
than the precept itself, taken as an abstract truth.
Now it cannot be denied that these maxims borrowed
by Jesus from his predecessors, produce quite a different effect in the Gospel to that in the ancient Law, in
the *Pirké Aboth,* or in the Talmud. It is neither the
ancient Law nor the Talmud which has conquered and
changed the world. Little original in itself — if we
mean by that that one might recompose it almost entirely by the aid of older maxims—the morality of the
Gospels remains, nevertheless, the highest creation of
human conscience—the most beautiful code of perfect
life that any moralist has traced.

Jesus did not speak against the Mosaic law, but it is
clear that he saw its insufficiency, and allowed it to be
seen that he did so. He repeated unceasingly that
more must be done than the ancient sages had commanded.[3] He forbade the least harsh word;[4] he prohibited divorce,[5] and all swearing;[6] he censured re-

---

[1] Matt. xxiii. 12; Luke xiv. 11, xviii. 14. The sentences quoted
by St. Jerome from the "Gospel according to the Hebrews"
(Comment. in *Epist. ad Ephes.,* v. 4; in Ezek. xviii.; *Dial. adv.
Pelag.,* iii. 2), are imbued with the same spirit.
[2] *Deut.* xxiv., xxv., xxvi., &c.; Isa. lviii. 7; *Prov.* xix. 17; *Pirké
Aboth,* i.; Talmud of Jerusalem, *Peah,* i. 1; Talmud of Babylon,
Shabbath, 63 a.
[3] Matt. v. 20, and following.   [4] Matt. v. 22.
[5] Matt. v. 31, and following. Compare Talmud of Babylon, *San-
edrim,* 22 a.   [6] Matt. v. 33, and following.

venge;[1] he condemned usury;[2] he considered voluptuous desire as criminal as adultery;[3] he insisted upon a
universal forgiveness of injuries.[4] The motive on
which he rested these maxims of exalted charity was
always the same . . . "That ye may be the children of your Father which is in heaven: for He maketh
His sun to rise on the evil and the good. For if ye
love them which love you, what reward have ye? do
not even the publicans the same? And if ye salute
your brethren only, what do ye more than others? do
not even the publicans so? Be ye therefore perfect,
even as your Father which is in heaven is perfect."[5]

A pure worship, a religion without priests and external observances, resting entirely on the feelings of the
heart, on the imitation of God,[6] on the direct relation
of the conscience with the heavenly Father, was the
result of these principles. Jesus never shrank from
this bold conclusion, which made him a thorough revo-
lutionist in the very centre of Judaism. Why should
there be mediators between man and his Father? As
God only sees the heart, of what good are these purifi-
cations, these observances relating only to the body?[7]
Even tradition, a thing so sacred to the Jews, is nothing compared to sincerity.[8] The hypocrisy of the
Pharisees, who, in praying, turned their heads to see if
they were observed, who gave their alms with ostenta-

---

[1]Matt. v. 38, and following.
[2]Matt. v. 42. The Law prohibited it also (*Deut.* xv. 7, 8), but
less formally, and custom authorized it (Luke vii. 41, and following).
[3]Matt. xxvii. 28. Compare Talmud, *Masséket Kalla* (edit.
Fürth, 1793), fol. 34 *b*.   [4]Matt. v. 23, and following.
[5]Matt. v. 45, and following. Compare *Lev.* xi. 44, xix. 2.
[6]Compare Philo, *De Migr. Abr.,* § 23 and 24; *De Vita Contemp.*
the whole.
[7]Matt. xv. 11, and following; Mark vii. 6, and following.
[8]Mark vii. 6, and following.

tion, and put marks upon their garments, that they might be recognized as pious persons — all these grimaces of false devotion disgusted him. "They have their recompense," said he; "but thou, when thou doest thine alms, let not thy left hand know what thy right hand doeth, that thy alms may be in secret, and thy Father, which seeth in secret, Himself shall reward thee openly."[1] "And when thou prayest, thou shalt not be as the hypocrites are: for they love to pray standing in the synagogues, and in the corners of the streets, that they may be seen of men. Verily I say unto you, They have their reward. But thou, when thou prayest, enter into thy closet; and when thou hast shut thy door, pray to thy Father which is in secret; and thy Father, which seeth in secret, shall reward thee openly. But when ye pray, use not vain repetitions, as the heathen do: for they think that they shall be heard for their much speaking. Your Father knoweth what things ye have need of before ye ask Him."[2]

He did not affect any external signs of asceticism, contenting himself with praying, or rather meditating, upon the mountains, and in the solitary places, where man has always sought God.[3] This high idea of the relations of man with God, of which so few minds, even after him, have been capable, is summed up in a prayer which he taught to his disciples :[4]

"Our Father which art in heaven, hallowed be thy name; thy kingdom come; thy will be done on earth as it is in heaven. Give us this day our daily bread. Forgive us our trespasses, as we forgive those who trespass against us. Lead us not into temptation;

[1] Matt. vi. 1, and following. Compare *Ecclesiasticus* xvii. 18, xxix. 15; Talm. of Bab., *Chagigah*, 5 *a; Baba Bathra*, 9 *b.*
[2] Matt. vi. 5-8.　　　　[3] Matt. xiv. 23; Luke iv. 42, v. 16, vi. 12.
[4] Matt. vi. 9, and following; Luke xi. 2, and following.

deliver us from the evil one."[1] He insisted particularly upon the idea, that the heavenly Father knows better than we what we need, and that we almost sin against Him in asking Him for this or that particular thing.[2]

Jesus in this only carried out the consequences of the great principles which Judaism had established, but which the official classes of the nation tended more and more to despise. The Greek and Roman prayers were almost always mere egotistical verbiage. Never had Pagan priest said to the faithful, "If thou bring thy offering to the altar, and there rememberest that thy brother hath aught against thee; leave there thy gift before the altar, and go thy way; first be reconciled with thy brother, and then come and offer thy gift."[3] Alone in antiquity, the Jewish prophets, especially Isaiah, had, in their antipathy to the priesthood, caught a glimpse of the true nature of the worship man owes to God. "To what purpose is the multitude of your sacrifices unto me: I am full of the burnt offerings of rams, and the fat of fed beasts; and I delight not in the blood of bullocks, or of lambs, or of he-goats. . . . Incense is an abomination unto me: for your hands are full of blood; cease to do evil, learn to do well, seek judgment, and then come."[4] In later times, certain doctors, Simeon the just,[5] Jesus, son of Sirach,[6] Hillel,[7] almost reached this point, and declared that the sum of the Law was righteousness. Philo, in the Judæo-Egyptian world, attained at the same time as Jesus

[1] *i. e.*, the devil.   [2] Luke xi. 5, and following.
[3] Matt. v. 23, 24.
[4] Isaiah i. 11, and following. Compare ibid., lviii. entirely; Hosea vi. 6; Malachi i. 10, and following.
[5] *Pirké Aboth*, i. 2.
[6] *Ecclesiasticus* xxxv. 1, and following.
[7] Talm. of Jerus., *Pesachim*, vi. 1. Talm. of Bab., the same treatise 66 *a; Shabbath*, 31 *a.*

ideas of a high moral sanctity, the consequence of which was the disregard of the observances of the Law.[1]   Shemaïa and Abtalion also more than once proved themselves to be very liberal casuists.[2]   Rabbi Johanan ere long placed works of mercy above even the study of the Law![3]   Jesus alone, however, proclaimed these principles in an effective manner.   Never has any one been less a priest than Jesus, never a greater enemy of forms, which stifle religion under the pretext of protecting it.   By this we are all his disciples and his successors; by this he has laid the eternal foundation-stone of true religion; and if religion is essential to humanity, he has by this deserved the Divine rank the world has accorded to him.   An absolutely new idea, the idea of a worship founded on purity of heart, and on human brotherhood, through him entered into the world—an idea so elevated, that the Christian Church ought to make it its distinguishing feature, but an idea which, in our days, only few minds are capable of embodying.

An exquisite sympathy with Nature furnished him each moment with expressive images.   Sometimes a remarkable ingenuity, which we call wit, adorned his aphorisms; at other times, their liveliness consisted in the happy use of popular proverbs.   "How wilt thou say to thy brother, Let me pull out the mote out of thine eye; and, behold, a beam is in thine own eye? Thou hypocrite, first cast out the beam out of thine own eye, and then thou shalt see clearly to cast out the mote out of thy brother's eye."[4]

[1] *Quod Deus Immut.*, § i. and 2; *De Abrahamo*, § 22; *Quis Rerum Divin. Hæres*, § 13, and following; 55, 58, and following; *De Profugis*, § 7 and 8; *Quod Omnis Probus Liber*, entirely; *De Vita Contemp.*, entirely.   [2] Talm. of Bab., *Pesachim*, 67 *b*.
[3] Talmud of Jerus., *Péah*, i. 1.
[4] Matt. vii. 4, 5.   Compare Talmud of Babylon, *Baba Bathra*, 15 *b*, *Erachin*, 16 *b*.

These lessons, long hidden in the heart of the young Master, soon gathered around him a few disciples. The spirit of the time favored small churches; it was the period of the Essenes or Therapeutæ. Rabbis, each having his distinctive teaching, Shemaïa, Abtalion, Hillel, Shammai, Judas the Gaulonite, Gamaliel, and many others, whose maxims form the Talmud,[1] appeared on all sides. They wrote very little; the Jewish doctors of this time did not write books; everything was done by conversations, and in public lessons, to which it was sought to give a form easily remembered.[2] The proclamation by the young carpenter of Nazareth of these maxims, for the most part already generally known, but which, thanks to him, were to regenerate the world, was therefore no striking event. It was only one rabbi more (it is true, the most charming of all), and around him some young men, eager to hear him, and thirsting for knowledge. It requires time to command the attention of men. As yet there were no Christians; though true Christianity was founded, and, doubtless, it was never more perfect than at this first period. Jesus added to it nothing durable afterward. Indeed, in one sense, he compromised it; for every movement, in order to triumph, must make sacrifices; we never come from the contest of life unscathed.

To conceive the good, in fact, is not sufficient; it must be made to succeed amongst men. To accomplish this, less pure paths must be followed. Certainly, if the Gospel was confined to some chapters of Matthew and Luke, it would be more perfect, and would not now

---

[1] See especially *Pirké Aboth*, ch. i.
[2] The Talmud, a *résumé* of this vast movement of the schools, was scarcely commenced till the second century of our era.

be open to so many objections; but would Jesus have
converted the world without miracles? If he had died
at the period of his career we have now reached, there
would not have been in his life a single page to wound
us; but, greater in the eyes of God, he would have remained unknown to men; he would have been lost in
the crowd of great unknown spirits, himself the greatest of all; the truth would not have been promulgated,
and the world would not have profited from the great
moral superiority with which his Father had endowed
him. Jesus, son of Sirach, and Hillel, had uttered
aphorisms almost as exalted as those of Jesus. Hillel,
however, will never be accounted the true founder of
Christianity. In morals, as in art, precept is nothing,
practice is everything. The idea which is hidden in a
picture of Raphael is of little moment; it is the picture
itself which is prized. So, too, in morals, truth is but
little prized when it is a mere sentiment, and only attains its full value when realized in the world as fact.
Men of indifferent morality have written very good
maxims. Very virtuous men, on the other hand, have
done nothing to perpetuate in the world the tradition
of virtue. The palm is his who has been mighty both
in words and in works, who has discerned the good,
and at the price of his blood has caused its triumph.
Jesus, from this double point of view, is without equal;
his glory remains entire, and will ever be renewed.

CHAPTER VI.

JOHN THE BAPTIST—VISIT OF JESUS TO JOHN, AND HIS ABODE IN THE DESERT OF JUDEA—ADOPTION OF THE BAPTISM OF JOHN.

An extraordinary man, whose position, from the absence of documentary evidence, remains to us in some degree enigmatical, appeared about this time, and was unquestionably to some extent connected with Jesus. This connection tended rather to make the young prophet of Nazareth deviate from his path; but it suggested many important accessories to his religious institution, and, at all events, furnished a very strong authority to his disciples in recommending their Master in the eyes of a certain class of Jews.

About the year 28 of our era (the fifteenth year of the reign of Tiberius) there spread throughout Palestine the reputation of a certain Johanan, or John, a young ascetic full of zeal and enthusiasm. John was of the priestly race,[1] and born, it seems, at Juttah near Hebron, or at Hebron itself.[2] Hebron, the patriarchal city *par excellence*, situated at a short distance from the desert of Judea, and within a few hours' journey of the great desert of Arabia, was at this period what it is to-

[1] Luke i. 5; passage from the Gospel of the Ebionites, preserved by Epiphanius, (*Adv. Hær.*, xxx. 13.)

[2] Luke i. 39. It has been suggested, not without probability, that "the city of Juda" mentioned in this passage of Luke, is the town of *Jutta* (Josh. xv. 55, xxi. 16). Robinson (*Biblical Researches,* i. 494, ii. 206) has discovered this *Jutta,* still bearing the same name, at two hours' journey south of Hebron.

day—one of the bulwarks of Semitic ideas, in their
most austere form. From his infancy, John was
Nazir—that is to say, subjected by vow to certain ab-
stinences.[1] The desert by which he was, so to speak,
surrounded, early attracted him.[2] He led there the life
of a Yogi of India, clothed with skins or stuffs of
camel's hair, having for food only locusts and wild
honey.[3] A certain number of disciples were grouped
around him, sharing his life and studying his severe
doctrine. We might imagine ourselves transported to
the banks of the Ganges, if particular traits had not
revealed in this recluse the last descendant of the great
prophets of Israel.

From the time that the Jewish nation had begun to
reflect upon its destiny with a kind of despair, the
imagination of the people had reverted with much com-
placency to the ancient prophets. Now, of all the personages of the past, the remembrance of whom came
like the dreams of a troubled night to awaken and agitate the people, the greatest was Elias. This giant of
the prophets, in his rough solitude of Carmel, sharing
the life of savage beasts, dwelling in the hollows of the
rocks, whence he came like a thunderbolt, to make and
unmake kings, had become, by successive transformations, a sort of superhuman being, sometimes visible,
sometimes invisible, and as one who had not tasted
death. It was generally believed that Elias would return and restore Israel.[4] The austere life which he
had led, the terrible remembrances he had left behind

[1] Luke i. 15.
[2] Luke i. 80.
[3] Matt. iii. 4; Mark i. 6; fragm. of the Gospel of the Ebionites,
in Epiph., *Adv. Hær.*, xxx. 13.
[4] Malachi iv. 5, 6; (iii. 23, 24, according to the Vulg.); *Ecclesiasticus* xlviii. 10; Matt. xvi. 14, xvii. 10, and following; Mark vi.
15, viii. 28, ix. 10, and following; Luke ix. 8, 19; John i. 21, 25.

him—the impression of which is still powerful in the East[1]—the sombre image which, even in our own time, causes trembling and death—all this mythology, full of vengeance and terror, vividly struck the mind of the people, and stamped as with a birth-mark all the creations of the popular mind. Whoever aspired to act powerfully upon the people, must imitate Elias; and, as solitary life had been the essential characteristic of this prophet, they were accustomed to conceive "the man of God" as a hermit. They imagined that all the holy personages had had their days of penitence, of solitude, and of austerity.[2] The retreat to the desert thus became the condition and the prelude of high destinies.

No doubt this thought of imitation had occupied John's mind.[3] The anchorite life, so opposed to the spirit of the ancient Jewish people, and with which the vows, such as those of the Nazirs and the Rechabites, had no relation, pervaded all parts of Judea. The Essenes or Therapeutæ were grouped near the birth-place of John, on the eastern shores of the Dead Sea.[4] It was imagined that the chiefs of sects ought to be recluses, having rules and institutions of their own, like the founders of religious orders. The teachers of the young were also at times species of anchorites,[5] somewhat resembling the *gourous*[6] of Brahminism. In fact, might there not in this be a remote influence of the *mounis* of India? Perhaps some of those wandering Buddhist monks who overran the world, as the first

[1] The ferocius Abdallah, pacha of St. Jean d'Acre, nearly died from fright at seeing him in a dream, standing erect on his mountain. In the pictures of the Christian churches, he is surrounded with decapitated heads. The Mussulmans dread him.
[2] *Isaiah* ii. 9-11.
[3] *Luke* i. 17.
[4] Pliny, *Hist. Nat.*, v. 17; Epiph., *Adv. Hær.*, xix. 1 and 2.
[5] Josephus, *Vita*, 2.   [6] Spiritual preceptors.

Franciscans did in later times, preaching by their actions and converting people who knew not their language, might have turned their steps toward Judea, as they certainly did toward Syria and Babylon?[1] On this point we have no certainty. Babylon had become for some time a true focus of Buddhism. Boudasp (Bodhisattva) was reputed a wise Chaldean, and the founder of Sabeism. *Sabeism* was, as its etymology indicates,[2] *baptism*—that is to say, the religion of many baptisms—the origin of the sect still existing called "Christians of St. John," or Mendaites, which the Arabs call *el-Mogtasila*, "the Baptists."[3] It is difficult to unravel these vague analogies. The sects floating between Judaism, Christianity, Baptism, and Sabeism, which we find in the region beyond the Jordan during the first centuries of our era,[4] present to criticism the most singular problem, in consequence of the confused accounts of them which have come down to us. We may believe, at all events, that many of the external practices of John, of the Essenes,[5] and of the Jewish spiritual teachers of this time, were derived from influences then but recently received from the far East. The fundamental practice which characterized the sect

---

[1] I have developed this point elsewhere. *Hist. Génér. des Langues Sémitiques*, III. iv. 1; *Journ. Asiat.*, February-March, 1856.

[2] The Aramean word *seba*, origin of the name of *Sabians*, is synonymous with βαπτίζω.

[3] I have treated of this at greater length in the *Journal Asiatique*, Nov.-Dec., 1853, and August-Sept., 1855. It is remarkable that the Elchasaites, a Sabian or Baptist sect, inhabited the same district as the Essenes, (the eastern bank of the Dead Sea), and were confounded with them (Epiph. *Adv. Hær.*, xix. 1, 2, 4, xxx. 16, 17, liii. 1, 2; *Philosophumena*, IX. iii. 15, 16, x. xx. 29).

[4] See the remarks of Epiphanius on the Essenes, Hemero-Baptists, Nazarites, Ossenes, Nazorenes, Ebionites, Samsonites (*Adv. Hær.*, books i. and ii.), and those of the author of the *Philosophumena* on the Elchasaites (books ix. and x).

[5] Epiph., *Adv. Hær.*, xix., xxx., liii.

of John, and gave it its name, has always had its centre in lower Chaldea, and constitutes a religion which is perpetuated there to the present day.

This practice was baptism, or total immersion. Ablutions were already familiar to the Jews, as they were to all religions of the East.[1] The Essenes had given them a peculiar extension.[2] Baptism had become an ordinary ceremony on the introduction of proselytes into the bosom of the Jewish religion, a sort of initiatory rite.[3] Never before John the Baptist, however, had either this importance or this form been given to immersion. John had fixed the scene of his activity in that part of the desert of Judea which is in the neighborhood of the Dead Sea.[4] At the periods when he administered baptism, he went to the banks of the Jordan,[5] either to Bethany or Bethabara,[6] upon the eastern shore, probably opposite to Jericho, or to a place called *Ænon,* or "the Fountains,"[7] near Salim, where there was much water.[8] Considerable crowds,

---

[1] Mark vii. 4; Jos., *Ant.*, XVIII. v. 2; Justin, *Dial. cum Tryph.,* 17, 29, 80; Epiph., *Adv. Hær.*, xvii.

[2] Jos., *B. J.*, II., viii. 5, 7, 9, 13.

[3] Mishnah, *Pesachim,* viii. 8; Talmud of Babylon, *Jebamoth,* 46 *b; Kerithuth,* 9 *a; Aboda Zara,* 57 *a; Masséket Gérim* (edit. Kirchheim, 1851), pp. 38-40.

[4] Matt. iii. 1; Mark i. 4.

[5] Luke iii. 3.

[6] John i. 28, iii. 26. All the manuscripts say *Bethany;* but, as no one knows of Bethany in these places, Origen (*Comment. in Joann.*, vi. 24) has proposed to substitute *Bethabara,* and his correction has been generally accepted. The two words have, moreover, analogous meanings, and seem to indicate a place where there was a ferry-boat to cross the river.

[7] *Ænon* is the Chaldean plural, *Ænawan,* "fountains."

[8] John iii. 23. The locality of this place is doubtful. The circumstance mentioned by the evangelist would lead us to believe that it was not very near the Jordan. Nevertheless, the synoptics are agreed in placing the scene of the baptisms of John on the banks of that river (Matt. iii. 6; Mark i. 5; Luke iii. 3). The comparison of verses 22 and 23 of chap. iii. of John, and of verses 3 and 4 of chap. iv. of the same Gospel, would lead us to believe

especially of the tribe of Judah, hastened to him to be baptized.[1] In a few months he thus became one of the most influential men in Judea, and acquired much importance in the general estimation.

The people took him for a prophet,[2] and many imagined that it was Elias who had risen again.[3] The belief in these resurrections was widely spread;[4] it was thought that God would raise from the tomb certain of the ancient prophets to guide Israel toward its final destiny. Others held John to be the Messiah himself, although he made no such pretensions.[5] The priests and the scribes, opposed to this revival of prophetism, and the constant enemies of enthusiasts, despised him. But the popularity of the Baptist awed them, and they dared not speak against him.[6] It was a victory which the ideas of the multitude gained over the priestly aristocracy. When the chief priests were compelled to declare themselves explicitly on this point, they were considerably embarrassed.[7]

Baptism with John was only a sign destined to make an impression, and to prepare the minds of the people for some great movement. No doubt he was possessed in the highest degree with the Messianic hope, and that his principal action was in accordance with it. "Re-

that Salim was in Judea, and consequently in the oasis of Jericho, near the mouth of the Jordan; since it would be difficult to find in any other district of the tribe of Judah a single natural basin in which any one might be totally immersed. Saint Jerome wishes to place Salim much more north, near Beth-Schean or Scythopolis. But Robinson (*Bibl. Res.*, iii. 333) has not been able to find anything at these places that justifies this assertion.

[1] Mark i. 5; Josephus, *Ant.*, XVIII. v. 2.
[2] Matt. xiv. 5, xxi. 26.
[3] Matt. vi. 14; Mark vi. 15; John i. 21.
[4] Matt. xiv. 2; Luke ix. 8.
[5] Luke iii. 15, and following; John i. 20.
[6] Matt. xxi. 25, and following; Luke vii. 30.
[7] Matt., *loc. cit.*

pent," said he, "for the kingdom of heaven is at hand."[1]
He announced a "great wrath," that is to say, terrible
calamities which should come to pass,[2] and declared
that the axe was already laid at the root of the tree,
and that the tree would soon be cast into the fire. He
represented the Messiah with a fan in his hand, col-
lecting the good wheat and burning the chaff. Repentance, of which baptism was the type, the giving of
alms, the reformation of habits,[3] were in John's view
the great means of preparation for the coming events,
though we do not know exactly in what light he conceived them. It is, however, certain that he preached
with much power against the same adversaries as
Jesus, against rich priests, the Pharisees, the doctors,
in one word, against official Judaism; and that, like
Jesus, he was specially welcomed by the despised
classes.[4] He made no account of the title "son of
Abraham," and said that God could raise up sons unto
Abraham from the stones of the road.[5] It does not
seem that he possessed even the germ of the great idea
which led to the triumph of Jesus, the idea of a pure
religion; but he powerfully served this idea in substituting a private rite for the legal ceremonies which required priests, as the Flagellants of the Middle Ages
were the precursors of the Reformation, by depriving
the official clergy of the monopoly of the sacraments
and of absolution. The general tone of his sermons
was stern and severe. The expressions which he used
against his adversaries appear to have been most violent.[6] It was a harsh and continuous invective. It is
probable that he did not remain quite a stranger to

[1] Matt. iii. 2. [2] Matt. iii. 7.
[3] Luke iii. 11-14; Josephus, *Ant.*, XVIII. v. 2.
[4] Matt. xxi. 32; Luke iii. 12-14.
[5] Matt. iii. 9.
[6] Matt. iii. 7; Luke iii. 7.

politics. Josephus, who, through his teacher Banou,
was brought into almost direct connection with John,
suggests as much by his ambiguous words,[1] and the
catastrophe which put an end to John's life seems to
imply this. His disciples led a very austere life,[2] fasted
often, and affected a sad and anxious demeanor. We
have at times glimpses of communism—the rich man
being ordered to share all that he had with the poor.[3]
The poor man appeared as the one who would be
specially benefited by the kingdom of God.

Although the centre of John's action was Judea, his
fame quickly penetrated to Galilee and reached Jesus,
who, by his first discourses, had already gathered
around himself a small circle of hearers. Enjoying as
yet little authority, and doubtless impelled by the desire
to see a teacher whose instruction had so much in common with his own, Jesus quitted Galilee and repaired
with his small group of disciples to John.[4] The new-

---

[1] *Ant.* XVIII. v. 2. We must observe that, when Josephus described the secret and more or less seditious doctrines of his
countrymen, he suppressed everything which had reference to the
Messianic beliefs, and, in order not to give umbrage to the Romans, spread over these doctrines a vulgar and commonplace air,
which made all the heads of Jewish sects appear as mere profes-
sors of morals or stoics.

[2] Matt. ix. 14.   [3] Luke iii. 11.

[4] Matt. iii. 13, and following; Mark i. 9, and following; Luke
iii. 21, and following; John i. 29, and following; iii. 22, and following. The synoptics make Jesus come to John, before he had
played any public part. But if it is true, as they state, that John
recognized Jesus from the first and welcomed him, it must be
supposed that Jesus was already a somewhat renowned teacher.
The fourth Gospel brings Jesus to John twice, the first time while
yet unknown, the second time with a band of disciples. Without
touching here the question of the precise journeys of Jesus (an
insoluble question, seeing the contradictions of the documents and
the little care the evangelists had in being exact in such matters),
and without denying that Jesus might have made a journey to
John when he had as yet no notoriety, we adopt the information
furnished by the fourth Gospel (iii. 22, and following), namely,
that Jesus, before beginning to baptize like John, had formed a

comers were baptized like every one else. John welcomed this group of Galilean disciples, and did not object to their remaining distinct from his own. The two teachers were young; they had many ideas in common; they loved one another, and publicly vied with each other in exhibitions of kindly feeling. At the first glance, such a fact surprises us in John the Baptist, and we are tempted to call it in question. Humility has never been a feature of strong Jewish minds. It might have been expected that a character so stubborn, a sort of Lamennais always irritated, would be very passionate, and suffer neither rivalry nor half adhesion. But this manner of viewing things rests upon a false conception of the person of John. We imagine him an old man; he was, on the contrary, of the same age as Jesus,[1] and very young according to the ideas of the time. In mental development, he was the brother rather than the father of Jesus. The two young enthusiasts, full of the same hopes and the same hatreds, were able to make common cause, and mutually to support each other. Certainly an aged teacher, seeing a man without celebrity approach him, and maintain toward him an aspect of independence, would have rebelled; we have scarcely an example of a leader of a school receiving with eagerness his future successor. But youth is capable of any sacrifice, and we may admit that John, having recognized in Jesus a spirit akin to his own, accepted him without any personal reservation. These good relations became after-

school. We must remember, besides, that the first pages of the fourth Gospel are notes tacked together without rigorous chronological arrangement.

[1] Luke i., although indeed all the details of the narrative, especially those which refer to the relationship of John with Jesus, are legendary.

ward the starting-point of a whole system developed
by the evangelists, which consisted in giving the Divine
mission of Jesus the primary basis of the attestation
of John.   Such was the degree of authority acquired
by the Baptist, that it was not thought possible to find
in the world a better guarantee.   But far from John
abdicating in favor of Jesus, Jesus, during all the time
that he passed with him, recognized him as his superior, and only developed his own genius with timidity.

It seems, in fact, that, notwithstanding his profound
originality, Jesus, during some weeks at least, was the
imitator of John.   His way as yet was not clear before
him.   At all times, moreover, Jesus yielded much to
opinion, and adopted many things which were not in
exact accordance with his own ideas, or for which he
cared little, merely because they were popular; but
these accessories never injured his principal idea, and
were always subordinate to it.   Baptism had been
brought by John into very great favor; Jesus thought
himself obliged to do like John; therefore he baptized,
and his disciples baptized also.[1]   No doubt he accompanied baptism with preaching, similar to that of John.
The Jordan was thus covered on all sides with Baptists,
whose discourses were more or less successful.   The
pupil soon equaled the master, and his baptism was
much sought after.   There was on this subject some
jealousy among the disciples;[2] the disciples of John
came to complain to him of the growing success of the
young Galilean, whose baptism would, they thought,
soon supplant his own.   But the two teachers remained

[1] John iii. 22-26, iv. 1, 2.   The parenthesis of ver. 2 appears to
be an interpolation, or perhaps a tardy scruple of John correcting
himself.
[2] John iii. 26, iv. 1.

superior to this meanness. The superiority of John was, besides, too indisputable for Jesus, still little known, to think of contesting it. Jesus only wished to increase under John's protection; and thought himself obliged, in order to gain the multitude, to employ the external means which had given John such astonishing success. When he recommenced to preach after John's arrest, the first words put into his mouth are but the repetition of one of the familiar phrases of the Baptist.[1] Many other of John's expressions may be found repeated verbally in the discourses of Jesus.[2] The two schools appear to have lived long on good terms with each other;[3] and after the death of John, Jesus, as his trusty friend, was one of the first to be informed of the event.[4]

John, in fact, was soon cut short in his prophetic career. Like the ancient Jewish prophets, he was, in the highest degree, a censurer of the established authorities.[5] The extreme vivacity with which he expressed himself at their expense could not fail to bring him into trouble. In Judea, John does not appear to have been disturbed by Pilate; but in Perea, beyond the Jordan, he came into the territory of Antipas. This tyrant was uneasy at the political leaven which was so little concealed by John in his preaching. The great assemblages of men gathered around the Baptist, by religious and patriotic enthusiasm, gave rise to suspicion.[6] An entirely personal grievance was also added to these motives of state, and rendered the death of the austere censor inevitable.

One of the most strongly marked characters of this

[1]Matt. iii. 2, iv. 17.   [2]Matt. iii. 7, xii. 34, xxiii. 33.
[3]Matt. xi. 2-13.   [4]Matt. xiv. 12.   [5]Luke iii. 19.
[6]Jos., *Ant*, xviii. v. 2.

tragical family of the Herods was Herodias, grand-daughter of Herod the Great. Violent, ambitious, and passionate, she detested Judaism, and despised its laws.[1] She had been married, probably against her will, to her uncle Herod, son of Mariamne,[2] whom Herod the Great had disinherited,[3] and who never played any public part. The inferior position of her husband, in respect to the other persons of the family, gave her no peace; she determined to be sovereign at whatever cost.[4]   Antipas was the instrument of whom she made use. This feeble man having become desperately enamored of her, promised to marry her, and to repudiate his first wife, daughter of Hareth, king of Petra, and emir of the neighboring tribes of Perea. The Arabian princess, receiving a hint of this design, resolved to fly. Concealing her intention, she pretended that she wished to make a journey to Machero, in her father's territory, and caused herself to be conducted thither by the officers of Antipas.[5]

Makaur,[6] or Machero, was a colossal fortress built by Alexander Jannaeus, and rebuilt by Herod, in one of the most abrupt wâdys to the east of the Dead Sea.[7] It was a wild and desolate country, filled with strange legends, and believed to be haunted by demons.[8]   The fortress was just on the boundary of the lands of Hareth and of Antipas. At that time it was in the pos-

[1] Jos., *Ant.*, xviii. v. 4.
[2] Matthew (chap. xiv. 3, in the Greek text) and Mark (chap. vi. 17) have it that this was Philip; but this is certainly an inadvertency (see Jos., *Ant.*, xviii. v. 1, 4). The wife of Philip was Salome, daughter of Herodias.   [3] Jos., *Ant.*, xvii. iv. 2.
[4] Ibid., xviii. vii. 1, 2; *B. J.*, ii. ix. 6.   [5] Ibid., xviii. v. 1.
[6] This form is found in the Talmud of Jerusalem (*Shebiit*, ix. 2), and in the Targums of Jonathan and of Jerusalem (*Numb.* xxii. 35).
[7] Now Mkaur, in the wâdy Zerka Main. This place has not been visited since Seetzen was there.
[8] Josephus, *De Bell. Jud.*, vii. vi. 1, and following.

session of Hareth.[1] The latter having been warned,
had prepared everything for the flight of his daughter,
who was conducted from tribe to tribe to Petra.

The almost incestuous[2] union of Antipas and Herodias then took place. The Jewish laws on marriage
were a constant rock of offence between the irreligious
family of the Herods and the strict Jews.[3] The members of this numerous and rather isolated dynasty being
obliged to marry amongst themselves, frequent viola-
tions of the limits prescribed by the Law necessarily
took place. John, in energetically blaming Antipas,
was the echo of the general feeling.[4] This was more
than sufficient to decide the latter to follow up his
suspicions. He caused the Baptist to be arrested, and
ordered him to be shut up in the fortress of Machero,
which he had probably seized after the departure of the
daughter of Hareth.[5]

More timid than cruel, Antipas did not desire to put
him to death. According to certain rumors, he feared
a popular sedition.[6] According to another version,[7]
he had taken pleasure in listening to the prisoner, and
these conversations had thrown him into great perplexities. It is certain that the detention was prolonged, and that John, in his prison, preserved an extended influence. He corresponded with his disciples,
and we find him again in connection with Jesus. His
faith in the near approach of the Messiah only became
firmer; he followed with attention the movements outside, and sought to discover in them the signs favorable
to the accomplishment of the hopes which he cherished.

---

[1] Jos., *Ant.*, XVIII. v. 1.   [2] *Lev.* xviii. 16.   [3] Jos., *Ant.*, XV. vii. 10.
[4] Matt. xiv. 4; Mark vi. 18; Luke iii. 19.   [5] Jos., *Ant.*, XVIII. v. 2.
[6] Matt. xiv. 5.
[7] Mark vi. 20. I read ἠπόρει, and not ἐποίει.

CHAPTER VII.

DEVELOPMENT OF THE IDEAS OF JESUS RESPECTING THE KINGDOM OF GOD.

Up to the arrest of John, which took place about the summer of the year 29, Jesus did not quit the neighborhood of the Dead Sea and of the Jordan. An abode in the desert of Judea was generally considered as the preparation for great things, as a sort of "retreat" before public acts. Jesus followed in this respect the example of others, and passed forty days with no other companions than savage beasts, maintaining a rigorous fast. The disciples speculated much concerning this sojourn. The desert was popularly regarded as the residence of demons.[1] There exist in the world few regions more desolate, more abandoned by God, more shut out from life, than the rocky declivity which forms the western shore of the Dead Sea. It was believed that during the time which Jesus passed in this frightful country, he had gone through terrible trials; that Satan had assailed him with his illusions, or tempted him with seductive promises; that afterward, in order to recompense him for his victory, the angels had come to minister to him.[2]

It was probably in coming from the desert that

[1] *Tobit* viii. 3; Luke xi. 24.

[2] Matt. iv. 1, and following; Mark i. 12, 13; Luke iv. 1, and following. Certainly, the striking similarity that these narratives present to the analogous legends of the *Vendidad* (farg. xix.) and of the *Lalitavistara* (chap. xvii., xviii., xxi.) would lead us to regard them only as myths. But the meagre and concise narrative of Mark, which evidently represents on this point the primitive compilation, leads us to suppose a real fact, which furnished later the theme of legendary developments.

Jesus learned of the arrest of John the Baptist. He had no longer any reason to prolong his stay in a country which was partly strange to him. Perhaps he feared also being involved in the severities exercised toward John, and did not wish to expose himself, at a time in which, seeing the little celebrity he had, his death could in no way serve the progress of his ideas. He regained Galilee,[1] his true home, ripened by an important experience, and having, through contact with a great man, very different from himself, acquired a consciousness of his own originality.

On the whole, the influence of John had been more hurtful than useful to Jesus. It checked his development; for everything leads us to believe that he had, when he descended toward the Jordan, ideas superior to those of John, and that it was by a sort of concession that he inclined for a time toward baptism. Perhaps if the Baptist, whose authority it would have been difficult for him to escape, had remained free, Jesus would not have been able to throw off the yoke of external rites and ceremonies, and would then, no doubt, have remained an unknown Jewish sectary; for the world would not have abandoned its old ceremonies merely for others of a different kind. It has been by the power of a religion, free from all external forms, that Christianity has attracted elevated minds. The Baptist once imprisoned, his school was soon diminished, and Jesus found himself left to his own impulses. The only things he owed to John, were lessons in preaching and in popular action. From this moment, in fact, he preached with greater power, and spoke to the multitude with authority.[2]

[1] Matt. iv. 12; Mark i. 14; Luke iv. 14; John iv. 3.
[2] Matt. vii. 29; Mark i. 22; Luke iv. 32.

It seems also that his sojourn with John had, not so much by the influence of the Baptist, as by the natural progress of his own thought, considerably ripened his ideas on "the kingdom of heaven." His watchword, henceforth, is the "good tidings," the announcement that the kingdom of God is at hand.[1] Jesus is no longer simply a delightful moralist, aspiring to express sublime lessons in short and lively aphorisms; he is the transcendent revolutionary, who essays to renovate the world from its very basis, and to establish upon earth the ideal which he had conceived. "To await the kingdom of God" is henceforth synonymous with being a disciple of Jesus.[2] This phrase, "kingdom of God," or "kingdom of heaven," was, as we have said, already long familiar to the Jews. But Jesus gave it a moral sense, a social application, which even the author of the Book of Daniel, in his apocalyptic enthusiasm, had scarcely dared to imagine.

He declared that in the present world evil is the reigning power. Satan is "the prince of this world,"[3] and everything obeys him. The kings kill the prophets. The priests and the doctors do not that which they command others to do; the righteous are persecuted, and the only portion of the good is weeping. The "world" is in this manner the enemy of God and His saints:[4] but God will awaken and avenge His saints. The day is at hand, for the abomination is at its height. The reign of goodness will have its turn.

The advent of this reign of goodness will be a great

[1] Mark i. 14, 15.
[2] Mark xv. 43.
[3] John xii. 31, xiv. 30, xvi. 11. (Comp. 2 *Cor.* iv. 4; *Ephes.* ii. 2.)
[4] John i. 10, vii. 7, xiv. 17, 22, 27, xv. 18, and following; xvi. 8, 20, 33, xvii. 9, 14, 16, 25. This meaning of the word "world" is especially applied in the writings of Paul and John.

and sudden revolution. The world will seem to be turned upside down; the actual state being bad, in order to represent the future, it suffices to conceive nearly the reverse of that which exists. The first shall be last.[1] A new order shall govern humanity. Now the good and the bad are mixed, like the tares and the good grain in a field. The master lets them grow together; but the hour of violent separation will arrive.[2] The kingdom of God will be as the casting of a great net, which gathers both good and bad fish; the good are preserved, and the rest are thrown away.[3] The germ of this great revolution will not be recognizable in its beginning. It will be like a grain of mustard-seed, which is the smallest of seeds, but which, thrown into the earth, becomes a tree under the foliage of which the birds repose;[4] or it will be like the leaven which, deposited in the meal, makes the whole to ferment.[5] A series of parables, often obscure, was designed to express the suddenness of this event, its apparent injustice, and its inevitable and final character.[6]

Who was to establish this kingdom of God? Let us remember that the first thought of Jesus, a thought so deeply rooted in him that it had probably no beginning, and formed part of his very being, was that he was the Son of God, the friend of his Father, the doer of his will. The answer of Jesus to such a question could not therefore be doubtful. The persuasion that he was to establish the kingdom of God took absolute

[1] Matt. xix. 30, xx. 16; Mark x. 31; Luke xiii. 30.
[2] Matt. xiii. 24, and following.
[3] Matt. xiii. 47, and following.
[4] Matt. xiii. 31, and following; Mark iv. 31, and following; Luke xiii. 19, and following.
[5] Matt. xiii. 33; Luke xiii. 21.
[6] Matt. xiii. entirely; xviii. 23, and following; xx. 1, and following; Luke xiii. 18, and following.

possession of his mind. He regarded himself as the universal reformer. The heavens, the earth, the whole of nature, madness, disease, and death, were but his instruments. In his paroxysm of heroic will, he believed himself all powerful. If the earth would not submit to this supreme transformation, it would be broken up, purified by fire, and by the breath of God. A new heaven would be created, and the entire world would be peopled with the angels of God.[1]

A radical revolution,[2] embracing even nature itself, was the fundamental idea of Jesus. Henceforward, without doubt, he renounced politics; the example of Judas, the Gaulonite, had shown him the inutility of popular seditions. He never thought of revolting against the Romans and tetrarchs. His was not the unbridled and anarchical principle of the Gaulonite. His submission to the established powers, though really derisive, was in appearance complete. He paid tribute to Cæsar, in order to avoid disturbance. Liberty and right were not of this world, why should he trouble his life with vain anxieties? Despising the earth, and convinced that the present world was not worth caring for, he took refuge in his ideal kingdom; he established the great doctrine of transcendent disdain,[3] the true doctrine of liberty of souls, which alone can give peace. But he had not yet said, "My kingdom is not of this world." Much darkness mixed itself with even his most correct views. Sometimes strange temptations crossed his mind. In the desert of Judea, Satan had offered him the kingdoms of the earth. Not knowing the power of the Roman empire, he might, with the enthusiasm there was in the heart of Judea, and which

[1] Matt. xxii. 30.   [2] $'A\pi o\chi\alpha\tau\acute{\alpha}\acute{o}\tau\alpha\acute{o}\iota\varsigma$ $\pi\acute{\alpha}\nu\tau\omega\nu$, *Acts* iii. 21.
[3] Matt. xvii. 23-26; xxii. 16-22.

ended soon after in so terrible an outbreak, hope to
establish a kingdom by the number and the daring of
his partisans.   Many times, perhaps, the supreme question presented itself—will the kingdom of God be
realized by force or by gentleness, by revolt or by
patience?   One day, it is said, the simple men of Galilee wished to carry him away and make him king,[1] but
Jesus fled into the mountain and remained there some
time alone.   His noble nature preserved him from the
error which would have made him an agitator, or a
chief of rebels, a Theudas or a Barkokeba.

The revolution he wished to effect was always a
moral revolution; but he had not yet begun to trust to
the angels and the last trumpet for its execution.   It
was upon men and by the aid of men themselves that
he wished to act.   A visionary who had no other idea
than the proximity of the last judgment, would not
have had this care for the amelioration of man, and
would not have given utterance to the finest moral
teaching that humanity has received.   Much vague-
ness no doubt tinged his ideas, and it was rather a noble
feeling than a fixed design, that urged him to the
sublime work which was realized by him, though in a
very different manner to what he imagined.

It was indeed the kingdom of God, or in other words,
the kingdom of the Spirit, which he founded; and if
Jesus, from the bosom of his Father, sees his work bear
fruit in the world, he may indeed say with truth, "This
is what I have desired."   That which Jesus founded,
that which will remain eternally his, allowing for the
imperfections which mix themselves with everything
realized by humanity, is the doctrine of the liberty of
the soul.   Greece had already had beautiful ideas on

[1] John vi 15.

this subject.[1]   Various stoics had learned how to be free even under a tyrant.   But in general the ancient world had regarded liberty as attached to certain political forms; freedom was personified in Harmodius and Aristogiton, Brutus and Cassius.   The true Christion enjoys more real freedom; here below he is an exile; what matters it to him who is the transitory governor of this earth, which is not his home?   Liberty for him is truth.[2]   Jesus did not know history sufficiently to understand that such a doctrine came most opportunely at the moment when republican liberty ended, and when the small municipal constitutions of antiquity were absorbed in the unity of the Roman empire.   But his admirable good sense, and the truly prophetic instinct which he had of his mission, guided him with marvelous certainty.   By the sentence, "Render unto Cæsar the things which are Cæsar's, and to God the things which are God's," he created something apart from politics, a refuge for souls in the midst of the empire of brute force.   Assuredly, such a doctrine had its dangers.   To establish as a principle that we must recognize the legitimacy of a power by the inscription on its coins, to proclaim that the perfect man pays tribute with scorn and without question, was to destroy republicanism in the ancient form, and to favor all tyranny.   Christianity, in this sense, has contributed much to weaken the sense of duty of the citizen, and to deliver the world into the absolute power of existing circumstances.   But in constituting an immense free association, which during three hundred years was able to dispense with politics, Christianity amply compensated for the wrong it had done to civic

[1]See Stobæus, *Florilegium*, ch. lxii., lxxvii., lxxxvi., and following.   [2]John viii. 32, and following.

virtues. The power of the state was limited to the things of earth; the mind was freed, or at least the terrible rod of Roman omnipotence was broken forever.

The man who is especially preoccupied with the duties of public life, does not readily forgive those who attach little importance to his party quarrels. He especially blames those who subordinate political to social questions, and profess a sort of indifference for the former. In one sense he is right, for exclusive power is prejudicial to the good government of human affairs. But what progress have "parties" been able to effect in the general morality of our species? If Jesus, instead of founding his heavenly kingdom, had gone to Rome, had expended his energies in conspiring against Tiberius, or in regretting Germanicus, what would have become of the world? As an austere republican, or zealous patriot, he would not have arrested the great current of the affairs of his age, but in declaring that politics are insignificant, he has revealed to the world this truth, that one's country is not everything, and that the man is before, and higher than, the citizen.

Our principles of positive science are offended by the dreams contained in the programme of Jesus. We know the history of the earth; cosmical revolutions of the kind which Jesus expected are only produced by geological or astronomical causes, the connection of which with spiritual things has never yet been demonstrated. But, in order to be just to great originators, they must not be judged by the prejudices in which they have shared. Columbus discovered America, though starting from very erroneous ideas; Newton believed his foolish explanation of the Apocalypse to be as true as his system of the world. Shall we place an ordinary man of our time above a Francis d'Assisi, a St. Bernard, a Joan of Arc, or a Luther, because he is free from errors which these last have professed? Should we measure men by the correctness of their ideas of physics, and by the more or less exact knowledge which they possess of the true system of the world? Let us understand better the position of Jesus and that which made his power. The Deism of the eighteenth century, and a certain kind of Protestantism, have accustomed us to consider the founder of the Christian faith only as a great moralist, a benefactor of mankind. We see nothing more in the Gospel than good maxims; we throw a prudent veil over the strange intellectual state in which it was originated. There are even persons who regret that the French Revolution departed more than once from principles, and that it was not brought about by wise and moderate men. Let us not impose our petty and commonplace ideas on these extraordinary movements so far above our everyday life. Let us continue to admire the "morality of the gospel"—let us suppress in our religious teachings the chimera which was its soul; but do not let us believe that with the simple ideas of happiness, or of individual morality, we stir the world. The idea of Jesus was much more profound; it was the most revolutionary idea ever formed in a human brain; it should be taken in its totality, and not with those timid suppressions which deprive it of precisely that which has rendered it efficacious for the regeneration of humanity.

The ideal is ever a Utopia. When we wish nowadays to represent the Christ of the modern conscience, the consoler, and the judge of the new times, what course do we take? That which Jesus himself did eighteen hundred and thirty years ago. We suppose the conditions of the real world quite other than what they are; we represent a moral liberator breaking without weapons the chains of the negro, ameliorating the condition of the poor, and giving liberty to oppressed nations. We forget that this implies the subversion of the world, the climate of Virginia and that of Congo modified, the blood and the race of millions of men changed, our social complications restored to a chimerical simplicity, and the political stratifications of Europe displaced from their natural order. The "restitution of all things"[1] desired by Jesus was not more difficult. This new earth, this new heaven, this new Jerusalem which comes from above, this cry: "Behold I make all things new!"[2] are the common characteristics of reformers. The contrast of the ideal with the sad reality, always produces in mankind those revolts against unimpassioned reason which inferior minds regard as folly, till the day arrives in which they triumph, and in which those who have opposed them are the first to recognize their reasonableness.

That there may have been a contradiction between the belief in the approaching end of the world and the general moral system of Jesus, conceived in prospect of a permanent state of humanity, nearly analogous to that which now exists, no one will attempt to deny.[3] It was exactly this contradiction that insured the success of his work. The millenarian alone would have done nothing lasting; the moralist alone would have done nothing powerful. The millenarianism gave the impulse, the moralist insured the future. Hence Christianity united the two conditions of great success

[1] *Acts* iii. 21.   [2] *Rev.* xxi. 1, 2, 5.
[3] The millenarian sects of England present the same contrast, I mean the belief in the near end of the world, notwithstanding much good sense in the conduct of life, and an extraordinary understanding of commercial affairs and industry.

in this world, a revolutionary starting-point, and the
possibility of continuous life. Everything which is intended to succeed ought to respond to these two wants;
for the world seeks both to change and to last. Jesus,
at the same time that he announced an unparalleled subversion in human affairs, proclaimed the principles
upon which society has reposed for eighteen hundred
years.

That which in fact distinguishes Jesus from the agi-
tators of his time, and from those of all ages, is his
perfect idealism. Jesus, in some respects, was an
anarchist, for he had no idea of civil government. That
government seemed to him purely and simply an abuse.
He spoke of it in vague terms, and as a man of the
people who had no idea of politics. Every magistrate
appeared to him a natural enemy of the people of God;
he prepared his disciples for contests with the civil
powers, without thinking for a moment that there was
anything in this to be ashamed of.[1] But he never
shows any desire to put himself in the place of the rich
and the powerful. He wishes to annihilate riches and
power, but not to appropriate them. He predicts persecution and all kinds of punishment to his disciples;[2]
but never once does the thought of armed resistance
appear. The idea of being all-powerful by suffering
and resignation, and of triumphing over force by purity of heart, is indeed an idea peculiar to Jesus. Jesus
is not a spiritualist, for to him everything tended to a
palpable realization; he had not the least notion of a
soul separated from the body. But he is a perfect
idealist, matter being only to him the sign of the idea,

[1] Matt. x. 17, 18; Luke xii. 11.
[2] Matt. v. 10, and following; x. entirely; Luke vi. 22, and following; John xv. 18, and following; xvi. 2, and following, 20, 33;
xvii. 14.

and the real, the living expression of that which does not appear.

To whom should we turn, to whom should we trust to establish the kingdom of God? The mind of Jesus on this point never hesitated. That which is highly esteemed among men, is abomination in the sight of God.[1] The founders of the kingdom of God are the simple. Not the rich, not the learned, not priests; but women, common people, the humble, and the young.[2] The great characteristic of the Messiah is, that "the poor have the gospel preached to them."[3] The idyllic and gentle nature of Jesus here resumed the superiority. A great social revolution, in which rank will be overturned, in which all authority in this world will be humiliated, was his dream. The world will not believe him; the world will kill him. But his disciples will not be of the world.[4] They will be a little flock of the humble and the simple, who will conquer by their very humility. The idea which has made "Christian" the antithesis of "worldly," has its full justification in the thoughts of the master.[5]

[1] Luke xvi. 15.
[2] Matt. v. 3, 10, xviii. 3, xix. 14, 23, 24, xxi. 31, xxii 2, and following; Mark x. 14, 15, 23-25; Luke iv. 18, and following; vi. 20, xviii. 16, 17, 24, 25.
[3] Matt. xi. 5.
[4] John xv. 19, xvii. 14, 16.
[5] See especially chapter xvii. of St. John, expressing, if not a real discourse delivered by Jesus, at least a sentiment which was very deeply rooted in his disciples, and which certainly came from him.

CHAPTER VIII.

JESUS AT CAPERNAUM.

BESET by an idea, gradually becoming more and more imperious and exclusive, Jesus proceeds henceforth with a kind of fatal impassibility in the path marked out by his astonishing genius and the extraordinary circumstances in which he lived. Hitherto he had only communicated his thoughts to a few persons secretly attracted to him; henceforward his teaching was sought after by the public. He was about thirty years of age.[1] The little group of hearers who had accompanied him to John the Baptist had, doubtless, increased, and perhaps some disciples of John had attached themselves to him.[2] It was with this first nucleus of a church that he boldly announced, on his return into Galilee, the "good tidings of the kingdom of God." This kingdom was approaching, and it was he, Jesus, who was that "Son of Man" whom Daniel had beheld in his vision as the divine herald of the last and supreme revelation.

We must remember, that in the Jewish ideas, which were averse to art and mythology, the simple form of man had a superiority over that of *Cherubs,* and of the fantastic animals which the imagination of the people, since it had been subjected to the influence of Assyria, had ranged around the Divine Majesty. Already in Ezekiel,[3] the Being seated on the supreme throne, far

[1] Luke iii. 23; Gospel of the Ebionites, in Epiph., *Adv. Hær.,* xxx. 13.
[2] John i. 37, and following.   [3] Chap. i. 5, 26, and following.

above the monsters of the mysterious chariot, the great
revealer of prophetic visions, had the figure of a man.
In the book of Daniel, in the midst of the vision of the
empires, represented by animals, at the moment when
the great judgment commences, and when the books
are opened, a Being "like unto a Son of Man," ad-
vances toward the Ancient of days, who confers on
him the power to judge the world, and to govern it for
eternity.[1] *Son of Man,* in the Semitic languages, especially in the Aramean dialects, is a simple synonym
of *man.* But this chief passage of Daniel struck the
mind; the words, *Son of Man,* became, at least in certain schools,[2] one of the titles of the Messiah, regarded
as judge of the world, and as king of the new era about
to be inaugurated.[3] The application which Jesus
made of it to himself was therefore the proclamation
of his Messiahship, and the affirmation of the coming
catastrophe in which he was to figure as judge, clothed
with the full powers which had been delegated to him
by the Ancient of days.[4]

The success of the teaching of the new prophet was
this time decisive. A group of men and women, all
characterized by the same spirit of juvenile frankness
and simple innocence, adhered to him, and said, "Thou
art the Messiah." As the Messiah was to be the son
of David, they naturally conceded him this title, which
was synonymous with the former. Jesus allowed it

[1] Daniel vii. 13, 14; comp. viii. 15. x. 16.
[2] In John xii. 34, the Jews do not appear to be aware of the
meaning of this word.
[3] Book of Enoch, xlvi. 1-3, xlviii. 2, 3, lxii. 9, 14, lxx. 1 (division
of Dilmann); Matt. x. 23, xiii. 41, xvi. 27, 28, xix. 28, xxiv. 27,
30, 37, 39, 44, xxv. 31, xxvi. 64; Mark xiii. 26, xiv. 62; Luke xii.
40, xvii. 24, 26, 30, xxi. 27, 36, xxii. 69; *Acts* vii. 55. But the
most significant passage is John v. 27, compared with *Rev.* i. 13,
xiv. 14. The expression "Son of woman," for the Messiah, occurs
once in the book of Enoch, lxii. 5.　[4] John v. 22, 27.

with pleasure to be given to him, although it might cause him some embarrassment, his birth being well known. The name which he preferred himself was that of "Son of Man," an apparently humble title, but one which connected itself directly with the Messianic hopes. This was the title by which he designated himself,[1] and he used "The Son of Man" as synonymous with the pronoun "I," which he avoided. But he was never thus addressed, doubtless because the name in question would be fully applicable to him only on the day of his future appearance.

His centre of action, at this epoch of his life, was the little town of Capernaum, situated on the shore of the lake of Gennesareth. The name of Capernaum, containing the word *caphar,* "village," seems to designate a small town of the ancient character, in opposition to the great towns built according to the Roman method, like Tiberias.[2] That name was so little known that Josephus, in one passage of his writings,[3] takes it for the name of a fountain, the fountain having more celebrity than the village situated near it. Like Nazareth, Capernaum had no history, and had in no way participated in the profane movement favored by the Herods. Jesus was much attached to this town, and made it a second home.[4] Soon after his return, he attempted to commence his work at Nazareth, but without success.[5] He could not perform any miracle there.

[1] This title occurs eighty-three times in the Gospels, and always in the discourses of Jesus.

[2] It is true that Tell-Houm, which is generally identified with Capernaum, contains the remains of somewhat fine monuments. But, besides this identification being doubtful, these monuments may be of the second or third century after Christ.

[3] *B. J.,* iii. x. 8.

[4] Matt. ix. 1; Mark ii. 1.

[5] Matt. xiii. 54, and following; Mark vi. 1, and following; Luke iv. 16, and following, 23-24; John iv. 44.

according to the simple remark of one of his biographers.[1] The knowledge which existed there about his family, not an important one, injured his authority too much. People could not regard as the son of David, one whose brother, sister, and brother-in-law they saw every day, and it is remarkable besides, that his family were strongly opposed to him, and plainly refused to believe in his mission.[2] The Nazarenes, much more violent, wished, it is said, to kill him by throwing him from a steep rock.[3] Jesus aptly remarked that this treatment was the fate of all great men, and applied to himself the proverb, "No one is a prophet in his own country."

This check far from discouraged him. He returned to Capernaum,[4] where he met with a much more favorable reception, and from thence he organized a series of missions among the small surrounding towns. The people of this beautiful and fertile country were scarcely ever assembled except on Saturday. This was the day which he chose for his teaching. At that time each town had its synagogue, or place of meeting. This was a rectangular room, rather small, with a portico, decorated in the Greek style. The Jews not having any architecture of their own, never cared to give these edifices an original style. The remains of many ancient synagogues still exist in Galilee.[5] They are all constructed of large and good materials; but their

[1] Mark vi. 5; cf. Matt. xii. 58; Luke iv. 23.
[2] Matt. xiii. 57; Mark vi. 4; John vii. 3, and following.
[3] Luke iv. 29. Probably the rock referred to here is the peak which is very near Nazareth, above the present church of the Maronites, and not the pretended *Mount of Precipitation*, at an hour's journey from Nazareth. See Robinson, ii. 335, and following.
[4] Matt. iv. 13; Luke iv. 31.
[5] ▲: Tell-Houm, Irbid (Arbela), Meiron (Mero), Jisch (Giscala), Kasyoun, Nabartein, and two at Kefr-Bereim.

style is somewhat paltry, in consequence of the profusion of floral ornaments, foliage, and twisted work, which characterize the Jewish buildings.[1]　In the interior there were seats, a chair for public reading, and a closet to contain the sacred rolls.[2]　These edifices, which had nothing of the character of a temple, were the centre of the whole Jewish life.　There the people assembled on the Sabbath for prayer, and reading of the law and the prophets.　As Judaism, except in Jerusalem, had, properly speaking, no clergy, the first comer stood up, gave the lessons of the day (*parasha* and *haphtara*), and added thereto a *midrash,* or entirely personal commentary, in which he expressed his own ideas.[3]　This was the origin of the "homily," the finished model of which we find in the small treatises of Philo.　The audience had the right of making objections and putting questions to the reader; so that the meeting soon degenerated into a kind of free assembly.　It had a president,[4] "elders,"[5] a *hazzan, i. e.,* a recognized reader, or apparitor,[6] deputies,[7] who were

---

[1] I dare not decide upon the age of those buildings, nor consequently affirm that Jesus taught in any of them.　How great would be the interest attaching to the synagogue of Tell-Houm were we to admit such an hypothesis!　The great synagogue of Kefr-Bereim seems to me the most ancient of all.　Its style is moderately pure.　That of Kasyoun bears a Greek inscription of the time of Septimus Severus.　The great importance which Judaism acquired in Upper Galilee after the Roman war, leads us to believe that several of these edifices only date back to the third century—a time in which Tiberias became a sort of capital of Judaism.

[2] 2 *Esdras* viii. 4; Matt. xxiii. 6; Epist. James ii. 3; Mishnah, *Megilla,* iii. 1; *Rosh Hasshana,* iv. 7, etc.　See especially the curious description of the synagogue of Alexandria in the Talmud of Babylon, *Sukka,* 51 *b.*

[3] Philo, quoted in Eusebius, *Præp. Evang.,* viii. 7, and *Quod Omnis Probus Liber,* § 12; Luke iv. 16; *Acts* xiii. 15, xv. 21; Mishnah, *Megilla,* iii. 4, and following.

[4] Ἀρχισυνάγωγος.　　　　[5] Πρεσβύτεροι.
[6] Ὑπηρέτης.　　　　[7] Ἀπόστολοι, or ἄγγελοι.

secretaries or messengers, and conducted the corre-
spondence between one synagogue and another, *a sham-
mash,* or sacristan.[1] The synagogues were thus really
little independent republics, having an extensive juris-
diction. Like all municipal corporations, up to an
advanced period of the Roman empire, they issued
honorary decrees,[2] voted resolutions, which had the
force of law for the community, and ordained corporal
punishments, of which the *hazzan* was the ordinary
executor.[3]

With the extreme activity of mind which has always
characterized the Jews, such an institution, notwithstanding the arbitrary rigors it tolerated, could not fail
to give rise to very animated discussions. Thanks to
the synagogues, Judaism has been able to sustain intact
eighteen centuries of persecution. They were like so
many little separate worlds, in which the national spirit
was preserved, and which offered a ready field for in-
testine struggles. A large amount of passion was expended there. The quarrels for precedence were of
constant occurrence. To have a seat of honor in the
first rank was the reward of great piety, or the most
envied privilege of wealth.[4] On the other hand, the
liberty, accorded to every one, of instituting himself
reader and commentator of the sacred text, afforded
marvelous facilities for the propagation of new ideas.

---

[1] *Διάκονος.* Mark v. 22, 35, and following; Luke iv. 20, vii. 3,
viii. 41, 49, xiii. 14; *Acts* xiii. 15, xviii. 8, 17; *Rev.* ii. 1; Mishnah,
Joma, vii. 1; *Rosh Hasshana,* iv. 9; Talm. of Jerus., *Sanhedrim,*
i. 7; Epiph., *Adv. Hær.,* xxx. 4, 11.

[2] Inscription of Berenice, in the *Corpus Inscr. Græc.,* No. 5361;
inscription of Kasyoun, in the *Mission de Phenicie,* book iv. [in
the press.]

[3] Matt. v. 25, x. 17, xxiii. 34; Mark xiii. 9; Luke xx. 11, xxi.
12; *Acts* xxii. 19, xxvi. 11; *2 Cor.* xi. 24; Mishnah, *Maccoth,* iii.
12; Talmud of Babylon, *Megilla,* 7 *b;* Epiph., *Adv. Hær.,* xxx. 11.

[4] Matt. xxiii. 6; Epist. James ii. 3; Talmud. of Bab., *Sukka,* 51 *b.*

This was one of the great instruments of power wielded by Jesus, and the most habitual means he employed to propound his doctrinal instruction.[1] He entered the synagogue, and stood up to read; the *hazzan* offered him the book, he unrolled it, and reading the *parasha* or the *haphtara* of the day, he drew from this reading a lesson in conformity with his own ideas.[2] As there were few Pharisees in Galilee, the discussion did not assume that degree of vivacity, and that tone of acrimony against him, which at Jerusalem would have arrested him at the outset. These good Galileans had never heard discourses so adapted to their cheerful imaginations.[3] They admired him, they encouraged him, they found that he spoke well, and that his reasons were convincing. He answered the most difficult objections with confidence; the charm of his speech and his person captivated the people, whose simple minds had not yet been cramped by the pedantry of the doctors.

The authority of the young master thus continued increasing every day, and, naturally, the more people believed in him, the more he believed in himself. His sphere of action was very limited. It was confined to the valley in which the Lake of Tiberias is situated, and even in this valley there was one region which he preferred. The lake is five or six leagues long and three or four broad; although it presents the appearance of an almost perfect oval, it forms, commencing from Tiberias up to the entrance of the Jordan, a sort of gulf, the curve of which measures about three leagues. Such is the field in which the seed sown by Jesus found at last a well-prepared soil. Let us run

---

[1] Matt. iv. 23, ix. 35; Mark i. 21, 39, vi. 2; Luke iv. 15, 16, 31, 44, xiii. 10; John xviii. 20.

[2] Luke iv. 16, and following. Comp. Mishnah, *Joma*, vii. 1.

[3] Matt. vii. 28, xiii. 54; Mark i. 22, vi. 1; Luke iv. 22, 32.

over it step by step, and endeavor to raise the mantle of aridity and mourning with which it has been covered by the demon of Islamism.

On leaving Tiberias, we find at first steep rocks, like a mountain which seems to roll into the sea. Then the mountains gradually recede; a plain (*El Ghoueir*) opens almost at the level of the lake. It is a delightful copse of rich verdure, furrowed by abundant streams which proceed partly from a great round basin of ancient construction (*Ain-Medawara*). At the entrance of this plain, which is, properly speaking, the country of Gennesareth, there is the miserable village of *Medjdel*. At the other extremity of the plain (always following the sea), we come to the site of a town (*Khan-Minyeh*), with very beautiful streams (*Ain-et-Tin*), a pretty road, narrow and deep, cut out of the rock, which Jesus often traversed, and which serves as a passage between the plain of Gennesareth and the northern slopes of the lake. A quarter of an hour's journey from this place, we cross a stream of salt water (*Ain-Tabiga*), issuing from the earth by several large springs at a little distance from the lake, and entering it in the midst of a dense mass of verdure. At last, after a journey of forty minutes further, upon the arid declivity which extends from Ain-Tabiga to the mouth of the Jordan, we find a few huts and a collection of monumental ruins, called *Tell-Houm*.

Five small towns, the names of which mankind will remember as long as those of Rome and Athens, were, in the time of Jesus, scattered in the space which extends from the village of Medjdel to Tell-Houm. Of these five towns, Magdala, Dalmanutha, Capernaum, Bethsaida, and Chorazin,[1] the first alone can be found

[1] The ancient Kinnereth had disappeared or changed its name.

at the present time with any certainty. The repulsive village of Medjdel has no doubt preserved the name and the place of the little town which gave to Jesus his most faithful female friend.[1] Dalmanutha[2] was probably near there. It is possible that Chorazin was a little more inland, on the northern side.[3] As to Bethsaida and Capernaum, it is in truth almost at hazard that they have been placed at Tell-Houm, Ain-et-Tin, Khan-Minyeh, and Ain-Medawara.[4] We might say that in topography, as well as in history, a profound design has wished to conceal the traces of the great founder. It is doubtful whether we shall ever be able, upon this extensively devastated soil, to ascertain the places where mankind would gladly come to kiss the imprint of his feet.

The lake, the horizon, the shrubs, the flowers, are all that remain of the little canton, three or four leagues in extent, where Jesus founded his Divine work. The trees have totally disappeared. In this country, in which the vegetation was formerly so brilliant that Josephus saw in it a kind of miracle—Nature, accord-

---

[1] We know in fact that it was very near Tiberias.—Talmud of Jerusalem, *Maasaroth,* iii. 1 ; *Shebiit,* ix. 1 ; *Erubin,* v. 7.
[2] Mark viii. 10. Comp. Matt. xv. 39.
[3] In the place named *Khorazi* or *Bir-kerazeh,* above Tell-Houm.
[4] The ancient hypothesis which identified Tell-Houm with Capernaum, though strongly disputed some years since, has still numerous defenders. The best argument we can give in its favor is the name of *Tell-Houm* itself, *Tell* entering into the names of many villages, and being a substitute for *Caphar.* It is impossible, on the other hand, to find near Tell-Houm a fountain corresponding to that mentioned by Josephus (*B. J.,* iii. x. 8.) This fountain of Capernaum seems to be Ain-Medawara, but Ain-Medawara is half an hour's journey from the lake, while Capernaum was a fishing town on the borders of the lake (Matt. iv. 13; John vi. 17.) The difficulties about Bethsaida are still greater; for the hypothesis, somewhat generally admitted, of two Bethsaidas, the one on the eastern, the other on the western shore of the lake, and at two or three leagues from one another, is rather singular.

ing to him, being pleased to bring hither side by side the plants of cold countries, the productions of the torrid zone, and the trees of temperate climates, laden all the year with flowers and fruits[1]—in this country travellers are obliged now to calculate a day beforehand the place where they will the next day find a shady resting-place. The lake has become deserted. A single boat in the most miserable condition now ploughs the waves once so rich in life and joy. But the waters are always clear and transparent.[2] The shore, composed of rocks and pebbles, is that of a little sea, not that of a pond, like the shores of Lake Huleh. It is clean, neat, free from mud, and always beaten in the same place by the light movement of the waves. Small promontories, covered with rose laurels, tamarisks, and thorny caper bushes, are seen there; at two places, especially at the mouth of the Jordan, near Tarichea, and at the boundary of the plain of Gennesareth, there are enchanting parterres, where the waves ebb and flow over masses of turf and flowers. The rivulet of Ain-Tabiga makes a little estuary, full of pretty shells. Clouds of aquatic birds hover over the lake. The horizon is dazzling with light. The waters, of an empyrean blue, deeply imbedded amid burning rocks, seem, when viewed from the height of the mountains of Safed, to lie at the bottom of a cup of gold. On the north, the snowy ravines of Hermon are traced in white lines upon the sky; on the west, the high, undulating plateaux of Gaulonitis and Perea, absolutely arid, and clothed by the sun with a sort of velvety atmosphere, form one compact mountain, or rather a

[1] *B. J.* III. x. 8.
[2] *B. J.,* III. x. 7; Jac. de Vitri, in the *Gesta Dei per Francos,* i. 1075.

long and very elevated terrace, which from Cæsarea Philippi runs indefinitely toward the south.

The heat on the shore is now very oppressive. The lake lies in a hollow six hundred and fifty feet below the level of the Mediterranean,[1] and thus participates in the torrid conditions of the Dead Sea.[2] An abundant vegetation formerly tempered these excessive heats; it would be difficult to understand that a furnace, such as the whole basin of the lake now is, commencing from the month of May, had ever been the scene of great activity. Josephus, moreover, considered the country very temperate.[3] No doubt there has been here, as in the *campagna* of Rome, a change of climate introduced by historical causes. It is Islamism, and especially the Mussulman reaction against the Crusades, which has withered as with a blast of death the district preferred by Jesus. The beautiful country of Gennesareth never suspected that beneath the brow of this peaceful wayfarer its highest destinies lay hidden.

Dangerous countryman! Jesus has been fatal to the country which had the formidable honor of bearing him. Having become a universal object of love or of hate, coveted by two rival fanaticisms, Galilee, as the price of its glory, has been changed to a desert. But who would say that Jesus would have been happier, if he had lived obscure in his village to the full age of man? And who would think of these ungrateful Nazarenes, if one of them had not, at the risk of compromising the future of their town, recognized his Father, and proclaimed himself the Son of God?

---

[1] This is the estimate of Captain Lynch (in Ritter, *Erdkunde* xv., 1st part, p. 20.) It nearly agrees with that of M. de Bertou (*Bulletin de la Soc. de Geogr.*, 2d series, xii., p. 146.)

[2] The depression of the Dead Sea is twice as much.

[3] *B. J.*, iii. x. 7 and 8.

Four or five large villages, situated at half an hour's journey from one another, formed the little world of Jesus at the time of which we speak.   He appears never to have visited Tiberias, a city inhabited for most part by Pagans, and the habitual residence of Antipas.[1] Sometimes, however, he wandered from his favorite region.   He went by boat to the eastern shore, to Gergesa, for instance.[2]   Toward the north we see him at Paneas or Cæsarea Philippi,[3] at the foot of Mount Hermon.   Lastly, he journeyed once in the direction of Tyre and Sidon,[4] a country which must have been marvellously flourishing at that time.   In all these countries he was in the midst of Paganism.[5]   At Cæsarea, he saw the celebrated grotto of *Panium*, thought to be the source of the Jordan, and with which the popular belief had associated strange legends;[6] he could admire the marble temple which Herod had erected near there in honor of Augustus;[7] he probably stopped before the numerous votive statues to Pan, to

[1]Jos., *Ant.*, xviii. ii. 3 ; *Vita,* 12, 13, 64.

[2]I adopt the opinion of Dr. Thomson (*The Land and the Book,* ii. 34, and following), according to which the Gergesa of Matthew viii. 28, identical with the Canaanite town of *Girgash* (*Gen.* x. 16, xv. 21 ; *Deut.* vii. 1 ; *Josh.* xxiv. 11), would be the site now named *Kersa* or *Gersa,* on the eastern shore, nearly opposite Magdala. Mark v. 1, and Luke viii. 26, name *Gadara* or *Gerasa* instead of Gergesa.   *Gerasa* is an impossible reading, the evangelists teaching us that the town in question was near the lake and opposite Galilee. As to Gadara, now *Om-Keis,* at a journey of an hour and a half from the lake and from the Jordan, the local circumstances given by Mark and Luke scarcely suit it. It is possible, moreover, that *Gergesa* may have become *Gerasa,* a much more common name, and that the topographical impossibilities which this latter reading offered may have caused Gadara to be adopted. —Cf. Orig., *Comment. in Joann.,* vi. 24, x. 10 ; Eusebius and St. Jerome, *De situ et nomin. loc. hebr.,* at the words Γεργεδά, Γεργαδεί.

[3]Matt. xvi. 13 ; Mark viii. 27.   [4]Matt. xv. 21 ; Mark vii. 24, 31.
[5]Jos., *Vita,* 13.
[6]Jos., *Ant.,* xv. x. 3 ; *B. J.,* i. xxi. 3, iii. x. 7 ; Benjamin of Tudela, p. 46, edit. Asher.   [7]Jos., *Ant.,* xv. x. 3.

the Nymphs, to the Echo of the Grotto, which piety had already begun to accumulate in this beautiful place.[1]

A rationalistic Jew, accustomed to take strange gods for deified men or for demons, would consider all these figurative representations as idols. The seductions of the naturalistic worships, which intoxicated the more sensitive nations, never affected him. He was doubtless ignorant of what the ancient sanctuary of Melkarth, at Tyre, might still contain of a primitive worship more or less analogous to that of the Jews.[2] The Paganism which, in Phœnicia, had raised a temple and a sacred grove on every hill, all this aspect of great industry and profane riches,[3] interested him but little. Monotheism takes away all aptitude for comprehending the Pagan religion; the Mussulman, thrown into polytheistic countries, seems to have no eyes. Jesus assuredly learned nothing in these journeys. He returned always to his well-beloved shore of Gennesareth. There was the centre of his thoughts; there he found faith and love.

[1] *Corpus inscr. gr.,* Nos. 4537, 4538, 4538 *b,* 4539.
[2] Lucianus (ut fertur), *De Dea Syria,* 3.
[3] The traces of the rich Pagan civilization of that time still cover all the Beled-Besharrah, and especially the mountains which form the group of Cape Blanc and Cape Nakoura.

CHAPTER IX.

THE DISCIPLES OF JESUS.

In this terrestrial paradise, which the great revolutions of history had till then scarcely touched, there lived a population in perfect harmony with the country itself, active, honest, joyous, and tender-hearted. The Lake of Tiberias is one of the best supplied with fish of any in the world.[1] Very productive fisheries were established, especially at Bethsaida, and at Capernaum, and had produced a certain degree of wealth. These families of fishermen formed a gentle and peaceable society, extending by numerous ties of relationship through the whole district of the lake which we have described. Their comparatively easy life left entire freedom to their imagination. The ideas about the kingdom of God found in these small companies of worthy people more credence than anywhere else. Nothing of that which we call civilization, in the Greek and worldly sense, had reached them. Neither was there any of our Germanic and Celtic earnestness; but, although goodness amongst them was often superficial and without depth, their habits were quiet, and they were in some degree intelligent and shrewd. We may imagine them as somewhat analogous to the better populations of the Lebanon, but with the gift, not possessed by the latter, of producing great men. Jesus met here his true family. He installed himself as one

[1] Matt. iv. 18; Luke v. 44, and following; John i. 44, xxi. 1, and following; Jos., *B. J.*, iii. x. 7; Jac. de Vitri, in the *Gesta Dei per Francos*, i. p. 1075.

of them; Capernaum became "his own city;"[1] in the centre of the little circle which adored him, he forgot his sceptical brothers, ungrateful Nazareth and its mocking incredulity.

One house especially at Capernaum offered him an agreeable refuge and devoted disciples. It was that of two brothers, both sons of a certain Jonas, who probably was dead at the period when Jesus came to stay on the borders of the lake. These two brothers were Simon, surnamed *Cephas* or *Peter,* and Andrew. Born at Bethsaida,[2] they were established at Capernaum when Jesus commenced his public life. Peter was married and had children; his mother-in-law lived with him.[3] Jesus loved this house and dwelt there habitually.[4] Andrew appears to have been a disciple of John the Baptist, and Jesus had perhaps known him on the banks of the Jordan.[5] The two brothers continued always, even at the period in which it seems they must have been most occupied with their master, to follow their business as fishermen.[6] Jesus, who loved to play upon words, said at times that he would make them fishers of men.[7] In fact, among all his disciples he had none more faithfully attached.

Another family, that of Zabdia or Zebedee, a well-to-do fisherman and owner of several boats,[8] gave Jesus a welcome reception. Zebedee had two sons: James, who was the elder, and a younger son, John, who later

[1] Matt. ix. 1; Mark ii. 1, 2.
[2] John i. 44.
[3] Matt. viii. 14; Mark i. 30; Luke iv. 38; 1 *Cor.* ix. 5; 1 Peter v. 13; Clem. Alex., *Strom.,* iii. 6, vii. 11; Pseudo-Clem., *Recogn.,* vii. 25; Eusebius, *H. E.,* iii. 30.
[4] Matt. viii. 14, xvii. 24; Mark i. 29-31; Luke iv. 38.
[5] John i. 40, and following.
[6] Matt. iv. 18; Mark i. 16; Luke v. 3; John xxi. 3.
[7] Matt. iv. 19; Mark i. 17; Luke v. 10.
[8] Mark i. 20; Luke v. 10, viii. 3; John xix. 27.

was called to play so prominent a part in the history of infant Christianity. Both were zealous disciples. Salome, wife of Zebedee, was also much attached to Jesus, and accompanied him until his death.[1]

Women, in fact, received him with eagerness. He manifested toward them those reserved manners which render a very sweet union of ideas possible between the two sexes. The separation of men from women, which has prevented all refined development among the Semitic peoples, was no doubt then, as in our days, much less rigorous in the rural districts and villages than in the large towns. Three or four devoted Galilean women always accompanied the young master, and disputed the pleasure of listening to and of tending him in turn.[2] They infused into the new sect an element of enthusiasm and of the marvellous, the importance of which had already begun to be understood. One of them, Mary of Magdala, who has rendered the name of this poor town so celebrated in the world, appears to have been of a very enthusiastic temperament. According to the language of the time, she had been possessed by seven demons.[3] That is, she had been affected with nervous and apparently inexplicable maladies. Jesus, by his pure and sweet beauty, calmed this troubled nature. The Magdalene was faithful to him, even unto Golgotha, and on the day but one after his death, played a prominent part; for, as we shall see later, she was the principal means by which faith in the resurrection was established. Joanna, wife of Chuza, one of the stewards of Antipas, Susanna, and others who have remained unknown, followed him constantly

[1]Matt. xxvii. 56; Mark xv. 40, xvi. 1.
[2]Matt. xxvii. 55, 56; Mark xv. 40, 41; Luke viii. 2. 3, xxiii. 49.
[3]Mark xvi. 9; Luke viii. 2; cf. *Tobit* iii. 8, vi. 14.

and ministered unto him.[1] Some were rich, and by their fortune enabled the young prophet to live without following the trade which he had until then practiced.[2]

Many others followed him habitually, and recognized him as their master—a certain Philip of Bethsaida; Nathanael, son of Tolmai or Ptolemy, of Cana, perhaps a disciple of the first period;[3] and Matthew, probably the one who was the Xenophon of the infant Christianity. The latter had been a publican, and, as such, doubtless handled the *Kalam* more easily than the others. Perhaps it was this that suggested to him the idea of writing the *Logia*,[4] which are the basis of what we know of the teachings of Jesus. Among the disciples are also mentioned Thomas, or Didymus,[5] who doubted sometimes, but who appears to have been a man of warm heart and of generous sympathies;[6] one Lebbæus, or Thaddeus; Simon Zelotes,[7] perhaps a disciple of Judas the Gaulonite, belonging to the party of the *Kenaim,* which was formed about that time, and which was soon to play so great a part in the movements of the Jewish people. Lastly, Judas, son of Simon, of the town of Kerioth, who was an exception in the faithful flock, and drew upon himself such a terrible notoriety. He was the only one who was not a Galilean. Kerioth was a town at the extreme south of the tribe of Judah,[8] a day's journey beyond Hebron.

---

[1] Luke viii. 3, xxiv. 10.
[2] Luke viii. 3.
[3] John i. 44, and following; xxi. 2. I admit the identification of Nathanael with the apostle who figures in the lists under the name of Bartholomew.
[4] Papias, in Eusebius, *Hist. Eccl.,* iii. 39.
[5] This second name is the Greek translation of the first.
[6] John xi. 16, xx. 24, and following.
[7] Matt. x. 4; Mark iii. 18; Luke vi. 15; *Acts* i. 13; Gospel of the Ebionites, in Epiphanes, *Adv. Hær.,* xxx. 13.
[8] Now *Kuryétein,* or *Kereitein.*

We have seen that in general the family of Jesus were little inclined toward him.[1]   James and Jude, however, his cousins by Mary Cleophas, henceforth became his disciples, and Mary Cleophas herself was one of the women who followed him to Calvary.[2]   At this period we do not see his mother beside him.   It was only after the death of Jesus that Mary acquired great importance,[3] and that the disciples sought to attach her to themselves.[4]   It was then, also, that the members of the family of the founder, under the title of "brothers of the Lord," formed an influential group, which was a long time at the head of the church of Jerusalem, and which, after the sack of the city, took refuge in Batanea.[5]   The simple fact of having been familiar with him became a decisive advantage, in the same manner as, after the death of Mahomet, the wives and daughters of the prophet, who had no importance in his life, became great authorities.

In this friendly group Jesus had evidently his favorites, and, so to speak, an inner circle.   The two sons of Zebedee, James and John, appear to have been in the first rank.   They were full of fire and passion.   Jesus had aptly surnamed them "sons of thunder," on account of their excessive zeal, which, if it could have controlled the thunder, would often have made use of it.[6]   John, especially, appears to have been on very familiar terms with Jesus.   Perhaps the warm affec-

---

[1] The circumstance related in John xix. 25-27 seems to imply that at no period of the public life of Jesus did his own brothers become attached to him.

[2] Matt. xxvii. 56; Mark xv. 40; John xix. 25.

[3] *Acts* i. 14.   Compare Luke i. 28, ii. 35, already implying a great respect for Mary.

[4] John xix. 25, and following.

[5] Julius Africanus, in Eusebius, *H. E.*, i. 7.

[6] Mark iii. 17, ix. 37, and following; x. 35, and following; Luke ix. 49, and following; 54, and following.

tion which the master felt for this disciple has been exaggerated in his Gospel, in which the personal interests of the writer are not sufficiently concealed.[1]   The most significant fact is, that, in the synoptical Gospels, Simon Bar-jona, or Peter, James, son of Zebedee, and John, his brother, form a sort of intimate council, which Jesus calls at certain times, when he suspects the faith and intelligence of the others.[2]   It seems, moreover, that they were all three associated in their fishing.[3]   The affection of Jesus for Peter was strong. The character of the latter—upright, sincere, impulsive —pleased Jesus, who at times permitted himself to smile at his resolute manners.   Peter, little of a mystic, communicated to the master his simple doubts, his repugnances, and his entirely human weaknesses,[4] with an honest frankness which recalls that of Joinville toward St. Louis.   Jesus chided him, in a friendly manner, full of confidence and esteem.   As to John, his youth,[5] his exquisite tenderness of heart,[6] and his lively imagination,[7] must have had a great charm.   The personality of this extraordinary man, who has exerted so peculiar an influence on infant Christianity, did not develop itself till afterward.   When old, he wrote that

[1] John xiii. 23, xviii. 15, and following, xix. 26, 27, xx. 2, 4, xxi. 7, 20, and following.

[2] Matt. xvii. 1, xxvi. 37; Mark v. 37, ix. 1, xiii. 3, xiv. 33; Luke ix. 28.   The idea that Jesus had communicated to these three disciples a Gnosis, or secret doctrine, was very early spread.   It is singular that John, in his Gospel, does not once mention James, his brother.

[3] Matt. iv. 18-22; Luke v. 10; John xxi. 2, and following.

[4] Matt. xiv. 28, xvi. 22; Mark viii. 32, and following.

[5] He appears to have lived till near the year 100.   See his Gospel, xxi. 15-23, and the ancient authorities collected by Eusebius, H. E., iii. 20, 23.

[6] See the epistles attributed to him, which are certainly by the same author as the fourth Gospel.

[7] Nevertheless we do not mean to affirm that the Apocalypse is by him.

strange Gospel,[1] which contains such precious teaching, but in which, in our opinion, the character of Jesus is falsified upon many points. The nature of John was too powerful and too profound for him to bend himself to the impersonal tone of the first evangelists. He was the biographer of Jesus, as Plato was of Socrates. Accustomed to ponder over his recollections with the feverish restlessness of an excited mind, he transformed his master in wishing to describe him, and sometimes he leaves it to be suspected (unless other hands have altered his work) that perfect good faith was not invariably his rule and law in the composition of this singular writing.

No hierarchy, properly speaking, existed in the new sect. They were to call each other "brothers;" and Jesus absolutely proscribed titles of superiority, such as *rabbi*, "master," father—he alone being master, and God alone being father. The greatest was to become the servant of the others.[2] Simon Bar-jona, however, was distinguished amongst his fellows by a peculiar degree of importance. Jesus lived with him, and taught in his boat;[3] his house was the centre of the Gospel preaching. In public he was regarded as the chief of the flock; and it is to him that the overseers of the tolls address themselves to collect the taxes which were due from the community.[4] He was the first who had recognized Jesus as the Messiah.[5] In a moment of unpopularity, Jesus, asking of his disciples, "Will ye also go away?" Simon answered, "Lord, to whom

[1] The common tradition seems sufficiently justified to me on this point. It is evident, besides, that the school of John retouched his Gospel (see the whole of chap. xxi.)
[2] Matt. xviii. 4, xx. 25-26, xxiii. 8-12; Mark ix. 34, x. 42-46.
[3] Luke v. 3.
[4] Matt. xvii. 23.
[5] Matt. xvi. 16, 17.

should we go? Thou hast the words of eternal life."[1]
Jesus, at various times, gave him a certain priority in
his church;[2] and gave him the Syrian surname of
Kepha (stone), by which he wished to signify by that,
that he made him the corner-stone of the edifice.[3]   At
one time he seems even to promise him "the keys of the
kingdom of heaven," and to grant him the right of pronouncing upon earth decisions which should always be
ratified in eternity.[4]

No doubt, this priority of Peter excited a little jealousy. Jealousy was kindled especially in view of the
future—and of this kingdom of God, in which all the
disciples would be seated upon thrones, on the right
and on the left of the master, to judge the twelve tribes
of Israel.[5]   They asked who would then be nearest to
the Son of man, and act in a manner as his prime minister and assessor.   The two sons of Zebedee aspired
to this rank.   Preoccupied with such a thought, they
prompted their mother Salome, who one day took Jesus
aside, and asked him for the two places of honor for
her sons.[6]   Jesus evaded the request by his habitual
maxim that he who exalteth himself shall be humbled,
and that the kingdom of heaven will be possessed by
the lowly.   This created some disturbance in the community; there was great discontent against James and
John.[7]   The same rivalry appears to show itself in the
Gospel of John, where the narrator unceasingly de-

[1] John vi. 68-70.
[2] Matt. x. 2; Luke xxii. 32; John xxi. 15, and following; *Acts* i.,
ii., v., etc.; *Gal.* i. 18, ii. 7, 8.
[3] Matt. xvi. 18; John i. 42.
[4] Matt. xvi. 19.   Elsewhere, it is true (Matt. xviii. 18), the same
power is granted to all the apostles.
[5] Matt. xviii. 1, and following; Mark ix. 33; Luke ix. 46, xxii.
30.
[6] Matt. xx. 20, and following; Mark x. 35, and following.
[7] Mark x. 41.

clares himself to be "the disciple whom Jesus loved," to whom the master in dying confided his mother, and seeks systematically to place himself near Simon Peter, and at times to put himself before him, in important circumstances where the older evangelists had omitted mentioning him.[1]

Among the preceding personages, all those of whom we know anything had begun by being fishermen. At all events, none of them belonged to a socially elevated class. Only Matthew or Levi, son of Alpheus,[2] had been a publican. But those to whom they gave this name in Judea were not the farmers-general of taxes, men of elevated rank (always Roman patricians), who were called at Rome *publicani*.[3] They were the agents of these contractors, employés of low rank, simply officers of the customs. The great route from Acre to Damascus, one of the most ancient routes of the world, which crossed Galilee, skirting the lake,[4] made this class of employé very numerous there.   Capernaum,

[1] John xviii. 15, and following, xix. 26, 27, xx. 2, and following, xxi. 7, 21. Comp. i. 35, and following, in which the disciple referred to is probably John.

[2] Matt. ix. 9, x. 3; Mark ii. 14, iii. 18; Luke v. 27, vi. 15; *Acts* i. 13. Gospel of the Ebionites, in Epiph., *Adv. Hær.*, xxx. 13. We must suppose, however strange it may seem, that these two names were borne by the same personage. The narrative, Matt. ix. 9, conceived in accordance with the ordinary model of legends, describing the call to apostleship, is, it is true, somewhat vague, and has certainly not been written by the apostle in question. But we must remember that, in the existing Gospel of Matthew, the only part which is by the apostle consists of the Discourses of Jesus. See Papias, in Eusebius, *Hist. Eccl.*, iii. 39.

[3] Cicero, *De Provinc. Consular.*, 5; *Pro Plancio*, 9; Tac., *Ann.*, iv. 6; Pliny, *Hist. Nat.*, xii. 32; Appian, *Bell. Civ.*, ii. 13.

[4] It remained celebrated, up to the time of the Crusades, under the name of *Via Maris*. Cf. Isaiah ix. 1; Matt. iv. 13-15; Tobit, i. 1. I think that the road cut in the rock near Ain-et-Tin formed part of it, and that the route was directed from thence toward the *Bridge of the Daughters of Jacob*, just as it is now. A part of the road from Ain-et-Tin to this bridge is of ancient construction.

which was perhaps on the road, possessed a numerous staff of them.[1] This profession is never popular, but with the Jews it was considered quite criminal. Taxation, new to them, was the sign of their subjection; one school, that of Judas the Gaulonite, maintained that to pay it was an act of paganism. The customs-officers, also, were abhorred by the zealots of the law. They were only named in company with assassins, highway robbers, and men of infamous life.[2] The Jews who accepted such offices were excommunicated, and became incapable of making a will; their money was accursed, and the casuists forbade the changing of money with them.[3] These poor men, placed under the ban of society, visited amongst themselves. Jesus accepted a dinner offered him by Levi, at which there were, according to the language of the time, "many publicans and sinners." This gave great offense.[4] In these ill-reputed houses there was a risk of meeting bad society. We shall often see him thus, caring little to shock the prejudices of well-disposed persons, seeking to elevate the classes humiliated by the orthodox, and thus exposing himself to the liveliest reproaches of the zealots.

Jesus owed these numerous conquests to the infinite charm of his person and his speech. A penetrating word, a look falling upon a simple conscience, which only wanted awakening, gave him an ardent disciple. Sometimes Jesus employed an innocent artifice, which Joan of Arc also used: he affected to know something

---

[1] Matt. ix. 9, and following.

[2] Matt. v. 46, 47, ix. 10, 11, xi. 19, xviii. 17, xxi. 31, 32; Mark ii. 15, 16; Luke v. 30, vii. 34, xv. 1, xviii. 11, xix. 7; Lucian, *Necyomant*, ii.; Dio Chrysost., orat. iv., p. 85, orat. xiv., p. 269 (edit. Emperius); Mishnah, *Nedarim*, iii. 4.

[3] Mishnah, *Baba Kama*, x. 1; Talmud of Jerusalem, *Demai*, ii 3; Talmud of Bab., *Sanhedrim*, 25 b.

[4] Luke v. 29, and following.

intimate respecting him whom he wished to gain, or he would perhaps recall to him some circumstance dear to his heart. It was thus that he attracted Nathanael,[1] Peter,[2] and the Samaritan woman.[3] Concealing the true source of his strength—his superiority over all that surrounded him—he permitted people to believe (in order to satisfy the ideas of the time—ideas which, moreover, fully coincided with his own) that a revelation from on high revealed to him all secrets and laid bare all hearts. Every one thought that Jesus lived in a sphere superior to that of humanity. They said that he conversed on the mountains with Moses and Elias;[4] they believed that in his moments of solitude the angels came to render him homage, and established a super-natural intercourse between him and heaven.[5]

[1] John i. 48, and following.
[2] John i. 42
[3] John iv. 17, and following.
[4] Matt. xvii. 3; Mark ix. 3; Luke ix. 30-31.
[5] Matt. iv. 11; Mark i. 13.

CHAPTER X.

THE PREACHINGS ON THE LAKE.

SUCH was the group which, on the borders of the
lake of Tiberias, gathered around Jesus. The aristocracy was represented there by a customs-officer and
by the wife of one of Herod's stewards. The rest were
fishermen and common people. Their ignorance was
extreme; their intelligence was feeble; they believed in
apparitions and spirits.[1] Not one element of Greek
culture had penetrated this first assembly of the saints.
They had very little Jewish instruction; but heart and
good-will overflowed. The beautiful climate of Galilee made the life of these honest fishermen a perpetual
delight. They truly preluded the kingdom of God—
simple, good, and happy—rocked gently on their delightful little sea, or at night sleeping on its shores.
We do not realize to ourselves the intoxication of a life
which thus glides away in the face of heaven — the
sweet yet strong love which this perpetual contact with
Nature gives, and the dreams of these nights passed in
the brightness of the stars, under an azure dome of
infinite expanse. It was during such a night that
Jacob, with his head resting upon a stone, saw in the
stars the promise of an innumerable posterity, and the
mysterious ladder by which the angels of God came
and went from heaven to earth. At the time of Jesus
the heavens were not closed, nor the earth grown cold.
The cloud still opened above the Son of man; the

[1] Matt. xiv. 26; Mark vi. 49; Luke xxiv. 39; John vi. 19.

angels ascended and descended upon his head;[1] the visions of the kingdom of God were everywhere, for man carried them in his heart. The clear and mild eyes of these simple souls contemplated the universe in its ideal source. The world unveiled perhaps its secret to the divinely enlightened conscience of these happy children, whose purity of heart deserved one day to behold God.

Jesus lived with his disciples almost always in the open air. Sometimes he got into a boat, and instructed his hearers, who were crowded upon the shore.[2] Sometimes he sat upon the mountains which bordered the lake, where the air is so pure and the horizon so luminous. The faithful band led thus a joyous and wandering life, gathering the inspirations of the master in their first bloom. An innocent doubt was sometimes raised, a question slightly sceptical; but Jesus, with a smile or a look, silenced the objection. At each step—in the passing cloud, the germinating seed, the ripening corn — they saw the sign of the Kingdom drawing nigh, they believed themselves on the eve of seeing God, of being masters of the world; tears were turned into joy; it was the advent upon earth of universal consolation.

"Blessed," said the master, "are the poor in spirit: for theirs is the kingdom of heaven.

"Blessed are they that mourn: for they shall be comforted.

"Blessed are the meek: for they shall inherit the earth.

"Blessed are they which do hunger and thirst after righteousness: for they shall be filled.

[1] John i. 51.
[2] Matt. xiii. 1, 2; Mark iii. 9, iv. 1; Luke v. 3.

"Blessed are the merciful: for they shall obtain mercy.

"Blessed are the pure in heart: for they shall see God.

"Blessed are the peacemakers: for they shall be called the children of God.

"Blessed are they which are persecuted for righteousness' sake: for theirs is the kingdom of heaven."[1]

His preaching was gentle and pleasing, breathing Nature and the perfume of the fields. He loved the flowers, and took from them his most charming lessons. The birds of heaven, the sea, the mountains, and the games of children, furnished in turn the subject of his instructions. His style had nothing of the Grecian in it, but approached much more to that of the Hebrew parabolists, and especially of sentences from the Jewish doctors, his contemporaries, such as we read them in the *"Pirké Aboth."* His teachings were not very extended, and formed a species of sorites in the style of the Koran, which, joined together, afterward composed those long discourses which were written by Matthew.[2] No transition united these diverse pieces; generally, however, the same inspiration penetrated them and made them one. It was, above all, in parable that the master excelled. Nothing in Judaism had given him the model of this delightful style.[3] He created it. It is true that we find in the Buddhist books parables of exactly the same tone and the same charac-

---

[1] Matt. v. 3-10; Luke vi. 20-25.

[2] This is what the *Λόγια κυριακά* were called. Papias, in Euse-bius, *H. E.,* iii. 39.

[3] The apologue, as we find it in *Judges* ix. 8, and following, *2 Sam.* xii. 1, and following, only resembles the Gospel parable in form. The profound originality of the latter is in the thought with which it is filled.

ter as the Gospel parables;[1] but it is difficult to admit that a Buddhist influence has been exercised in these. The spirit of gentleness and the depth of feeling which equally animate infant Christianity and Buddhism, suffice perhaps to explain these analogies.

A total indifference to exterior life and the vain appanage of the "comfortable," which our drearier countries make necessary to us, was the consequence of the sweet and simple life lived in Galilee. Cold climates, by compelling man to a perpetual contest with external nature, cause too much value to be attached to researches after comfort and luxury. On the other hand, the countries which awaken few desires are the countries of idealism and of poesy. The accessories of life are there insignificant compared with the pleasure of living. The embellishment of the house is superfluous, for it is frequented as little as possible. The strong and regular food of less generous climates would be considered heavy and disagreeable. And as to the luxury of garments, what can rival that which God has given to the earth and the birds of heaven? Labor in climates of this kind appears useless; what it gives is not equal to what it costs. The animals of the field are better clothed than the most opulent man, and they do nothing. This contempt, which, when it is not caused by idleness, contributes greatly to the elevation of the soul, inspired Jesus with some charming apologues: "Lay not up for yourselves treasures upon earth," said he, "where moth and rust doth corrupt, and where thieves break through and steal, but lay up for yourselves treasures in heaven, where neither moth nor rust doth corrupt, and where thieves do not break through nor steal: for where your treasure is, there will your

[1] See especially the *Lotus of the Good Law*, chap. iii. and iv.

heart be also.[1] No man can serve two masters: for either he will hate the one and love the other; or else he will hold to one and despise the other. Ye cannot serve God and Mammon.[2] Therefore I say unto you, take no thought for your life, what ye shall eat, or what ye shall drink; nor yet for your body, what ye shall put on. Is not the life more than meat, and the body than raiment? Behold the fowls of the air: for they sow not, neither do they reap, nor gather into barns; yet your heavenly Father feedeth them. Are ye not much better than they? Which of you by taking thought can add one cubit unto his stature? And why take ye thought for raiment? Consider the lilies of the field, how they grow; they toil not, neither do they spin; and yet I say unto you, That even Solomon in all his glory was not arrayed like one of these. Wherefore, if God so clothe the grass of the field, which to-day is, and to-morrow is cast into the oven, shall he not much more clothe you, O ye of little faith? Therefore take no thought, saying, What shall we eat? or, What shall we drink? or, Wherewithal shall we be clothed? For after all these things do the Gentiles seek; for your heavenly Father knoweth that ye have need of all these things. But seek ye first the kingdom of God,[3] and his righteousness; and all these things shall be added unto you. Take therefore no thought for the morrow: for the morrow shall take thought of the things of itself. Sufficient unto the day is the evil thereof."[4]

[1] Compare Talm. of Bab., *Baba Bathra*, 11 a.

[2] The god of riches and hidden treasures, a kind of Plutus in the Phœnician and Syrian mythology.

[3] I here adopt the reading of Lachmann and Tischendorf.

[4] Matt. vi. 19-21, 24-34. Luke xii. 22-31, 33, 34, xvi. 13. Compare the precepts in Luke x. 7, 8, full of the same simple sentiment, and Talmud of Babylon. *Sota,* 48 b.

This essentially Galilean sentiment had a decisive influence on the destiny of the infant sect. The happy flock, relying on the heavenly Father for the satisfaction of its wants, had for its first principle the regarding of the cares of life as an evil which choked the germ of all good in man.[1] Each day they asked of God the bread for the morrow.[2] Why lay up treasure? The kingdom of God is at hand. "Sell that ye have and give alms," said the master. "Provide yourselves bags which wax not old, a treasure in the heavens that faileth not."[3] What more foolish than to heap up treasures for heirs whom thou wilt never behold?[4] As an example of human folly, Jesus loved to cite the case of a man who, after having enlarged his barns and amassed wealth for long years, died before having enjoyed it![5] The brigandage which was deeply rooted in Galilee,[6] gave much force to these views. The poor, who did not suffer from it, would regard themselves as the favored of God; whilst the rich, having a less sure possession, were the truly disinherited. In our societies, established upon a very rigorous idea of property, the position of the poor is horrible; they have literally no place under the sun. There are no flowers, no grass, no shade, except for him who possesses the earth. In the East, these are gifts of God which belong to no one. The proprietor has but a slender privilege; nature is the patrimony of all.

The infant Christianity, moreover, in this only followed the footsteps of the Essenes, or Therapeutæ, and

[1] Matt. xiii. 22; Mark iv. 19; Luke viii. 14.
[2] Matt. vi. 11; Luke xi. 3. This is the meaning of the word ἐπιούσιος.
[3] Luke xii. 33, 34.
[4] Luke xii. 20.
[5] Luke xii. 16, and following.
[6] Jos., Ant., XVII. x. 4, and following; Vita, 11, etc.

of the Jewish sects founded on the monastic life. A communistic element entered into all these sects, which were equally disliked by Pharisees and Sadducees. The Messianic doctrine, which was entirely political among the orthodox Jews, was entirely social amongst them. By means of a gentle, regulated, contemplative existence, leaving its share to the liberty of the individual, these little churches thought to inaugurate the heavenly kingdom upon earth. Utopias of a blessed life, founded on the brotherhood of men and the worship of the true God, occupied elevated souls, and produced from all sides bold and sincere, but short-lived attempts to realize these doctrines.

Jesus, whose relations with the Essenes are difficult to determine (resemblances in history not always implying relations), was on this point certainly their brother. The community of goods was for some time the rule in the new society.[1] Covetousness was the cardinal sin.[2] Now it must be remarked that the sin of covetousness, against which Christian morality has been so severe, was then the simple attachment to property. The first condition of becoming a disciple of Jesus was to sell one's property and to give the price of it to the poor. Those who recoiled from this extremity were not admitted into the community.[3] Jesus often repeated that he who has found the kingdom of God ought to buy it at the price of all his goods, and that in so doing he makes an advantageous bargain. "The kingdom of heaven is like unto treasure hid in a field; the which when a man hath found, he hideth, and for joy thereof goeth and selleth all that he hath and

[1] Acts iv. 32, 34-37; v. 1, and following.
[2] Matt. xiii. 22; Luke xii. 15, and following.
[3] Matt. xix. 21; Mark x. 21, and following, 29, 30; Luke xviii. 22, 23, 28.

buyeth that field. Again, the kingdom of heaven is like unto a merchantman seeking goodly pearls; who, when he had found one pearl of great price, went and sold all that he had and bought it."[1] Alas! the inconveniences of this plan were not long in making themselves felt. A treasurer was wanted. They chose for that office Judas of Kerioth. Rightly or wrongly, they accused him of stealing from the common purse;[2] it is certain that he came to a bad end.

Sometimes the master, more versed in things of heaven than those of earth, taught a still more singular political economy. In a strange parable, a steward is praised for having made himself friends among the poor at the expense of his master, in order that the poor might in their turn introduce him into the kingdom of heaven. The poor, in fact, becoming the dispensers of this kingdom, will only receive those who have given to them. A prudent man, thinking of the future, ought therefore to seek to gain their favor. "And the Pharisees also," says the evangelist, "who were covetous, heard all these things: and they derided him."[3] Did they also hear the formidable parable which follows? "There was a certain rich man, which was clothed in purple and fine linen, and fared sumptuously every day: and there was a certain beggar named Lazarus, which was laid at his gate, full of sores, and desiring to be fed with the crumbs which fell from the rich man's table: moreover the dogs came and licked his sores. And it came to pass, that the beggar died, and was carried by the angels into Abraham's bosom: the rich man also died, and was buried;[4] and in hell he lifted up his eyes, being in torments, and

[1]Matt. xiii. 44-46.   [2]John xii. 6.   [3]Luke xvi. 1-14.
[4]See the Greek text.

seeth Abraham afar off, and Lazarus in his bosom.
And he cried and said, Father Abraham, have mercy on
me, and send Lazarus that he may dip the tip of his
finger in water, and cool my tongue; for I am tormented in this flame. But Abraham said, Son, remember that thou in thy lifetime receivedst thy good
things; and likewise Lazarus evil things: but now he
is comforted and thou art tormented."[1]   What more
just?   Afterward this parable was called that of the
"wicked rich man."   But it is purely and simply the
parable of the "rich man."   He is in hell because he is
rich, because he does not give his wealth to the poor,
because he dines well, while others at his door dine
badly.   Lastly, in a less extravagant moment, Jesus
does not make it obligatory to sell one's goods and
give them to the poor except as a suggestion toward
greater perfection.   But he still makes this terrible
declaration: "It is easier for a camel to go through
the eye of a needle than for a rich man to enter into the
kingdom of God."[2]

An admirable idea governed Jesus in all this, as well
as the band of joyous children who accompanied him
and made him for eternity the true creator of the peace
of the soul, the great consoler of life.   In disengaging
man from what he called "the cares of the world,"
Jesus might go to excess and injure the essential conditions of human society; but he founded that high

---

[1]Luke xvi. 19-25. Luke, I am aware, has a very decided communistic tendency (comp. vi. 20, 21, 25, 26), and I think he has
exaggerated this shade of the teaching of Jesus. But the features
of the Λόγια of Matthew are sufficiently significant.

[2]Matt. xix. 24; Mark x. 25; Luke xviii. 25. This proverbial
phrase is found in the Talmud (Bab., *Berakoth*, 55 b, *Baba metsia*,
38 b) and in the Koran (Sur., vii. 38.) Origen and the Greek
interpreters, ignorant of the Semitic proverb, thought that it
meant a cable (ϰάμιλοϛ.)

spiritualism which for centuries has filled souls with joy in the midst of this vale of tears. He saw with perfect clearness that man's inattention, his want of philosophy and morality, come mostly from the distractions which he permits himself, the cares which besiege him, and which civilization multiplies beyond measure.[1] The Gospel, in this manner, has been the most efficient remedy for the weariness of ordinary life, a perpetual *sursum corda,* a powerful diversion from the miserable cares of earth, a gentle appeal like that of Jesus in the ear of Martha—"Martha, Martha, thou art careful and troubled about many things; but one thing is needful." Thanks to Jesus, the dullest existence, that most absorbed by sad or humiliating duties, has had its glimpse of heaven. In our busy civilizations the remembrance of the free life of Galilee has been like perfume from another world, like the "dew of Hermon,"[2] which has prevented drought and barrenness from entirely invading the field of God.

[1] Matt. xiii. 22.
[2] Psalm cxxxiii. 3.

CHAPTER XI.

THE KINGDOM OF GOD CONCEIVED AS THE INHERITANCE OF THE POOR.

THESE maxims, good for a country where life is nourished by the air and the light, and this delicate communism of a band of children of God reposing in confidence on the bosom of their Father, might suit a simple sect constantly persuaded that its Utopia was about to be realized. But it is clear that they could not satisfy the whole of society. Jesus understood very soon, in fact, that the official world of his time would by no means adopt his kingdom. He took his resolution with extreme boldness. Leaving the world, with its hard heart and narrow prejudices on one side, he turned toward the simple. A vast substitution of classes would take place. The kingdom of God was made—1st, for children, and those who resemble them; 2d, for the outcasts of this world, victims of that social arrogance which repulses the good but humble man; 3d, for heretics and schismatics, publicans, Samaritans, and Pagans of Tyre and Sidon. An energetic parable explained this appeal to the people and justified it.[1] A king has prepared a wedding feast, and sends his servants to seek those invited. Each one excuses himself; some ill-treat the messengers. The king, therefore, takes a decided step. The great people have not accepted his invitation. Be it so. His guests shall be the first comers; the people collected

[1] Matt. xxii. 2, and following; Luke xiv. 16, and following. Comp. Matt. viii. 11, 12, xxi. 33, and following.

from the highways and byways, the poor, the beggars, and the lame; it matters not who, the room must be filled. "For I say unto you," said he, "that none of those men which were bidden shall taste of my supper."

Pure *Ebionism*—that is, the doctrine that the poor (*ebionim*) alone shall be saved, that the reign of the poor is approaching—was, therefore, the doctrine of Jesus. "Woe unto you that are rich," said he, "for ye have received your consolation. Woe unto you that are full, for ye shall hunger. Woe unto you that laugh now, for ye shall mourn and weep."[1] "Then said he also to him that bade him, When thou makest a dinner or a supper, call not thy friends, nor thy brethren, neither thy kinsmen, nor thy rich neighbors, lest they also bid thee again, and a recompense be made thee. But when thou makest a feast, call the poor, the maimed, the lame, the blind: and thou shalt be blessed; for they cannot recompense thee; for thou shalt be recompensed at the resurrection of the just."[2] It is perhaps in an analogous sense that he often repeated, "Be good bankers."[3]—that is to say, make good investments for the kingdom of God, in giving your wealth to the poor, conformably to the old proverb, "He that hath pity upon the poor, lendeth unto the Lord."[4]

This, however, was not a new fact. The most exalted democratic movement of which humanity has preserved the remembrance (the only one, also, which has succeeded, for it alone has maintained itself in the domain of pure thought), had long disturbed the Jewish race. The thought that God is the avenger of

---

[1] Luke vi. 24, 25.   [2] Luke xiv. 12, 14.
[3] A saying preserved by very ancient tradition, and much used, Clement of Alexandria, *Strom.* i. 28. It is also found in Origen, St. Jerome, and a great number of the Fathers of the Church.
[4] Prov. xix. 17.

the poor and the weak, against the rich and the power-ful, is found in each page of the writings of the Old Testament. The history of Israel is of all histories that in which the popular spirit has most constantly predominated. The prophets, the true, and, in one sense, the boldest tribunes, had thundered incessantly against the great, and established a close relation, on the one hand, between the words "rich, impious, violent, wicked," and, on the other, between the words "poor, gentle, humble, pious."[1] Under the Seleucidæ, the aristocrats having almost all apostatized and gone over to Hellenism, these associations of ideas only became stronger. The Book of Enoch contains still more violent maledictions than those of the Gospel against the world, the rich, and the powerful.[2] Luxury is there depicted as a crime. The "Son of man," in this strange Apocalypse, dethrones kings, tears them from their voluptuous life, and precipitates them into hell.[3] The initiation of Judea into secular life, the recent introduction of an entirely worldly element of luxury and comfort, provoked a furious reaction in favor of patriarchal simplicity. "Woe unto you who despise the humble dwelling and inheritance of your fathers! Woe unto you who build your palaces with the sweat of others! Each stone, each brick, of which it is built, is a sin."[4] The name of "poor" (ebion) had become a synonym of "saint," of "friend of God." This was the name that the Galilean disciples of Jesus loved to

---

[1] See, in particular, Amos ii. 6; Isa. lxiii. 9; Ps. xxv. 9, xxxvii. 11, lxix. 33; and, in general, the Hebrew dictionaries, at the words:

עֶבְיוֹן, דַּל, עָנִי, עָנָו, חָסִיד, עָשִׁיר, הוֹלְלִים, עָרִיץ.

[2] Ch. lxii., lxiii., xcvii., c., civ.
[3] *Enoch,* ch. xlvi. 4-8.
[4] *Enoch.* xcix. 13, 14.

give themselves; it was for a long time the name of the Judaizing Christians of Batanea and of the Hauran (Nazarenes, Hebrews) who remained faithful to the tongue, as well as to the primitive instructions of Jesus, and who boasted that they possessed amongst themselves the descendants of his family.[1] At the end of the second century, these good sectaries, having remained beyond the reach of the great current which had carried away all the other churches, were treated as heretics (*Ebionites*), and a pretended heretical leader (*Ebion*) was invented to explain their name.[2]

We may see, in fact, without difficulty, that this exaggerated taste for poverty could not be very lasting. It was one of those Utopian elements which always mingle in the origin of great movements, and which time rectifies. Thrown into the centre of human society, Christianity very easily consented to receive rich men into her bosom, just as Buddhism, exclusively monkish in its origin, soon began, as conversions multiplied, to admit the laity. But the mark of origin is ever preserved. Although it quickly passed away and became forgotten, *Ebionism* left a leaven in the whole history of Christian institutions which has not been lost. The collection of the *Logia*, or discourses of Jesus, was formed in the Ebionitish centre of Batanea.[3]

---

[1] Julius Africanus in Eusebius, *H. E.*, i. 7; Eus., *De situ et nom. loc. hebr.*, at the word Χωβά; Orig., *Contra Celsus*, ii. 1, v. 61; Epiph., *Adv. Hær.*, xxix. 7, 9, xxx. 2, 18.

[2] See especially Origen, *Contra Celsus*, ii. 1; *De Principiis*, iv. 22. Compare Epiph., *Adv. Hær.*, xxx. 17. Irenæus, Origen, Eusebius, and the apostolic Constitutions, ignore the existence of such a personage. The author of the *Philosophumena* seems to hesitate (vii. 34 and 35, x. 22 and 23.) It is by Tertullian, and especially by Epiphanes, that the fable of one *Ebion* has been spread. Besides, all the Fathers are agreed on the etymology, Ἐβίων=πτωχός.

[3] Epiph., *Adv. Hær.*, xix., xxix., and xxx., especially xxix. 9.

"Poverty" remained an ideal from which the true followers of Jesus were never after separated. To possess nothing was the truly evangelical state; mendicancy became a virtue, a holy condition. The great Umbrian movement of the thirteenth century, which, among all the attempts at religious construction, most resembles the Galilean movement, took place entirely in the name of poverty. Francis d'Assisi, the man who, more than any other, by his exquisite goodness, by his delicate, pure, and tender intercourse with universal life, most resembled Jesus, was a poor man. The mendicant orders, the innumerable communistic sects of the middle ages (*Pauvres de Lyon, Bégards, Bons-Hommes, Fratricelles, Humiliés, Pauvres évangéliques,* &c.) grouped under the banner of the "Everlasting Gospel," pretended to be, and in fact were, the true disciples of Jesus. But even in this case the most impracticable dreams of the new religion were fruitful in results. Pious mendicity, so impatiently borne by our industrial and well-organized communities, was in its day, and in a suitable climate, full of charm. It offered to a multitude of mild and contemplative souls the only condition suited to them. To have made poverty an object of love and desire, to have raised the beggar to the altar, and to have sanctified the coat of the poor man, was a master-stroke which political economy may not appreciate, but in the presence of which the true moralist cannot remain indifferent. Humanity, in order to bear its burdens, needs to believe that it is not paid entirely by wages. The greatest service which can be rendered to it is to repeat often that it lives not by bread alone.

Like all great men, Jesus loved the people, and felt himself at home with them. The Gospel, in his idea, is made for the poor; it is to them he brings the glad tidings of salvation.[1]   All the despised ones of ortho- dox Judaism were his favorites.   Love of the people, and pity for its weakness (the sentiment of the demo- cratic chief, who feels the spirit of the multitude live in him, and recognize him as its natural interpreter), shine forth at each moment in his acts and discourses.[2]

The chosen flock presented, in fact, a very mixed character, and one likely to astonish rigorous moral- ists.   It counted in its fold men with whom a Jew, respecting himself, would not have associated.[3]   Per- haps Jesus found in this society, unrestrained by ordi- nary rules, more mind and heart than in a pedantic and formal middle-class, proud of its apparent morality. The Pharisees, exaggerating the Mosaic prescriptions, had come to believe themselves defiled by contact with men less strict than themselves; in their meals they almost rivalled the puerile distinctions of caste in India. Despising these miserable aberrations of the religious sentiment, Jesus loved to eat with those who suffered from them;[4] by his side at table were seen persons said to lead wicked lives, perhaps only so called because they did not share the follies of the false devotees. The Pharisees and the doctors protested against the scandal. "See," said they, "with what men he eats!"   Jesus returned subtle answers, which exasperated the hypo- crites: "They that be whole need not a physician."[5] Or again: "What man of you, having an hundred sheep, if he lose one of them, doth not leave the ninety and nine in the wilderness, and go after that which is

[1]Matt. xi. 5; Luke vi. 20, 21.
[2]Matt. ix. 36; Mark vi. 34.
[3]Matt. ix. 10, and following; Luke xv. entirely.
[4]Matt. ix. 11; Mark ii. 16; Luke v. 30.
[5]Matt. ix. 12.

lost until he find it? And when he hath found it, **he**
layeth it on his shoulders rejoicing."[1] Or again: "The
Son of Man is come to save that which was lost."[2]
Or again: "I am not come to call the righteous, but
sinners."[3] Lastly, that delightful parable of the prodigal son, in which he who is fallen is represented as
having a kind of privilege of love above him who has
always been righteous. Weak or guilty women, surprised at so much that was charming, and realizing,
for the first time, the attractions of contact with virtue,
approached him freely. People were astonished that
he did not repulse them. "Now when the Pharisee
which had bidden him saw it, he spake within himself,
saying, This man, if he were a prophet, would have
known who and what manner of woman this is that
toucheth him: for she is a sinner." Jesus replied by
the parable of a creditor who forgives his debtors' unequal debts, and he did not hesitate to prefer the lot of
him to whom was remitted the greater debt.[4] He
appreciated conditions of soul only in proportion to
the love mingled therein. Women, with tearful hearts,
and disposed through their sins to feelings of humility,
were nearer to his kingdom than ordinary natures, who
often have little merit in not having fallen. We may
conceive, on the other hand, that these tender souls,
finding in their conversion to the sect an easy means

[1]Luke xv. 4, and following.
[2]Matt. xviii. 11; Luke xix. 10.   [3]Matt. ix. 13.
[4]Luke vii. 36, and following. Luke, who likes to bring out in
relief everything that relates to the forgiveness of sinners (comp.
x. 30, and following, xv. entirely, xvii. 16, and following, xix. 2,
and following, xxiii. 39-43), has included in this narrative passages from another history, that of the anointing of feet, which
took place at Bethany some days before the death of Jesus. But
the pardon of sinful women was undoubtedly one of the essential
features of the anecdotes of the life of Jesus.—Cf. John viii. 3,
and following; Papias, in Eusebius, *Hist. Eccl.,* iii. 39.

of restoration, would passionately attach themselves to him.

Far from seeking to soothe the murmurs stirred up by his disdain for the social susceptibilities of the time, he seemed to take pleasure in exciting them. Never did any one avow more loftily this contempt for the "world," which is the essential condition of great things and of great originality. He pardoned a rich man, but only when the rich man, in consequence of some prejudice, was disliked by society.[1] He greatly preferred men of equivocal life and of small consideration in the eyes of the orthodox leaders. "The publicans and the harlots go into the kingdom of God before you. For John came unto you and ye believed him not: but the publicans and the harlots believed him."[2] We can understand how galling the reproach of not having followed the good example set by prostitutes must have been to men making a profession of seriousness and rigid morality.

He had no external affectation or show of austerity. He did not fly from pleasure; he went willingly to marriage feasts. One of his miracles was performed to enliven a wedding at a small town. Weddings in the East take place in the evening. Each one carries a lamp; and the lights coming and going produce a very agreeable effect. Jesus liked this gay and animated aspect, and drew parables from it.[3] Such conduct, compared with that of John the Baptist, gave offence.[4] One day, when the disciples of John and the Pharisees were observing the fast, it was asked, "Why do the disciples of John and the Pharisees fast,

---

[1] Luke xix. 2, and following.
[2] Matt. xxi. 31, 32.
[3] Matt. xxv. 1, and following.
[4] Mark ii. 18; Luke v. 33.

but thy disciples fast not? And Jesus said unto them, Can the children of the bridechamber fast, while the bridegroom is with them? As long as they have the bridegroom with them, they cannot fast. But the days will come when the bridegroom shall be taken away from them, and then they shall fast in those days."[1] His gentle gaiety found expression in lively ideas and amiable pleasantries. "But whereunto," said he, "shall I liken this generation? It is like unto children sitting in the markets, and calling unto their fellows, and saying, We have piped unto you, and ye have not danced; we have mourned unto you, and ye have not lamented.[2] For John came neither eating nor drinking, and they say, He hath a devil. The Son of man came eating and drinking, and they say, Behold a man gluttonous, and a winebibber, a friend of publicans and sinners. But Wisdom is justified of her children."[3]

He thus traversed Galilee in the midst of a continual feast. He rode on a mule. In the East this is a good and safe mode of traveling; the large, black eyes of the animal, shaded by long eyelashes, give it an expression of gentleness. His disciples sometimes surrounded him with a kind of rustic pomp, at the expense of their garments, which they used as carpets. They placed them on the mule which carried him, or extended them on the earth in his path.[4] His entering a house was considered a joy and a blessing. He stopped in the villages and the large farms, where he received an

[1] Matt. ix. 14, and following; Mark ii. 18, and following; Luke v. 33, and following.
[2] An allusion to some children's game.
[3] Matt. xi. 16, and following; Luke vii. 34, and following. A proverb which means "The opinion of men is blind. The wisdom of the works of God is only proclaimed by His works themselves." I read ἔργων, with the manuscript B. of the Vatican, and not τέκνων.   [4] Matt. xxi. 7, 8.

eager hospitality. In the East, the house into which a stranger enters becomes at once a public place. All the village assembles there, the children invade it, and though dispersed by the servants, always return. Jesus could not permit these simple auditors to be treated harshly; he caused them to be brought to him and embraced them.[1] The mothers, encouraged by such a reception, brought him their children in order that he might touch them.[2] Women came to pour oil upon his head, and perfume on his feet. His disciples sometimes repulsed them as troublesome; but Jesus, who loved the ancient usages, and all that indicated simplicity of heart, repaired the ill done by his too zealous friends. He protected those who wished to honor him.[3] Thus children and women adored him. The reproach of alienating from their families these gentle creatures, always easily misled, was one of the most frequent charges of his enemies.[4]

The new religion was thus in many respects a movement of women and children. The latter were like a young guard around Jesus for the inauguration of his innocent royalty, and gave him little ovations which much pleased him, calling him "son of David," crying *Hosanna*,[5] and bearing palms around him. Jesus, like Savonarola, perhaps made them serve as instruments

[1]Matt. xix. 13, and following; Mark ix. 35, x. 13, and following; Luke xviii. 15, 16.

[2]Ibid.

[3]Matt. xxvi. 7, and following; Mark xiv. 3, and following; Luke vii. 37, and following.

[4]Gospel of Marcion, addition to ver. 2 of chap. xxiii. of Luke (Epiph., *Adv. Hær.*, xlii. 11.) If the suppressions of Marcion are without critical value, such is not the case with his additions, when they proceed, not from a special view, but from the condition of the manuscripts which he used.

[5]A cry which was raised at the feast of tabernacles, amidst the waving of palms. Mishnah, *Sukka*, iii. 9. This custom still exists among the Israelites.

for pious missions; he was very glad to see these young apostles, who did not compromise him, rush into the front and give him titles which he dared not take himself. He let them speak, and when he was asked if he heard, he replied in an evasive manner that the praise which comes from young lips is the most agreeable to God.[1]

He lost no opportunity of repeating that the little ones are sacred beings,[2] that the kingdom of God belongs to children,[3] that we must become children to enter there,[4] that we ought to receive it as a child,[5] that the heavenly Father hides his secrets from the wise and reveals them to the little ones.[6] The idea of disciples is in his mind almost synonymous with that of children.[7] On one occasion, when they had one of those quarrels for precedence, which were not uncommon, Jesus took a little child, placed him in their midst, and said to them, "Whosoever therefore shall humble himself as this little child, the same is greatest in the kingdom of heaven."[8]

It was infancy, in fact, in its divine spontaneity, in its simple bewilderments of joy, which took possession of the earth. Every one believed at each moment that the kingdom so much desired was about to appear. Each one already saw himself seated on a throne[9] beside the master. They divided amongst themselves the positions of honor in the new kingdom,[10] and strove to

[1] Matt. xxi. 15, 16.
[2] Matt. xviii. 5, 10, 14; Luke xvii. 2.
[3] Matt. xix. 14; Mark x. 14; Luke xviii. 16.
[4] Matt. xviii. 1, and following; Mark ix. 33, and following; Luke ix. 46.
[5] Mark x. 15.
[6] Matt. xi. 25; Luke x. 21.
[7] Matt. x. 42, xviii. 5, 14; Mark ix. 36; Luke xvii. 2.
[8] Matt. xviii. 4; Mark ix. 33-36; Luke ix. 46-48.
[9] Luke xxii. 30.   [10] Mark x. 37, 40, 41.

reckon the precise date of its advent. This new doctrine was called the "Good Tidings;" it had no other
name. An old word, *"paradise,"* which the Hebrew,
like all the languages of the East, had borrowed from
the Persian, and which at first designated the parks of
the Achæmenidæ, summed up the general dream; a
delightful garden, where the charming life which was
led here below would be continued forever.[1] How
long this intoxication lasted we know not. No one,
during the course of this magical apparition, measured
time any more than we measure a dream. Duration
was suspended; a week was an age. But whether it
filled years or months, the dream was so beautiful that
humanity has lived upon it ever since, and it is still
our consolation to gather its weakened perfume. Never
did so much joy fill the breast of man. For a moment
humanity, in this the most vigorous effort she ever
made to rise above the world, forgot the leaden weight
which binds her to earth and the sorrows of the life
below. Happy he who has been able to behold this
divine unfolding, and to share, were it but for one day,
this unexampled illusion! But still more happy, Jesus
would say to us, is he who, freed from all illusion, shall
reproduce in himself the celestial vision, and, with no
millenarian dream, no chimerical paradise, no signs in
the heavens, but by the uprightness of his will and the
poetry of his soul, shall be able to create anew in his
heart the true kingdom of God!

[1] Luke xxiii. 43; 2 Cor. xii. 4. Comp. *Carm. Sibyll., procem,* 86;
Talm. of Bab., *Chagigah,* 14 *b.*

CHAPTER XII.

EMBASSY FROM JOHN IN PRISON TO JESUS—DEATH OF JOHN—RELATIONS OF HIS SCHOOL WITH THAT OF JESUS.

WHILST joyous Galilee was celebrating in feasts the coming of the well-beloved, the sorrowful John, in his prison of Machero, was pining away with expectation and desire. The success of the young master, whom he had seen some months before as his auditor, reached his ears. It was said that the Messiah predicted by the prophets, he who was to re-establish the kingdom of Israel, was come, and was proving his presence in Galilee by marvelous works. John wished to inquire into the truth of this rumor, and as he communicated freely with his disciples, he chose two of them to go to Jesus in Galilee.[1]

The two disciples found Jesus at the height of his fame. The air of gladness which reigned around him surprised them. Accustomed to fasts, to persevering prayer, and to a life of aspiration, they were astonished to see themselves transported suddenly into the midst of the joys attending the welcome of the Messiah.[2] They told Jesus their message: "Art thou he that should come? Or do we look for another?" Jesus, who from that time hesitated no longer respecting his peculiar character as Messiah, enumerated the works which ought to characterize the coming of the kingdom of God—such as the healing of the sick, and the good

[1]Matt. xi. 2, and following; Luke vii. 18, and following.
[2]Matt. ix. 14, and following.

tidings of a speedy salvation preached to the poor. He did all these works. "And blessed is he," said Jesus, "whosoever shall not be offended in me." We know not whether this answer found John the Baptist living, or in what temper it put the austere ascetic. Did he die consoled and certain that he whom he had announced already lived, or did he remain doubtful as to the mission of Jesus? There is nothing to inform us. Seeing, however, that his school continued to exist a considerable time parallel with the Christian churches, we are led to think that, notwithstanding his regard for Jesus, John did not look upon him as the one who was to realize the divine promises. Death came, moreover, to end his perplexities. The untamable freedom of the ascetic was to crown his restless and stormy career by the only end which was worthy of it.

The leniency which Antipas had at first shown toward John was not of long duration. In the conversations which, according to the Christian tradition, John had had with the tetrarch, he did not cease to declare to him that his marriage was unlawful, and that he ought to send away Herodias.[1] We can easily imagine the hatred which the granddaughter of Herod the Great must have conceived toward this importunate counsellor. She only waited an opportunity to ruin him.

Her daughter, Salome, born of her first marriage, and like her ambitious and dissolute, entered into her designs. That year (probably the year 30) Antipas was at Machero on the anniversary of his birthday. Herod the Great had constructed in the interior of the fortress a magnificent palace, where the tetrarch fre-

[1] Matt. xiv. 4, and following; Mark vi. 18, and following; Luke iii. 19.

quently resided.[1]   He gave a great feast there, during
which Salome executed one of those dances in character
which were not considered in Syria as unbecoming a
distinguished person.   Antipas being much pleased,
asked the dancer what she most desired, and she replied, at the instigation of her mother, "Give me here
John Baptist's head in a charger."[2]   Antipas was sorry,
but he did not like to refuse.   A guard took the dish,
went and cut off the head of the prisoner, and brought
it.[3]

The disciples of the Baptist obtained his body and
placed it in a tomb, but the people were much displeased.   Six years after, Hareth, having attacked
Antipas, in order to recover Machero and avenge the
dishonor of his daughter, Antipas was completely
beaten; and his defeat was generally regarded as a
punishment for the murder of John.[4]

The news of John's death was brought to Jesus by
the disciples of the Baptist.[5]   John's last act toward
Jesus had effectually united the two schools in the most
intimate bonds.   Jesus, fearing an increase of ill-will
on the part of Antipas, took precautions and retired to
the desert,[6] where many people followed him.   By
exercising an extreme frugality, the holy band was
enabled to live there, and in this there was naturally
seen a miracle.[7]   From this time Jesus always spoke of
John with redoubled admiration.   He declared unhesi-
tatingly[8] that he was more than a prophet, that the

[1] Jos., De Bello jud., VII. vi. 2.
[2] A portable dish on which liquors and viands are served in the
East.
[3] Matt. xiv. 3, and following; Mark vi. 14-29; Jos., Ant., XVIII.
v. 2.   [4] Josephus, Ant., XVIII. v. 1, 2.
[5] Matt. xiv. 12.   [6] Matt. xiv. 13.
[7] Matt. xiv. 15, and following; Mark vi. 35, and following;
Luke ix. 11, and following; John vi. 2, and following.
[8] Matt. xi. 7. and following; Luke vii. 24, and following.

Law and the ancient prophets had force only until he came,[1] that he had abrogated them, but that the kingdom of heaven would displace him in turn. In fine, he attributed to him a special place in the economy of the Christian mystery, which constituted him the link of union between the Old Testament and the advent of the new reign.

The prophet Malachi, whose opinion in this matter was soon brought to bear,[2] had announced with much energy a precursor of the Messiah, who was to prepare men for the final renovation, a messenger who should come to make straight the paths before the elected one of God. This messenger was no other than the prophet Elias, who, according to a widely spread belief, was soon to descend from heaven, whither he had been carried, in order to prepare men by repentance for the great advent, and to reconcile God with his people.[3] Sometimes they associated with Elias, either the patriarch Enoch, to whom for one or two centuries they had attributed high sanctity;[4] or Jeremiah,[5] whom they considered as a sort of protecting genius of the people, constantly occupied in praying for them before the throne of God.[6] This idea, that two ancient prophets should rise again in order to serve as precursors to the Messiah, is discovered in so striking a form in the doctrine of the Parsees that we feel much inclined to believe that it comes from that source.[7] However this

---

[1] Matt. xi. 12, 13; Luke xvi. 16.
[2] Malachi iii. and iv.; *Ecclesiasticus* xlviii. 10. See *ante*, Chap. VI.
[3] Matt. xi. 14, xvii. 10; Mark vi. 15, viii. 28, ix. 10, and following; Luke ix. 8, 19.   [4] *Ecclesiasticus* xliv. 16.
[5] Matt. xvi. 14.   [6] 2 *Macc.* v. 13, and following.
[7] Texts cited by Anquetil-Duperron, *Zend-Avesta,* i. 2d part, p. 46, corrected by Spiegel, in the *Zeitschrift der deutschen morgenländischen Gesellschaft,* i. 261, and following; extracts from

may be, it formed at the time of Jesus an integral portion of the Jewish theories about the Messiah.   It was
admitted that the appearance of "two faithful witnesses," clothed in garments of repentance, would be
the preamble of the great drama about to be unfolded,
to the astonishment of the universe.[1]

It will be seen that, with these ideas, Jesus and his
disciples could not hesitate about the mission of John
the Baptist.   When the scribes raised the objection
that the Messiah could not have come because Elias
had not yet appeared,[2] they replied that Elias was come,
that John was Elias raised from the dead.[3]   By his
manner of life, by his opposition to the established
political authorities, John in fact recalled that strange
figure in the ancient history of Israel.[4]   Jesus was not
silent on the merits and excellencies of his forerunner.
He said that none greater was born among the children
of men.   He energetically blamed the Pharisees and
the doctors for not having accepted his baptism, and
for not being converted at his voice.[5]

The disciples of Jesus were faithful to these principles of their master.   This respect for John continued
during the whole of the first Christian generation.[6]
He was supposed to be a relative of Jesus.[7]   In order to
establish the mission of the latter upon testimony admitted by all, it was declared that John, at the first

the *Jamasp-Nameh*, in the *Avesta* of Spiegel, i., p. 34.   None of
the Parsee texts, which truly imply the idea of resuscitated
prophets and of precursors, are ancient; but the ideas contained
in them appear to be much anterior to the time of the compilation
itself.

[1] *Rev.* xi. 3, and following.   [2] Mark ix. 10.
[3] Matt. xi. 14, xvii. 10-13; Mark vi. 15, ix. 10-12; Luke ix. 8;
John i. 21-25.
[4] Luke i. 17.
[5] Matt. xxi. 32; Luke vii. 29, 30.
[6] *Acts* xix. 4.   [7] Luke i.

sight of Jesus, proclaimed him the Messiah; that he recognized himself his inferior, unworthy to unloose the latchets of his shoes; that he refused at first to baptize him, and maintained that it was he who ought to be baptized by Jesus.[1] These were exaggerations, which are sufficiently refuted by the doubtful form of John's last message.[2] But, in a more general sense, John remains in the Christian legend that which he was in reality—the austere forerunner, the gloomy preacher of repentance before the joy on the arrival of the bridegroom, the prophet who announces the kingdom of God and dies before beholding it. This giant in the early history of Christianity, this eater of locusts and wild honey, this rough redresser of wrongs, was the bitter which prepared the lip for the sweetness of the kingdom of God. His beheading by Herodias inaugurated the era of Christian martyrs; he was the first witness for the new faith. The worldly, who recognized in him their true enemy, could not permit him to live; his mutilated corpse, extended on the threshold of Christianity, traced the bloody path in which so many others were to follow.

The school of John did not die with its founder. It lived some time distinct from that of Jesus, and at first a good understanding existed between the two. Many years after the death of the two masters, people were baptized with the baptism of John. Certain persons belonged to the two schools at the same time—for example, the celebrated Apollos, the rival of St. Paul (toward the year 50), and a large number of the Christians of Ephesus.[3] Josephus placed himself (year 53)

---

[1] Matt. iii. 14, and following; Luke iii. 16; John i. 15, and following, v. 32, 33.
[2] Matt. xi. 2, and following; Luke vii. 18, and following.
[3] *Acts* xviii. 25, xix. 1-5.   Cf. Epiph., *Adv. Hær.*, xxx. 16.

in the school of an ascetic named Banou,[1] who presents
the greatest resemblance to John the Baptist, and who
was perhaps of his school. This Banou[2] lived in the
desert, clothed with the leaves of trees; he supported
himself only on wild plants and fruits, and baptized
himself frequently, both day and night, in cold water,
in order to purify himself. James, he who was called
the "brother of the Lord" (there is here perhaps some
confusion of homonyms), practised a similar asceticism.[3] Afterward, toward the year 80, Baptism was
in strife with Christianity, especially in Asia Minor.
John the evangelist appears to combat it in an indirect
manner.[4] One of the Sibylline[5] poems seems to proceed from this school. As to the sects of Hemero-
baptists, Baptists, and Elchasaïtes (*Sabiens Mogtasila*
of the Arabian writers[6]), who, in the second century,
filled Syria, Palestine and Babylonia, and whose representatives still exist in our days among the Mendaites,
called "Christians of St. John;" they have the same
origin as the movement of John the Baptist, rather than
an authentic descent from John. The true school of
the latter, partly mixed with Christianity, became a
small Christian heresy, and died out in obscurity. John
had foreseen distinctly the destiny of the two schools. If
he had yielded to a mean rivalry, he would to-day have
been forgotten in the crowd of sectaries of his time.
By his self-abnegation he has attained a glorious and
unique position in the religious pantheon of humanity.

---

[1] *Vita*, 2.
[2] Would this be the Bounaï who is reckoned by the Talmud
(Bab., *Sanhedrim*, 43 *a*) amongst the disciples of Jesus?
[3] Hegesippus, in Eusebius, *H. E.*, ii. 23.
[4] Gospel, i. 26, 33, iv. 2; 1st Epistle, v. 6. Cf. *Acts* x. 47.
[5] Book iv. See especially v. 157, and following.
[6] *Sabiens* is the Aramean equivalent of the word "Baptists."
Mogtasila has the same meaning in Arabic.

CHAPTER XIII.

FIRST ATTEMPTS ON JERUSALEM.

JESUS, almost every year, went to Jerusalem for the feast of the passover. The details of these journeys are little known, for the synoptics do not speak of them,[1] and the notes of the fourth Gospel are very confused on this point.[2] It was, it appears, in the year 31, and certainly after the death of John, that the most important of the visits of Jesus to Jerusalem took place. Many of the disciples followed him. Although Jesus attached from that time little value to the pilgrimage, he conformed himself to it in order not to wound Jewish opinion, with which he had not yet broken. These journeys, moreover, were essential to his design; for he felt already that in order to play a

[1] They, however, imply them obscurely (Matt. xxiii. 37; Luke xiii. 34). They knew as well as John the relation of Jesus with Joseph of Arimathea. Luke even (x. 38-42) knew the family of Bethany. Luke (ix. 51-54) has a vague idea of the system of the fourth Gospel respecting the journeys of Jesus. Many discourses against the Pharisees and the Sadducees, said by the synoptics to have been delivered in Galilee, have scarcely any meaning, except as having been given at Jerusalem. And again, the lapse of eight days is much too short to explain all that happened between the arrival of Jesus in that city and his death.

[2] Two pilgrimages are clearly indicated (John ii. 13, and v. 1), without speaking of his last journey (vii. 10), after which Jesus returned no more to Galilee. The first took place while John was still baptizing. It would belong consequently to the Easter of the year 29. But the circumstances given as belonging to this journey are of a more advanced period. (Comp. especially John ii. 14, and following, and Matt. xxi. 12, 13; Mark xi. 15-17; Luke xix. 45, 46.) There are evidently transpositions of dates in these chapters of John, or rather he has mixed the circumstances of different journeys.

leading part, he must go from Galilee, and attack
Judaism in its stronghold, which was Jerusalem.

The little Galilean community were here far from
being at home. Jerusalem was then nearly what it is
to-day, a city of pedantry, acrimony, disputes, hatreds,
and littleness of mind. Its fanaticism was extreme,
and religious seditions very frequent. The Pharisees
were dominant; the study of the Law, pushed to the
most insignificant minutiæ, and reduced to questions of
casuistry, was the only study. This exclusively theological and canonical culture contributed in no respect
to refine the intellect. It was something analogous to
the barren doctrine of the Mussulman fakir, to that
empty science discussed round about the mosques, and
which is a great expenditure of time and useless argumentation, by no means calculated to advance the right
discipline of the mind. The theological education of
the modern clergy, although very dry, gives us no idea
of this, for the Renaissance has introduced into all our
teachings, even the most irregular, a share of *belles
lettres* and of method, which has infused more or less
of the *humanities* into scholasticism. The science of
the Jewish doctor, of the *sofer* or scribe, was purely
barbarous, unmitigatedly absurd, and denuded of all
moral element.[1] To crown the evil, it filled with
ridiculous pride those who had wearied themselves in
acquiring it. The Jewish scribe, proud of the pretended knowledge which had cost him so much trouble,
had the same contempt for Greek culture which the
learned Mussulman of our time has for European civilization, and which the old catholic theologian had for
the knowledge of men of the world. The tendency of

[1] We may judge of it by the Talmud, the echo of the Jewish
scholasticism of that time

this scholastic culture was to close the mind to all that was refined, to create esteem only for those difficult triflings on which they had wasted their lives, and which were regarded as the natural occupation of persons professing a degree of seriousness.[1]

This odious society could not fail to weigh heavily on the tender and susceptible minds of the north. The contempt of the Hierosolymites for the Galileans rendered the separation still more complete. In the beautiful temple which was the object of all their desires, they often only met with insult. A verse of the pilgrim's psalm,[2] "I had rather be a doorkeeper in the house of my God," seemed made expressly for them. A contemptuous priesthood laughed at their simple devotion, as formerly in Italy the clergy, familiarized with the sanctuaries, witnessed coldly and almost jestingly the fervor of the pilgrim come from afar. The Galileans spoke a rather corrupt dialect; their pronunciation was vicious; they confounded the different aspirations of letters, which led to mistakes which were much laughed at.[3] In religion, they were considered as ignorant and somewhat heterodox;[4] the expression, "foolish Galileans," had become proverbial.[5] It was believed (not without reason) that they were not of pure Jewish blood, and no one expected Galilee to produce a prophet.[6] Placed thus on the confines of Judaism, and almost outside of it, the poor Galileans had only one badly interpreted passage in Isaiah to build their hopes upon.[7] "Land of Zebulon, and land of

[1] Jos., *Ant.,* xx., xi. 2.
[2] Ps. lxxxiv. (Vulg. lxxxiii.) 11.
[3] Matt. xxvi. 73; Mark xiv. 70; *Acts* ii. 7; Talm. of Bab., *Erubin* 53 *a,* and following; Bereschith Rabba, 26 *c.*
[4] Passage from the treatise *Erubin,* loc. cit.
[5] *Erubin,* loc. sit., 53 *b.*   [6] John vii. 52.
[7] Isa. ix. 1, 2; Matt. iv. 13, and following.

Naphtali, way of the sea, Galilee of the nations! The people that walked in darkness have seen a great light: they that dwell in the land of the shadow of death, upon them hath the light shined." The reputation of the native city of Jesus was particularly bad. It was a popular proverb, "Can there any good thing come out of Nazareth?"[1]

The parched appearance of Nature in the neighborhood of Jerusalem must have added to the dislike Jesus had for the place. The valleys are without water; the soil arid and stony. Looking into the valley of the Dead Sea, the view is somewhat striking; elsewhere it is monotonous. The hill of Mizpeh, around which cluster the most ancient historical remembrances of Israel, alone relieves the eye. The city presented, at the time of Jesus, nearly the same form that it does now. It had scarcely any ancient monuments, for, until the time of the Asmoneans, the Jews had remained strangers to all the arts. John Hyrcanus had begun to embellish it, and Herod the Great had made it one of the most magnificent cities of the East. The Herodian constructions, by their grand character, perfection of execution, and beauty of material, may dispute superiority with the most finished works of antiquity.[2] A great number of superb tombs, of original taste, were raised at the same time in the neighborhood of Jerusalem.[3] The style of these monuments was Grecian, but appropriate to the customs of the Jews, and considerably modified in accordance with their principles. The ornamental sculptures of the human figure which

[1] John i. 46.
[2] Jos., *Ant.*, xv. viii. xi.; *B. J.*, v. v. 6; Mark xiii. 1, 2.
[3] Tombs, namely, of the Judges, Kings, Absalom, Zechariah, Jehoshaphat, and of St. James. Compare the description of the tomb of the Maccabees at Modin (1 Macc. xiii. 27, and following).

the Herods had sanctioned, to the great discontent of the purists, were banished, and replaced by floral decorations. The taste of the ancient inhabitants of Phœnicia and Palestine for monoliths in solid stone seemed to be revived in these singular tombs cut in the rock, and in which Grecian orders are so strangely applied to an architecture of troglodytes. Jesus, who regarded works of art as a pompous display of vanity, viewed these monuments with displeasure.[1] His absolute spiritualism, and his settled conviction that the form of the old world was about to pass away, left him no taste except for things of the heart.

The temple, at the time of Jesus, was quite new, and the exterior works of it were not completed. Herod had begun its reconstruction in the year 20 or 21 before the Christian era, in order to make it uniform with his other edifices. The body of the temple was finished in eighteen months; the porticos took eight years;[2] and the accessory portions were continued slowly, and were only finished a short time before the taking of Jerusalem.[3] Jesus probably saw the work progressing, not without a degree of secret vexation. These hopes of a long future were like an insult to his approaching advent. Clearer-sighted than the unbelievers and the fanatics, he foresaw that these superb edifices were destined to endure but for a short time.[4]

The temple formed a marvelously imposing whole, of which the present *haram,*[5] notwithstanding its

---

[1]Matt. xxiii, 27, 29, xxiv. 1, and following; Mark xiii. 1, and following; Luke xix. 44, xxi. 5, and following. Compare *Book of Enoch,* xcvii. 13, 14; Talmud of Babylon, *Shabbath,* 33 *b.*
[2]Jos., *Ant.,* xv. xi. 5, 6.　　[3]Jos., *Ant.,* xx. ix. 7; John ii. 20.
[4]Matt. xxiv. 2, xxvi. 61, xxvii. 40; Mark xiii. 2, xiv. 58, xv. 29; Luke xxi. 6; John ii. 19, 20.
[5]The temple and its enclosure doubtless occupied the site of the mosque of Omar and the *haram,* or Sacred Court, which sur-

beauty, scarcely gives us any idea.   The courts and the
surrounding porticos served as the daily rendezvous for
a considerable number of persons—so much so, that
this great space was at once temple, forum, tribunal,
and university.   All the religious discussions of the
Jewish schools, all the canonical instruction, even the
legal processes and civil causes — in a word, all the
activity of the nation was concentrated there.[1]   It was
an arena where arguments were perpetually clashing,
a battlefield of disputes, resounding with sophisms and
subtle questions.   The temple had thus much analogy
with a Mahometan mosque.   The Romans   at   this
period treated all strange religions with respect, when
kept within proper limits,[2] and carefully refrained
from entering the sanctuary; Greek and Latin inscriptions marked the point up to which those who were not
Jews were permitted to advance.[3]   But the tower of
Antonia, the headquarters of the Roman forces, commanded the whole enclosure, and allowed all that
passed therein to be seen.[4]   The guarding of the
temple belonged to the Jews; the entire superintendence
was committed to a captain, who caused the gates to be
opened and shut, and prevented any one from crossing
the enclosure with a stick in his hand, or with dusty
shoes, or when carrying parcels, or to shorten his path.[5]
They were especially scrupulous in watching that no
one entered within the inner gates in a state of

rounds the mosque. The foundation of the haram is, in some
parts, especially at the place where the Jews go to weep, the exact
base of the temple of Herod.

[1] Luke ii. 46, and following; Mishnah, *Sanhedrim*, x. 2.

[2] Suet., *Aug.* 93.   [3] Philo, *Legatio ad Caium*, § 31; Jos., *B. J.*,
v. v. 2, vi. ii. 4; *Acts* xxi. 28.

[4] Considerable traces of this tower are still seen in the northern
part of the haram.

[5] Mishnah, *Berakoth*, ix. 5; Talm. of Babyl., *Jebamoth*, 6 *b;*
Mark xi. 16.

legal impurity. The women had an entirely separate court.

It was in the temple that Jesus passed his days, whilst he remained at Jerusalem. The period of the feasts brought an extraordinary concourse of people into the city. Associated in parties of ten to twenty persons, the pilgrims invaded everywhere, and lived in that disordered state in which Orientals delight.[1] Jesus was lost in the crowd, and his poor Galileans grouped around him were of small account. He probably felt that he was in a hostile world which would receive him only with disdain. Everything he saw set him against it. The temple, like much-frequented places of devotion in general, offered a not very edifying spectacle. The accessories of worship entailed a number of repulsive details, especially of mercantile operations, in consequence of which real shops were established within the sacred enclosure. There were sold beasts for the sacrifices; there were tables for the exchange of money; at times it seemed like a bazaar. The inferior officers of the temple fulfilled their functions doubtless with the irreligious vulgarity of the sacristans of all ages. This profane and heedless air in the handling of holy things wounded the religious sentiment of Jesus, which was at times carried even to a scrupulous excess.[2] He said that they had made the house of prayer into a den of thieves. One day, it is even said, that, carried away by his anger, he scourged the vendors with a "scourge of small cords," and overturned their tables.[3] In general, he had little love for the temple. The worship

[1] Jos., *B. J.,* ii. xiv. 3, vi. ix. 3. Comp. Ps cxxxiii. (Vulg. cxxxii.)
[2] Mark xi. 16.
[3] Matt. xxi. 12, and following; Mark xi. 15, and following; Luke xix. 45, and following; John ii. 14, and following.

which he had conceived for his Father had nothing in common with scenes of butchery. All these old Jewish institutions displeased him, and he suffered in being obliged to conform to them. Except among the Judaizing Christians, neither the temple nor its site inspired pious sentiments. The true disciples of the new faith held this ancient sanctuary in aversion. Constantine and the first Christian emperors left the pagan construction of Adrian existing there,[1] and only the enemies of Christianity, such as Julian, remembered the temple.[2] When Omar entered into Jerusalem, he found the site designedly polluted in hatred of the Jews.[3] It was Islamism, that is to say, a sort of resurrection of Judaism in its exclusively Semitic form, which restored its glory. The place has always been anti-Christian.

The pride of the Jews completed the discontent of Jesus, and rendered his stay in Jerusalem painful. In the degree that the great ideas of Israel ripened, the priesthood lost its power. The institution of synagogues had given to the interpreter of the Law, to the doctor, a great superiority over the priest. There were no priests except at Jerusalem, and even there, reduced to functions entirely ritual, almost, like our parish priests, excluded from preaching, they were surpassed by the orator of the synagogue, the casuist, and the *sofer* or scribe, although the latter was only a layman. The celebrated men of the Talmud were not priests; they were learned men according to the ideas of the time. The high priesthood of Jerusalem held, it is true, a very elevated rank in the nation; but it was by

---

[1] *Itin. a Burdig. Hierus.*, p. 152 (edit. Schott); S. Jerome, in *Is.* i. 8, and in *Matt.* xxiv. 15.

[2] Ammianus Marcellinus, xxiii. 1.

[3] Eutychius, *Ann.*. II. 286, and following (Oxford. 1659).

no means at the head of the religious movement. The
sovereign pontiff, whose dignity had already been degraded by Herod,[1] became more and more a Roman
functionary,[2] who was frequently removed in order to
divide the profits of the office. Opposed to the Pharisees, who were very warm lay zealots, the priests were
almost all Sadducees, that is to say, members of that
unbelieving aristocracy which had been formed around
the temple, and which lived by the altar, while they
saw the vanity of it.[3] The sacerdotal caste was separated to such a degree from the national sentiment
and from the great religious movement which dragged
the people along, that the name of "Sadducee"
(*sadoki*), which at first simply designated a member
of the sacerdotal family of Sadok, had become synonymous with "Materialist" and with "Epicurean."

A still worse element had begun, since the reign of
Herod the Great, to corrupt the high-priesthood.
Herod having fallen in love with Mariamne, daughter
of a certain Simon, son of Boëthus of Alexandria, and
having wished to marry her (about the year 28 B.C.),
saw no other means of ennobling his father-in-law and
raising him to his own rank than by making him high-
priest. This intriguing family remained master, almost without interruption, of the sovereign pontificate
for thirty-five years.[4] Closely allied to the reigning
family, it did not lose the office until after the deposition of Archelaus, and recovered it (the year 42 of our
era) after Herod Agrippa had for some time re-enacted
the work of Herod the Great. Under the name of

---

[1] Jos., *Ant.*, xv. iii. 1, 3.   [2] Ibid., XVIII. ii.
[3] *Acts* iv. 1, and following, v. 17; Jos., *Ant.*, xx. ix. 1; *Pirké
Aboth*, i. 10.
[4] Jos., *Ant.*, xv., ix. 3, XVII. vi. 4, xiii. 1, XVIII. i. 1, ii. 1,
XIX. vi. 2, viii. 1.

Boëthusim,[1] a new sacerdotal nobility was formed, very worldly, and little devotional, and closely allied to the Sadokites. The *Boëthusim,* in the Talmud and the rabbinical writings, are depicted as a kind of unbelievers, and always reproached as Sadducees.[2] From all this there resulted a miniature court of Rome around the temple, living on politics, little inclined to excesses of zeal, even rather fearing them, not wishing to hear of holy personages or of innovators, for it profited from the established routine. These epicurean priests had not the violence of the Pharisees; they only wished for quietness; it was their moral indifference, their cold irreligion, which revolted Jesus. Although very different, the priests and the Pharisees were thus confounded in his antipathies. But a stranger, and without influence, he was long compelled to restrain his discontent within himself, and only to communicate his sentiments to the intimate friends who accompanied him.

Before his last stay, which was by far the longest of all that he made at Jerusalem, and which was terminated by his death, Jesus endeavored, however, to obtain a hearing. He preached; people spoke of him;

---

[1] This name is only found in the Jewish documents. I think that the "Herodians" of the gospel are the *Boëthusim.*

[2] The treatise of *Aboth Nathan,* 5; *Soferim,* iii., hal. 5; Mishnah, *Menachoth,* x. 3; Talmud of Babylon, *Shabbath,* 118 *a.* The name of *Boëthusim* is often changed in the Talmudic books with that of the Sadduccees, or with the word *Minim* (heretics). Compare Thosiphta, *Joma,* i., with the Talm. of Jerus., the same treatise, i. 5, and Talm. of Bab., same treatise, 19 *b;* Thos. *Sukka,* iii. with the Talm. of Bab., same treatise, 43 *b;* Thos. ibid., further on, with the Talm. of Bab., same treatise, 48 *b;* Thos. *Rosh hasshana,* i. with Mishnah, same treatise ii. 1; Talm. of Jerus., same treatise, ii. 1; and Talm. of Bab., same treatise, 22 *b;* Thos. *Menachoth,* x. with Mishnah, same treatise, x. 3; Talm. of Bab., same treatise, 65 *a;* Mishnah, *Chagigah,* ii. 4; and Megillath Taanith, i.; Thos. *Iadaim,* ii. with Talm. of Jerus.; *Baba Bathra,* viii. 1; Talm. of Bab., same treatise, 115 *b;* and Megillath Taanith, v.

and they conversed respecting certain deeds of his which were looked upon as miraculous. But from all that, there resulted neither an established church at Jerusalem nor a group of Hierosolymite disciples. The charming teacher, who forgave every one provided they loved him, could not find much sympathy in this sanctuary of vain disputes and obsolete sacrifices. The only result was that he formed some valuable friendships, the advantage of which he reaped afterward. He does not appear at that time to have made the acquaintance of the family of Bethany, which, amidst the trials of the latter months of his life, brought him so much consolation. But very early he attracted the attention of a certain Nicodemus, a rich Pharisee, a member of the Sanhedrim, and a man occupying a high position in Jerusalem.[1] This man, who appears to have been upright and sincere, felt himself attracted toward the young Galilean. Not wishing to compromise himself, he came to see Jesus by night, and had a long conversation with him.[2] He doubtless preserved a favorable impression of him, for afterward he defended Jesus against the prejudices of his colleagues,[3] and, at the death of Jesus, we shall find him tending with pious care the corpse of the master.[4] Nicodemus did not become a Christian; he had too much regard for his position to take part in a revolutionary movement which as yet counted no men of note amongst its

---

[1] It seems that he is referred to in the Talmud. Talm. of Bab., *Taanith*, 20 *a; Gittin*, 56 *a; Ketuboth*, 66 *b;* treatise *Aboth Nathan*, vii.; Midrash Rabba, *Eka*, 64 *a*. The passage *Taanith* identifies him with Bounaï, who, according to *Sanhedrim* (see ante, p. 212, note 2), was a disciple of Jesus. But if Bounaï is the Banou of Josephus, this identification will not hold good.

[2] John iii. 1, and following, vii. 50. We are certainly free to believe that the exact text of the conversation is but a creation of John's.

[3] John vii. 50, and following.   [4] John xix. 39.

adherents.   But he evidently felt great friendship for
Jesus, and rendered him service, though unable to
rescue him from a death which even at this period was
all but decreed.

As to the celebrated doctors of the time, Jesus does
not appear to have had any connection with them.
Hillel and Shammai were dead; the greatest authority
of the time was Gamaliel, grandscn of Hillel.   He was
of a liberal spirit, and a man of the world, not opposed
to secular studies, and inclined to tolerance by his
intercourse with good society.[1]   Unlike the very strict
Pharisees, who walked veiled or with closed eyes, he
did not scruple to gaze even upon Pagan women.[2]
This, as well as his knowledge of Greek, was tolerated
because he had access to the court.[3]   After the death
of Jesus, he expressed very moderate views respecting
the new sect.[4]   St. Paul sat at his feet,[5] but it is not
probable that Jesus ever entered his school.

One idea, at least, which Jesus brought from Jerusalem, and which henceforth appears rooted in his
mind, was that there was no union possible between
him and the ancient Jewish religion.   The abolition
of the sacrifices which had caused him so much disgust,
the suppression of an impious and haughty priesthood,
and, in a general sense, the abrogation of the law,
appeared to him absolutely necessary.   From this time
he appears no more as a Jewish reformer, but as a
destroyer of Judaism.   Certain advocates of the Messianic ideas had already admitted that the Messiah
would bring a new law, which should be common to

[1] Mishnah, *Baba Metsia,* v. 8; Talm. of Bab., *Sota,* 49 *b.*
[2] Talm. of Jerus., *Berakoth,* ix. 2.
[3] Passage *Sota,* before cited, and *Baba Kama,* 83 *a.*
[4] *Acts* v. 34, and following.
[5] *Acts* xxii. 3.

all the earth.[1] The Essenes, who were scarcely Jews,
also appear to have been indifferent to the temple and
to the Mosaic observances. But these were only isolated or unavowed instances of boldness. Jesus was
the first who dared to say that from his time, or rather
from that of John,[2] the Law was abolished. If sometimes he used more measured terms,[3] it was in order
not to offend existing prejudices too violently. When
he was driven to extremities, he lifted the veil entirely,
and declared that the Law had no longer any force.
On this subject he used striking comparisons. "No
man putteth a piece of new cloth into an old garment,
neither do men put new wine into old bottles."[4] This
was really his chief characteristic as teacher and creator. The temple excluded all except Jews from its
enclosure by scornful announcements. Jesus had no
sympathy with this. The narrow, hard, and unchari-
table Law was only made for the children of Abraham.
Jesus maintained that every well-disposed man, every
man who received and loved him, was a son of Abraham.[5] The pride of blood appeared to him the great
enemy which was to be combated. In other words,
Jesus was no longer a Jew. He was in the highest
degree revolutionary; he called all men to a worship
founded solely on the fact of their being children of
God. He proclaimed the rights of man, not the rights
of the Jew; the religion of man, not the religion of the

[1] *Orac. Sib.*, book iii. 573, and following, 715, and following, 756-
58. Compare the Targum of Jonathan, Isa. xii. 3.
[2] Luke xvi. 16. The passage in Matt. xi. 12, 13, is less clear,
but can have no other meaning.
[3] Matt. v. 17, 18 (Cf. Talm. of Bab., *Shabbath*, 116 *b*). This
passage is not in contradiction with those in which the abolition
of the Law is implied. It only signifies that in Jesus all the types
of the Old Testament are realized. Cf. Luke xvi. 17.
[4] Matt. ix. 16, 17; Luke v. 36, and following.
[5] Luke xix. 9.

Jew; the deliverance of man, not the deliverance of the Jew.[1] How far removed was this from a Gaulonite Judas or a Matthias Margaloth, preaching revolution in the name of the Law! The religion of humanity, established, not upon blood, but upon the heart, was founded. Moses was superseded, the temple was rendered useless, and was irrevocably condemned.

[1] Matt. xxiv. 14, xxviii. 19; Mark xiii. 10, xvi. 15; Luke xxiv. 47.

CHAPTER XIV.

INTERCOURSE OF JESUS WITH THE PAGANS AND THE SAMARITANS.

FOLLOWING out these principles, Jesus despised all religion which was not of the heart. The vain practices of the devotees,[1] the exterior strictness, which trusted to formality for salvation, had in him a mortal enemy. He cared little for fasting.[2] He preferred forgiveness to sacrifice.[3] The love of God, charity and mutual forgiveness, were his whole law.[4] Nothing could be less priestly. The priest, by his office, ever advocates public sacrifice, of which he is the appointed minister; he discourages private prayer, which has a tendency to dispense with his office.

We should seek in vain in the Gospel for one religious rite recommended by Jesus. Baptism to him was only of secondary importance;[5] and with respect to prayer, he prescribes nothing, except that it should proceed from the heart. As is always the case, many thought to substitute mere good-will for genuine love of goodness, and imagined they could win the kingdom of heaven by saying to him, "Rabbi, Rabbi." He rebuked them, and proclaimed that his religion consisted in doing good.[6] He often quoted the passage in Isaiah, which says: "This people honor me with their lips, but their heart is far from me."[7]

[1] Matt. xv. 9.   [2] Matt. ix. 14, xi. 19.
[3] Matt. v. 23, and following, ix. 13, xii. 7.
[4] Matt. xxii. 37, and following; Mark xii. 28, and following; Luke x. 25, and following.
[5] Matt. iii. 15; 1 Cor. i. 17.   [6] Matt. vii. 21; Luke vi. 46.
[7] Matt. xv. 8; Mark vii. 6. Cf. Isaiah xxix. 13.

The observance of the Sabbath was the principal point upon which was raised the whole edifice of Pharisaic scruples and subtleties.   This ancient and excellent institution had become a pretext for the miserable disputes of casuists, and a source of superstitious beliefs.[1]   It was believed that Nature observed it; all intermittent springs were accounted "Sabbatical."[2] This was the point upon which Jesus loved best to defy his adversaries.[3]   He openly violated the Sabbath, and only replied by subtle raillery to the reproaches that were heaped upon him.   He despised still more a multitude of modern observances, which tradition had added to the Law, and which were dearer than any other to the devotees on that very account.   Ablutions, and the too subtle distinctions between pure and impure things, found in him a pitiless opponent: "There is nothing from without a man," said he, "that entering into him can defile him: but the things which come out of him, those are they that defile the man."   The Pharisees, who were the propagators of these mummeries, were unceasingly denounced by him.   He accused them of exceeding the Law, of inventing impossible precepts, in order to create occasions of sin: "Blind leaders of the blind," said he, "take care lest ye also fall into the ditch."   "O generation of vipers, how can ye, being evil, speak good things? for out of the abundance of the heart the mouth speaketh."[4]

[1] See especially the treatise *Shabbath* of the Mishnah and the *Livre des Jubilés* (translated from the Ethiopian in the *Jahrbücher* of Ewald, years 2 and 3), chap. 1.

[2] Jos., *B. J.*, VII. v. 1; Pliny, *H. N.*, xxxi. 18. Cf. Thomson, *The Land and the Book*, i. 406, and following.

[3] Matt. xii. 1-14; Mark ii. 23-28; Luke vi. 1-5, xiii. 14, and following, xiv. 1, and following.

[4] Matt. xii. 34, xv. 1, and following, 12, and following, xxiii. entirely; Mark vii. 1, and following, 15, and following; Luke vi. 45, xi. 39, and following.

He did not know the Gentiles sufficiently to think of founding anything lasting upon their conversion. Galilee contained a great number of pagans, but, as it appears, no public and organized worship of false gods.[1] Jesus could see this worship displayed in all its splendor in the country of Tyre and Sidon, at Cæsarea Philippi and in the Decapolis, but he paid little attention to it. We never find in him the wearisome pedantry of the Jews of his time, those declamations against idolatry, so familiar to his co-religionists from the time of Alexander, and which fill, for instance, the book of "Wisdom."[2] That which struck him in the pagans was not their idolatry, but their servility.[3] The young Jewish democrat agreeing on this point with Judas the Gaulonite, and admitting no master but God, was hurt at the honors with which they surrounded the persons of sovereigns, and the frequently mendacious titles given to them. With this exception, in the greater number of instances in which he comes in contact with pagans, he shows great indulgence to them; sometimes he professes to conceive more hope of them than of the Jews.[4] The kingdom of God would be transferred to them. "When the lord, therefore, of the vineyard cometh, what will he do unto these husbandmen? He will miserably destroy those

[1] I believe the pagans of Galilee were found especially on the frontiers—at Kedes, for example; but that the very heart of the country, the city of Tiberias excepted, was entirely Jewish. The line where the ruins of temples end, and those of synagogues begin, is to-day plainly marked as far north as Lake Huleh (Samachonites). The traces of pagan sculpture, which were thought to have been found at Tell-Houm, are doubtful. The coast—the town of Acre, in particular—did not form part of Galilee.

[2] Chap. XIII. and following.

[3] Matt. xx. 25; Mark x. 42; Luke xxii. 25.

[4] Matt. viii. 5, and following, xv. 22, and following; Mark vii. 25, and following; Luke iv. 25, and following.

wicked men, and will let out his vineyard unto other husbandmen, which shall render him the fruits in their seasons."[1]   Jesus adhered so much the more to this idea, as the conversion of the Gentiles was, according to Jewish ideas, one of the surest signs of the advent of the Messiah.[2]   In his kingdom of God he represents, as seated at a feast, by the side of Abraham, Isaac, and Jacob, men come from the four winds of heaven, whilst the lawful heirs of the kingdom are rejected.[3]   Sometimes, it is true, there seems to be an entirely contrary tendency in the commands he gives to his disciples: he seems to recommend them only to preach salvation to the orthodox Jews,[4] he speaks of pagans in a manner conformable to the prejudices of the Jews.[5]   But we must remember that the disciples, whose narrow minds did not share in this supreme indifference for the privileges of the sons of Abraham, may have given the instruction of their master the bent of their own ideas. Besides, it is very possible that Jesus may have varied on this point, just as Mahomet speaks of the Jews in the Koran, sometimes in the most honorable manner, sometimes with extreme harshness, as he had hope of winning their favor or otherwise.   Tradition, in fact, attributes to Jesus two entirely opposite rules of proselytism, which he may have practised in turn: "He that is not against us is on our part."   "He that is not with me, is against me."[6]   Impassioned conflict involves almost necessarily this kind of contradictions.

[1] Matt. xxi. 41; Mark xii. 9; Luke xx. 16.
[2] Isa. ii. 2, and following, lx.; Amos ix. 11, and following; Jer. iii. 17; Mal. i. 11; *Tobit,* xiii. 13, and following; *Orac. Sibyll.,* iii. 715, and following.   Comp. Matt. xxiv. 14; *Acts* xv. 15, and following.
[3] Matt. viii. 11, 12, xxi. 33, and following, xxii. 1, and following.
[4] Matt. vii. 6, x. 5, 6, xv. 24, xxi. 43.
[5] Matt. v. 46, and following, vi. 7, 32, xviii. 17; Luke vi. 32, and following, xii. 30.   [6] Matt. xii. 30; Mark ix. 39; Luke ix. 50, xi. 23.

It is certain that he counted among his disciples many men whom the Jews called "Hellenes."[1] This word had in Palestine divers meanings. Sometimes it designated the pagans; sometimes the Jews, speaking Greek, and dwelling among the pagans;[2] sometimes men of pagan origin converted to Judaism.[3] It was probably in the last-named category of Hellenes that Jesus found sympathy.[4] The affiliation with Judaism had many degrees; but the proselytes always remained in a state of inferiority in regard to the Jew by birth. Those in question were called "proselytes of the gate," or "men fearing God," and were subject to the precepts of Noah, and not to those of Moses.[5] This very inferiority was doubtless the cause which drew them to Jesus, and gained them his favor.

He treated the Samaritans in the same manner. Shut in, like a small island, between the two great provinces of Judaism (Judea and Galilee), Samaria formed in Palestine a kind of enclosure in which was preserved the ancient worship of Gerizim, closely resembling and rivalling that of Jerusalem. This poor sect, which had neither the genius nor the learned organization of Judaism, properly so called, was treated by the Hierosolymites with extreme harshness.[6] They placed them in the same rank as pagans, but hated them more.[7] Jesus, from a feeling of opposition, was well disposed

---

[1] Josephus confirms this (*Ant.*, xviii. iii. 3). Comp. John vii. 35, xii. 20, 21.

[2] Talm. of Jerus., *Sota*, vii. 1.

[3] See in particular, John vii. 35, xii. 20; *Acts* xiv. 1, xvii. 4, xviii. 4, xxi. 28. [4] John xii. 20; *Acts* viii. 27.

[5] Mishnah, *Baba Metsia*, ix. 12; Talm. of Bab., *Sanh.*, 56 *b*; Acts viii. 27, x. 2, 22, 35, xiii. 16, 26, 43, 50, xvi. 14, xvii. 4, 17, xviii. 7; Gal. ii. 3; Jos., *Ant.*, xiv. vii. 2.

[6] *Ecclesiasticus* l. 27, 28; John viii. 48; Jos., *Ant.*, ix. xiv. 3, xi. viii. 6, xii. v. 5; Talm. of Jerus., *Aboda zara*, v. 4; *Pesachim*, i. 1.

[7] Matt. x. 5; Luke xvii. 18. Comp. Talm. of Bab., *Cholin*, 6 *a*.

toward Samaria, and often preferred the Samaritans to the orthodox Jews. If, at other times, he seems to forbid his disciples preaching to them, confining his gospel to the Israelites proper,[1] this was no doubt a precept arising from special circumstances, to which the apostles have given too absolute a meaning. Sometimes, in fact, the Samaritans received him badly, because they thought him imbued with the prejudices of his co-religionists;[2] — in the same manner as in our days the European free-thinker is regarded as an enemy by the Mussulman, who always believes him to be a fanatical Christian. Jesus raised himself above these misunderstandings.[3] He had many disciples at Shechem, and he passed at least two days there.[4] On one occasion he meets with gratitude and true piety from a Samaritan only.[5] One of his most beautiful parables is that of the man wounded on the way to Jericho. A priest passes by and sees him, but goes on his way; a Levite also passes, but does not stop; a Samaritan takes pity on him, approaches him, and pours oil into his wounds, and bandages them.[6] Jesus argues from this that true brotherhood is established among men by charity, and not by creeds. The "neighbor" who in Judaism was specially the co-religionist, was in his estimation the man who has pity on his kind without distinction of sect. Human brotherhood in its widest sense overflows in all his teaching.

These thoughts, which beset Jesus on his leaving Jerusalem, found their vivid expression in an anecdote which has been preserved respecting his return. The road from Jerusalem into Galilee passes at the distance

[1] Matt. x. 5, 6.
[2] Luke ix. 53.
[3] Luke ix. 56.
[4] John iv. 39-43.
[5] Luke xvii. 16.
[6] Luke x. 30, and following.

of half an hour's journey from Shechem,[1] in front of the opening of the valley commanded by mounts Ebal and Gerizim. This route was in general avoided by the Jewish pilgrims, who preferred making in their journeys the long detour through Perea, rather than expose themselves to the insults of the Samaritans, or ask anything of them. It was forbidden to eat and drink with them.[2] It was an axiom of certain casuists, that "a piece of Samaritan bread is the flesh of swine."[3] When they followed this route, provisions were always laid up beforehand; yet they rarely avoided conflict and ill-treatment.[4] Jesus shared neither these scruples nor these fears. Having come to the point where the valley of Shechem opens on the left, he felt fatigued, and stopped near a well. The Samaritans were then as now accustomed to give to all the localities of their valley names drawn from patriarchal reminiscences. They regarded this well as having been given by Jacob to Joseph; it was probably the same which is now called *Bir-Iakoub*. The disciples entered the valley and went to the city to buy provisions. Jesus seated himself at the side of the well, having Gerizim before him.

It was about noon. A woman of Shechem came to draw water. Jesus asked her to let him drink, which excited great astonishment in the woman, the Jews generally forbidding all intercourse with the Samaritans. Won by the conversation of Jesus, the woman recognized in him a prophet, and expecting some reproaches about her worship, she anticipated him: "Sir," said she, "our fathers worshipped in this moun-

---

[1] Now Nablous.
[2] Luke ix. 53; John iv. 9.
[3] Mishnah, *Shebiit*, viii. 10.
[4] Jos., *Ant.*, xx. v. 1; *B. J.*, ii. xii. 3; *Vita*, 52.

tain, and ye say that in Jerusalem is the place where men ought to worship. Jesus saith unto her, Woman, believe me, the hour cometh when ye shall neither in this mountain, nor yet at Jerusalem, worship the Father. But the hour cometh, and now is, when the true worshippers shall worship the Father in spirit and in truth."[1]

The day on which he uttered this saying, he was truly Son of God. He pronounced for the first time the sentence upon which will repose the edifice of eternal religion. He founded the pure worship, of all ages, of all lands, that which all elevated souls will practice until the end of time. Not only was his religion on this day the best religion of humanity, it was the absolute religion; and if other planets have inhabitants gifted with reason and morality, their religion cannot be different from that which Jesus proclaimed near the well of Jacob. Man has not been able to maintain this position; for the ideal is realized but transitorily. This sentence of Jesus has been a brilliant light amidst gross darkness; it has required eighteen hundred years for the eyes of mankind (what do I say! for an infinitely small portion of mankind) to become accustomed to it. But the light will become the full day, and, after having run through all the cycles of error, mankind will return to this sentence, as the immortal expression of its faith and its hope.

[1] John iv. 21-23. Verse 22, at least the latter clause of it, which expresses an idea opposed to that of verses 21 and 23, appears to have been interpolated. We must not insist too much on the historical reality of such a conversation, since Jesus, or his interlocutor, alone would have been able to relate it. But the anecdote in chapter iv. of John, certainly represents one of the most intimate thoughts of Jesus, and the greater part of the circumstances have a striking appearance of truth.

CHAPTER XV.

JESUS returned to Galilee, having completely lost his Jewish faith, and filled with revolutionary ardor. His ideas are now expressed with perfect clearness. The innocent aphorisms of the first part of his prophetic career, in part borrowed from the Jewish rabbis anterior to him, and the beautiful moral precepts of his second period, are exchanged for a decided policy. The Law would be abolished; and it was to be abolished by him.[1] The Messiah had come, and he was the Messiah. The kingdom of God was about to be revealed; and it was he who would reveal it. He knew well that he would be the victim of his boldness; but the kingdom of God could not be conquered without violence; it was by crises and commotions that it was to be established.[2] The Son of man would reappear in glory, accompanied by legions of angels, and those who had rejected him would be confounded.

The boldness of such a conception ought not to surprise us. Long before this, Jesus had regarded his relation to God as that of a son to his father. That

---

[1] The hesitancy of the immediate disciples of Jesus, of whom a considerable portion remained attached to Judaism, might cause objections to be raised to this. But the trial of Jesus leaves no room for doubt. We shall see that he was there treated as a "corrupter." The Talmud gives the procedure adopted against him as an example of that which ought to be followed against "corrupters," who seek to overturn the Law of Moses. (Talm. of Jerus., *Sanhedrim,* xiv. 16; Talm. of Bab., *Sanhedrim* 43 *a.* 67 *a.*)

[2] Matt. xi. 12; Luke xvi. 16.

which in others would be an insupportable pride, ought not in him to be regarded as presumption.

The title of "Son of David" was the first which he accepted, probably without being concerned in the innocent frauds by which it was sought to secure it to him. The family of David had, as it seems, been long extinct;[1] the Asmoneans being of priestly origin, could not pretend to claim such a descent for themselves; neither Herod nor the Romans dreamt for a moment that any representative whatever of the ancient dynasty existed in their midst. But from the close of the Asmonean dynasty the dream of an unknown descendant of the ancient kings, who should avenge the nation of its enemies, filled every mind. The universal belief was, that the Messiah would be son of David, and like him would be born at Bethlehem.[2] The first idea of Jesus was not precisely this. The remembrance of David, which was uppermost in the minds of the Jews, had nothing in common with his heavenly reign. He believed himself the Son of God, and not the son of David. His kingdom, and the deliverance which he meditated, were of quite another order. But public opinion on this point made him do violence to himself. The immediate consequence of the proposition, "Jesus is the Messiah," was this other proposition, "Jesus is the son of David." He allowed a title to be given him, without which he could not hope for success. He ended, it seems, by taking pleasure therein, for he performed most willingly the miracles which were asked

[1] It is true that certain doctors—such as Hillel, Gamaliel—are mentioned as being of the race of David. But these are very doubtful allegations. If the family of David still formed a distinct and prominent group, how is it that we never see it figure, by the side of the Sadokites, Boëthusians, the Asmoneans, and Herods, in the great struggles of the time?

[2] Matt. ii. 5, 6, xxii. 42; Luke i. 32; John vii. 41, 42; *Acts* ii. 30.

of him by those who used this title in addressing him.[1]
In this, as in many other circumstances of his life,
Jesus yielded to the ideas which were current in his
time, although they were not precisely his own. He
associated with his doctrine of the "kingdom of God"
all that could warm the heart and the imagination. It
was thus that we have seen him adopt the baptism of
John, although it could not have been of much importance to him.

One great difficulty presented itself — his birth at
Nazareth, which was of public notoriety. We do not
know whether Jesus strove against this objection.
Perhaps it did not present itself in Galilee, where the
idea that the son of David should be a Bethlehemite
was less spread. To the Galilean idealist, moreover,
the title of "son of David" was sufficiently justified, if
he to whom it was given revived the glory of his race,
and brought back the great days of Israel. Did Jesus
authorize by his silence the fictitious genealogies which
his partisans invented in order to prove his royal descent?[2] Did he know anything of the legends invented
to prove that he was born at Bethlehem; and particularly of the attempt to connect his Bethlehemite origin
with the census which had taken place by order of the
imperial legate, Quirinus?[3] We know not. The inexactitude and the contradictions of the genealogies[4]

[1] Matt. ix. 27, xii. 23, xv. 22, xx. 30, 31; Mark x. 47, 52; Luke
xviii. 38.
[2] Matt. i. 1, and following; Luke iii. 23, and following.
[3] Matt. ii. 1, and following; Luke ii. 1, and following.
[4] The two genealogies are quite contradictory, and do not agree
with the lists of the Old Testament. The narrative of Luke on
the census of Quirinus implies an anachronism. See ante, p. 81,
note 4. It is natural to suppose, besides, that the legend may have
laid hold of this circumstance. The census made a great impression on the Jews, overturned their narrow ideas, and was remembered by them for a long period. Cf. *Acts* v. 37.

lead to the belief that they were the result of popular
ideas operating at various points, and that none of
them were sanctioned by Jesus.[1] Never does he designate himself as son of David. His disciples, much less
enlightened than he, frequently magnified that which
he said of himself; but, as a rule, he had no knowledge
of these exaggerations. Let us add, that during the
first three centuries, considerable portions of Christendom[2] obstinately denied the royal descent of Jesus and
the authenticity of the genealogies.

The legends about him were thus the fruit of a great
and entirely spontaneous conspiracy, and were developed around him during his lifetime. No great event
in history has happened without having given rise to a
cycle of fables; and Jesus could not have put a stop to
these popular creations, even if he had wished to do so.
Perhaps a sagacious observer would have recognized
from this point the germ of the narratives which were
to attribute to him a supernatural birth, and which
arose, it may be, from the idea, very prevalent in antiquity, that the incomparable man could not be born of
the ordinary relations of the two sexes; or, it may be,
in order to respond to an imperfectly understood chapter of Isaiah,[3] which was thought to foretell that the
Messiah should be born of a virgin; or, lastly, it may
be in consequence of the idea that the "breath of God,"
already regarded as a divine hypostasis, was a principle
of fecundity.[4] Already, perhaps, there was current

[1] Julius Africanus (in Eusebius, *H. E.*, i. 7) supposes that it was
the relations of Jesus, who, having taken refuge in Batanea, attempted to recompose the genealogies.
[2] The *Ebionites,* the "Hebrews," the "Nazarenes," Tatian, Marcion. Cf. Epiph., *Adv. Hær.*, xxix. 9, xxx. 3, 14, xlvi. 1; Theodoret, *Hæret. fab.*, i. 20; Isidore of Pelusium, Epist. i. 371, ad
Pansophium.   Matt. i. 22, 23.
[4] Gen. i. 2. For the analogous idea among the Egyptians, se

more than one anecdote about his infancy, conceived
with the intention of showing in his biography the accomplishment of the Messianic ideal;[1] or, rather, of the
prophecies which the allegorical exegesis of the time
referred to the Messiah.   At other times they connected him from his birth with celebrated men, such as
John the Baptist, Herod the Great, Chaldean astrolo-
gers, who, it was said, visited Jerusalem about this
time,[2] and two aged persons, Simeon and Anna, who
had left memories of great sanctity.[3]   A rather loose
chronology characterized these combinations, which
for the most part were founded upon real facts traves-
tied.[4]   But a singular spirit of gentleness and goodness, a profoundly popular sentiment, permeated all
these fables, and made them a supplement to his preaching.[5]   It was especially after the death of Jesus that
such narratives became greatly developed; we may,
however, believe that they circulated even during his
life, exciting only a pious credulity and simple admiration.

That Jesus never dreamt of making himself pass for
an incarnation of God, is a matter about which there
can be no doubt.   Such an idea was entirely foreign to
the Jewish mind; and there is no trace of it in the
synoptical gospels,[6] we only find it indicated in portions of the Gospel of John, which cannot be accepted

Herodotus, iii. 28; Pomp. Mela, i. 9; Plutarch, *Quæst. symp.*,
VIII. i. 3; *De Isid. et Osir.*, 43.
    [1]Matt. i. 15, 23; Isa. vii. 14, and following.
    [2]Matt. ii. 1, and following.   [3]Luke ii. 25, and following.
    [4]Thus the legend of the massacre of the Innocents probably re-
fers to some cruelty exercised by Herod near Bethlehem. Comp.
Jos., *Ant.*, XIV. ix. 4.
    [5]Matt. i., ii.; Luke i., ii.; S. Justin., *Dial. cum Tryph.*, 78, 106;
Protoevang. of James (Apoca.). 18, and following.
    [6]Certain passages, such as *Acts* ii. 22, expressly exclude this
idea.

as expressing the thoughts of Jesus. Sometimes
Jesus even seems to take precautions to put down such
a doctrine.[1]   The accusation that he made himself
God, or the equal of God, is presented, even in the Gospel of John, as a calumny of the Jews.[2]   In this last
Gospel he declares himself less than his Father.[3]   Elsewhere he avows that the Father has not revealed everything to him.[4]   He believes himself to be more than an
ordinary man, but separated from God by an infinite
distance.   He is Son of God, but all men are, or may
become so, in divers degrees.[5]   Every one ought daily
to call God his father; all who are raised again will be
sons of God.[6]   The divine son-ship was attributed in
the Old Testament to beings whom it was by no means
pretended were equal with God.[7]   The word "son" has
the widest meanings in the Semitic language, and in
that of the New Testament.[8]   Besides, the idea Jesus
had of man was not that low idea which a cold Deism
has introduced.   In his poetic conception of Nature,
one breath alone penetrates the universe: the breath of
man is that of God; God dwells in man, and lives by

[1] Matt. xix. 17; Mark x. 18; Luke xviii. 19.
[2] John v. 18, and following, x. 33, and following.
[3] John xiv. 28.
[4] Mark xiii. 35.
[5] Matt. v. 9, 45; Luke iii. 38, vi. 35, xx. 36; John i. 12, 13, x. 34,
35.   Comp. *Acts* xvii. 28, 29; Rom. viii. 14, 19, 21, ix. 26; 2 Cor.
vi. 18; Gal. iii. 26; and in the Old Testament, *Deut.* xiv. 1; and
especially *Wisdom,* ii. 13, 18.
[6] Luke xx. 36.
[7] Gen. vi. 2; Job i. 6, ii. 1, xxviii. 7; Ps. ii. 7, lxxxii. 6; 2 Sam.
vii. 14.
[8] The child of the devil (Matt. xiii. 38; *Acts* xiii. 10); the children of this world (Mark iii. 17; Luke xvi. 8, xx. 34); the children of light (Luke xvi. 8; John xii. 36); the children of the
resurrection (Luke xx. 36); the children of the kingdom (Matt.
viii. 12, xiii. 38); the children of the bride-chamber (Matt. ix.
15; Mark ii. 19; Luke v. 34); the children of hell (Matt. xxiii.
15); the children of peace (Luke x. 6), &c. Let us remember that
the Jupiter of paganism is πατὴρ ἀνδρῶν τε θεῶν τε.

man, the same as man dwells in God, and lives by God.[1] The transcendent idealism of Jesus never permitted him to have a very clear notion of his own personality. He is his Father, his Father is he. He lives in his disciples; he is everywhere with them;[2] his disciples are one, as he and his Father are one.[3] The idea to him is everything; the body, which makes the distinction of persons, is nothing.

The title "Son of God," or simply "Son,"[4] thus became for Jesus a title analogous to "Son of man," and, like that, synonymous with the "Messiah," with the sole difference that he called himself "Son of man," and does not seem to have made the same use of the phrase, "Son of God."[5] The title, Son of man, expressed his character as judge; that of Son of God his power and his participation in the supreme designs. This power had no limits. His Father had given him all power. He had the power to alter even the Sabbath.[6] No one could know the Father except through him.[7] The Father had delegated to him exclusively the right of judging.[8] Nature obeyed him; but she obeys also all who believe and pray, for faith can do everything.[9] We must remember that no idea of the laws of Nature marked the limit of the impossible, either in his own mind, or in that of his hearers. The witnesses of his

[1] Comp. *Acts* xvii. 28.
[2] Matt. xviii. 20, xxviii. 20.
[3] John x. 30, xvii. 21. See in general the later discourses of John, especially chap. xvii., which express one side of the psychological state of Jesus, though we cannot regard them as true historical documents.
[4] The passages in support of this are too numerous to be referred to here.
[5] It is only in the Gospel of John that Jesus uses the expression "Son of God," or "Son," in speaking of himself.
[6] Matt. xii. 8; Luke vi. 5.
[7] Matt. xi. 27.
[8] John v. 22.   [9] Matt. xvii. 18, 19; Luke xvii. 6.

miracles thanked God "for having given such power unto men."[1]   He pardoned sins;[2] he was superior to David, to Abraham, to Solomon, and to the prophets.[3] We do not know in what form, nor to what extent, these affirmations of himself were made.   Jesus ought not to be judged by the law of our petty conventionalities.   The admiration of his disciples overwhelmed him and carried him away.   It is evident that the title of *Rabbi,* with which he was at first contented, no longer sufficed him; even the title of prophet or messenger of God responded no longer to his ideas.   The position which he attributed to himself was that of a superhuman being, and he wished to be regarded as sustaining a higher relationship to God than other men. But it must be remarked that these words, "superhuman" and "supernatural," borrowed from our petty theology, had no meaning in the exalted religious consciousness of Jesus.   To him Nature and the development of humanity were not limited kingdoms apart from God—paltry realities subjected to the laws of a hopeless empiricism.   There was no supernatural for him, because there was no Nature.   Intoxicated with infinite love, he forgot the heavy chain which holds the spirit captive; he cleared at one bound the abyss, impossible to most, which the weakness of the human faculties has created between God and man.

We cannot mistake in these affirmations of Jesus the germ of the doctrine which was afterward to make of him a divine hypostasis,[4] in identifying him with the

[1] Matt. ix. 8.

[2] Matt. ix. 2, and following; Mark ii. 5, and following; Luke v. 20, vii. 47, 48.

[3] Matt. xii. 41, 42, xxii. 43, and following; John viii. 52, and following.

[4] See especially John xiv., and following. But it is doubtful whether we have here the authentic teaching of Jesus.

Word, or "second God,"[1] or eldest Son of God,[2] or Angel Metathronos,[3] which Jewish theology created apart from him.[4] A kind of necessity caused this theology, in order to correct the extreme rigor of the old Monotheism, to place near God an assessor, to whom the eternal Father is supposed to delegate the government of the universe. The belief that certain men are incarnations of divine faculties or "powers," was widespread; the Samaritans possessed about the same time a thaumaturgus named Simon, whom they identified with the "great power of God."[5] For nearly two centuries, the speculative minds of Judaism had yielded to the tendency to personify the divine attributes, and certain expressions which were connected with the Divinity. Thus, the "breath of God," which is often referred to in the Old Testament, is considered as a separate being, the "Holy Spirit." In the same manner

[1] Philo cited in Eusebius, *Præp. Evang.*, vii. 13.

[2] Philo, *De migr. Abraham,* § 1; *Quod Deus immut.*, § 6; *De confus. ling.*, § 9, 14 and 28; De profugis, § 20; *De Somniis,* i. § 37; *De Agric. Noë,* § 12; *Quis rerum divin. hæres,* § 25, and following, 48, and following, &c.

[3] Μεταθρονος, that is, sharing the throne of God; a kind of divine secretary, keeping the register of merits and demerits: *Bereshith Rabba,* v. 6 c; Talm. of Bab., *Sanhedr.*, 38 b; *Chagigah,* 15 a; Targum of Jonathan, *Gen.*, v. 24.

[4] This theory of the Λόγος contains no Greek elements. The comparisons which have been made between it and the *Honover* of the Parsees are also without foundation. The *Minokhired* or "Divine Intelligence," has much analogy with the Jewish Λόγος. (See the fragments of the book entitled *Minokhired* in Spiegel, *Parsi-Grammatik,* pp. 161, 162.) But the development which the doctrine of the *Minokhired* has taken among the Parsees is modern, and may imply a foreign influence. The "Divine Intelligence" (*Maiyu-Khratû*) appears in the Zend books; but it does not there serve as basis to a theory; it only enters into some invocations. The comparisons which have been attempted between the Alexandrian theory of the Word and certain points of Egyptian theology may not be entirely without value. But nothing indicates that, in the centuries which preceded the Christian era, Palestinian Judaism had borrowed anything from Egypt.

[5] *Acts* viii. 10.

the "Wisdom of God" and the "Word of God" became
distinct personages. This was the germ of the process
which has engendered the *Sephiroth* of the Cabbala, the
Æons of Gnosticism, the hypostasis of Christianity,
and all that dry mythology, consisting of personified
abstractions, to which Monotheism is obliged to resort
when it wishes to pluralize the Deity.

Jesus appears to have remained a stranger to these
refinements of theology, which were soon to fill the
world with barren disputes. The metaphysical theory
of the Word, such as we find it in the writings of his
contemporary Philo, in the Chaldean Targums, and
even in the book of "Wisdom,"[1] is neither seen in the
Logia of Matthew, nor in general in the synoptics, the
most authentic interpreters of the words of Jesus.
The doctrine of the Word, in fact, had nothing in common with Messianism. The "Word" of Philo, and of
the Targums, is in no sense the Messiah. It was John
the Evangelist, or his school, who afterward endeavored to prove that Jesus was the Word, and who
created, in this sense, quite a new theology, very different from that of the "kingdom of God."[2] The essential character of the Word was that of Creator and of
Providence. Now, Jesus never pretended to have created the world, nor to govern it. His office was to
judge it, to renovate it. The position of president at
the final judgment of humanity was the essential attribute which Jesus attached to himself, and the charac-

---

[1] ix. 1, 2, xvi. 12. Comp. vii. 12, viii. 5, and following, ix., and
in general ix.-xi. These prosopopœia of Wisdom personified are
found in much older books. Prov. viii., ix.; Job xxviii.; *Rev.*
xix. 13.

[2] John, Gospel, i. 1-14; 1 Epistle v. 7; moreover, it will be remarked, that, in the Gospel of John, the expression of "the Word"
does not occur except in the prologue, and that the narrator never
puts it into the mouth of Jesus.

ter which all the first Christians attributed to him.[1]
Until the great day, he will sit at the right hand of God,
as his Metathronos, his first minister, and his future
avenger.[2]   The superhuman Christ of the Byzantine
apsides, seated as judge of the world, in the midst of
the apostles in the same rank with him, and superior to
the angels who only assist and serve, is the exact repre-
sentation of that conception of the "Son of man," of
which we find the first features so strongly indicated in
the book of Daniel.

At all events, the strictness of a studied theology by
no means existed in such a state of society.   All the
ideas we have just stated formed in the mind of the
disciples a theological system so little settled, that the
Son of God, this species of divine duplicate, is made to
act purely as man.   He is tempted—he is ignorant of
many things—he corrects himself[3]—he is cast down,
discouraged—he asks his Father to spare him trials—
he is submissive to God as a son.[4]   He who is to judge
the world does not know the day of judgment.[5]   He
takes precautions for his safety.[6]   Soon after his birth,
he is obliged to be concealed to avoid powerful men
who wish to kill him.[7]   In exorcisms, the devil cheats
him, and does not come out at the first command.[8]   In
his miracles we are sensible of painful effort—an exhaustion, as if something went out of him.[9]   All these

---

[1] *Acts* x. 42.
[2] Matt. xxvi. 64; Mark xvi. 19; Luke xxii. 69; *Acts* vii. 55;
Rom. viii. 34; Ephes. i. 20; Coloss. iii. 1; Heb. i. 3, 13, viii. 1, x
12, xii. 2; 1 Peter iii. 22.   See the passages previously cited on the
character of the Jewish Metathronos.
[3] Matt. x. 5, compared with xxviii. 19.
[4] Matt. xxvi. 39; John xii. 27.   [5] Mark xiii. 32.
[6] Matt. xii. 14-16, xiv. 13; Mark iii. 6, 7, ix. 29, 30; John vii. 1,
and following.   [7] Matt. ii. 20.
[8] Matt. xvii. 20; Mark ix. 25.
[9] Luke viii. 45, 46; John xi. 33, 38.

are simply the acts of a messenger of God, of a man protected and favored by God.[1] We must not look here for either logic or sequence. The need Jesus had of obtaining credence, and the enthusiasm of his disciples, heaped up contradictory notions. To the Messianic believers of the millenarian school, and to the enthusiastic readers of the books of Daniel and of Enoch, he was the Son of man—to the Jews holding the ordinary faith, and to the readers of Isaiah and Micah, he was the Son of David—to the disciples he was the Son of God, or simply the Son. Others, without being blamed by the disciples, took him for John the Baptist risen from the dead, for Elias, for Jeremiah, conformable to the popular belief that the ancient prophets were about to reappear, in order to prepare the time of the Messiah.[2]

An absolute conviction, or rather the enthusiasm, which freed him from even the possibility of doubt, shrouded all these boldnesses. We little understand, with our cold and scrupulous natures, how any one can be so entirely possessed by the idea of which he has made himself the apostle. To the deeply earnest races of the West, conviction means sincerity to one's self. But sincerity to one's self has not much meaning to Oriental peoples, little accustomed to the subtleties of a critical spirit. Honesty and imposture are words which, in our rigid consciences, are opposed as two irreconcilable terms. In the East, they are connected by numberless subtle links and windings. The authors of the Apocryphal books (of "Daniel" and of "Enoch," for instance), men highly exalted, in order to aid their

[1] *Acts* ii. 22.
[2] Matt. xiv. 2, xvi. 14, xvii. 3, and following; Mark vi. 14, 15, viii. 28; Luke ix. 8, and following, 19.

cause, committed, without a shadow of scruple, an act which we should term a fraud. The literal truth has little value to the Oriental; he sees everything through the medium of his ideas, his interests, and his passions.

History is impossible, if we do not fully admit that there are many standards of sincerity. All great things are done through the people; now we can only lead the people by adapting ourselves to its ideas. The philosopher who, knowing this, isolates and fortifies himself in his integrity, is highly praiseworthy. But he who takes humanity with its illusions, and seeks to act with it and upon it, cannot be blamed. Cæsar knew well that he was not the son of Venus; France would not be what it is, if it had not for a thousand years believed in the Holy Ampulla of Rheims. It is easy for us, who are so powerless, to call this falsehood, and, proud of our timid honesty, to treat with contempt the heroes who have accepted the battle of life under other conditions. When we have effected by our scruples what they accomplished by their falsehoods, we shall have the right to be severe upon them. At least, we must make a marked distinction between societies like our own, where everything takes place in the full light of reflection, and simple and credulous communities, in which the beliefs that have governed ages have been born. Nothing great has been established which does not rest on a legend. The only culprit in such cases is the humanity which is willing to be deceived

CHAPTER XVI.

MIRACLES.

Two means of proof—miracles and the accomplishment of prophecies—could alone, in the opinion of the contemporaries of Jesus, establish a supernatural mission. Jesus, and especially his disciples, employed these two processes of demonstration in perfect good faith. For a long time, Jesus had been convinced that the prophets had written only in reference to him. He recognized himself in their sacred oracles; he regarded himself as the mirror in which all the prophetic spirit of Israel had read the future. The Christian school, perhaps even in the lifetime of its founder, endeavored to prove that Jesus responded perfectly to all that the prophets had predicted of the Messiah.[1] In many cases, these comparisons were quite superficial, and are scarcely appreciable by us. They were most frequently fortuitous or insignificant circumstances in the life of the master which recalled to the disciples certain passages of the Psalms and the Prophets, in which, in consequence of their constant preoccupation, they saw images of him.[2] The exegesis of the time consisted thus almost entirely in a play upon words, and in quotations made in an artificial and arbitrary manner. The synagogue had no officially settled list of the passages which related to the future reign. The Messianic references were very liberally created, and constituted artifices of style rather than serious reasoning.

[1] For example, Matt. i. 22, ii. 5, 6, 15, 18, iv. 15.
[2] Matt. i. 23, iv. 6, 14, xxvi. 31, 54, 56, xxvii. 9, 35; Mark xiv. 27, xv. 28; John xii. 14, 15, xviii. 9, xix. 19, 24, 28, 36.

As to miracles, they were regarded at this period as the indispensable mark of the divine, and as the sign of the prophetic vocation. The legends of Elijah and Elisha were full of them. It was commonly believed that the Messiah would perform many.[1] In Samaria, a few leagues from where Jesus was, a magician, named Simon, acquired an almost divine character by his illusions.[2] Afterward, when it was sought to establish the reputation of Apollonius of Tyana, and to prove that his life had been the sojourn of a god upon the earth, it was not thought possible to succeed therein except by inventing a vast cycle of miracles.[3] The Alexandrian philosophers themselves, Plotinus and others, are reported to have performed several.[4] Jesus was, therefore, obliged to choose between these two alternatives—either to renounce his mission, or to become a thaumaturgus. It must be remembered that all antiquity, with the exception of the great scientific schools of Greece and their Roman disciples, accepted miracles; and that Jesus not only believed therein, but had not the least idea of an order of Nature regulated by fixed laws. His knowledge on this point was in no way superior to that of his contemporaries. Nay, more, one of his most deeply rooted opinions was, that by faith and prayer man has entire power over Nature.[5] The faculty of performing miracles was regarded as a privilege frequently conferred by God upon men,[6] and it had nothing surprising in it.

[1] John vii. 34; *IV. Esdras*, xiii. 50.
[2] *Acts* viii. 9, and following.
[3] See his biography by Philostratus.
[4] See the Lives of the Sophists, by Eunapius; the Life of Plotinus, by Porphyry; that of Proclus, by Marinus; and that of Isidorus, attributed to Damascius.
[5] Matt. xvii. 19, xxi. 21, 22; Mark xi. 23, 24.
[6] Matt. ix. 8.

The lapse of time has changed that which constituted the power of the great founder of Christianity into something offensive to our ideas, and if ever the worship of Jesus loses its hold upon mankind, it will be precisely on account of those acts which originally inspired belief in him. Criticism experiences no embarrassment in presence of this kind of historical phenomenon. A thaumaturgus of our days, unless of an extreme simplicity, like that manifested by certain stigmatists of Germany, is odious; for he performs miracles without believing in them; and is a mere charlatan. But, if we take a Francis d'Assisi, the question becomes altogether different; the series of miracles attending the origin of the order of St. Francis, far from offending us, affords us real pleasure. The founder of Christianity lived in as complete a state of poetic ignorance as did St. Clair and the *tres socii*. The disciples deemed it quite natural that their master should have interviews with Moses and Elias, that he should command the elements, and that he should heal the sick. We must remember, besides, that every idea loses something of its purity, as soon as it aspires to realize itself. Success is never attained without some injury being done to the sensibility of the soul. Such is the feebleness of the human mind that the best causes are ofttimes gained only by bad arguments. The demonstrations of the primitive apologists of Christianity are supported by very poor reasonings. Moses, Christopher Columbus, Mahomet, have only triumphed over obstacles by constantly making allowance for the weakness of men, and by not always giving the true reasons for the truth. It is probable that the hearers of Jesus were more struck by his miracles than by his eminently divine discourses. Let us add, that doubtless popular rumor, both before and after the death of Jesus, exaggerated enormously the number of occurrences of this kind. The types of the gospel miracles, in fact, do not present much variety; they are repetitions of each other and seem fashioned from a very small number of models, accommodated to the taste of the country.

It is impossible, amongst the miraculous narratives so tediously enumerated in the Gospels, to distinguish the miracles attributed to Jesus by public opinion from those in which he consented to play an active part. It is especially impossible to ascertain whether the offensive circumstances attending them, the groanings, the strugglings, and other features savoring of jugglery,[1] are really historical, or whether they are the fruit of the belief of the compilers, strongly imbued with theurgy, and living, in this respect, in a world analogous to that of the "spiritualists" of our times.[2] Almost all the miracles which Jesus thought he performed, appear to have been miracles of healing. Medicine was at this period in Judea, what it still is in the East, that is to say, in no respect scientific, but absolutely surrendered to individual inspiration. Scientific medicine, founded by Greece five centuries before, was at the time of Jesus unknown to the Jews of Palestine. In such a state of knowledge, the presence of a superior man, treating the diseased with gentleness, and giving him by some sensible signs the assurance of his recovery, is often a decisive remedy. Who would dare to say that in many cases, always excepting certain pecul-

---

[1] Luke viii. 45, 46; John xi. 33 and 38.
[2] Acts. ii. 2, and following, iv. 31, viii. 15, and following, x. 44 and following. For nearly a century, the apostles and their disciples dreamed only of miracles. See the Acts, the writings of St. Paul, the extracts from Papias, in Eusebius, Hist. Eccl., iii. 39 &c. Comp. Mark iii. 15, xvi. 17, 18, 20.

iar injuries, the touch of a superior being is not equal
to all the resources of pharmacy? The mere pleasure
of seeing him cures. He gives only a smile, or a hope,
but these are not in vain.

Jesus had no more idea than his countrymen of a
rational medical science; he believed, like every one
else, that healing was to be effected by religious practices, and such a belief was perfectly consistent. From
the moment that disease was regarded as the punishment of sin,[1] or as the act of a demon,[2] and by no
means as the result of physical causes, the best physician was the holy man who had power in the supernatural world. Healing was considered a moral act;
Jesus, who felt his moral power, would believe himself
specially gifted to heal. Convinced that the touching
of his robe,[3] the imposition of his hands,[4] did good to
the sick, he would have been unfeeling, if he had refused to those who suffered, a solace which it was in his
power to bestow. The healing of the sick was considered as one of the signs of the kingdom of God, and
was always associated with the emancipation of the
poor.[5] Both were the signs of the great revolution
which was to end in the redress of all infirmities.

One of the species of cure which Jesus most frequently performed, was exorcism, or the expulsion of
demons. A strange disposition to believe in demons
pervaded all minds. It was a universal opinion, not
only in Judea, but in the whole world, that demons
seized hold of the bodies of certain persons and made
them act contrary to their will. A Persian *div,* often

[1]John v. 14, ix. 1, and following, 34.
[2]Matt. ix. 32, 33, xii. 22; Luke xiii. 11, 16.
[3]Luke viii. 45, 46.
[4]Luke iv. 40.
[5]Matt. xi. 5, xv. 30, 31; Luke ix. 1, 2, 6.

named in the Avesta,[1] *Aeschma-daëva,* the "div of con-
cupiscence," adopted by the Jews under the name of
Asmodeus,[2] became the cause of all the hysterical af-
flictions of women.[3] Epilepsy, mental and nervous
maladies,[4] in which the patient seems no longer to belong to himself, and infirmities, the cause of which is
not apparent, as deafness, dumbness,[5] were explained
in the same manner. The admirable treatise, "On
Sacred Disease," by Hippocrates, which set forth the
true principles of medicine on this subject, four centuries and a half before Jesus, had not banished from
the world so great an error. It was supposed that
there were processes more or less efficacious for driving
away the demons; and the occupation of exorcist was a
regular profession like that of physician.[6] There is
no doubt that Jesus had in his lifetime the reputation of
possessing the greatest secrets of this art.[7] There
were at that time many lunatics in Judea, doubtless in
consequence of the great mental excitement. These
mad persons, who were permitted to go at large, as
they still are in the same districts, inhabited the abandoned sepulchral caves, which were the ordinary retreat of vagrants. Jesus had great influence over these
unfortunates.[8] A thousand singular incidents were

---

[1] *Vendidad,* xi. 26; *Yaçna,* x. 18.
[2] *Tobit,* iii. 8, vi. 14; Talm. of Bab., *Gittin,* 68 *a.*
[3] Comp. Mark xvi. 9; Luke viii. 2; *Gospel of the Infancy,* 16, 33;
Syrian Code, published in the *Anecdota Syriaca* of M. Land, i.,
p. 152.
[4] Jos., *Bell. Jud.,* VII. vi. 3; Lucian, *Philopseud.,* 16; Philostratus,
Life of Apoll., iii. 38, iv. 20; Aretus, *De causis morb. chron.,* i. 4.
[5] Matt. ix. 33, xii. 22; Mark ix. 16, 24; Luke xi. 14.
[6] *Tobit,* viii. 2, 3; Matt. xii. 27; Mark ix. 38; *Acts* xix. 13;
Josephus, *Ant.,* VIII. ii. 5; Justin, *Dial. cum Tryph.,* 85; Lucian,
Epigr., xxiii. (xvii. Dindorf).
[7] Matt. xvii. 20; Mark ix. 24, and following.
[8] Matt. viii. 28, ix. 34, xii. 43, and following, xvii. 14, and following, 20; Mark v. 1, and following; Luke viii. 27, and following.

related in connection with his cures, in which the credulity of the time gave itself full scope. But still these difficulties must not be exaggerated. The disorders which were explained by "possessions" were often very slight. In our times, in Syria, they regard as mad or possessed by a demon (these two ideas were expressed by the same word, *medjnoun*[1]) people who are only somewhat eccentric. A gentle word often suffices in such cases to drive away the demon. Such were doubtless the means employed by Jesus. Who knows if his celebrity as exorcist was not spread almost without his own knowledge? Persons who reside in the East are occasionally surprised to find themselves, after some time, in possession of a great reputation, as doctors, sorcerers, or discoverers of treasures, without being able to account to themselves for the facts which have given rise to these strange fancies.

Many circumstances, moreover, seem to indicate that Jesus only became a thaumaturgus late in life and against his inclination. He often performs his miracles only after he has been besought to do so, and with a degree of reluctance, reproaching those who asked them for the grossness of their minds.[2] One singularity, apparently inexplicable, is the care he takes to perform his miracles in secret, and the request he addresses to those whom he heals to tell no one.[3] When the demons wish to proclaim him the Son of God, he

---

[1] The phrase, *Dæmonium habes* (Matt. xi. 18; Luke vii. 33; John vii. 20, viii. 48, and following, x. 20, and following) should be translated by: "Thou art mad," as we should say in Arabic: *Medjnoun enté*. The verb δαιμονᾶν has also, in all classical antiquity, the meaning of "to be mad."

[2] Matt. xii. 39, xvi. 4, xvii. 16; Mark viii. 17, and following, ix. 18; Luke ix. 41.

[3] Matt. viii. 4. ix. 30, 31, xii. 16, and following; Mark i. 44, vii. 24, and following, viii. 26.

forbids them to open their mouths; but they recognize
him in spite of himself.[1] These traits are especially
characteristic in Mark, who is pre-eminently the evangelist of miracles and exorcisms. It seems that the
disciple, who has furnished the fundamental teachings
of this Gospel, importuned Jesus with his admiration
of the wonderful, and that the master, wearied of a
reputation which weighed upon him, had often said to
him, "See thou say nothing to any man." Once this
discordance evoked a singular outburst,[2] a fit of im-
patience, in which the annoyance these perpetual demands of weak minds caused Jesus, breaks forth. One
would say, at times, that the character of thaumaturgus
was disagreeable to him, and that he sought to give as
little publicity as possible to the marvels which, in a
manner, grew under his feet. When his enemies asked
a miracle of him, especially a celestial miracle, a "sign
from heaven," he obstinately refused.[3] We may therefore conclude that his reputation of thaumaturgus was
imposed upon him, that he did not resist it much, but
also that he did nothing to aid it, and that, at all events,
he felt the vanity of popular opinion on this point.

We should neglect to recognize the first principles of
history if we attached too much importance to our repugnances on this matter, and if, in order to avoid the
objections which might be raised against the character
of Jesus, we attempted to suppress facts which, in the
eyes of his contemporaries, were considered of the
greatest importance.[4] It would be convenient to say
that these are the additions of disciples much inferior
to their Master who, not being able to conceive his true

[1] Mark i. 24, 25, 34, iii. 12: Luke iv. 41.
[2] Matt. xvii. 16; Mark ix. 18; Luke ix. 41.
[3] Matt. xii. 38, and following, xvi. 1, and following; Mark viii. 11.
[4] Josephus, *Ant.*, xviii. iii. 3.

grandeur, have sought to magnify him by illusions unworthy of him. But the four narrators of the life of
Jesus are unanimous in extolling his miracles; one of
them, Mark, interpreter of the apostle Peter,[1] insists
so much on this point, that, if we trace the character of
Christ only according to this Gospel, we should represent him as an exorcist in possession of charms of rare
efficacy, as a very potent sorcerer, who inspired fear,
and whom the people wished to get rid of.[2] We will
admit, then, without hesitation, that acts which would
now be considered as acts of illusion or folly, held a
large place in the life of Jesus. Must we sacrifice to
these uninviting features the sublimer aspect of such a
life? God forbid. A mere sorcerer, after the manner
of Simon the magician, would not have brought about
a moral revolution like that effected by Jesus. If the
thaumaturgus had effaced in Jesus the moralist and the
religious reformer, there would have proceeded from
him a school of theurgy, and not Christianity.

The problem, moreover, presents itself in the same
manner with respect to all saints and religious founders. Things now considered morbid, such as epilepsy
and seeing of visions, were formerly principles of
power and greatness. Physicians can designate the
disease which made the fortune of Mahomet.[3] Almost
in our own day, the men who have done the most for
their kind (the excellent Vincent de Paul himself!)
were, whether they wished it or not, thaumaturgi. If
we set out with the principle that every historical per-

---

[1] Papias, in Eusebius, *Hist. Eccl.,* iii. 39.

[2] Mark iv. 40, v. 15, 17, 33, 36, vi. 50, x. 32; cf. Matt. viii. 27, 34,
ix. 8, xiv. 27, xvii. 6, 7, xxviii. 5, 10; Luke iv. 36, v. 17, viii. 25,
35, 37, ix. 34. The Apocryphal Gospel, said to be by Thomas the
Israelite, carries this feature to the most offensive absurdity.
Compare the *Miracles of the Infancy,* in Philo, *Cod. Apocr. N.T.*
p. cx., note.   [3] *Hysteria Muscularis* of Shoenlein.

sonage to whom acts have been attributed, which we in the nineteenth century hold to be irrational or savoring of quackery, was either a madman or a charlatan, all criticism is nullified. The school of Alexandria was a noble school, but, nevertheless, it gave itself up to the practices of an extravagant theurgy. Socrates and Pascal were not exempt from hallucinations. Facts ought to explain themselves by proportionate causes. The weaknesses of the human mind only engender weakness; great things have always great causes in the nature of man, although they are often developed amidst a crowd of littlenesses which, to superficial minds, eclipse their grandeur.

In a general sense, it is therefore true to say that Jesus was only thaumaturgus and exorcist in spite of himself. Miracles are ordinarily the work of the public much more than of him to whom they are attributed. Jesus persistently shunned the performance of the wonders which the multitude would have created for him; the greatest miracle would have been his refusal to perform any; never would the laws of history and popular psychology have suffered so great a derogation. The miracles of Jesus were a violence done to him by his age, a concession forced from him by a passing necessity. The exorcist and the thaumaturgus have alike passed away; but the religious reformer will live eternally.

Even those who did not believe in him were struck with these acts, and sought to be witnesses of them.[1] The pagans, and persons unacquainted with him, experienced a sentiment of fear, and sought to remove him from their district.[2] Many thought perhaps to

[1] Matt. xiv. 1, and following; Mark vi. 14; Luke ix. 7, xxiii. 8.
[2] Matt. viii. 34; Mark v. 17, viii. 37.

abuse his name by connecting it with seditious movements.[1]   But the purely moral and in no respect political tendency of the character of Jesus saved him from
these entanglements.   His kingdom was in the circle
of disciples, whom a like freshness of imagination and
the same foretaste of heaven had grouped and retained
around him.

[1]John vi. 14, 15,

CHAPTER XVII.

DEFINITIVE FORM OF THE IDEAS OF JESUS RESPECTING THE KINGDOM OF GOD.

WE suppose that this last phase of the activity of Jesus continued about eighteen months from the time of his return from the Passover of the year 31, until his journey to the feast of tabernacles of the year 32.[1] During this time, the mind of Jesus does not appear to have been enriched by the addition of any new element; but all his old ideas grew and developed with an ever-increasing degree of power and boldness.

The fundamental idea of Jesus from the beginning, was the establishment of the kingdom of God. But this kingdom of God, as we have already said, appears to have been understood by Jesus in very different senses. At times, we should take him for a democratic leader desiring only the triumph of the poor and the disinherited. At other times, the kingdom of God is the literal accomplishment of the apocalyptic visions of Daniel and Enoch. Lastly, the kingdom of God is often a spiritual kingdom, and the approaching deliverance is a deliverance of the spirit. In this last sense, the revolution desired by Jesus was the one which has really taken place; the establishment of a new worship, purer than that of Moses. All these thoughts appear to have existed at the same time in the mind of Jesus. The first one, however—that of a temporal revolution

---

[1] John v. 1, vii. 2. We follow the system of John, according to whom the public life of Jesus lasted three years. The synoptics on the contrary, group all the facts within the space of one year.

—does not appear to have impressed him much; he never regarded the earth or the riches of the earth, or material power, as worth caring for. He had no worldly ambition. Sometimes by a natural consequence, his great religious importance was in danger of being converted into mere social importance. Men came requesting him to judge and arbitrate on questions affecting their material interests. Jesus rejected these proposals with haughtiness, treating them as insults.[1] Full of his heavenly ideal, he never abandoned his disdainful poverty. As to the other two conceptions of the kingdom of God, Jesus appears always to have held them simultaneously. If he had been only an enthusiast, led away by the apocalypses on which the popular imagination fed, he would have remained an obscure sectary, inferior to those whose ideas he followed. If he had been only a puritan, a sort of Channing or "Savoyard vicar," he would undoubtedly have been unsuccessful. The two parts of his system, or, rather, his two conceptions of the kingdom of God, rest one on the other, and this mutual support has been the cause of his incomparable success. The first Christians were dreamers, living in a circle of ideas which we should term visionary; but, at the same time, they were the heroes of that social war which has resulted in the enfranchisement of the conscience, and in the establishment of a religion from which the pure worship, proclaimed by the founder, will eventually proceed.

The apocalyptic ideas of Jesus, in their most complete form, may thus be summed up. The existing condition of humanity is approaching its termination. This termination will be an immense revolution, "an anguish" similar to the pains of child-birth; a *palin-*

[1] Luke xii. 13, 14.

genesis, or, in the words of Jesus himself, a "new birth,"[1] preceded by dark calamities and heralded by strange phenomena.[2] In the great day, there will appear in the heavens the sign of the Son of man; it will be a startling and luminous vision like that of Sinai, a great storm rending the clouds, a fiery meteor flashing rapidly from east to west. The Messiah will appear in the clouds, clothed in glory and majesty, to the sound of trumpets and surrounded by angels. His disciples will sit by his side upon thrones. The dead will then arise, and the Messiah will proceed to judgment.[3]

At this judgment men will be divided into two classes according to their deeds.[4] The angels will be the executors of the sentences.[5] The elect will enter into delightful mansions, which have been prepared for them from the foundation of the world;[6] there they will be seated, clothed with light, at a feast presided over by Abraham,[7] the patriarchs and the prophets.

[1] Matt. xix. 28.

[2] Matt. xxiv. 3, and following; Mark xiii. 4, and following; Luke xvii. 22, and following, xxi. 7, and following. It must be remarked that the picture of the end of time attributed to Jesus by the synoptics, contains many features which relate to the siege of Jerusalem. Luke wrote some time after the siege (xxi. 9, 20, 24). The compilation of Matthew, on the contrary (xxvi. 15, 16, 22, 29), carries us back exactly to this precise period, or very shortly afterward. There is no doubt, however, that Jesus predicted that great terrors would precede his reappearance. These terrors were an integral part of all the Jewish apocalypses. *Enoch,* xcix., c., cii., ciii. (division of Dillman); *Carm. sibyll.,* iii. 334, and following, 633, and following, iv. 168, and following, v. 511, and following. According to Daniel also, the reign of the saints will only come after the desolation shall have reached its height. Chap. vii. 25, and following, viii. 23, and following, ix. 26, 27, xii. 1.

[3] Matt. xvi. 27, xix. 28, xx. 21, xxiv. 30, and following, xxv. 31, and following, xxvi. 64; Mark xiv. 62; Luke xxii. 30; 1 Cor. xv. 52; 1 Thess. iv. 15, and following.

[4] Matt. xiii. 38, and following, xxv. 33.

[5] Matt. xiii. 39, 41, 49.   [6] Matt. xxv. 34. Comp. John xiv. 2.

[7] Matt. viii. 11, xiii. 43, xxvi. 29; Luke xiii. 28, xvi. 22, xxii. 30.

They will be the smaller number.[1] The rest will depart into *Gehenna*. Gehenna was the western valley of Jerusalem. There the worship of fire had been practised at various times, and the place had become a kind of sewer. Gehenna was, therefore, in the mind of Jesus, a gloomy, filthy valley, full of fire. Those excluded from the kingdom will there be burnt and eaten by the never-dying worm, in company with Satan and his rebel angels.[2] There, there will be wailing and gnashing of teeth.[3] The kingdom of heaven will be as a closed room, lighted from within, in the midst of a world of darkness and torments.[4]

This new order of things will be eternal. Paradise and Gehenna will have no end. An impassable abyss separates the one from the other.[5] The Son of man, seated on the right hand of God, will preside over this final condition of the world and of humanity.[6]

That all this was taken literally by the disciples and by the master himself at certain moments, appears clearly evident from the writings of the time. If the first Christian generation had one profound and constant belief, it was that the world was near its end,[7] and

---

[1]Luke xiii. 23, and following.

[2]Matt xxv. 41. The idea of the fall of the angels, detailed in the Book of Enoch, was universally admitted in the circle of Jesus. Epistle of Jude 6, and following; 2d Epistle attributed to Saint Peter. ii. 4, 11; *Revelation* xii. 9; Gospel of John viii. 44.

[3]Matt. v. 22, viii. 12, x. 28, xiii. 40, 42, 50, xviii. 8, xxiv. 51, xxv. 30; Mark ix, 43, &c.

[4]Matt. viii. 12, xxii. 13, xxv. 30. Comp. Jos., *B. J.*, iii. viii. 5.

[5]Luke xvi. 28.

[6]Mark iii. 29; Luke xxii. 69; *Acts* vii. 55.

[7]*Acts* ii. 17, iii. 19, and following; 1 Cor. xv. 23, 24, 52; 1 Thess. iii. 13, iv. 14, and following, v. 23; 2 Thess. ii. 8; 1 Tim. vi. 14; 2 Tim. iv. 1; Tit. ii. 13; Epistle of James v. 3, 8; Epistle of Jude 18; 2d Epistle of Peter, iii. entirely; *Revelations* entirely, and in particular, i. 1, ii. 5, 16, iii. 11, xi. 14, xxii. 6, 7, 12, 20. Comp. 4th Book of Esdras, iv. 26.

that the great "revelation"[1] of Christ was about to take place. The startling proclamation, "The time is at hand,"[2] which commences and closes the Apocalypse; the incessantly reiterated appeal, "He that hath ears to hear let him hear!"[3] were the cries of hope and encouragement for the whole apostolic age. A Syrian expression, *Maran atha,* "Our Lord cometh!"[4] became a sort of password, which the believers used amongst themselves to strengthen their faith and their hope. The Apocalypse, written in the year 68 of our era,[5] declares that the end will come in three years and a half.[6] The "Ascension of Isaiah"[7] adopts a calculation very similar to this.

Jesus never indulged in such precise details. When he was interrogated as to the time of his advent, he always refused to reply; once even he declared that the date of this great day was known only by the Father, who had revealed it neither to the angels nor to the Son.[8] He said that the time when the kingdom of God was most anxiously expected, was just that in which it would not appear.[9] He constantly repeated that it would be a surprise, as in the times of Noah and of Lot; that we must be on our guard, always ready to depart; that each one must watch and keep his lamp trimmed as for a wedding procession, which arrives

---

[1]Luke xvii. 30; 1. Cor. i. 7, 8; 2 Thess. i. 7; 1 Peter i. 7, 13; *Revelations* i. 1. [2]*Revelations* i. 3, xxii. 10.
[3]Matt. xi. 15, xiii. 9, 43; Mark iv. 9, 23, vii. 16; Luke viii. 8, xiv. 35; *Revelations* ii. 7, 11, 27, 29, iii. 6, 13, 22, xiii. 9.
[4]1 Cor. xvi. 22.
[5]*Revelations* xvii. 9, and following. The sixth emperor, whom the author represents as reigning, is Galba. The dead emperor, who was to return, is Nero, whose name is given in figures (xiii. 18).
[6]*Revelations* xi. 2, 3, xii. 14. Comp. Daniel vii. 25, xii. 7.
[7]Chap. iv., v. 12 and 14. Comp. Cedrenus, p. 68 (Paris, 1647).
[8]Matt. xxiv. 36; Mark xiii. 32.
[9]Luke xvii. 20. Comp. Talmud of Babyl., *Sanhedrim,* 97 a.

unforeseen;[1] that the Son of man would come like a thief, at an hour when he would not be expected;[2] that he would appear as a flash of lightning, running from one end of the heavens to the other.[3] But his declarations on the nearness of the catastrophe leave no room for any equivocations.[4] "This generation," said he, "shall not pass till all these things be fulfilled. There be some standing here, which shall not taste of death, till they see the Son of man coming in his kingdom."[5] He reproaches those who do not believe in him, for not being able to read the signs of the future kingdom. "When it is evening, ye say, It will be fair weather; for the sky is red. And in the morning, It will be foul weather to-day; for the sky is red and lowering. O ye hypocrites, ye can discern the face of the sky; but can ye not discern the signs of the times?"[6] By an illusion common to all great reformers, Jesus imagined the end to be much nearer than it really was; he did not take into account the slowness of the movements of humanity; he thought to realize in one day that which, eighteen centuries later, has still to be accomplished.

These formal declarations preoccupied the Christian family for nearly seventy years. It was believed that some of the disciples would see the day of the final revelation before dying. John, in particular, was considered as being of this number;[7] many believed that

[1] Matt. xxiv. 36, and following; Mark xiii. 32, and following; Luke xii. 35, and following, xvii. 20, and following.

[2] Luke xii. 40; 2 Peter iii. 10.

[3] Luke xvii. 24.

[4] Matt. x. 23, xxiv., xxv. entirely, and especially xxiv. 29, 34; Mark xiii. 30; Luke xiii. 35, xxi. 28, and following.

[5] Matt. xvi. 28, xxiii. 36, 39, xxiv. 34; Mark viii. 39; Luke ix. 27, xxi. 32.

[6] Matt. xvi. 2-4; Luke xii. 54-56.

[7] John xxi. 22, 23.

he would never die. Perhaps this was a later opinion suggested toward the end of the first century, by the advanced age which John seems to have reached; this age having given rise to the belief that God wished to prolong his life indefinitely until the great day, in order to realize the words of Jesus. However this may be, at his death the faith of many was shaken, and his disciples attached to the prediction of Christ a more subdued meaning.[1]

At the same time that Jesus fully admitted the Apocalyptic beliefs, such as we find them in the apocryphal Jewish books, he admitted the doctrine, which is the complement, or rather the condition of them all, namely, the resurrection of the dead. This doctrine, as we have already said, was still somewhat new in Israel; a number of people either did not know it, or did not believe it.[2] It was the faith of the Pharisees, and of the fervent adherents of the Messianic beliefs.[3] Jesus accepted it unreservedly, but always in the most idealistic sense. Many imagined that in the resuscitated world they would eat, drink, and marry. Jesus, indeed, admits into his kingdom a new passover, a table, and a new wine;[4] but he expressly excludes marriage from it. The Sadducees had on this subject an apparently coarse argument, but one which was really in conformity with the old theology. It will be remembered that according to the ancient sages, man survived only in his children. The Mosaic code had

[1] John xxi. 22, 23. Chapter xxi. of the fourth Gospel is an addition, as is proved by the final clause of the primitive compilation, which concludes at verse 31 of chapter xx. But the addition is almost contemporaneous with the publication of the Gospel itself.
[2] Mark ix. 9; Luke xx. 27, and following.
[3] Dan. xii. 2, and following; 2 Macc. vii. entirely, xii. 45, 46, xiv. 46; *Acts* xxiii. 6, 8; Jos., *Ant.*, XVIII. i. 3; *B. J.*, II. viii. 14, III. viii. 5.
[4] Matt. xxvi. 29; Luke xxii. 30.

consecrated this patriarchal theory by a strange institution, the levirate law. The Sadducees drew from thence subtle deductions against the resurrection. Jesus escaped them by formally declaring that in the life eternal there would no longer exist differences of sex, and that men would be like the angels.[1] Sometimes he seems to promise resurrection only to the righteous,[2] the punishment of the wicked consisting in complete annihilation.[3] Oftener, however, Jesus declares that the resurrection shall bring eternal confusion to the wicked.[4]

It will be seen that nothing in all these theories was absolutely new. The Gospels and the writings of the apostles scarcely contain anything as regards apocalyptic doctrines but what might be found already in "Daniel,"[5] "Enoch,"[6] and the "Sibylline Oracles,"[7] of Jewish origin. Jesus accepted the ideas, which were generally received among his contemporaries. He made them his basis of action, or rather one of his bases; for he had too profound an idea of his true work to establish it solely upon such fragile principles—principles so liable to be decisively refuted by facts.

It is evident, indeed, that such a doctrine, taken by itself in a literal manner, had no future. The world, in continuing to exist, caused it to crumble. One generation of man at the most was the limit of its endur-

---

[1] Matt. xxii. 24, and following; Luke xx. 34-38; Ebionite Gospel, entitled, "Of the Egyptians," in Clem. of Alex., *Strom.* ii. 9, 13; Clem. Rom., Epist. ii. 12.

[2] Luke xiv. 14, xx. 35, 36. This is also the opinion of St. Paul: 1 Cor. xv. 23, and following; 1 Thess. iv. 12, and following.

[3] Comp. 4th book of Esdras, ix. 22.

[4] Matt. xxv. 32, and following.

[5] See especially chaps. ii., vi.-viii., x.-xiii.

[6] Chaps. i., xlv., lii., lxii., xciii. 9, and following.

[7] Book iii. 573, and following; 652, and following; 766, and following; 795, and following.

ance. The faith of the first Christian generation is intelligible, but the faith of the second generation is no longer so. After the death of John, or of the last survivor, whoever he might be, of the group which had seen the master, the word of Jesus was convicted of falsehood.[1] If the doctrine of Jesus had been simply belief in an approaching end of the world, it would certainly now be sleeping in oblivion. What is it, then, which has saved it? The great breadth of the Gospel conceptions, which has permitted doctrines suited to very different intellectual conditions to be found under the same creed. The world has not ended, as Jesus announced, and as his disciples believed. But it has been renewed, and in one sense renewed as Jesus desired. It is because his thought was two-sided that it has been fruitful. His chimera has not had the fate of so many others which have crossed the human mind, because it concealed a germ of life which having been introduced, thanks to a covering of fable, into the bosom of humanity, has thus brought forth eternal fruits.

And let us not say that this is a benevolent interpretation, imagined in order to clear the honor of our great master from the cruel contradiction inflicted on his dreams by reality. No, no: this true kingdom of God, this kingdom of the spirit, which makes each one king and priest; this kingdom which, like the grain of mustard-seed, has become a tree which overshadows the world, and amidst whose branches the birds have their nests, was understood, wished for, and founded by Jesus. By the side of the false, cold, and impos-

---

[1] These pangs of Christian conscience are rendered with simplicity in the second epistle attributed to St. Peter, iii. 8, and following.

sible idea of an ostentatious advent, he conceived the real city of God, the true "palingenesis," the Sermon on the Mount, the apotheosis of the weak, the love of the people, regard for the poor, and the re-establishment of all that is humble, true, and simple. This re-establishment he has depicted as an incomparable artist, by features which will last eternally. Each of us owes that which is best in himself to him. Let us pardon him his hope of a vain apocalypse, and of a second coming in great triumph upon the clouds of heaven. Perhaps these were the errors of others rather than his own; and if it be true that he himself shared the general illusion, what matters it, since his dream rendered him strong against death, and sustained him in a struggle, to which he might otherwise have been unequal?

We must, then, attach several meanings to the divine city conceived by Jesus. If his only thought had been that the end of time was near, and that we must prepare for it, he would not have surpassed John the Baptist. To renounce a world ready to crumble, to detach one's self little by little from the present life, and to aspire to the kingdom about to come, would have formed the gist of his preaching. The teaching of Jesus had always a much larger scope. He proposed to himself to create a new state of humanity, and not merely to prepare the end of that which was in exist= ence. Elias or Jeremiah, reappearing in order to prepare men for the supreme crisis, would not have preached as he did. This is so true that this morality, attributed to the latter days, is found to be the eternal morality, that which has saved humanity. Jesus himself in many cases makes use of modes of speech which do not accord with the apocalyptic theory. He often declares that the kingdom of God has already commenced; that every man bears it within himself; and can, if he be worthy, partake of it; that each one silently creates this kingdom by the true conversion of the heart.[1] The kingdom of God at such times is only the highest form of good.[2] A better order of things than that which exists, the reign of justice, which the faithful, according to their ability, ought to help in establishing; or, again, the liberty of the soul, something analogous to the Buddhist "deliverance," the fruit of the soul's separation from matter and absorption in the divine essence. These truths, which are purely abstract to us, were living realities to Jesus. Everything in his mind was concrete and substantial. Jesus, of all men, believed most thoroughly in the reality of the ideal.

In accepting the Utopias of his time and his race, Jesus thus was able to make high truths of them, thanks to the fruitful misconceptions of their import. His kingdom of God was no doubt the approaching apocalypse, which was about to be unfolded in the heavens. But it was still, and probably above all the kingdom of the soul, founded on liberty and on the filial sentiment which the virtuous man feels when resting on the bosom of his Father. It was a pure religion, without forms, without temple, and without priest; it was the moral judgment of the world, delegated to the conscience of the just man, and to the arm of the people. This is what was destined to live; this is what has lived. When, at the end of a century of vain expectation, the materialistic hope of a near end of the world was exhausted, the true kingdom of God became apparent. Accommodating explanations threw

[1] Matt. vi. 10, 33; Mark xii. 34; Luke xi. 2, xii. 31, xvii. 20, 21, and following. [2] See especially Mark xii. 34.

a veil over the material kingdom, which was then seen to be incapable of realization. The Apocalypse of John, the chief canonical book of the New Testament,[1] being too formally tied to the idea of an immediate catastrophe, became of secondary importance, was held to be unintelligible, tortured in a thousand ways and almost rejected. At least, its accomplishment was adjourned to an indefinite future. Some poor benighted ones who, in a fully enlightened age, still preserved the hopes of the first disciples, became heretics (Ebionites, Millenarians), lost in the shallows of Christianity. Mankind had passed to another kingdom of God. The degree of truth contained in the thought of Jesus had prevailed over the chimera which obscured it.

Let us not, however, despise this chimera, which has been the thick rind of the sacred fruit on which we live. This fantastic kingdom of heaven, this endless pursuit after a city of God, which has constantly preoccupied Christianity during its long career, has been the principle of that great instinct of futurity which has animated all reformers, persistent believers in the Apocalypse, from Joachim of Flora down to the Protestant sectary of our days. This impotent effort to establish a perfect society has been the source of the extraordinary tension which has always made the true Christian an athlete struggling against the existing order of things. The idea of the "kingdom of God," and the Apocalypse, which is the complete image of it, are thus, in a sense, the highest and most poetic expressions of human progress. But they have necessarily given rise to great errors. The end of the world, suspended as a perpetual menace over mankind, was, by the periodical panics which it caused during centuries, a great hin-

[1] Justin, *Dial. cum Tryph.*, 81.

drance to all secular development. Society being no longer certain of its existence, contracted therefrom a degree of trepidation, and those habits of servile humility, which rendered the Middle Ages so inferior to ancient and modern times.[1] A profound change had also taken place in the mode of regarding the coming of Christ. When it was first announced to mankind that the end of the world was about to come, like the infant which receives death with a smile, it experienced the greatest access of joy that it has ever felt. But in growing old, the world became attached to life. The day of grace, so long expected by the simple souls of Galilee, became to these iron ages a day of wrath: *Dies iræ, dies illa!* But, even in the midst of barbarism, the idea of the kingdom of God continued fruitful. In spite of the feudal church, of sects, and of religious orders, holy persons continued to protest, in the name of the Gospel, against the iniquity of the world. Even in our days, troubled days, in which Jesus has no more authentic followers than those who seem to deny him, the dreams of an ideal organization of society, which have so much analogy with the aspirations of the primitive Christian sects, are only in one sense the blossoming of the same idea. They are one of the branches of that immense tree in which germinates all thought of a future, and of which the "kingdom of God" will be eternally the root and stem. All the social revolutions of humanity will be grafted on this phrase. But, tainted by a coarse materialism, and aspiring to the impossible, that is to say, to found universal happiness upon political and economical measures, the "so-

---

[1] See, for example, the prologue of Gregory of Tours to his *Histoire Ecclesiastique des Francs,* and the numerous documents of the first half of the Middle Ages, beginning by the formula, "On the approach of the night of the world. . . . ."

cialist" attempts of our time will remain unfruitful until they take as their rule the true spirit of Jesus, I mean absolute idealism—the principle that, in order to possess the world, we must renounce it.

The phrase, "kingdom of God," expresses also, very happily, the want which the soul experiences of a supplementary destiny, of a compensation for the present life. Those who do not accept the definition of man as a compound of two substances, and who regard the Deistical dogma of the immortality of the soul as in contradiction with physiology, love to fall back upon the hope of a final reparation, which under an unknown form shall satisfy the wants of the heart of man. Who knows if the highest term of progress after millions of ages may not evoke the absolute conscience of the universe, and in this conscience the awakening of all that has lived? A sleep of a million of years is not longer than the sleep of an hour. St. Paul, on this hypothesis, was right in saying, *In ictu oculi!*[1] It is certain that moral and virtuous humanity will have its reward, that one day the ideas of the poor but honest man will judge the world, and that on that day the ideal figure of Jesus will be the confusion of the frivolous who have not believed in virtue, and of the selfish who have not been able to attain to it. The favorite phrase of Jesus continues, therefore, full of an eternal beauty. A kind of exalted divination seems to have maintained it in a vague sublimity, embracing at the same time various orders of truths.

[1] 1 Cor. xv. 52.

CHAPTER XVIII.

INSTITUTIONS OF JESUS.

THAT Jesus was never entirely absorbed in his apocalyptic ideas is proved, moreover, by the fact that at the very time he was most preoccupied with them, he laid with rare forethought the foundation of a church destined to endure. It is scarcely possible to doubt that he himself chose from among his disciples those who were pre-eminently called the "apostles," or the "twelve," since on the day after his death we find them forming a distinct body, and filling up by election the vacancies that had arisen in their midst.[1] They were the two sons of Jonas; the two sons of Zebedee; James, son of Cleophas; Philip; Nathaniel bar-Tolmai; Thomas; Levi, or Matthew, the son of Alphæus; Simon Zelotes; Thaddeus or Lebbæus; and Judas of Kerioth.[2] It is probable that the idea of the twelve tribes of Israel had had some share in the choice of this number.[3]

The "twelve," at all events, formed a group of privileged disciples, among whom Peter maintained a fraternal priority,[4] and to them Jesus confided the propagation of his work. There was nothing, however, which presented the appearance of a regularly organized sacerdotal school. The lists of the "twelve," which have been preserved, contain many uncertainties

[1] *Acts* i. 15, and following; 1 Cor. xv. 5; Gal. i. 10.
[2] Matt. x. 2. and following; Mark iii. 16, and following; Luke vi. 14, and following; *Acts* i. 13; Papias, in Eusebius, *Hist. Eccl.,* iii. 39.
[3] Matt. xix. 28; Luke xxii. 30.
[4] *Acts* i. 15, ii. 14, v. 2, 3, 29, viii. 19, xv. 7; Gal. i. 18.

and contradictions; two or three of those who figure in them have remained completely obscure. Two, at least, Peter and Philip,[1] were married and had children.

Jesus evidently confided secrets to the twelve, which he forbade them to communicate to the world.[2] It seems as if his plan at times was to surround himself with a degree of mystery, to postpone the most important testimony respecting himself till after his death, and to reveal himself completely only to his disciples, confiding to them the care of demonstrating him afterward to the world.[3] "What I tell you in darkness, that speak ye in light; and what ye hear in the ear, that preach ye upon the housetops." This spared him the necessity of too precise declarations, and created a kind of medium between the public and himself. It is clear that there were certain teachings confined to the apostles, and that he explained many parables to them, the meaning of which was ambiguous to the multitude.[4] An enigmatical form and a degree of oddness in connecting ideas were customary in the teachings of the doctors, as may be seen in the sentences of the *Pirké Aboth.* Jesus explained to his intimate friends whatever was peculiar in his apothegms or in his apologues, and showed them his meaning stripped of the wealth of illustration which sometimes obscured it.[5] Many of these explanations appear to have been carefully preserved.[6]

[1]For Peter. see ante, p. 174; for Philip, see Papias, Polycrates, and Clement of Alexandria, quoted by Eusebius, *Hist. Eccl.,* iii. 30, 31, 39, v. 24.   [2]Matt. xvi. 20, xvii. 9; Mark viii. 30, ix. 8. [3]Matt. x. 26, 27; Mark iv. 21, and following; Luke viii. 17, xii. 2, and following; John xiv. 22.
[4]Matt. xiii. 10, and following, 34 and following; Mark iv. 10, and following, 33, and following; Luke viii. 9, and following; xii. 41.
[5]Matt. xvi. 6, and following; Mark vii. 17-23.
[6]Matt. xiii. 18, and following; Mark vii. 18, and following.

During the lifetime of Jesus, the apostles preached,[1] but without ever departing far from him. Their preaching, moreover, was limited to the announcement of the speedy coming of the kingdom of God.[2] They went from town to town, receiving hospitality, or rather taking it themselves, according to the custom of the country. The guest in the East has much authority; he is superior to the master of the house, who has the greatest confidence in him. This fireside preaching is admirably adapted to the propagation of new doctrines. The hidden treasure is communicated, and payment is thus made for what is received; politeness and good feeling lend their aid; the household is touched and converted. Remove Oriental hospitality, and it would be impossible to explain the propagation of Christianity. Jesus, who adhered greatly to good old customs, encouraged his disciples to make no scruple of profiting by this ancient public right, probably already abolished in the great towns where there were hostelries.[3] "The laborer," said he, "is worthy of his hire!" Once installed in any house, they were to remain there, eating and drinking what was offered them, as long as their mission lasted.

Jesus desired that, in imitation of his example, the messengers of the glad tidings should render their preaching agreeable by kindly and polished manners. He directed that, on entering into a house, they should give the salaam or greeting. Some hesitated; the salaam being then, as now, in the East, a sign of religious communion, which is not risked with persons of a doubtful faith. "Fear nothing," said Jesus; "if

[1] Luke ix. 6.
[2] Luke x. 11.
[3] The Greek word πανδοκεῖον, in all the languages of the Semitic East. designates an hostelry.

no one in the house is worthy of your salute, it will return unto you."[1] Sometimes, in fact, the apostles of the kingdom of God were badly received, and came to complain to Jesus, who generally sought to soothe them. Some of them, persuaded of the omnipotence of their master, were hurt at this forbearance. The sons of Zebedee wanted him to call down fire from heaven upon the inhospitable towns.[2] Jesus received these outbursts with a subtle irony, and stopped them by saying: "The Son of man is not come to destroy men's lives, but to save them."

He sought in every way to establish as a principle that his apostles were as himself.[3] It was believed that he had communicated his marvellous virtues to them. They cast out demons, prophesied, and formed a school of renowned exorcists,[4] although certain cases were beyond their power.[5] They also wrought cures, either by the imposition of hands, or by the anointing with oil,[6] one of the fundamental processes of Oriental medicine. Lastly, like the Psylli, they could handle serpents and could drink deadly potions with impunity.[7] The further we get from Jesus—the more offensive does this theurgy become. But there is no doubt that it was generally received by the primitive Church, and that it held an important place in the estimation of the world around.[8] Charlatans, as generally happens, took advantage of this movement of popular credulity.

[1] Matt. x. 11, and following; Mark vi. 10, and following; Luke x. 5, and following. Comp. 2 Epistle of John, 10, 11.
[2] Luke ix. 52, and following.
[3] Matt. x. 40, 42, xxv. 35, and following; Mark ix. 40; Luke x. 16; John xiii. 20.
[4] Matt. vii. 22, x. 1; Mark iii. 15, vi. 13; Luke x. 17.
[5] Matt. xvii. 18, 19.
[6] Mark vi. 13, xvi. 18; Epist. Jas. v. 14.
[7] Mark xvi. 18; Luke x. 19.
[8] Mark xvi. 20.

Even in the lifetime of Jesus, many, without being his disciples, cast out demons in his name. The true disciples were much displeased at this, and sought to prevent them. Jesus, who saw that this was really an homage paid to his renown, was not very severe toward them.[1] It must be observed, moreover, that the exercise of these gifts had to some degree become a trade. Carrying the logic of absurdity to the extreme, certain men cast out demons by Beelzebub,[2] the prince of demons. They imagined that this sovereign of the infernal regions must have entire authority over his subordinates, and that in acting through him they were certain to make the intruding spirit depart.[3] Some even sought to buy from the disciples of Jesus the secret of the miraculous powers which had been conferred upon them.[4] The germ of a church from this time began to appear. This fertile idea of the power of men in association (*ecclesia*) was doubtless derived from Jesus. Full of the purely idealistic doctrine that it is the union of love which brings souls together, he declared that whenever men assembled in his name, he would be in their midst. He confided to the Church the right to bind and to unbind (that is to say, to render certain things lawful or unlawful), to remit sins, to reprimand, to warn with authority, and to pray with the certainty of being heard favorably.[5] It is possible that many of these words may have been attributed to the master, in order to give a warrant to the collective authority which was afterward sought to be substituted for that of Jesus. At all events, it was only after his

[1] Mark ix. 37, 38; Luke ix. 49, 50.
[2] An ancient god of the Philistines, transformed by the Jews into a demon.
[3] Matt. xii. 24, and following.   [4] *Acts* viii. 18, and following
[5] Matt. xviii. 17, and following; John xx. 23.

death that particular churches were established, and even this first constitution was made purely and simply on the model of the synagogue. Many personages who had loved Jesus much, and had founded great hopes upon him, as Joseph of Arimathea, Lazarus, Mary Magdalen, and Nicodemus, did not, it seems, join these churches, but clung to the tender or respectful memory which they had preserved of him.

Moreover, there is no trace, in the teaching of Jesus, of an applied morality or of a canonical law, ever so slightly defined. Once only, respecting marriage, he spoke decidedly, and forbade divorce.[1] Neither was there any theology or creed. There were indefinite views respecting the Father, the Son, and the Spirit,[2] from which, afterward, were drawn the Trinity and the Incarnation, but they were then only in a state of indeterminate imagery. The later books of the Jewish canon recognized the Holy Spirit, a sort of divine hypostasis, sometimes identified with Wisdom or the Word.[3] Jesus insisted upon this point,[4] and announced to his disciples a baptism by fire and by the spirit,[5] as much preferable to that of John, a baptism which they believed they had received, after the death of Jesus, in the form of a great wind and tongues of fire.[6] The Holy Spirit thus sent by the Father was to teach them all truth, and testify to that which Jesus himself had promulgated.[7] In order to designate this Spirit, Jesus made use of the word *Peraklit,* which the Syro-Chal-

---

[1]Matt. xix. 3, and following.
[2]Matt. xxviii. 19. Comp. Matt. iii. 16, 17; John xv. 26.
[3]*Sap.* i. 7, vii. 7, ix. 17, xii. 1; *Eccles.* i. 9, xv. 5, xxiv. 27; xxxix. 8; *Judith* xvi. 17.
[4]Matt. x. 20; Luke xii. 12, xxiv. 49; John xiv. 26, xv. 26.
[5]Matt. iii. 11; Mark i. 8; Luke iii. 16; John i. 26, iii. 5; *Acts* i. 5, 8, x. 47.   [6]*Acts* ii. 1-4, xi. 15, xix. 6. Cf. John vii. 39.
[7]John xv. 26, xvi. 13.

daic had borrowed from the Greek ($\pi\alpha\rho\acute{\alpha}\kappa\lambda\eta\tau\sigma$), and which appears to have had in his mind the meaning of "advocate,"[1] "counsellor,"[2] and sometimes that of "interpreter of celestial truths," and of "teacher charged to reveal to men the hitherto hidden mysteries."[3] He regarded himself as a *Peraklit* to his disciples,[4] and the Spirit which was to come after his death would only take his place. This was an application of the process which the Jewish and Christian theologies would follow during centuries, and which was to produce a whole series of divine assessors, the *Metathronos,* the *Synadelphe* or *Sandalphon,* and all the personifications of the Cabbala. But in Judaism, these creations were to remain free and individual speculations, whilst in Christianity, commencing with the fourth century, they were to form the very essence of orthodoxy and of the universal doctrine.

It is unnecessary to remark how remote from the thought of Jesus was the idea of a religious book, containing a code and articles of faith. Not only did he not write, but it was contrary to the spirit of the infant sect to produce sacred books. They believed themselves on the eve of the great final catastrophe. The Messiah came to put the seal upon the Law and the Prophets, not to promulgate new Scriptures. With the exception of the Apocalypse, which was in one sense the only revealed book of the infant Christianity, all the other writings of the apostolic age were works evoked by existing circumstances, making no pretensions to furnish a completely dogmatic whole. The

---

[1] To *Peraklit* was opposed *Katigor,* ($\kappa\alpha\tau\acute{\eta}\gamma o\rho os$), the "accuser."
[2] John xiv. 16; 1st Epistle of John ii. 1.
[3] John xiv. 26, xv. 26, xvi. 7, and following. Comp. Philo, *De Mundi opificio,* § 6.
[4] John xiv. 16. Comp. the epistle before cited, *l. c.*

Gospels had at first an entirely personal character, and much less authority than tradition.[1]

Had the sect, however, no sacrament, no rite, no sign of union? It had one which all tradition ascribes to Jesus. One of the favorite ideas of the master was that he was the new bread, bread very superior to manna, and on which mankind was to live. This idea, the germ of the Eucharist, was at times expressed by him in singularly concrete forms. On one occasion especially, in the synagogue of Capernaum, he took a decided step, which cost him several of his disciples. "Verily, verily, I say unto you, Moses gave you not that bread from heaven; but my Father giveth you the true bread from heaven."[2] And he added, "I am the bread of life: he that cometh to me shall never hunger, and he that believeth on me shall never thirst."[3] These words excited much murmuring. "The Jews then murmured at him because he said, I am the bread which came down from heaven. And they said, Is not this Jesus the son of Joseph, whose father and mother we know? how is it then that he saith, I came down from heaven?" But Jesus insisting with still more force, said, "I am that bread of life; your fathers did eat manna in the wilderness and are dead. This is the bread which cometh down from heaven, that a man may eat thereof, and not die. I am the living bread which came down from heaven; if any man eat of this bread, he shall live for ever: and the bread that I will give is my flesh, which I will give for the life of the world."[4] The offence was now at its height: "How

[1] Papias, in Eusebius, *Hist. Eccl.*, iii. 39.
[2] John vi. 32, and following.
[3] We find an analogous form of expression provoking a similar misunderstanding, in John iv. 10, and following.
[4] All these discourses bear too strongly the imprint of the style

can this man give us his flesh to eat?" Jesus going still further, said: "Verily, verily, I say unto you, except ye eat the flesh of the Son of man, and drink his blood, ye have no life in you. Whoso eateth my flesh and drinketh my blood, hath eternal life, and I will raise him up at the last day. For my flesh is meat indeed, and my blood is drink indeed. He that eateth my flesh and drinketh my blood dwelleth in me, and I in him. As the living Father has sent me, and I live by the Father: so he that eateth me, even he shall live by me. This is that bread which came down from heaven: not as your fathers did eat manna, and are dead: he that eateth of this bread shall live for ever." Several of his disciples were offended at such obstinacy in paradox, and ceased to follow him. Jesus did not retract; he only added: "It is the spirit that quickeneth; the flesh profiteth nothing. The words that I speak unto you, they are spirit, and they are life." The twelve remained faithful, notwithstanding this strange preaching. It gave to Cephas, in particular, an opportunity of showing his absolute devotion, and of proclaiming once more, "Thou art that Christ, the Son of the living God."

It is probable that from that time, in the common repasts of the sect, there was established some custom which was derived from the discourse so badly received by the men of Capernaum. But the apostolic traditions on this subject are very diverse and probably intentionally incomplete. The synoptical gospels suppose that a unique sacramental act served as basis to the mysterious rite, and declare this to have been "the last

peculiar to John, for them to be regarded as exact. The anecdote related in chapter vi. of the fourth Gospel cannot, however, be entirely stripped of historical reality.

supper." John, who has preserved the incident at the synagogue of Capernaum, does not speak of such an act, although he describes the last supper at great length. Elsewhere we see Jesus recognized in the breaking of bread,[1] as if this act had been to those who associated with him the most characteristic of his person. When he was dead, the form under which he appeared to the pious memory of his disciples, was that of president of a mysterious banquet, taking the bread, blessing it, breaking and presenting it to those present.[2] It is probable that this was one of his habits, and that at such times he was particularly loving and tender. One material circumstance, the presence of fish upon the table (a striking indication, which proves that the rite had its birth on the shore of Lake Tiberias[3]), was itself almost sacramental, and became a necessary part of the conceptions of the sacred feast.[4]

Their repasts were among the sweetest moments of the infant community. At these times they all assembled; the master spoke to each one, and kept up a charming and lively conversation. Jesus loved these seasons, and was pleased to see his spiritual family thus grouped around him.[5] The participation of the same bread was considered as a kind of communion, a reciprocal bond. The master used, in this respect, extremely

[1] Luke xxiv. 30, 35.   [2] Luke *l. c.;* John xxi. 13.

[3] Comp. Matt. vii. 10, xiv. 17, and following, xv. 34, and following; Mark vi. 38, and following, Luke ix. 13, and following, xi. 11, xxiv. 42; John vi. 9, and following, xxi. 9, and following. The district round Lake Tiberias is the only place in Palestine where fish forms a considerable portion of the diet.

[4] John xxi. 13; Luke xxiv. 42, 43. Compare the oldest representations of the Lord's Supper, related or corrected by M. de Rossi, in his dissertation on the ΙΧΘΥΣ (*Spicilegium Solesmense* de dom Pitra, v. iii., p. 568, and following). The meaning of the anagram which the word ΙΧΘΥΣ contains, was probably combined with a more ancient tradition on the place of fish in the Gospel repasts.

[5] Luke xxii. 15.

strong terms, which were afterward taken in a very
literal sense. Jesus was, at the same time, very idealistic in his conceptions, and very materialistic in his
expression of them. Wishing to express the thought
that the believer only lives by him, that altogether
(body, blood, and soul) he was the life of the truly
faithful, he said to his disciples, "I am your nourishment"—a phrase which, turned in figurative style,
became, "My flesh is your bread, my blood your drink."
Added to this, the modes of speech employed by Jesus,
always strongly subjective, carried him still further.
At table, pointing to the food, he said, "I am here"—
holding the bread—"this is my body;" and of the
wine, "This is my blood"—all modes of speech which
were equivalent to, "I am your nourishment."

This mysterious rite obtained great importance in
the lifetime of Jesus. It was probably established
some time before the last journey to Jerusalem, and it
was the result of a general doctrine much more than a
determinate act. After the death of Jesus, it became
the great symbol of Christian communion,[1] and it is to
the most solemn moment of the life of the Saviour that
its establishment is referred. It was wished to see, in
the consecration of bread and wine, a farewell memorial
which Jesus, at the moment of quitting life, had left to
his disciples.[2] They recognized Jesus himself in this
sacrament. The wholly spiritual idea of the presence
of souls, which was one of the most familiar to the
Master, which made him say, for instance, that he was
personally with his disciples[3] when they were assembled in his name, rendered this easily admissible. Jesus,
we have already said, never had a very defined notion

---

[1] *Acts* ii. 42, 46.
[3] I *Cor.* xi. 20, and following.   [2] *Matt.* xviii. 20.

of that which constitutes individuality.   In the degree
of exaltation to which he had attained, the ideal surpassed everything to such an extent that the body
counted for nothing.   We are one when we love one
another, when we live in dependence on each other;
it was thus that he and his disciples were one.[1]   His
disciples adopted the same language.   Those who for
years had lived with him, had seen him constantly take
the bread and the cup "between his holy and venerable
hands,"[2] and thus offer himself to them.   It was he
whom they ate and drank; he became the true passover,
the former one having been abrogated by his blood.
It is impossible to translate into our essentially determined idiom, in which a rigorous distinction between
the material and the metaphorical must always be observed, habits of style the essential character of which
is to attribute to metaphor, or rather to the idea it
represents, a complete reality.

[1] John xii. entirely.
[2] Canon of the Greek Masses and the Latin Mass (very ancient).

CHAPTER XIX.

INCREASING PROGRESSION OF ENTHUSIASM AND OF EXALTATION.

It is clear that such a religious society, founded solely on the expectation of the kingdom of God, must be in itself very incomplete. The first Christian generation lived almost entirely upon expectations and dreams. On the eve of seeing the world come to an end, they regarded as useless everything which only served to prolong it. Possession of property was interdicted.[1] Everything which attaches man to earth, everything which draws him aside from heaven, was to be avoided. Although several of the disciples were married, there was to be no more marriage on becoming a member of the sect.[2] The celibate was greatly preferred; even in marriage continence was recommended.[3] At one time the master seems to approve of those who should mutilate themselves in prospect of the kingdom of God.[4] In this he was consistent with his principle—"If thy hand or thy foot offend thee, cut them off, and cast them from thee; it is better for thee to enter into life halt or maimed, rather than having two hands or two feet to be cast into everlasting fire. And if thine eye offend thee, pluck it out, and cast it from thee; it is better for thee to enter into life with one eye, rather than having two eyes to be cast into

[1] Luke xiv. 33; *Acts* iv. 32, and following, v. 1-11.
[2] Matt. xix. 10, and following; Luke xviii. 29, and following.
[3] This is the constant doctrine of Paul. Comp. *Rev.* xiv. 4.
[4] Matt. xix. 12.

hell-fire."[1] The cessation of generation was often considered as the sign and condition of the kingdom of God.[2]

Never, we perceive, would this primitive Church have formed a lasting society but for the great variety of germs deposited by Jesus in his teaching. It required more than a century for the true Christian Church—that which has converted the world—to disengage itself from this little sect of "latter-day saints," and to become a framework applicable to the whole of human society. The same thing, indeed, took place in Buddhism, which at first was founded only for monks. The same thing would have happened in the order of St. Francis, if that order had succeeded in its pretension of becoming the rule of the whole of human society. Essentially Utopian in their origin, and succeeding by their very exaggeration, the great systems of which we have just spoken have only laid hold of the world by being profoundly modified, and by abandoning their excesses. Jesus did not advance beyond this first and entirely monachal period, in which it was believed that the impossible could be attempted with impunity. He made no concession to necessity. He boldly preached war against nature, and total severance from ties of blood. "Verily I say unto you," said he, "there is no man that hath left house, or parents, or brethren, or wife, or children, for the kingdom of God's sake, who shall not receive manifold more in this present time, and in the world to come life everlasting."[3]

The teachings which Jesus is reputed to have given

[1] Matt. xviii. 8, 9. Cf. Talmud of Babylon, *Niddah*, 13 *b*.
[2] Matt. xxii. 30; Mark xii. 25; Luke xx. 35; Ebionite Gospel, entitled "Of the Egyptians," in Clem. of Alex., *Strom.* iii. 9, 13, and Clem. Rom., Epist. ii. 12.   [3] Luke xviii. 29, 30.

to his disciples breathe the same exaltation.[1] He who was so tolerant to the world outside, he who contented himself sometimes with half adhesions,[2] exercised toward his own an extreme rigor. He would have no "all buts." We should call it an "order," constituted by the most austere rules. Faithful to his idea that the cares of life trouble man, and draw him downward, Jesus required from his associates a complete detachment from the earth, an absolute devotion to his work. They were not to carry with them either money or provisions for the way, not even a scrip, or change of raiment. They must practise absolute poverty, live on alms and hospitality. "Freely ye have received, freely give,"[3] said he, in his beautiful language. Arrested and arraigned before the judges, they were not to prepare their defence; the *Peraklit,* the heavenly advocate, would inspire them with what they ought to say. The Father would send them his Spirit from on high, which would become the principle of all their acts, the director of their thoughts, and their guide through the world.[4] If driven from any town, they were to shake the dust from their shoes, declaring always the proximity of the kingdom of God, that none might plead ignorance. "Ye shall not have gone over the cities of Israel," added he, "till the Son of man be come."

A strange ardor animates all these discourses, which may in part be the creation of the enthusiasm of his disciples,[5] but which even in that case came indirectly

[1] Matt. x., entirely, xxiv. 9; Mark vi. 8, and following, ix. 40, xiii. 9-13; Luke x. 3, and following, x. 1, and following, xii. 4, and following, xxi. 17; John xv. 18, and following, xvii. 14.

[2] Mark ix. 38, and following.

[3] Matt. x. 8. Comp. Midrash Ialkout, *Deut.,* sect. 824.

[4] Matt. x. 20; John xiv. 16, and following, 26, xv. 26, xvi. 7, 13.

[5] The expressions in Matt. x. 38, xvi. 24; Mark viii. 34; Luke xiv. 27, can only have been conceived after the death of Jesus.

from Jesus, for it was he who had inspired the enthusiasm. He predicted for his followers severe persecutions and the hatred of mankind. He sent them forth as lambs in the midst of wolves. They would be scourged in the synagogues, and dragged to prison. Brother should deliver up brother to death, and the father his son. When they were persecuted in one country they were to flee to another. "The disciple," said he, "is not above his master, nor the servant above his lord. Fear not them which kill the body, but are not able to kill the soul. Are not two sparrows sold for a farthing? and one of them shall not fall to the ground without your Father. But the very hairs of your head are all numbered. Fear ye not, therefore, ye are of more value than many sparrows."[1] "Whosoever, therefore," continued he, "shall confess me before men, him will I confess also before my Father which is in heaven. But whosoever shall deny me before men, him will I also deny before my Father which is in heaven."[2]

In these fits of severity he went so far as to abolish all natural ties. His requirements had no longer any bounds. Despising the healthy limits of man's nature, he demanded that he should exist only for him, that he should love him alone. "If any man come to me," said he, "and hate not his father, and mother, and wife, and children, and brethren, and sisters, and his own life also, he cannot be my disciple."[3] "So likewise, whosoever he be of you that forsaketh not all that he hath, he cannot be my disciple."[4] There was, at such

[1] Matt. x. 24-31; Luke xii. 4-7.
[2] Matt. x. 32, 33; Mark viii. 38; Luke ix. 26, xii. 8, 9.
[3] Luke xiv. 26. We must here take into account the exaggeration of Luke's style.
[4] Luke xiv. 33.

times, something strange and more than human in his
words; they were like a fire utterly consuming life, and
reducing everything to a frightful wilderness. The
harsh and gloomy feeling of distaste for the world, and
of excessive self-abnegation which characterizes Christian perfection, was originated, not by the refined and
cheerful moralist of earlier days, but by the sombre
giant whom a kind of grand presentiment was with-
drawing, more and more, out of the pale of humanity.
We should almost say that, in these moments of conflict with the most legitimate cravings of the heart,
Jesus had forgotten the pleasure of living, of loving, of
seeing, and of feeling. Employing still more unmeas-
ured language, he even said, "If any man will come
after me, let him deny himself and follow me. He that
loveth father or mother more than me, is not worthy
of me; and he that loveth son or daughter more than
me, is not worthy of me. He that findeth his life shall
lose it, and he that loseth his life for my sake and the
gospel's, shall find it. What is a man profited if he
shall gain the whole world, and lose his own soul?"[1]
Two anecdotes of the kind we cannot accept as historical, but which, although they were exaggerations,
were intended to represent a characteristic feature,
clearly illustrate this defiance of nature. He said to
one man, "Follow me!"—"But he said, Lord, suffer
me first to go and bury my father." Jesus answered,
"Let the dead bury their dead: but go thou and preach
the kingdom of God." Another said to him, Lord,
I will follow thee; but let me first go bid them farewell, which are at home at my house." Jesus replied,
"No man, having put his hand to the plough, and look-

[1]Matt. x. 37-39, xvi. 24, 25; Luke ix. 23-25, xiv. 26, 27, xvii. 33;
John xii. 25.

ing back, is fit for the kingdom of God."[1]   An extraordinary confidence, and at times accents of singular sweetness, reversing all our ideas of him, caused these exaggerations to be easily received.   "Come unto me," cried he, "all ye that labor and are heavy laden, and I will give you rest.   Take my yoke upon you, and learn of me: for I am meek and lowly in heart: and ye shall find rest unto your souls.   For my yoke is easy, and my burden is light."[2]

A great danger threatened the future of this exalted morality, thus expressed in hyperbolical language and with a terrible energy.   By detaching man from earth the ties of life were severed.   The Christian would be praised for being a bad son, or a bad patriot, if it was for Christ that he resisted his father and fought against his country.   The ancient city, the parent republic, the state, or the law common to all, were thus placed in hostility with the kingdom of God.   A fatal germ of theocracy was introduced into the world.

From this point, another consequence may be perceived.   This morality, created for a temporary crisis, when introduced into a peaceful country, and in the midst of a society assured of its own duration, must seem impossible.   The Gospel was thus destined to become a Utopia for Christians, which few would care to realize.   These terrible maxims would, for the greater number, remain in profound oblivion, an oblivion encouraged by the clergy itself; the Gospel man would prove a dangerous man.   The most selfish, proud, hard and worldly of all human beings, a Louis XIV. for instance, would find priests to persuade him, in spite of the Gospel, that he was a Christian.   But, on the other hand, there would always be found holy men who

[1] Matt. viii. 21, 22 ; Luke ix. 59-62.   [2] Matt. xi. 28-30.

would take the sublime paradoxes of Jesus literally. Perfection being placed beyond the ordinary conditions of society, and a complete Gospel life being only possible away from the world, the principle of asceticism and of monasticism was established. Christian societies would have two moral rules; the one moderately heroic for common men, the other exalted in the extreme for the perfect man; and the perfect man would be the monk, subjected to rules which professed to realize the gospel ideal. It is certain that this ideal, if only on account of the celibacy and poverty it imposed, could not become the common law. The monk would be thus, in one sense, the only true Christian. Common sense revolts at these excesses; and if we are guided by it, to demand the impossible, is a mark of weakness and error. But common sense is a bad judge where great matters are in question. To obtain little from humanity we must ask much. The immense moral progress which we owe to the Gospel is the result of its exaggerations. It is thus that it has been, like stoicism, but with infinitely greater fulness, a living argument for the divine powers in man, an exalted monument of the potency of the will.

We may easily imagine that to Jesus, at this period of his life, everything which was not the kingdom of God had absolutely disappeared. He was, if we may say so, totally outside nature: family, friendship, country, had no longer any meaning for him. No doubt from this moment he had already sacrificed his life. Sometimes we are tempted to believe that, seeing in his own death a means of founding his kingdom, he deliberately determined to allow himself to be killed.[1] At other times, although such a thought only afterward

[1]Matt. xvi. 21-23, xvii. 12, 21, 22.

became a doctrine, death presented itself to him as a sacrifice, destined to appease his Father and to save mankind.[1] A singular taste for persecution and torments[2] possessed him. His blood appeared to him as the water of a second baptism with which he ought to be baptized, and he seemed possessed by a strange haste to anticipate this baptism, which alone could quench his thirst.[3]

The grandeur of his views upon the future was at times surprising. He did not conceal from himself the terrible storm he was about to cause in the world. "Think not," said he, with much boldness and beauty, "that I am come to send peace on earth: I came not to send peace, but a sword. There shall be five in one house divided, three against two, and two against three. I am come to set a man at variance against his father, and the daughter against her mother, and the daughter-in-law against her mother-in-law. And a man's foes shall be they of his own household."[4] "I am come to send fire on the earth; and what will I, if it be already kindled?"[5] "They shall put you out of the synagogues," he continued; "yea, the time cometh, that whosoever killeth you, will think that he doeth God service."[6] "If the world hate you, ye know that it hated me before it hated you. Remember the word that I said unto you: The servant is not greater than his lord. If they have persecuted me, they will also persecute you."[7]

Carried away by this fearful progression of enthusiasm, and governed by the necessities of a preaching becoming daily more exalted, Jesus was no longer

[1] Mark x. 45.   [2] Luke vi. 22, and following.   [3] Luke xii. 50.
[4] Matt. x. 34-36; Luke xii. 51-53. Compare Micah vii. 5, 6.
[5] Luke xii. 49. See the Greek text.
[6] John xvi. 2.   [7] John xv. 18-20.

free; he belonged to his mission, and, in one sense, to mankind. Sometimes one would have said that his reason was disturbed. He suffered great mental anguish and agitation.[1] The great vision of the kingdom of God, glistening before his eyes, bewildered him. His disciples at times thought him mad.[2] His enemies declared him to be possessed.[3] His excessively impassioned temperament carried him incessantly beyond the bounds of human nature. He laughed at all human systems, and his work not being a work of the reason, that which he most imperiously required was "faith."[4] This was the word most frequently repeated in the little guest-chamber. It is the watchword of all popular movements. It is clear that none of these movements would take place if it were necessary that their author should gain his disciples one by one by force of logic. Reflection leads only to doubt. If the authors of the French Revolution, for instance, had had to be previously convinced by lengthened meditations, they would all have become old without accomplishing anything; Jesus, in like manner, aimed less at convincing his hearers than at exciting their enthusiasm. Urgent and imperative, he suffered no opposition: men must be converted, nothing less would satisfy him. His natural gentleness seemed to have abandoned him; he was sometimes harsh and capricious.[5] His disciples at times did not understand him, and experienced in his presence a feeling akin to fear.[6] Sometimes his displeasure at the slightest opposition

---

[1] John xii. 27.   [2] Mark iii. 21, and following.
[3] Mark iii. 22; John vii. 20, viii. 48, and following, x. 20, and following.
[4] Matt. viii. 10, ix. 2, 22, 28, 29, xvii. 19; John vi. 29, etc.
[5] Matt. xvii. 16; Mark iii. 5, ix. 18; Luke viii. 45, ix. 41.
[6] It is in Mark especially that this feature is visible; iv. 40, v. 15, ix. 31, x. 32.

led him to commit inexplicable and apparently absurd acts.[1]

It was not that his virtue deteriorated; but his struggle for the ideal against the reality became insupportable. Contact with the world pained and revolted him. Obstacles irritated him. His idea of the Son of God became disturbed and exaggerated. The fatal law which condemns an idea to decay as soon as it seeks to convert men applied to him. Contact with men degraded him to their level. The tone he had adopted could not be sustained more than a few months; it was time that death came to liberate him from an endurance strained to the utmost, to remove him from the impossibilities of an interminable path, and by delivering him from a trial in danger of being too prolonged, introduce him henceforth sinless into celestial peace.

[1]Mark xi. 12-14, 20, and following.

CHAPTER XX.

OPPOSITION TO JESUS.

DURING the first period of his career, it does not appear that Jesus met with any serious opposition. His preaching, thanks to the extreme liberty which was enjoyed in Galilee, and to the number of teachers who arose on all hands, made no noise beyond a restricted circle. But when Jesus entered upon a path brilliant with wonders and public successes, the storm began to gather. More than once he was obliged to conceal himself and fly.[1] Antipas, however, did not interfere with him, although Jesus expressed himself sometimes very severely respecting him.[2] At Tiberias, his usual residence, the Tetrarch was only one or two leagues distant from the district chosen by Jesus for the centre of his activity; he heard speak of his miracles, which he doubtless took to be clever tricks, and desired to see them.[3] The incredulous were at that time very curious about this class of illusions.[4] With his ordinary tact, Jesus refused to gratify him. He took care not to prejudice his position by mingling with an irreligious world, which wished to draw from him an idle amusement; he aspired only to gain the people; he reserved for the simple, means suitable to them alone.

On one occasion the report was spread that Jesus was no other than John the Baptist risen from the dead. Antipas became anxious and uneasy;[5] and employed

[1] Matt. xii. 14-16; Mark iii. 7, ix. 29, 30.
[2] Mark viii. 15; Luke xiii. 32. [3] Luke ix 9, xxiii. 8.
[4] *Lucius;* attributed to Lucian, 4.
[5] Matt. xiv. 1, and following; Mark vi. 14, and following; Luke ix. 7. and following.

artifice to rid his dominions of the new prophet. Certain Pharisees, under the pretence of regard for Jesus, came to tell him that Antipas was seeking to kill him. Jesus, notwithstanding his great simplicity, saw the snare, and did not depart.[1] His peaceful manners, and his remoteness from popular agitation, ultimately reassured the Tetrarch and dissipated the danger.

The new doctrine was by no means received with equal favor in all the towns of Galilee. Not only did incredulous Nazareth continue to reject him who was to become her glory; not only did his brothers persist in not believing in him,[2] but the cities of the lake themselves, in general well-disposed, were not all converted. Jesus often complained of the incredulity and hardness of heart which he encountered, and although it is natural that in such reproaches we make allowance for the exaggeration of the preacher, although we are sensible of that kind of *convicium seculi* which Jesus affected in imitation of John the Baptist,[3] it is clear that the country was far from yielding itself entirely a second time to the kingdom of God. "Woe unto thee, Chorazin! woe unto thee, Bethsaida!" cried he; "for if the mighty works which were done in you had been done in Tyre and Sidon, they would have repented long ago in sackcloth and ashes. But I say unto you, it shall be more tolerable for Tyre and Sidon at the day of judgment than for you. And thou, Capernaum, which art exalted unto heaven, shalt be brought down to hell; for if the mighty works which have been done in thee had been done in Sodom, it would have remained until this day. But I say unto you, That it shall be more toler-

---

[1] Luke xiii. 31, and following.
[2] John vii. 5.
[3] Matt. xii. 39, 45, xiii. 15, xvi. 4; Luke xi. 29.

able for the land of Sodom in the day of judgment than for thee."[1]   The queen of the south," added he, "shall rise up in the judgment of this generation, and shall condemn it: for she came from the uttermost parts of the earth to hear the wisdom of Solomon; and behold, a greater than Solomon is here.   The men of Nineveh shall rise in judgment with this generation, and shall condemn it: because they repented at the preaching of Jonas; and behold, a greater than Jonas is here."[2]   His wandering life, at first so full of charm, now began to weigh upon him.   "The foxes," said he, "have holes, and the birds of the air have nests; but the Son of man hath not where to lay his head."[3]   Bitterness and reproach took more and more hold upon him.   He accused unbelievers of not yielding to evidence, and said that, even at the moment in which the Son of man should appear in his celestial glory, there would still be men who would not believe in him.[4]

Jesus, in fact, was not able to receive opposition with the coolness of the philosopher, who, understanding the reason of the various opinions which divide the world, finds it quite natural that all should not agree with him.   One of the principal defects of the Jewish race is its harshness in controversy, and the abusive tone which it almost always infuses into it.   There never were in the world such bitter quarrels as those of the Jews among themselves.   It is the faculty of nice discernment which makes the polished and moderate man. Now, the lack of this faculty is one of the most constant features of the Semitic mind.   Subtle and refined works, the dialogues of Plato, for example, are alto-

[1] Matt. xi. 21-24; Luke x. 12-15.
[2] Matt. xii. 41, 42; Luke xi. 31, 32.
[3] Matt. viii. 20; Luke ix. 58.
[4] Luke xviii. 8.

gether unknown to these nations.   Jesus, who was exempt from almost all the defects of his race, and whose
leading quality was precisely an infinite delicacy, was
led in spite of himself to make use of the general style
in polemics.[1]   Like John the Baptist,[2] he employed
very harsh terms against his adversaries.   Of an exquisite gentleness with the simple, he was irritated at
incredulity, however little aggressive.[3]   He was no
longer the mild teacher who delivered the "Sermon on
the Mount," who had met with neither resistance nor
difficulty.   The passion that underlay his character led
him to make use of the keenest invectives.   This singular mixture ought not to surprise us.   M. de Lamennais, a man of our own times, has strikingly presented
the same contrast.   In his beautiful book, the "Words
of a Believer," the most immoderate anger and the
sweetest relentings alternate, as in a mirage.   This
man, who was extremely kind in the intercourse of
life, became madly intractable toward those who did
not agree with him.   Jesus, in like manner, applied to
himself, not without reason, the passage from Isaiah :[4]
"He shall not strive, nor cry; neither shall any man
hear his voice in the streets.   A bruised reed shall he
not break, and smoking flax shall he not quench."[5]
And yet many of the recommendations which he addressed to his disciples contain the germs of a true
fanaticism,[6] germs which the Middle Ages were to
develop in a cruel manner.   Must we reproach him for
this?   No revolution is effected without some harshness.   If Luther, or the actors in the French Revolution, had been compelled to observe the rules of polite-

[1]Matt. xii. 34, xv. 14, xxiii. 33.   [3]Matt. iii. 7.
[3]Matt. xii. 30; Luke xxi. 23.   [4]Isa. xlii. 2, 3.   [5]Matt. xii. 19-20.
[6]Matt. x. 14, 15, 21, and following, 34, and following; Luke
xix. 27.

ness, neither the Reformation nor the Revolution would have taken place. Let us congratulate ourselves in like manner that Jesus encountered no law which punished the invectives he uttered against one class of citizens. Had such a law existed, the Pharisees would have been inviolate. All the great things of humanity have been accomplished in the name of absolute principles. A critical philosopher would have said to his disciples: Respect the opinion of others; and believe that no one is so completely right that his adversary is completely wrong. But the action of Jesus has nothing in common with the disinterested speculation of the philosopher. To know that we have touched the ideal for a moment, and have been deterred by the wickedness of a few, is a thought insupportable to an ardent soul. What must it have been for the founder of a new world?

The invincible obstacle to the ideas of Jesus came especially from orthodox Judaism, represented by the Pharisees. Jesus became more and more alienated from the ancient Law. Now, the Pharisees were the true Jews; the nerve and sinew of Judaism. Although this party had its centre at Jerusalem, it had adherents either established in Galilee, or who often came there.[1] They were, in general, men of a narrow mind, caring much for externals; their devoutness was haughty, formal, and self-satisfied.[2] Their manners were ridiculous, and excited the smiles of even those who respected them. The epithets which the people gave them, and which savor of caricature, prove this. There

[1] Mark vii. 1; Luke v. 17, and following, vii. 36.
[2] Matt. vi. 2, 5, 16, ix. 11, 14, xii. 2, xxiii. 5, 15, 23; Luke v. 30, vi. 2, 7, xi. 39, and following, xviii. 12; John ix. 16; *Pirké Aboth*, i. 16; Jos., *Ant.*, XVII. ii. 4, XVIII. i. 3; *Vita*, 38; Talm. of Bab., *Sota*, 22 b.

was the "bandy-legged Pharisee" (*Nikfi*), who walked
in the streets dragging his feet and knocking them
against the stones; the "bloody-browed Pharisee"
(*Kizai*), who went with his eyes shut in order not to
see the women, and dashed his head so much against
the walls that it was always bloody; the "pestle Pharisee" (*Medinkia*), who kept himself bent double like the
handle of a pestle; the "Pharisee of strong shoulders'
(*Shikmi*), who walked with his back bent as if he
carried on his shoulders the whole burden of the Law;
the *"What-is-there-to-do?-I-do-it Pharisee,"* always on
the search for a precept to fulfil; and, lastly, the "dyed
Pharisee," whose externals of devotion were but a
varnish of hypocrisy.[1]   This strictness was, in fact,
often only apparent, and concealed in reality great
moral laxity.[2]   The people, nevertheless, were duped
by it.   The people, whose instinct is always right, even
when it is most astray respecting individuals, is very
easily deceived by false devotees.   That which it loves
in them is good and worthy of being loved; but it has
not sufficient penetration to distinguish the appearance
from the reality.

It is easy to understand the antipathy which, in such
an impassioned state of society, must necessarily break
out between Jesus and persons of this character. Jesus
recognized only the religion of the heart, whilst that of
the Pharisees consisted almost exclusively in obser-

[1] Talmud of Jerusalem, *Berakoth*, ix., sub fin.; *Sota*, v. 7; Talmud of Babylon, *Sota*, 22 b. The two compilations of this curious passage present considerable differences. We have, in general, followed the Babylonian compilation, which seems most
natural. Cf. Epiph., *Adv. Hær.*, xvi. 1. The passages in Epiphanes, and several of those of the Talmud, may, besides, relate
to an epoch posterior to Jesus, an epoch in which "Pharisee" had
become synonymous with "devotee."

[2] Matt. v. 20, xv. 4, xxiii. 3, 16, and following; John viii. 7;
Ios., *Ant.*, XII. ix. 1; XIII. x. 5.

vances. Jesus sought the humble and outcasts of all kinds, and the Pharisees saw in this an insult to their religion of respectability. The Pharisee was an infallible and faultless man, a pedant always right in his own conceit, taking the first place in the synagogue, praying in the street, giving alms to the sound of a trumpet, and caring greatly for salutations. Jesus maintained that each one ought to await the kingdom of God with fear and trembling. The bad religious tendency represented by Pharisaism did not reign without opposition. Many men before or during the time of Jesus, such as Jesus, son of Sirach (one of the true ancestors of Jesus of Nazareth), Gamaliel, Antigonus of Soco, and especially the gentle and noble Hillel, had taught much more elevated, and almost Gospel doctrines. But these good seeds had been choked. The beautiful maxims of Hillel, summing up the whole law as equity,[1] those of Jesus, son of Sirach, making worship consist in doing good,[2] were forgotten or anathematized.[3] Shammai, with his narrow and exclusive spirit, had prevailed. An enormous mass of "traditions" had stifled the Law,[4] under pretext of protecting and interpreting it. Doubtless these conservative measures had their share of usefulness; it is well that the Jewish people loved its Law even to excess, since it is this frantic love which, in saving Mosaism under Antiochus Epiphanes and under Herod, has preserved the leaven from which Christianity was to emanate. But taken in themselves, all these old precautions were only puerile. The synagogue, which was the depository of them, was no more than a parent of error. Its reign was ended · and yet

[1] Talm. of Bab., *Shabbath*, 31 *a; Joma*, 35 *b.*
[2] *Eccles.* xvii. 21, and following, xxxv. 1, and following.
[3] Talm. of Jerus., *Sanhedrim*, xi. 1; Talm. of Bab., *Sanhedrim*, 100 *b.*
[4] Matt. xv. 2

to require its abdication was to require the impossible, that which an established power has never done or been able to do.

The conflicts of Jesus with official hypocrisy were continual. The ordinary tactics of the reformers who appeared in the religious state which we have just described, and which might be called "traditional formalism," were to oppose the "text" of the sacred books to "traditions." Religious zeal is always an innovator, even when it pretends to be in the highest degree conservative. Just as the neo-Catholics of our days become more and more remote from the Gospel, so the Pharisees left the Bible at each step more and more. This is why the Puritan reformer is generally essentially "Biblical," taking the unchangeable text for his basis in criticising the current theology, which has changed with each generation. Thus acted later the Karaites and the Protestants. Jesus applied the axe to the root of the tree much more energetically. We see him sometimes, it is true, invoke the text against the false *Masores* or traditions of the Pharisees.[1] But in general he dwelt little on exegesis — it was the conscience to which he appealed. With one stroke he cut through both text and commentaries. He showed, indeed, to the Pharisees that they seriously perverted Mosaism by their traditions, but he by no means pretended himself to return to Mosaism. His mission was concerned with the future, not with the past. Jesus was more than the reformer of an obsolete religion; he was the creator of the eternal religion of humanity.

Disputes broke out especially respecting a number of external practices introduced by tradition, which

[1] Matt. xv. 2, and following; Mark vii. 2, and following.

neither Jesus nor his disciples observed.[1] The Pharisees reproached him sharply for this. When he dined with them, he scandalized them much by not observing the customary ablutions. "Give alms," said he, "of such things as ye have; and behold, all things are clean unto you."[2] That which in the highest degree hurt his refined feeling was the air of assurance which the Pharisees carried into religious matters; their paltry worship, which ended in a vain seeking after precedents and titles, to the utter neglect of the improvement of their hearts. An admirable parable rendered this thought with infinite charm and justice. "Two men," said he, "went up into the temple to pray; the one a Pharisee and the other a publican. The Pharisee stood and prayed thus with himself, God, I thank thee, that I am not as other men are, extortioners, unjust, adulterers, or even as this publican. I fast twice in the week, I give tithes of all that I possess. And the publican, standing afar off, would not lift up so much as his eyes unto heaven, but smote upon his breast, saying, God, be merciful to me a sinner. I tell you, this man went down to his house justified rather than the other."[3]

A hate, which death alone could satisfy, was the consequence of these struggles. John the Baptist had already provoked enmities of the same kind.[4] But the aristocrats of Jerusalem, who despised him, had allowed simple men to take him for a prophet.[5] In the case of Jesus, however, the war was to the death. A new spirit had appeared in the world, causing all that preceded to pale before it. John the Baptist was com-

[1] Matt. xv. 2, and following; Mark vii. 4, 8; Luke v. sub fin, and vi. init., xi. 38, and following.
[2] Luke xi. 41.
[3] Luke xviii. 9-14; comp. *ibid.*, xiv. 7-11.
[4] Matt. iii. 7, and following, xvii. 12, 13.
[5] Matt. xiv. 5, xxi. 26; Mark xi. 32; Luke xx. 6.

pletely a Jew; Jesus was scarcely one at all. Jesus always appealed to the delicacy of the moral sentiment. He was only a disputant when he argued against the Pharisees, his opponents forcing him, as generally happens, to adopt their tone.[1] His exquisite irony, his arch and provoking remarks, always struck home. They were everlasting stigmas, and have remained festering in the wound. This Nessus-shirt of ridicule which the Jew, son of the Pharisees, has dragged in tatters after him during eighteen centuries, was woven by Jesus with a divine skill. Masterpieces of fine raillery, their features are written in lines of fire upon the flesh of the hypocrite and the false devotee. Incomparable traits, worthy of a son of God! A god alone knows how to kill after this fashion. Socrates and Molière only touched the skin. He carried fire and rage to the very marrow.

But it was also just that this great master of irony should pay for his triumph with his life. Even in Galilee, the Pharisees sought to ruin him, and employed against him the manœuvre which ultimately succeeded at Jerusalem. They endeavored to interest in their quarrel the partisans of the new political faction which was established.[2] The facilities Jesus found for escape in Galilee, and the weakness of the government of Antipas, baffled these attempts. He ran into danger of his own free will. He saw clearly that his action, if he remained confined to Galilee, was necessarily limited. Judea drew him as by a charm; he wished to try a last effort to gain the rebellious city; and seemed anxious to fulfill the proverb — that a prophet must not die outside Jerusalem.[3]

[1] Matt. xii. 3-8, xxiii. 16, and following.
[2] Mark iii. 6.   [3] Luke xiii. 33.

CHAPTER XXI.

LAST JOURNEY OF JESUS TO JERUSALEM.

JESUS had for a long time been sensible of the dangers that surrounded him.[1] During a period of time which we may estimate at eighteen months, he avoided going on a pilgrimage to Jerusalem.[2] At the feast of Tabernacles of the year 32 (according to the hypothesis we have adopted), his relations, always malevolent and incredulous,[3] pressed him to go there. The evangelist John seems to insinuate that there was some hidden project to ruin him in this invitation. "Depart hence, and go into Judea, that thy disciples also may see the works that thou doest. For there is no man that doeth anything in secret, and he himself seeketh to be known openly. If thou do these things, show thyself to the world." Jesus, suspecting some treachery, at first refused; but when the caravan of pilgrims had set out, he started on the journey, unknown to every one, and almost alone.[4] It was the last farewell which he bade to Galilee. The feast of Tabernacles fell at the autumnal equinox. Six months still had to elapse before the fatal denouement. But during this interval, Jesus saw no more his beloved provinces of the north. The pleasant days had passed away; he must now traverse, step by step, the painful path that will terminate only in the anguish of death.

His disciples, and the pious women who tended him, met him again in Judea.[5] But how much everything

[1] Matt. xvi. 20, 21; Mark viii. 30, 31.
[2] John vii. 1.   [3] John vii. 5.   [4] John vii. 10.
[5] Matt. xxvii. 55; Mark xv. 41; Luke xxiii. 49, 55.

was changed for him there! Jesus was a stranger at Jerusalem. He felt that there was a wall of resistance he could not penetrate. Surrounded by snares and difficulties, he was unceasingly pursued by the ill-will of the Pharisees.[1] Instead of that illimitable faculty of belief, happy gift of youthful natures, which he found in Galilee—instead of those good and gentle people, amongst whom objections (always the fruit of some degree of ill-will and indocility) had no existence, he met there at each step an obstinate incredulity, upon which the means of action that had so well succeeded in the north had little effect. His disciples were despised as being Galileans. Nicodemus, who, on one of his former journeys, had had a conversation with him by night, almost compromised himself with the Sanhedrim, by having wished to defend him. "Art thou also of Galilee?" they said to him. "Search and look: for out of Galilee ariseth no prophet."[2]

The city, as we have already said, displeased Jesus. Until then he had always avoided great centres, preferring for his action the country and the towns of small importance. Many of the precepts which he gave to his apostles were absolutely inapplicable, except in a simple society of humble men.[3] Having no idea of the world, and accustomed to the kindly communism of Galilee, remarks continually escaped him, whose simplicity would at Jerusalem appear very singular.[4] His imagination and his love of Nature found themselves constrained within these walls. True religion does not proceed from the tumult of towns, but from the tranquil serenity of the fields.

[1] John vii. 20, 25, 30, 32.   [2] John vii. 50, and following.
[3] Matt. x. 11-13; Mark vi. 10; Luke x. 5-8.
[4] Matt. xxi. 2, xxvi. 18; Mark xi. 3, xiv. 13, 14; Luke xix. 31, xxii. 10-12.

The arrogance of the priests rendered the courts of
the temple disagreeable to him.   One day some of his
disciples, who knew Jerusalem better than he, wished
him to notice the beauty of the buildings of the temple,
the admirable choice of materials, and the richness of
the votive offerings that covered the walls.   "Seest
thou these buildings?" said he; "there shall not be left
one stone upon another."[1]   He refused to admire anything, except it was a poor widow who passed at that
moment, and threw a small coin into the box.   "She
has cast in more than they all," said he; "for all these
have of their abundance cast in unto the offerings of
God; but she of her penury hath cast in all the living
that she had."[2]   This manner of criticising all he observed at Jerusalem, of praising the poor who gave
little, of slighting the rich who gave much,[3] and of
blaming the opulent priesthood who did nothing for
the good of the people, naturally exasperated the sacerdotal caste.   As the seat of a conservative aristocracy,
the temple, like the Mussulman *haram* which succeeded
it, was the last place in the world where revolution
could prosper.   Imagine an innovator going in our
days to preach the overturning of Islamism round the
mosque of Omar!   There, however, was the centre of
the Jewish life, the point where it was necessary to
conquer or die.   On this Calvary, where certainly
Jesus suffered more than at Golgotha, his days passed
away in disputation and bitterness, in the midst of
tedious controversies respecting canonical law and exegesis, for which his great moral elevation, instead of
giving him the advantage, positively unfitted him.

[1]Matt. xxiv. 1, 2; Mark xiii. 1, 2; Luke xix. 44, xxi. 5, 6. Cf
Mark xi. 11.
[2]Mark xii. 41, and following; Luke xxi. 1, and following.
[3]Mark xii. 41.

In the midst of this troubled life, the sensitive and
kindly heart of Jesus found a refuge, where he enjoyed
moments of sweetness.   After having passed the day
disputing in the temple, toward evening Jesus descended into the valley of Kedron, and rested a while
in the orchard of a farming establishment (probably
for the making of oil) named Gethsemane,[1] which
served as a pleasure garden to the inhabitants.   Thence
he proceeded to pass the night upon the Mount of
Olives, which limits the horizon of the city on the east.[2]
This side is the only one, in the environs of Jerusalem,
which offers an aspect in any degree pleasing and ver-
dant.   The plantations of olives, figs, and palms were
numerous there, and gave their names to the villages,
farms, or enclosures of Bethphage, Gethsemane, and
Bethany.[3]   There were upon the Mount of Olives two
great cedars, the memory of which was long preserved
amongst the dispersed Jews; their branches served as
an asylum to clouds of doves, and under their shade
were established small bazaars.[4]   All this precinct was
in a manner the abode of Jesus and his disciples; they
knew it field by field and house by house.

The village of Bethany, in particular,[5] situated at the
summit of the hill, upon the incline which commands
the Dead Sea and the Jordan, at a journey of an hour
and a half from Jerusalem, was the place especially
beloved by Jesus.[6]   He there made the acquaintance of

[1] Mark xi. 19; Luke xxii. 39; John xviii. 1, 2. This orchard
could not be very far from the place where the piety of the Catho-
lics has surrounded some old olive-trees by a wall. The word
Gethsemane seems to signify "oil-press."
[2] Luke xxi. 37, xxii. 39; John viii. 1, 2.
[3] Talm. of Bab., *Pesachim*, 53 *a.*
[4] Talm. of Jerus., *Taanith*, iv. 8.
[5] Now *El-Azerié* (from *El-Azir*, the Arabic name of Lazarus);
in the Christian texts of the Middle Ages, *Lazarium.*
[6] Matt. xxi. 17, 18; Mark xi. 11, 12.

a family composed of three persons, two sisters and a
brother, whose friendship had a great charm for him.[1]
Of the two sisters, the one, named Martha, was an
obliging, kind, and assiduous person;[2] the other, named
Mary, on the contrary, pleased Jesus by a sort of lan-
guor,[3] and by her strongly developed speculative instincts. Seated at the feet of Jesus, she often forgot,
in listening to him, the duties of real life. Her sister,
upon whom fell all the duty at such times, gently complained. "Martha, Martha," said Jesus to her, "thou
art troubled, and carest about many things; now, one
thing only is needful. Mary has chosen the better part,
which will not be taken away."[4] Her brother, Eleazar,
or Lazarus, was also much beloved by Jesus.[5] Lastly,
a certain Simon, the leper, who was the owner of the
house, formed, it appears, part of the family.[6] It was
there, in the enjoyment of a pious friendship, that Jesus
forgot the vexations of public life. In this tranquil
home he consoled himself for the bickerings with which
the scribes and the Pharisees unceasingly surrounded
him. He often sat on the Mount of Olives, facing
Mount Moriah,[7] having beneath his view the splendid
perspective of the terraces of the temple, and its roofs
covered with glittering plates of metal. This view
struck strangers with admiration; at the rising of the
sun, especially, the sacred mountain dazzled the eyes,
and appeared like a mass of snow and of gold.[8] But a
profound feeling of sadness poisoned for Jesus the
spectacle that filled all other Israelites with joy and
pride. He cried out, in his moments of bitterness, "O
Jerusalem, Jerusalem, thou that killest the prophets,

---

[1] John xi. 5. [2] Luke x. 38-42; John xii. 2. [3] John xi. 20.
[4] Luke x. 38, and following. [5] John xi. 35, 36.
[6] Matt. xxvi. 6; Mark xiv. 3; Luke vii. 40-43; John xii. 1, and
following. [7] Mark xiii. 3. [8] Josephus, B. J., v. v. 6.

and stonest them which are sent unto thee, how often would I have gathered thy children together, even as a hen gathereth her chickens under her wings, and ye would not."[1]

It was not that many good people here, as in Galilee, were not touched; but such was the power of the dominant orthodoxy, that very few dared to confess it. They feared to discredit themselves in the eyes of the Hierosolymites by placing themselves in the school of a Galilean. They would have risked being driven from the synagogue, which, in a mean and bigoted society, was the greatest degradation.[2] Excommunication, besides, carried with it the confiscation of all possessions.[3] By ceasing to be a Jew, a man did not become a Roman; but remained without protection, in the power of a theocratic legislation of the most atrocious severity. One day, the inferior officers of the temple, who had been present at one of the discourses of Jesus, and had been enchanted with it, came to confide their doubts to the priests: "Have any of the rulers or of the Pharisees believed on him?" was the reply to them: "but this people who knoweth not the Law are cursed."[4] Jesus remained thus at Jerusalem, a provincial admired by provincials like himself, but rejected by all the aristocracy of the nation. The chiefs of schools and of sects were too numerous for any one to be stirred by seeing one more appear. His voice made little noise in Jerusalem. The prejudices of race and of sect, the direct enemies of the spirit of the Gospel, were too deeply rooted there.

His teaching in this new world necessarily became much modified. His beautiful discourses, the effect of

---

[1] Matt. xxiii. 37; Luke xiii. 34.
[2] John vii. 13, xii. 42, 43, xix. 38.
[3] 1 Esdr. x. 8; Epistle to Hebrews x. 34; Talmud. of Jerus., *Moëdkaton*, iii. 1.   [4] John vii. 45, and following.

which was always observable upon youthful imaginations and consciences morally pure, here fell upon
stone. He who was so much at his ease on the shores
of his charming little lake, felt constrained and not at
home in the company of pedants. His perpetual self-
assertion appeared somewhat fastidious.[1] He was
obliged to become controversialist, jurist, exegetist,
and theologian. His conversations, generally so full
of charm, became a rolling fire of disputes,[2] an interminable train of scholastic battles. His harmonious
genius was wasted in insipid argumentations upon the
Law and the prophets,[3] in which we should have preferred not seeing him sometimes play the part of
aggressor.[4] He lent himself with a condescension we
cannot but regret to the captious criticisms to which
the merciless cavillers subjected him.[5] In general, he
extricated himself from difficulties with much skill.
His reasonings, it is true, were often subtle (simplicity
of mind and subtlety touch each other; when simplicity
reasons, it is often a little sophistical); we find that
sometimes he courted misconceptions, and prolonged
them intentionally;[6] his reasoning, judged according to
the rules of Aristotelian logic, was very weak. But
when the unequaled charm of his mind could be displayed, he was triumphant. One day it was intended
to embarrass him by presenting to him an adulteress
and asking him what was to be done to her. We
know the admirable answer of Jesus.[7] The fine rail-

[1] John viii. 13, and following.   [2] Matt. xxi. 23-37.
[3] Matt. xxii. 23, and following.   [4] Matt. xxii. 42, and following.
[5] Matt. xxii. 36, and following, 46.
[6] See especially the discussions reported by John, chapter viii.,
for example; it is true that the authenticity of such passages is
only relative.
[7] John viii. 3, and following. This passage did not at first form
part of the Gospel of St. John; it is wanting in the more ancient

lery of a man of the world, tempered by a divine goodness, could not be expressed in a more exquisite manner. But the wit which is allied to moral grandeur is
that which fools forgive the least. In pronouncing
this sentence of so just and pure a taste: "He that is
without sin among you, let him first cast a stone at
her," Jesus pierced hypocrisy to the heart, and with the
same stroke sealed his own death-warrant.

It is probable, in fact, that but for the exasperation
caused by so many bitter shafts, Jesus might long have
remained unnoticed, and have been lost in the dreadful
storm which was soon about to overwhelm the whole
Jewish nation. The high priesthood and the Sadducees had rather disdained than hated him. The great
sacerdotal families, the *Boëthusim,* the family of
Hanan, were only fanatical in their conservatism.
The Sadducees, like Jesus, rejected the "traditions" of
the Pharisees.[1] By a very strange singularity, it was
these unbelievers who, denying the resurrection, the
oral Law, and the existence of angels, were the true
Jews. Or rather, as the old Law in its simplicity no
longer satisfied the religious wants of the time, those
who strictly adhered to it, and rejected modern inven-
tions, were regarded by the devotees as impious, just
as an evangelical Protestant of the present day is regarded as an unbeliever in Catholic countries. At all
events, from such a party no very strong reaction
against Jesus could proceed. The official priesthood,
with its attention turned toward political power, and

manuscripts, and the text is rather unsettled. Nevertheless, it is
from the primitive Gospel traditions, as is proved by the singular
peculiarities of verses 6 and 8, which are not in the style of Luke,
and compilers at second hand, who admitted nothing that does
not explain itself. This history is found, as it seems, in the Gospel according to the Hebrews. (Papias, quoted by Eusebius,
Hist. Eccl., iii. 39.)   [1]Jos. *Ant.,* XIII. x. 6, XVIII. i. 4.

intimately connected with it, did not comprehend these enthusiastic movements. It was the middle-class Pharisees, the innumerable *soferim,* or scribes, living on the science of "traditions," who took the alarm, and whose prejudices and interests were in reality threatened by the doctrine of the new teacher.

One of the most constant efforts of the Pharisees was to involve Jesus in the discussion of political questions, and to compromise him as connected with the party of Judas the Gaulonite. These tactics were clever; for it required all the deep wisdom of Jesus to avoid collision with the Roman authority, whilst proclaiming the kingdom of God. They wanted to break through this ambiguity, and compel him to explain himself. One day, a group of Pharisees, and of those politicians named "Herodians" (probably some of the *Boëthusim*), approached him, and, under pretense of pious zeal, said unto him, "Master, we know that thou art true, and teachest the way of God in truth, neither carest thou for any man. Tell us, therefore, what thinkest thou? Is it lawful to give tribute unto Cæsar, or not?" They hoped for an answer which would give them a pretext for delivering him up to Pilate. The reply of Jesus was admirable. He made them show him the image on the coin: "Render," said he, "unto Cæsar the things which are Cæsar's; and unto God the things that are God's."[1] Profound words, which have decided the future of Christianity! Words of a perfected spiritualism, and of marvellous justness, which have established the separation between the spiritual and the temporal, and laid the basis of true liberalism and civilization!

[1] Matt. xxii. 15, and following; Mark xii. 13, and following; Luke xx. 20, and following. Comp. Talm. of Jerus., *Sanhedrim,* ii. 3.

His gentle and penetrating genius inspired him when alone with his disciples, with accents full of tenderness. "Verily, verily, I say unto you, he that entereth not by the door into the sheepfold, but climbeth up some other way, the same is a thief and a robber. But he that entereth in by the door is the shepherd of the sheep. The sheep hear his voice: and he calleth his own sheep by name, and leadeth them out. He goeth before them, and the sheep follow him; for they know his voice. The thief cometh not, but for to steal, and to kill, and to destroy. But he that is an hireling, and not the shepherd, whose own the sheep are not, seeth the wolf coming, and leaveth the sheep, and fleeth. I am the good shepherd, and know my sheep, and am known of mine; and I lay down my life for the sheep."[1] The idea that the crisis of humanity was close at hand frequently recurred to him. "Now," said he, "learn a parable of the fig-tree: When his branch is yet tender, and putteth forth leaves, ye know that summer is nigh. Lift up your eyes, and look on the fields; for they are white already to harvest."[2]

His powerful eloquence always burst forth when contending with hypocrisy. "The scribes and Pharisees sit in Moses' seat. All, therefore, whatsoever they bid you observe, that observe and do; but do not ye after their works: for they say and do not. For they bind heavy burdens and grievous to be borne, and lay them on men's shoulders; but they themselves will not move them with one of their fingers.

"But all their works they do to be seen of men; they make broad their phylacteries,[3] enlarge the borders of

[1] John x. 1-16.
[2] Matt. xxiv. 32; Mark xiii. 28; Luke xxi. 30; John iv. 35.
[3] *Totafôth* or *tefillin,* plates of metal or strips of parchment, containing passages of the Law; which the devout Jews wore

their garments,[1] and love the uppermost rooms at feasts, and the chief seats in the synagogues, and greetings in the markets, and to be called of men, Rabbi, Rabbi. Woe unto them! . . .

"Woe unto you, scribes and Pharisees, hypocrites! for ye have taken away the key of knowledge, shut up the kingdom of heaven against men![2] for ye neither go in yourselves, neither suffer ye them that are entering to go in. Woe unto you, for ye devour widows' houses, and, for a pretense, make long prayers: therefore ye shall receive the greater damnation. Woe unto you, for ye compass sea and land to make one proselyte; and when he is made, ye make him twofold more the child of hell than yourselves! Woe unto you, for ye are as graves which appear not; and the men that walk over them are not aware of them.[3]

"Ye fools, and blind! for ye pay tithe of mint and anise and cummin, and have omitted the weightier matters of the law, judgment, mercy, and faith: these ought ye to have done, and not to leave the other undone. Ye blind guides, which strain at a gnat, and swallow a camel. Woe unto you!

"Woe unto you, scribes and Pharisees, hypocrites! for ye make clean the outside of the cup and of the

---

attached to the forehead and left arm, in literal fulfilment of the passages (*Ex.* xiii. 9; *Deut.* vi. 8, xi. 18.)

[1] *Zizith*, red borders or fringes which the Jews wore at the corner of their cloaks to distinguish them from the pagans (*Num.* xv. 38, 39; *Deut.* xxii. 12.)

[2] The Pharisees excluded men from the kingdom of God by their fastidious casuistry, which rendered entrance into it too difficult, and discouraged the unlearned.

[3] Contact with the tombs rendered any one impure. Great care was, therefore, taken to mark their extent on the ground. Talm. of Bab., *Baba Bathra*, 58 *a; Baba Metsia*, 45 *b*. Jesus here reproached the Pharisees for having invented a number of small precepts which might be violated unwittingly. and which only served to multiply infringements of the law.

platter;[1] but within they are full of extortion and excess. Thou blind Pharisee,[2] cleanse first that which is within the cup and platter, that the outside of them may be clean also.[3]

"Woe unto you, scribes and Pharisees, hypocrites; for ye are like unto whited sepulchres,[4] which indeed appear beautiful outward, but are within full of dead men's bones, and of all uncleanness. Even so ye also outwardly appear righteous unto men, but within ye are full of hypocrisy and iniquity.

"Woe unto you, scribes and Pharisees, hypocrites! because ye build the tombs of the prophets, and garnish the sepulchres of the righteous, and say, 'If we had been in the days of our fathers, we would not have been partakers with them in the blood of the prophets.' Wherefore, ye be witnesses unto yourselves, that ye are the children of them which killed the prophets. Fill ye up then the measure of your fathers. 'Therefore, also,' said the Wisdom of God,[5] 'I will send unto you prophets, and wise men, and scribes; and some of them ye shall kill and crucify; and some of them shall ye scourge in your synagogues, and persecute them from city to city. That upon you may come all the right-

---

[1]The purification of vessels was subjected, amongst the Pharisees, to the most complicated laws (Mark vii. 4.)

[2]This epithet, often repeated (Matt. xxiii. 16, 17, 19, 24, 26), perhaps contains an allusion to the custom which certain Pharisees had of walking with closed eyes in affectation of sanctity.

[3]Luke (xi. 37, and following) supposes, not without reason, that this verse was uttered during a repast, in answer to the vain scruples of the Pharisees.

[4]The tombs being impure, it was customary to whiten them with lime, to warn persons not to approach them. See p. 315, note 3, and Mishnah, *Maasar hensi*, v. 1; Talm. of Jerus., *Shekalim*, i. 1; *Maasar sheni*, v. 1; *Moëd katon*, i. 2; *Sota*, ix. 1; Talm. of Bab., *Moëd katon*, 5 a. Perhaps there is an allusion to the "dyed Pharisees" in this comparison which Jesus uses.

[5]We are ignorant from what book this quotation is taken.

eous blood shed upon the earth, from the blood of righteous Abel unto the blood of Zacharias, son of Barachias,[1] whom ye slew between the temple and the altar.' Verily, I say unto you, all these things shall come upon this generation."[2]

His terrible doctrine of the substitution of the Gentiles—the idea that the kingdom of God was about to be transferred to others, because those for whom it was destined would not receive it,[3] is used as a fearful menace against the aristocracy. The title "Son of God," which he openly assumed in striking parables,[4] wherein his enemies appeared as murderers of the heavenly messengers, was an open defiance to the Judaism of the Law. The bold appeal he addressed to the poor was still more seditious. He declared that he had "come that they which see not might see, and that they which see might be made blind."[5] One day, his dislike of the temple forced from him an imprudent speech : "I will destroy this temple that is made with hands, and within three days I will build another made without hands."[6] His disciples found strained allegories in this sentence; but we do not know what meaning Jesus

---

[1]There is a slight confusion here, which is also found in the Targum of Jonathan (*Lament.* ii. 20), between Zacharias, son of Jehoiadas, and Zacharias, son of Barachias, the prophet. It is the former that is spoken of (2 *Paral.* xxiv. 21.) The book of the Paralipomenes, in which the assassination of Zacharias, son of Jehoiadas, is related, closes the Hebrew canon. This murder is the last in the list of murders of righteous men, drawn up according to the order in which they are presented in the Bible. That of Abel is, on the contrary, the first.

[2]Matt. xxiii. 2-36; Mark xii. 38-40; Luke xi. 39-52, xx. 46, 47.

[3]Matt. viii. 11, 12. xx. 1, and following, xxi. 28, and following, 33, and following, 43, xxii. 1, and following; Mark xii. 1, and following; Luke xx. 9, and following.

[4]Matt. xxi. 37, and following; John x. 36, and following.

[5]John ix. 39.

[6]The most authentic form of this sentence appears to be in Mark xiv. 58, xv. 29. Cf. John ii. 19; Matt. xxvi. 61, xxvii. 40.

attached to it.   But as only a pretext was wanted, this
sentence was quickly laid hold of.   It reappeared in the
preamble of his death-warrant, and rang in his ears
amidst the last agonies of Golgotha.   These irritating
discussions always ended in tumult.   The Pharisees
threw stones at him;[1] in doing which they only fulfilled an article of the Law, which commanded every
prophet, even a thaumaturgus, who should turn the
people from the ancient worship, to be stoned without
a hearing.[2]   At other times they called him mad, possessed, Samaritan,[3] and even sought to kill him.[4]
These words were taken note of in order to invoke
against him the laws of an intolerant theocracy, which
the Roman government had not yet abrogated.[5]

[1]John viii. 39, x. 31, xi. 8.
[2]*Deuter.* xiii. 1, and following.   Comp. Luke xx. 6; John x.
33; 2 Cor. xi. 25.
[3]John x. 20.
[4]John v. 18, vii. 1, 20, 25, 30, viii. 37, 40.
[5]Luke xi. 53, 54.

CHAPTER XXII.

MACHINATIONS OF THE ENEMIES OF JESUS.

JESUS passed the autumn and a part of the winter at Jerusalem. This season is there rather cold. The portico of Solomon, with its covered aisles, was the place where he habitually walked.[1] This portico consisted of two galleries, formed by three rows of columns, and covered by a ceiling of carved wood.[2] It commanded the valley of Kedron, which was doubtless less covered with débris than it is at the present time. The depth of the ravine could not be measured, from the height of the portico; and it seemed, in consequence of the angle of the slopes, as if an abyss opened immediately beneath the wall.[3] The other side of the valley even at that time was adorned with sumptuous tombs. Some of the monuments, which may be seen at the present day, were perhaps those cenotaphs in honor of ancient prophets[4] which Jesus pointed out, when, seated under the portico, he denounced the official classes, who covered their hypocrisy or their vanity by these colossal piles.[5]

At the end of the month of December, he celebrated at Jerusalem the feast established by Judas Maccabeus in memory of the purification of the temple after the

---

[1]John x. 23.
[2]Jos., *B. J.,* v. v. 2. Comp. *Ant.,* xv. xi. 5, xx. ix. 7.
[3]Jos., places cited.
[4]See ante, p. 316. I am led to suppose that the tombs called those of Zachariah and of Absalom were monuments of this kind. Cf. *Itin. a Burdig. Hierus.,* p. 153 (edit. Schott.)
[5]Matt. xxiii. 29; Luke xi. 47.

sacrileges of Antiochus Epiphanes.[1]   It was also called
the "Feast of Lights," because, during the eight days
of the feast, lamps were kept lighted in the houses.[2]
Jesus undertook soon after a journey into Perea and to
the banks of the Jordan—that is to say, into the very
country he had visited some years previously, when he
followed the school of John,[3] and in which he had himself administered baptism.   He seems to have reaped
consolation from this journey, especially at Jericho.
This city, as the terminus of several important routes,
or, it may be, on account of its gardens of spices and its
rich cultivation,[4] was a customs station of importance.
The chief receiver, Zaccheus, a rich man, desired to see
Jesus.[5]   As he was of small stature, he climbed a syca-
more tree near the road which the procession had to
pass.   Jesus was touched with this simplicity in a person
of consideration, and at the risk of giving offense, he
determined to stay with Zaccheus.   There was much
dissatisfaction at his honoring the house of a sinner by
this visit.   In parting, Jesus declared his host to be a
good son of Abraham; and, as if to add to the vexation
of the orthodox, Zaccheus became a Christian; he gave,
it is said, the half of his goods to the poor, and restored
fourfold to those whom he might have wronged.   But
this was not the only pleasure which Jesus experienced
there.   On leaving the town, the beggar Bartimeus[6]
pleased him much by persisting in calling him "son of

[1]John x. 22. Comp. 1 Macc. iv. 52, and following; 2 Macc. x.
6, and following.
[2]Jos., *Ant.*, XII. vii. 7.
[3]John x. 40. Cf. Matt. xix. 1; Mark x. 1. This journey is
known to the synoptics. But they seem to think that Jesus made
it by coming from Galilee to Jerusalem through Perea.
[4]*Eccles.* xxiv. 18; Strabo, XVI. ii. 41; Justin., xxxvi. 3; Jos.,
Ant., IV. vi. 1, XIV. iv. 1, XV. iv. 2.
[5]Luke xix. 1, and following.
[6]Matt. xx. 29; Mark x. 46, and following; Luke xviii. 35.

David," although he was told to be silent. The cycle of Galilean miracles appeared for a time to recommence in this country, which was in many respects similar to the provinces of the north. The delightful oasis of Jericho, at that time well watered, must have been one of the most beautiful places in Syria. Josephus speaks of it with the same admiration as of Galilee, and calls it, like the latter province, a "divine country."[1]

After Jesus had completed this kind of pilgrimage to the scenes of his earliest prophetic activity, he returned to his beloved abode in Bethany, where a singular event occurred, which seems to have had a powerful influence on the remaining days of his life.[2] Tired of the cold reception which the kingdom of God found in the capital, the friends of Jesus wished for a great miracle which should strike powerfully the incredulity of the Hierosolymites. The resurrection of a man known at Jerusalem appeared to them most likely to carry conviction. We must bear in mind that the essential condition of true criticism is to understand the diversity of times, and to rid ourselves of the instinctive repugnances which are the fruit of a purely rational education. We must also remember that in this dull and impure city of Jerusalem, Jesus was no longer himself. Not by any fault of his own, but by that of others, his conscience had lost something of its original purity. Desperate, and driven to extremity, he was no longer his own master. His mission overwhelmed him, and he yielded to the torrent. As always happens in the lives of great and inspired men, he suffered the miracles opinion demanded of him rather than performed them. At this distance of time, and with only a single

[1] *B. J.*, IV. viii. 3. Comp. *ibid.*, I. vi. 6, I. xviii. 5, and *Antiq.* XV. iv. 2.
[2] John xi. 1, and following.

text, bearing evident traces of artifices of composition, it is impossible to decide whether in this instance the whole is fiction, or whether a real fact which happened at Bethany has served as a basis to the rumors which were spread about it. It must be acknowledged, however, that the way John narrates the incident differs widely from those descriptions of miracles, the off-spring of the popular imagination, which fill the synoptics. Let us add, that John is the only evangelist who has a precise knowledge of the relations of Jesus with the family of Bethany, and that it is impossible to believe that a mere creation of the popular mind could exist in a collection of remembrances so entirely personal. It is, then, probable that the miracle in question was not one of those purely legendary ones for which no one is responsible. In other words, we think that something really happened at Bethany which was looked upon as a resurrection.

Fame already attributed to Jesus two or three works of this kind.[1] The family of Bethany might be led, almost without suspecting it, into taking part in the important act which was desired. Jesus was adored by them. It seems that Lazarus was sick, and that in consequence of receiving a message from the anxious sisters Jesus left Perea.[2] They thought that the joy Lazarus would feel at his arrival might restore him to life. Perhaps, also, the ardent desire of silencing those who violently denied the divine mission of Jesus, carried his enthusiastic friends beyond all bounds. It may be that Lazarus, still pallid with disease, caused himself to be wrapped in bandages as if dead, and shut

---

[1] Matt. ix. 18, and following; Mark v. 22, and following; Luke vii. 11, and following, viii. 41, and following.

[2] John xi. 3, and following.

up in the tomb of his family. These tombs were large vaults cut in the rock, and were entered by a square opening, closed by an enormous stone. Martha and Mary went to meet Jesus, and without allowing him to enter Bethany, conducted him to the cave. The emotion which Jesus experienced at the tomb of his friend, whom he believed to be dead,[1] might be taken by those present for the agitation and trembling[2] which accompanied miracles. Popular opinion required that the divine virtue should manifest itself in man as an epileptic and convulsive principle. Jesus (if we follow the above hypothesis) desired to see once more him whom he had loved; and, the stone being removed, Lazarus came forth in his bandages, his head covered with a winding-sheet. This reappearance would naturally be regarded by every one as a resurrection. Faith knows no other law than the interest of that which it believes to be true. Regarding the object which it pursues as absolutely holy, it makes no scruple of invoking bad arguments in support of its thesis when good ones do not succeed. If such and such a proof be not sound many others are! If such and such a wonder be not real, many others have been! Being intimately persuaded that Jesus was a thaumaturgus, Lazarus and his two sisters may have aided in the execution of one of his miracles, just as many pious men who, convinced of the truth of their religion, have sought to triumph over the obstinacy of their opponents by means of whose weakness they were well aware. The state of their conscience was that of the stigmatists, of the convulsionists, of the possessed ones in convents, drawn, by the influence of the world in which they live, and by their own belief, into feigned

[1] John xi. 35, and following.   [2] John xi. 33, 38.

acts. As to Jesus, he was no more able than St. Bernard or St. Francis d'Assisi to moderate the avidity for the marvellous, displayed by the multitude, and even by his own disciples. Death, moreover, in a few days would restore him his divine liberty, and release him from the fatal necessities of a position which each day became more exacting, and more difficult to sustain.

Everything, in fact, seems to lead us to believe that the miracle of Bethany contributed sensibly to hasten the death of Jesus.[1] The persons who had been witnesses of it, were dispersed throughout the city, and spoke much about it. The disciples related the fact, with details as to its performance, prepared in expectation of controversy. The other miracles of Jesus were transitory acts, spontaneously accepted by faith, exaggerated by popular fame, and were not again referred to after they had once taken place. This was a real event, held to be publicly notorious, and one by which it was hoped to silence the Pharisees.[2] The enemies of Jesus were much irritated at all this fame. They endeavored, it is said, to kill Lazarus.[3] It is certain, that from that time a council of the chief priests[4] was assembled, and that in this council the question was clearly put: "Can Jesus and Judaism exist together?" To raise the question was to resolve it; and without being a prophet, as thought by the evangelist, the high priest could easily pronounce his cruel axiom: "It is expedient that one man should die for the people."

"The high priest of that same year," to use an expression of the fourth Gospel, which well expresses the state of abasement to which the sovereign pontificate

[1]John xi. 46, and following, xii. 2, 9, and following, 17, and following.   [2]John xii. 9, 10, 17. 18.   [3]John xii. 10.
[4]John xi. 47, and following.

was reduced, was Joseph Kaïapha, appointed by Valerius Gratus, and entirely devoted to the Romans.
From the time that Jerusalem had been under the government of procurators, the office of high priest had
been a temporary one; changes in it took place nearly
every year.[1] Kaïapha, however, held it longer than
any one else. He had assumed his office in the year
25, and he did not lose it till the year 36. His character is unknown to us, and many circumstances lead to
the belief that his power was only nominal. In fact,
another personage is always seen in conjunction with,
and even superior to him, who, at the decisive moment
we have now reached, seems to have exercised a pre-
ponderating power.

This personage was Hanan or Annas,[2] son of Seth,
and father-in-law of Kaïapha. He was formerly the
high priest, and had in reality preserved amidst the
numerous changes of the pontificate all the authority
of the office. He had received the high priesthood
from the legate Quirinius, in the year 7 of our era. He
lost his office in the year 14, on the accession of Tiberius; but he remained much respected. He was still
called "high priest," although he was out of office,[3] and
he was consulted upon all important matters. During
fifty years the pontificate continued in his family almost
uninterruptedly; five of his sons successively sustained
this dignity,[4] besides Kaïapha, who was his son-in-law.
His was called the "priestly family," as if the priesthood had become hereditary in it.[5] The chief offices
of the temple were almost all filled by them.[6] An-

[1] Jos., *Ant.*, xv. iii. 1, xviii. ii. 2, v. 3, xx. ix. 1, 4.
[2] The *Ananus* of Josephus. It is thus that the Hebrew name
Johanan became in Greek *Joannes* or *Joannas*.
[3] John xviii. 15-23; Acts iv. 6.   [4] Jos., *Ant.*, xx. ix. 1.
[5] Jos., *Ant.*, xv. iii. 1; *B. J.*, iv. v. 6 and 7; *Acts* iv. 6.
[6] Jos., *Ant.*, xx. ix. 3

other family, that of Boëthus, alternated, it is true, with that of Hanan's in the pontificate.[1] But the *Boëthusim*, whose fortunes were of not very honorable origin, were much less esteemed by the pious middle class. Hanan was then in reality the chief of the priestly party. Kaïapha did nothing without him; it was customary to associate their names, and that of Hanan was always put first.[2] It will be understood, in fact, that under this *régime* of an annual pontificate, changed according to the caprice of the procurators, an old high priest, who had preserved the secret of the traditions, who had seen many younger than himself succeed each other, and who had retained sufficient influence to get the office delegated to persons who were subordinate to him in family rank, must have been a very important personage. Like all the aristocracy of the temple,[3] he was a Sadducee, "a sect," says Josephus, "particularly severe in its judgments." All his sons also were violent persecutors.[4] One of them, named like his father, Hanan, caused James, the brother of the Lord, to be stoned, under circumstances not unlike those which surrounded the death of Jesus. The spirit of the family was haughty, bold, and cruel;[5] it had that particular kind of proud and sullen wickedness which characterizes Jewish politicians. Therefore, upon this Hanan and his family must rest the responsibility of all the acts which followed. It was Hanan (or the party he represented) who killed Jesus. Hanan was the principal actor in the terrible drama, and far more than Kaïapha, far more than Pilate, ought to bear the weight of the maledictions of mankind.

[1] Jos., *Ant.*, xv. ix. 3, xix. vi. 2, viii. 1.   [2] Luke iii. 2.
[3] *Acts* v. 17.   [4] Jos., *Ant.*, xx. ix. 1.
[5] Jos., *Ant.*, xx. ix. 1.

It is in the mouth of Kaïapha that the evangelist places the decisive words which led to the death of Jesus.[1] It was supposed that the high priest possessed a certain gift of prophecy; his declaration thus became an oracle full of profound meaning to the Christian community. But such an expression, whoever he might be that pronounced it, was the feeling of the whole sacerdotal party. This party was much opposed to popular seditions. It sought to put down religious enthusiasts, rightly foreseeing that by their excited preachings they would lead to the total ruin of the nation. Although the excitement created by Jesus was in nowise temporal, the priests saw, as an ultimate consequence of this agitation an aggravation of the Roman yoke and the overturning of the temple, the source of their riches and honors.[2] Certainly the causes which, thirty-seven years after, were to effect the ruin of Jerusalem, did not arise from infant Christianity. They arose in Jerusalem itself, and not in Galilee. We cannot, however, say that the motive alleged in this circumstance by the priests was so improbable that we must necessarily regard it as insincere. In a general sense, Jesus, if he had succeeded, would have really effected the ruin of the Jewish nation. According to the principles universally admitted by all ancient polity, Hanan and Kaïapha were right in saying: "Better the death of one man than the ruin of a people!" In our opinion this reasoning is detestable. But it has been that of conservative parties from the commencement of all human society. The "party of order" (I use this expression in its mean and narrow sense) has ever been the same. Deeming the highest duty of government to be the prevention of popular

[1] John xi. 49, 50. Cf. *ibid.*, xviii. 14.   [2] John xi. 48.

disturbances, it believes it performs an act of patriotism in preventing, by judicial murder, the tumultuous effusion of blood. Little thoughtful of the future, it does not dream that in declaring war against all innovations, it incurs the risk of crushing ideas destined one day to triumph. The death of Jesus was one of the thousand illustrations of this policy. The movement he directed was entirely spiritual, but it was still a movement; hence the men of order, persuaded that it was essential for humanity not to be disturbed, felt themselves bound to prevent the new spirit from extending itself. Never was seen a more striking example of how much such a course of procedure defeats its own object. Left free, Jesus would have exhausted himself in a desperate struggle with the impossible. The unintelligent hate of his enemies decided the success of his work, and sealed his divinity.

The death of Jesus was thus resolved upon from the month of February or the beginning of March.[1] But he still escaped for a short time. He withdrew to an obscure town called Ephraim or Ephron, in the direction of Bethel, a short day's journey from Jerusalem.[2] He spent a few days there with his disciples, letting the storm pass over. But the order to arrest him the moment he appeared at Jerusalem was given. The feast of the Passover was drawing nigh, and it was thought that Jesus, according to his custom, would come to celebrate it at Jerusalem.[3]

---

[1] John xi. 53.

[2] John xi. 54. Cf. 2 *Chron.* xiii. 19; Jos., *B. J.,* IV. ix. 9; Eusebius and St. Jerome, *De situ et nom. loc. hebr.,* at the words Εφρών and Εφραίμ.

[3] John xi. 55, 56. For the order of the events, in all this part we follow the system of John. The synoptics appear to have little information as to the period of the life of Jesus which precedes the Passion.

CHAPTER XXIII.

LAST WEEK OF JESUS.

Jesus did in fact set out with his disciples to see once more, and for the last time, the unbelieving city. The hopes of his companions were more and more exalted. All believed, in going up to Jerusalem, that the kingdom of God was about to be realized there.[1] The impiety of men being at its height, was regarded as a great sign that the consummation was at hand. The persuasion in this respect was such, that they already disputed for precedence in the kingdom.[2] This was, it is said, the moment chosen by Salome to ask, on behalf of her sons, the two seats on the right and left of the Son of man.[3] The Master, on the other hand, was beset by grave thoughts. Sometimes he allowed a gloomy resentment against his enemies to appear; he related the parable of a nobleman, who went to take possession of a kingdom in a far country; but no sooner had he gone than his fellow-citizens wished to get rid of him. The king returned, and commanded those who had conspired against him to be brought before him, and had them all put to death.[4] At other times he summarily destroyed the illusions of the disciples. As they marched along the stony roads to the north of Jerusalem, Jesus pensively preceded the group of his companions. All regarded him in silence, experiencing a feeling of fear, and not daring to interrogate him. Already, on various occasions, he had

[1]Luke xix. 11.　　　　　　　[2]Luke xxii. 24, and following.
[3]Matt. xx. 20, and following; Mark x. 35, and following.
[4]Luke xix. 12-27.

spoken to them of his future sufferings, and they had listened to him reluctantly.[1]   Jesus at last spoke to them, and no longer concealing his presentiments, discoursed to them of his approaching end.[2]   There was great sadness in the whole company.   The disciples were expecting soon to see the sign appear in the clouds.   The inaugural cry of the kingdom of God: "Blessed is he that cometh in the name of the Lord,"[3] resounded already in joyous accents in their ears.   The fearful prospect he foreshadowed, troubled them.   At each step of the fatal road, the kingdom of God became nearer or more remote in the mirage of their dreams. As to Jesus, he became confirmed in the idea that he was about to die, but that his death would save the world.[4]   The misunderstanding between him and his disciples became greater each moment.

The custom was to come to Jerusalem several days before the Passover, in order to prepare for it.   Jesus arrived late, and at one time his enemies thought they were frustrated in their hope of seizing him.[5]   The sixth day before the feast (Saturday, 8th of Nisan, equal to the 28th March[6]) he at last reached Bethany. He entered, according to his custom, the house of Lazarus, Martha and Mary, or of Simon the leper. They gave him a great reception.   There was a dinner at Simon the leper's,[7] where many persons were assembled, drawn thither by the desire of seeing him, and

[1] Matt. xvi. 21, and following; Mark viii. 31, and following.
[2] Matt. xx. 17, and following; Mark x. 31, and following; Luke xviii. 31, and following.
[3] Matt. xxiii. 39; Luke xiii. 35.
[4] Matt. xx. 28.
[5] John xi. 56.
[6] The Passover was celebrated on the 14th of Nisan. Now in the year 33, the 1st of Nisan corresponded with Saturday, 21st of March.
[7] Matt. xxvi. 6; Mark xiv. 3. Cf. Luke vii. 40, 43, 44.

also of seeing Lazarus, of whom for some time so
many things had been related.   Lazarus was seated at
the table, and attracted much attention.   Martha
served, according to her custom.[1]   It seems that they
sought, by an increased show of respect, to overcome
the coolness of the public, and to assert the high dignity
of their guest.   Mary, in order to give to the event a
more festive appearance, entered during dinner, bearing a vase of perfume which she poured upon the feet
of Jesus.   She afterward broke the vase, according to
an ancient custom by which the vessel that had been
employed in the entertainment of a stranger of distinction was broken.[2]   Then, to testify her worship in an
extraordinary manner, she prostrated herself at the feet
of her Master and wiped them with her long hair.[3]
All the house was filled with the odor of the perfume,
to the great delight of every one except the avaricious
Judas of Kerioth.   Considering the economical habits
of the community, this was certainly prodigality.   The
greedy treasurer calculated immediately how much the
perfume might have been sold for, and what it would
have realized for the poor.   This not very affectionate
feeling, which seemed to place something above Jesus,
dissatisfied him.   He liked to be honored, for honors
served his aim and established his title of Son of David.
Therefore, when they spoke to him of the poor, he replied rather sharply: "Ye have the poor always with
you; but me ye have not always."   And, exalting him-

---

[1] It is customary, in the East, for a person who is attached to
any one by a tie of affection or of domesticity, to attend upon him
when he goes to eat at the house of another.

[2] I have seen this custom still practised at Sour (Zoar.)

[3] We must remember that the feet of the guests were not, as
amongst us, concealed under the table, but extended on a level
with the body on the divan. or *triclinium.*

self, he promised immortality to the woman who in this critical moment gave him a token of love.[1]

The next day (Sunday, 9th of Nisan), Jesus descended from Bethany to Jerusalem.[2] When, at a bend of the road, upon the summit of the Mount of Olives, he saw the city spread before him, it is said he wept over it, and addressed to it a last appeal.[3] At the base of the mountain, at some steps from the gate, on entering the neighboring portion of the eastern wall of the city, which was called *Bethphage,* no doubt on account of the fig-trees with which it was planted,[4] he had experienced a momentary pleasure.[5] His arrival was noised abroad. The Galileans who had come to the feast were highly elated, and prepared a little triumph for him. An ass was brought to him, followed, according to custom, by its colt. The Galileans spread their finest garments upon the back of this humble animal as saddle-cloths, and seated him thereon. Others, however, spread their garments upon the road, and strewed it with green branches. The multitude which preceded and followed him, carrying palms, cried: "Hosanna to the son of David! Blessed is he that cometh in the name of the Lord!" Some persons even gave him the title of king of Israel.[6] "Master, rebuke

[1] Matt. xxvi. 6, and following; Mark xiv. 3, and following; John xi. 2, xii. 2, and following. Compare Luke vii. 36, and following.

[2] John xii. 12.   [3] Luke xix. 41, and following.

[4] Mishnah, *Menachoth,* xi. 2; Talm. of Bab., *Sanhedrim,* 14 *b; Pesachim,* 63 *b,* 91 *a; Sota,* 45 *a; Baba metsia,* 85 *a.* It follows from these passages that Bethphage was a kind of *pomœrium,* which extended to the foot of the eastern basement of the temple, and which had itself its wall of inclosure. The passages Matt. xxi. 1, Mark xi. 1, Luke xix. 29, do not plainly imply that Bethphage was a village, as Eusebius and St. Jerome have supposed.

[5] Matt. xxi. 1, and following; Mark xi. 1, and following; Luke xix. 29, and following; John xii. 12, and following.

[6] Luke xix. 38; John xii. 13.

thy disciples," said the Pharisees to him. "If these should hold their peace, the stones would immediately cry out," replied Jesus, and he entered into the city. The Hierosolymites, who scarcely knew him. asked who he was. "It is Jesus, the prophet of Nazareth, in Galilee," was the reply. Jerusalem was a city of about 50,000 souls.[1] A trifling event, such as the entrance of a stranger, however little celebrated, or the arrival of a band of provincials, or a movement of people to the avenues of the city, could not fail, under ordinary circumstances, to be quickly noised about. But at the time of the feast, the confusion was extreme.[2] Jerusalem at these times was taken possession of by strangers. It was amongst the latter that the excitement appears to have been most lively. Some proselytes, speaking Greek, who had come to the feast, had their curiosity piqued. and wished to see Jesus. They addressed themselves to his disciples;[3] but we do not know the result of the interview. Jesus, according to his custom, went to pass the night at his beloved village of Bethany.[4] The three following days (Monday, Tuesday, and Wednesday) he descended regularly to Jerusalem; and, after the setting of the sun, he returned either to Bethany, or to the farms on the western side of the Mount of Olives, where he had many friends.[5]

A deep melancholy appears, during these last days,

---

[1] The number of 120,000, given by Hecatæus (in Josephus, *Contra Apion*, I. xxii.), appears exaggerated. Cicero speaks of Jerusalem as of a paltry little town (*Ad Atticum*, II. ix.) The ancient boundaries, whichever calculation we adopt, do not allow of a population quadruple of that of the present time, which does not reach 15,000. See Robinson, *Bibl. Res.*, i. 421, 422 (2d edition); Fergusson, *Topogr. of Jerus.*, p. 51; Forster, *Syria and Palestine*, p. 82.

[2] Jos., *B. J.*, II. xiv. 3, VI. ix. 3.

[3] John xii. 20, and following.   [4] Matt. xxi. 17; Mark xi. 11.

[5] Matt. xxi. 17, 18; Mark xi. 11, 12, 19; Luke xxi. 37, 38.

to have filled the soul of Jesus, who was generally so
joyous and serene. All the narratives agree in relating
that, before his arrest, he underwent a short experience
of doubt and trouble; a kind of anticipated agony. According to some, he suddenly exclaimed, "Now is my
soul troubled. O Father, save me from this hour."[1]
It was believed that a voice from heaven was heard at
this moment: others said that an angel came to console
him.[2] According to one widely spread version, the
incident took place in the garden of Gethsemane.
Jesus, it was said, went about a stone's throw from his
sleeping disciples, taking with him only Peter and the
two sons of Zebedee, and fell on his face and prayed.
His soul was sad even unto death; a terrible anguish
weighed upon him; but resignation to the divine will
sustained him.[3] This scene, owing to the instinctive
art which regulated the compilation of the synoptics,
and often led them in the arrangement of the narrative
to study adaptability and effect, has been given as oc-
curring on the last night of the life of Jesus, and at the
precise moment of his arrest. If this version were the
true one, we should scarcely understand why John,
who had been the intimate witness of so touching an
episode, should not mention it in the very circumstan-
tial narrative which he has furnished of the evening of
the Thursday.[4] All that we can safely say is, that,

[1] John xii. 27, and following. We can easily imagine that the
exalted tone of John, and his exclusive pre-occupation with the
divine character of Jesus, may have effaced from the narrative
the circumstances of natural weakness related by the synoptics.

[2] Luke xxii. 43; John xii. 28, 29.

[3] Matt. xxvi. 36, and following; Mark xiv. 32, and following;
Luke xxii. 39, and following.

[4] This is the less to be understood, as John is affectedly particular in noticing the circumstances which were personal to him,
or of which he had been the only witness (xiii. 23, and following,
xviii. 15, and following, xix. 26, and following, 35, xx. 2, and
following, xxi. 20, and following.)

during his last days, the enormous weight of the mission he had accepted pressed cruelly upon Jesus. Human nature asserted itself for a time. Perhaps he began to hesitate about his work. Terror and doubt took possession of him, and threw him into a state of exhaustion worse than death. He who has sacrificed his repose, and the legitimate rewards of life, to a great idea, always experiences a feeling of revulsion when the image of death presents itself to him for the first time, and seeks to persuade him that all has been in vain. Perhaps some of those touching reminiscences which the strongest souls preserve, and which at times pierce like a sword, came upon him at this moment. Did he remember the clear fountains of Galilee where he was wont to refresh himself; the vine and the fig-tree under which he had reposed, and the young maidens who, perhaps, would have consented to love him? Did he curse the hard destiny which had denied him the joys conceded to all others? Did he regret his too lofty nature, and, victim of his greatness, did he mourn that he had not remained a simple artisan of Nazareth? We know not. For all these internal troubles evidently were a sealed letter to his disciples. They understood nothing of them, and supplied by simple conjectures that which in the great soul of their Master was obscure to them. It is certain, at least, that his divine nature soon regained the supremacy. He might still have avoided death; but he would not. Love for his work sustained him. He was willing to drink the cup to the dregs. Henceforth we behold Jesus entirely himself; his character unclouded. The subtleties of the polemic, the credulity of the thaumaturgus and of the exorcist, are forgotten. There remains only the incomparable hero of the Passion, the founder of the rights of free conscience, and the complete model which all suffering souls will contemplate in order to fortify and console themselves.

The triumph of Bethphage—that bold act of the provincials in celebrating at the very gates of Jerusalem the advent of their Messiah-King—completed the exasperation of the Pharisees and the aristocracy of the temple. A new council was held on the Wednesday (12th of Nisan) in the house of Joseph Kaïapha.[1] The immediate arrest of Jesus was resolved upon. A great idea of order and of conservative policy governed all their plans. The desire was to avoid a scene. As the feast of the Passover, which commenced that year on the Friday evening, was a time of bustle and excitement, it was resolved to anticipate it. Jesus being popular,[2] they feared an outbreak; the arrest was therefore fixed for the next day, Thursday. It was resolved, also, not to seize him in the temple, where he came every day,[3] but to observe his habits, in order to seize him in some retired place. The agents of the priests sounded his disciples, hoping to obtain useful information from their weakness or their simplicity. They found what they sought in Judas of Kerioth. This wretch, actuated by motives impossible to explain, betrayed his Master, gave all the necessary information, and even undertook himself (although such an excess of vileness is scarcely credible) to guide the troop which was to effect his arrest. The remembrance of horror which the folly or the wickedness of this man has left in the Christian tradition has doubtless given rise to some exaggeration on this point. Judas, until then, had been a disciple like the others; he had even the title of apostle; and he had performed miracles and driven out demons. Legend, which always uses strong and decisive language, describes the occupants of the little supper-room as eleven saints and one reprobate. Reality does not proceed by such absolute categories. Avarice, which the synoptics give as the motive of the crime in question, does not suffice to explain it. It would be very singular if a man who kept the purse, and who knew what he would lose by the death of his chief, were to abandon the profits of his occupation[1] in exchange for a very small sum of money.[2] Had the self-love of Judas been wounded by the rebuff which he had received at the dinner at Bethany? Even that would not explain his conduct. John would have us regard him as a thief, an unbeliever from the beginning,[3] for which, however, there is no probability. We would rather ascribe it to some feeling of jealousy or to some dissension amongst the disciples. The peculiar hatred John manifests toward Judas[4] confirms this hypothesis. Less pure in heart than the others, Judas had, from the very nature of his office, become unconsciously narrow-minded. By a caprice very common to men engaged in active duties, he had come to regard the interests of the treasury as superior even to those of the work for which it was intended. The treasurer had overcome the apostle. The murmurings which escaped him at Bethany seem to indicate that sometimes he thought the Master cost his spiritual family too dear. No doubt this mean economy had caused many other collisions in the little society.

[1] John xii. 6.
[2] John does not even speak of a payment in money.
[3] John vi. 65, xii. 6.
[4] John vi. 65, 71, 72, xii. 6; xiii. 2, 27, and following.

Without denying that Judas of Kerioth may have contributed to the arrest of his Master, we still believe that the curses with which he is loaded are somewhat unjust. There was, perhaps, in his deed more awkwardness than perversity. The moral conscience of the man of the people is quick and correct, but unstable and inconsistent. It is at the mercy of the impulse of the moment. The secret societies of the republican party were characterized by much earnestness and sincerity, and yet their denouncers were very numerous. A trifling spite sufficed to convert a partisan into a traitor. But if the foolish desire for a few pieces of silver turned the head of poor Judas, he does not seem to have lost the moral sentiment completely, since when he had seen the consequences of his fault he repented,[1] and, it is said, killed himself.

Each moment of this eventful period is solemn, and counts more than whole ages in the history of humanity. We have arrived at the Thursday, 13th of Nisan (2d April). The evening of the next day commenced the festival of the Passover, begun by the feast in which the Paschal lamb was eaten. The festival continued for seven days, during which unleavened bread was eaten. The first and the last of these seven days were peculiarly solemn. The disciples were already occupied with preparations for the feast.[2] As to Jesus, we are led to believe that he knew of the treachery of Judas, and that he suspected the fate that awaited him. In the evening he took his last repast with his disciples. It was not the ritual feast of the passover, as was afterward supposed, owing to an error of a day in reckon-

[1] Matt. xxvii. 3, and following.
[2] Matt. xxvi. 1, and following; Mark xiv. 12; Luke xxii. 7; John xiii. 29.

ing,[1] but for the primitive church this supper of the
Thursday was the true passover, the seal of the new
covenant. Each disciple connected with it his most
cherished remembrances, and numerous touching traits
of the Master which each one preserved were associated
with this repast, which became the corner-stone of
Christian piety, and the starting-point of the most
fruitful institutions.

Doubtless the tender love which filled the heart of
Jesus for the little church which surrounded him overflowed at this moment,[2] and his strong and serene soul
became buoyant, even under the weight of the gloomy
preoccupations that beset him. He had a word for
each of his friends; two among them especially, John
and Peter, were the objects of tender marks of attachment. John (at least according to his own account)
was reclining on the divan, by the side of Jesus, his
head resting upon the breast of the Master. Toward
the end of the repast, the secret which weighed upon
the heart of Jesus almost escaped him: he said, "Verily
I say unto you, that one of you shall betray me."[3] To
these simple men this was a moment of anguish; they
looked at each other, and each questioned himself.
Judas was present; perhaps Jesus, who had for some
time had reasons to suspect him, sought by this expression to draw from his looks or from his embarrassed
manner the confession of his fault. But the unfaithful

[1] This is the system of the synoptics (Matt. xxvi. 17, and following; Mark xiv. 12, and following; Luke xxii. 7, and following,
15.) But John, whose narrative of this portion has a greater
authority, expressly states that Jesus died the same day on which
the Paschal lamb was eaten (xiii. 1, 2, 29, xviii. 28, xix. 14, 31.)
The Talmud also makes Jesus to die "on the eve of the Passover" (Talm. of Bab., *Sanhedrim*, 43 *a*, 67 *a*.)
[2] John xiii. 1, and following.
[3] Matt. xxvi. 21, and following; Mark xiv. 18, and following;
Luke xx. 21, and following; John xiii. 21, and following, xxi. 20.

disciple did not lose countenance; he even dared, it is said, to ask with the others: "Master, is it I?"

Meanwhile, the good and upright soul of Peter was in torture. He made a sign to John to endeavor to ascertain of whom the Master spoke. John, who could converse with Jesus without being heard, asked him the meaning of this enigma. Jesus having only suspicions, did not wish to pronounce any name; he only told John to observe to whom he was going to offer a sop. At the same time he soaked the bread and offered it to Judas. John and Peter alone had cognizance of the fact. Jesus addressed to Judas words which contained a bitter reproach, but which were not understood by those present; and he left the company. They thought that Jesus was simply giving him orders for the morrow's feast.[1]

At the time, this repast struck no one; and apart from the apprehensions which the Master confided to his disciples, who only half understood them, nothing extraordinary took place. But after the death of Jesus, they attached to this evening a singularly solemn meaning, and the imagination of believers spread a coloring of sweet mysticism over it. The last hours of a cherished friend are those we best remember. By an inevitable illusion, we attribute to the conversations we have then had with him a meaning which death alone gives to them; we concentrate into a few hours the memories of many years. The greater part of the disciples saw their Master no more after the supper of which we have just spoken. It was the farewell banquet. In this repast, as in many others, Jesus practised his mysterious rite of the breaking of bread. As it

---

[1] John xiii. 21, and following, which shows the improbabilities of the narrative of the synoptics.

was early believed that the repast in question took place on the day of the Passover, and was the Paschal feast, the idea naturally arose that the Eucharistic institution was established at this supreme moment. Starting from the hypothesis that Jesus knew beforehand the precise moment of his death, the disciples were led to suppose that he reserved a number of important acts for his last hours. As, moreover, one of the fundamental ideas of the first Christians was that the death of Jesus had been a sacrifice, replacing all those of the ancient Law, the "Last Supper," which was supposed to have taken place, once for all, on the eve of the Passion, became the supreme sacrifice—the act which constituted the new alliance—the sign of the blood shed for the salvation of all.[1] The bread and wine, placed in connection with death itself, were thus the image of the new testament that Jesus had sealed with his sufferings—the commemoration of the sacrifice of Christ until his advent.[2]

Very early this mystery was embodied in a small sacramental narrative, which we possess under four forms,[3] very similar to one another. John, preoccupied with the Eucharistic ideas,[4] and who relates the Last Supper with so much prolixity, connecting with it so many circumstances and discourses[5] — and who was the only one of the evangelists whose testimony on this point has the value of an eye-witness—does not mention this narrative. This is a proof that he did not regard the Eucharist as a peculiarity of the Lord's Supper. For him the special rite of the Last Supper was the washing of feet. It is probable that in certain

---

[1] Luke xxii. 20. [2] 1 Cor. xi. 26.
[3] Matt. xxvi. 26-28; Mark xiv. 22-24; Luke xxii. 19-21; 1 Cor. xi. 23-25.
[4] Chap. vi. [5] Chaps. xiii.-xvii.

primitive Christian families this latter rite obtained an importance which it has since lost.[1] No doubt, Jesus, on some occasions, had practised it to give his disciples an example of brotherly humility. It was connected with the eve of his death, in consequence of the tendency to group around the Last Supper all the great moral and ritual recommendations of Jesus.

A high sentiment of love, of concord, of charity, and of mutual deference, animated, moreover, the remembrances which were cherished of the last hours of Jesus.[2] It is always the unity of his Church, constituted by him or by his Spirit, which is the soul of the symbols and of the discourses which Christian tradition referred to this sacred moment: "A new commandment I give unto you," said he, "that ye love one another; as I have loved you, that ye also love one another. By this shall all men know that ye are my disciples, if ye have love one to another. Henceforth I call you not servants; for the servant knoweth not what his lord doeth: but I have called you friends; for all things that I have heard of my Father I have made known unto you. These things I command you, that ye love one another."[3] At this last moment there were again evoked rivalries and struggles for precedence.[4] Jesus remarked, that if he, the Master, had been in the midst of his disciples as their servant, how much more

[1] John xiii. 14, 15. Cf. Matt. xx. 26, and following; Luke xxii. 26, and following.

[2] John xiii. 1, and following. The discourses placed by John after the narrative of the Last Supper cannot be taken as historical. They are full of peculiarities and of expressions which are not in the style of the discourses of Jesus; and which, on the contrary, are very similar to the habitual language of John. Thus the expression "little children" in the vocative (John xiii. 33) is very frequent in the First Epistle of John. It does not appear to have been familiar to Jesus.   [3] John xiii. 33-35, xv. 12-17.

[4] Luke xxii. 24-27. Cf. John xiii. 4, and following.

ought they to submit themselves to one another. According to some, in drinking the wine, he said, "I will not drink henceforth of this fruit of the vine until that day when I drink it new with you in my Father's kingdom."[1] According to others, he promised them soon a celestial feast, where they would be seated on thrones at his side.[2]

It seems that, toward the end of the evening, the presentiments of Jesus took hold of the disciples. All felt that a very serious danger threatened the Master, and that they were approaching a crisis. At one time Jesus thought of precautions, and spoke of swords. There were two in the company. "It is enough," said he.[3] He did not, however, follow out this idea; he saw clearly that timid provincials would not stand before the armed force of the great powers of Jerusalem. Peter, full of zeal, and feeling sure of himself, swore that he would go with him to prison and to death. Jesus, with his usual acuteness, expressed doubts about him. According to a tradition, which probably came from Peter himself, Jesus declared that Peter would deny him before the crowing of the cock. All, like Peter, swore that they would remain faithful to him.[4]

[1]Matt. xxvi. 29; Mark xiv. 25; Luke xxii. 18.
[2]Luke xxii. 29, 30.   [3]Luke xxii. 36-38.
[4]Matt. xxvi. 31, and following; Mark xiv. 29, and following; Luke xxii. 33, and following; John xiii. 36, and following.

CHAPTER XXIV.

ARREST AND TRIAL OF JESUS.

It was nightfall[1] when they left the room.[2] Jesus, according to his custom, passed through the valley of Kedron; and, accompanied by his disciples, went to the garden of Gethsemane, at the foot of the Mount of Olives,[3] and sat down there. Overawing his friends by his inherent greatness, he watched and prayed. They were sleeping near him, when all at once an armed troop appeared bearing lighted torches. It was the guards of the temple, armed with staves, a kind of police under the control of the priests. They were supported by a detachment of Roman soldiers with their swords. The order for the arrest emanated from the high priest and the Sanhedrim.[4] Judas, knowing the habits of Jesus, had indicated this place as the one where he might most easily be surprised. Judas, according to the unanimous tradition of the earliest times, accompanied the detachment himself;[5] and according to some,[6] he carried his hateful conduct even to betraying him by a kiss. However this may be, it is certain that there was some show of resistance on the

[1] John xiii. 30.
[2] The singing of a religious hymn, related by Matt. xxvi. 30, and Mark xiv. 26, proceeds from the opinion entertained by these two evangelists that the last repast of Jesus was the Paschal feast. Before and after the Paschal feast, psalms were sung. Talm. of Bab., *Pesachim,* cap. ix. hal. 3, and fol. 118 *a,* etc.
[3] Matt. xxvi. 36; Mark xiv. 32; Luke xxii. 39; John xviii. 1, 2.
[4] Matt. xxvi. 47; Mark xiv. 43; John xviii. 3, 12.
[5] Matt. xxvi. 47; Mark xiv. 43; Luke xxii. 47; John xviii. 3; *Acts* i. 16.
[6] This is the tradition of the synoptics. In the narrative of John, Jesus declares himself.

part of the disciples.[1] One of them (Peter, according
to eye-witnesses[2]) drew his sword, and wounded the
ear of one of the servants of the high priest, named
Malchus. Jesus restrained this opposition, and gave
himself up to the soldiers. Weak and incapable of
effectual resistance, especially against authorities who
had so much prestige, the disciples took flight, and became dispersed; Peter and John alone did not lose sight
of their Master. Another unknown young man followed him, covered with a light garment. They
sought to arrest him, but the young man fled, leaving
his tunic in the hands of the guards.[3]

The course which the priests had resolved to take
against Jesus was quite in conformity with the established law. The procedure against the "corrupter"
(*mésith*), who sought to injure the purity of religion,
is explained in the Talmud, with details, the naïve im-
pudence of which provokes a smile. A judicial am-
bush is there made an essential part of the examination
of criminals. When a man was accused of being a
"corrupter," two witnesses were suborned who were
concealed behind a partition. It was arranged to bring
the accused into a contiguous room, where he could be
heard by these two without his perceiving them. Two
candles were lighted near him, in order that it might be
satisfactorily proved that the witnesses "saw him."[4]
He was then made to repeat his blasphemy, and urged
to retract it. If he persisted, the witnesses who had
heard him conducted him to the tribunal, and he was
stoned to death. The Talmud adds, that this was the
manner in which they treated Jesus; that he was con-

[1] The two traditions are agreed on this point.
[2] John xviii. 10.   [3] Mark xiv. 51, 52.
[4] In criminal matters, eye-witnesses alone were admitted. Mishnah. *Sanhedrim*, iv. 5.

demned on the faith of two witnesses who had been suborned, and that the crime of "corruption" is, moreover, the only one for which the witnesses are thus prepared.[1]

We learn from the disciples of Jesus themselves that the crime with which their Master was charged was that of "corruption;"[2] and apart from some minutiæ, the fruit of the rabbinical imagination, the narrative of the Gospels corresponds exactly with the procedure described by the Talmud. The plan of the enemies of Jesus was to convict him, by the testimony of witnesses and by his own avowals, of blasphemy, and of outrage against the Mosaic religion, to condemn him to death according to law, and then to get the condemnation sanctioned by Pilate. The priestly authority, as we have already seen, was in reality entirely in the hands of Hanan. The order for the arrest probably came from him. It was before this powerful personage that Jesus was first brought.[3] Hanan questioned him as to his doctrine and his disciples. Jesus, with proper pride, refused to enter into long explanations. He referred Hanan to his teachings, which had been public; he declared he had never held any secret doctrine; and desired the ex-high priest to interrogate those who had listened to him. This answer was perfectly natural; but the exaggerated respect with which the old priest was surrounded made it appear audacious; and one of those present replied to it, it is said, by a blow.

Peter and John had followed their Master to the

---

[1] Talm. of Jerus., *Sanhedrim*, xiv. 16; Talm. of Bab., same treatise. 43 *a*, 67 *a*. Cf. *Shabbath*, 104 *b*.

[2] Matt. xxvii. 63; John vii. 12, 47.

[3] John xviii. 13, and following. This circumstance, which we only find in John, is the strongest proof of the historic value of the fourth Gospel.

dwelling of Hanan.   John, who was known in the house, was admitted without difficulty; but Peter was stopped at the entrance, and John was obliged to beg the porter to let him pass.   The night was cold.   Peter stopped in the antechamber, and approached a brasier, around which the servants were warming themselves. He was soon recognized as a disciple of the accused. The unfortunate man, betrayed by his Galilean accent, and pestered by questions from the servants, one of whom, a kinsman of Malchus, had seen him at Gethsemane, denied thrice that he had ever had the least connection with Jesus.   He thought that Jesus could not hear him, and never imagined that this cowardice, which he sought to hide by his dissimulation, was exceedingly dishonorable.   But his better nature soon revealed to him the fault he had committed.   A fortuitous circumstance, the crowing of the cock, recalled to him a remark that Jesus had made.   Touched to the heart, he went out and wept bitterly.[1]

Hanan, although the true author of the judicial murder about to be accomplished, had not power to pronounce the sentence upon Jesus; he sent him to his son-in-law, Kaïapha, who bore the official title.   This man, the blind instrument of his father-in-law, would naturally ratify everything that had been done.   The Sanhedrim was assembled at his house.[2]   The inquiry commenced; and several witnesses, prepared beforehand according to the inquisitorial process described in the Talmud, appeared before the tribunal.   The fatal sentence which Jesus had really uttered: "I am able to destroy the temple of God and to build it in three days,"

[1] Matt. xxvi. 69, and following; Mark xiv. 66, and following; Luke xxii. 54, and following; John xviii. 15, and following, 25, and following.

[2] Matt. xvi. 57; Mark xiv. 53; Luke xxii. 66.

was cited by two witnesses. To blaspheme the temple
of God was, according to the Jewish law, to blaspheme
God himself.[1] Jesus remained silent, and refused to
explain the incriminated speech. If we may believe
one version, the high priest then adjured him to say if
he were the Messiah; Jesus confessed it, and proclaimed
before the assembly the near approach of his heavenly
reign.[2] The courage of Jesus, who had resolved to
die, renders this narrative superfluous. It is probable
that here, as when before Hanan, he remained silent.
This was in general his rule of conduct during his last
moments. The sentence was settled; and they only
sought for pretexts. Jesus felt this, and did not un-
dertake a useless defense. In the light of orthodox
Judaism, he was truly a blasphemer, a destroyer of the
established worship. Now, these crimes were punished
by the law with death.[3] With one voice, the assembly
declared him guilty of a capital crime. The members
of the council who secretly leaned to him, were absent
or did not vote.[4] The frivolity which characterizes old
established aristocracies, did not permit the judges to
reflect long upon the consequences of the sentence they
had passed. Human life was at that time very lightly
sacrificed; doubtless the members of the Sanhedrim did
not dream that their sons would have to render account
to an angry posterity for the sentence pronounced with
such careless disdain.

The Sanhedrim had not the right to execute a sentence of death.[5] But in the confusion of powers which
then reigned in Judea, Jesus was, from that moment,

[1] Matt. xxiii. 16, and following.
[2] Matt. xxvi. 64; Mark xiv. 62; Luke xxii. 69. John knows
nothing of this scene.
[3] *Levit.* xxiv. 14, and following; *Deut.* xiii. 1, and following.
[4] Luke xxiii. 50, 51.   [5] John xviii. 31; Jos., *Ant.*, xx. ix. 1.

none the less condemned. He remained the rest of the night exposed to the ill-treatment of an infamous pack of servants, who spared him no indignity.[1]

In the morning the chief priests and the elders again assembled.[2] The point was, to get Pilate to ratify the condemnation pronounced by the Sanhedrim, which, since the occupation of the Romans, was no longer sufficient. The procurator was not invested, like the imperial legate, with the disposal of life and death. But Jesus was not a Roman citizen; it only required the authorization of the governor in order that the sentence pronounced against him should take its course. As always happens, when a political people subjects a nation in which the civil and the religious laws are confounded, the Romans had been brought to give to the Jewish law a sort of official support. The Roman law did not apply to Jews. The latter remained under the canonical law which we find recorded in the Talmud, just as the Arabs in Algeria are still governed by the code of Islamism. Although neutral in religion, the Romans thus very often sanctioned penalties inflicted for religious faults. The situation was nearly that of the sacred cities of India under the English dominion, or rather that which would be the state of Damascus if Syria were conquered by a European nation. Josephus asserts, though this may be doubted, that if a Roman trespassed beyond the pillars which bore inscriptions forbidding pagans to advance, the Romans themselves would have delivered him to the Jews to be put to death.[3]

The agents of the priests therefore bound Jesus and

[1] Matt. xxvi. 67, 68; Mark xiv. 65; Luke xxii. 63-65.
[2] Matt. xxvii. 1; Mark xv. 1; Luke xxii. 66, xxiii. 1; John xviii 28.
[3] Jos., *Ant.*, xv. xi. 5; *B. J.*, vi. ii. 4.

led him to the judgment-hall, which was the former palace of Herod,[1] adjoining the Tower of Antonia.[2] It was the morning of the day on which the Paschal lamb was to be eaten (Friday the 14th of Nisan, our 3d of April). The Jews would have been defiled by entering the judgment-hall, and would not have been able to share in the sacred feast. They therefore remained without.[3] Pilate being informed of their presence, ascended the *bima*[4] or tribunal, situated in the open air,[5] at the place named *Gabbatha,* or in Greek, *Lithostrotos,* on account of the pavement which covered the ground.

He had scarcely been informed of the accusation, before he displayed his annoyance at being mixed up with this affair.[6] He then shut himself up in the judgment-hall with Jesus. There a conversation took place, the precise details of which are lost, no witness having been able to repeat it to the disciples, but the tenor of which appears to have been well divined by John. His narrative, in fact, perfectly accords with what history teaches us of the mutual position of the two interlocutors.

The procurator, Pontius, surnamed Pilate, doubtless on account of the *pilum* or javelin of honor with which he or one of his ancestors was decorated,[7] had hitherto had no relation with the new sect. Indifferent to the

---

[1] Philo, *Legatio ad Caium,* § 38. Jos., *B. J.,* ii. xiv. 8.
[2] The exact place now occupied by the seraglio of the Pacha of Jerusalem.   [3] John xviii. 28.
[4] The Greek word $B\eta\mu\alpha$ had passed into the Syro-Chaldaic.
[5] Jos., *B. J.,* ii. ix. 3, xiv. 8; Matt. xxvii. 27; John xviii. 33.
[6] John xviii. 29.
[7] Virg., *Æn.,* xii. 121; Martial, *Epigr.,* i. xxxii., x. xlviii.; Plutarch, *Life of Romulus,* 29. Compare the *hasta pura,* a military decoration. Orelli and Henzen, *Inscr. Lat.,* Nos. 3574, 6852, etc. *Pilatus* is, on this hypothesis, a word of the same form as *Torquatus.*

internal quarrels of the Jews, he only saw in all these movements of sectaries, the results of intemperate imaginations and disordered brains. In general, he did not like the Jews, but the Jews detested him still more. They thought him hard, scornful, and passionate, and accused him of improbable crimes.[1]

Jerusalem, the centre of a great national fermentation, was a very seditious city, and an insupportable abode for a foreigner. The enthusiasts pretended that it was a fixed design of the new procurator to abolish the Jewish law.[2] Their narrow fanaticism, and their religious hatreds, disgusted that broad sentiment of justice and civil government which the humblest Roman carried everywhere with him. All the acts of Pilate which are known to us, show him to have been a good administrator.[3] In the earlier period of the exercise of his office, he had difficulties with those subject to him which he had solved in a very brutal manner; but it seems that essentially he was right. The Jews must have appeared to him a people behind the age; he doubtless judged them as a liberal prefect formerly judged the Bas-Bretons, who rebelled for such trifling matters as a new road, or the establishment of a school. In his best projects for the good of the country, notably in those relating to public works, he had encountered an impassable obstacle in the Law. The Law restricted life to such a degree that it opposed all change, and all amelioration. The Roman structures, even the most useful ones, were objects of great antipathy on the part of zealous Jews.[4] Two votive escutcheons with inscriptions, which he had set up at his residence near the sacred precincts, provoked a still

[1]Philo, *Leg. ad Caium,* § 38.   [2]Jos., *Ant.,* XVIII. iii. 1, init.
[3]Jos., *Ant.,* XVIII. ii.-iv.   [4]Talm. of Bab., *Shabbath,* 33 b

more violent storm.[1]   Pilate at first cared little for
these susceptibilities; and he was soon involved in san-
guinary suppressions of revolt,[2] which afterward ended
in his removal.[3]   The experience of so many conflicts
had rendered him very prudent in his relations with
this intractable people, which avenged itself upon its
governors by compelling them to use toward it hateful
severities.   The procurator saw himself, with extreme
displeasure, led to play a cruel part in this new affair,
for the sake of a law he hated.[4]   He knew that religious fanaticism, when it has obtained the sanction of
civil governments to some act of violence, is afterward
the first to throw the responsibility upon the government, and almost accuses them of being the author of
it.   Supreme injustice; for the true culprit is, in such
cases, the instigator!

Pilate, then, would have liked to save Jesus.   Perhaps the dignified and calm attitude of the accused
made an impression upon him.   According to a tradition,[5] Jesus found a supporter in the wife of the procurator himself.   She may have seen the gentle Galilean
from some window of the palace, overlooking the
courts of the temple.   Perhaps she had seen him again
in her dreams; and the idea that the blood of this beautiful young man was about to be spilt, weighed upon
her mind.   Certain it is that Jesus found Pilate pre-
possessed in his favor.   The governor questioned him
with kindness, and with the desire to find an excuse for
sending him away pardoned.

The title of "King of the Jews," which Jesus had
never taken upon himself, but which his enemies repre-

[1] Philo, *Leg. ad Caium*, § 38.
[2] Jos., *Ant.*, XVIII. iii. 1 and 2; Luke xiii. 1.
[3] Jos., *Ant.*, XVIII. iv. 1, 2.
[4] John xviii. 35.   [5] Matt. xxvii. 19.

sented as the sum and substance of his acts and pretensions, was naturally that by which it was sought to excite the suspicions of the Roman authority. They accused him on this ground of sedition, and of treason against the government. Nothing could be more unjust; for Jesus had always recognized the Roman government as the established power. But conservative religious bodies do not generally shrink from calumny. Notwithstanding his own explanation, they drew certain conclusions from his teaching; they transformed him into a disciple of Judas the Gaulonite; they pretended that he forbade the payment of tribute to Cæsar.[1] Pilate asked him if he was really the king of the Jews.[2] Jesus concealed nothing of what he thought. But the great ambiguity of speech which had been the source of his strength, and which, after his death, was to establish his kingship, injured him on this occasion. An idealist that is to say, not distinguishing the spirit from the substance, Jesus, whose words, to use the image of the Apocalypse, were as a two-edged sword, never completely satisfied the powers of earth. If we may believe John, he avowed his royalty, but uttered at the same time this profound sentence: "My kingdom is not of this world." He explained the nature of his kingdom, declaring that it consisted entirely in the possession and proclamation of truth Pilate understood nothing of this grand idealism.[3] Jesus doubtless impressed him as being an inoffensive dreamer. The total absence of religious and philosophical proselytism among the Romans of this epoch made them regard devotion to truth as a chi-

---

[1] Luke xxiii. 2, 5.
[2] Matt. xxvii. 11; Mark xv. 2; Luke xxiii. 3; John xviii. 33.
[3] John xviii. 38.

mera. Such discussions annoyed them, and appeared to them devoid of meaning. Not perceiving the element of danger to the empire that lay hidden in these new speculations, they had no reason to employ violence against them. All their displeasure fell upon those who asked them to inflict punishment for what appeared to them to be vain subtleties. Twenty years after, Gallio still adopted the same course toward the Jews.[1] Until the fall of Jerusalem, the rule which the Romans adopted in administration, was to remain completely indifferent to these sectarian quarrels.[2]

An expedient suggested itself to the mind of the governor by which he could reconcile his own feelings with the demands of the fanatical people, whose pressure he had already so often felt. It was the custom to deliver a prisoner to the people at the time of the Passover. Pilate, knowing that Jesus had only been arrested in consequence of the jealousy of the priests,[3] tried to obtain for him the benefit of this custom. He appeared again upon the *bima,* and proposed to the multitude to release the "King of the Jews." The proposition made in these terms, though ironical, was characterized by a degree of liberality. The priests saw the danger of it. They acted promptly,[4] and in order to combat the proposition of Pilate, they suggested to the crowd the name of a prisoner who enjoyed great popularity in Jerusalem. By a singular coincidence,

---

[1] *Acts* xviii. 14, 15.

[2] Tacitus (*Ann.,* xv. 44) describes the death of Jesus as a political execution by Pontius Pilate. But at the epoch in which Tacitus wrote, the Roman policy toward the Christians was changed; they were held guilty of secretly conspiring against the state. It was natural that the Latin historian should believe that Pilate, in putting Jesus to death, had been actuated by a desire for the public safety. Josephus is much more exact (*Ant.* xviii. iii. 3.)

[3] Mark xv. 10.

[4] Matt. xxvii. 20; Mark xv. 11.

he also was called Jesus,[1] and bore the surname of Bar-
Abba, or Bar-Rabban.[2]   He was a well-known personage,[3] and had been arrested for taking part in an up-
roar in which murder had been committed.[4]   A general clamor was raised, "Not this man; but Jesus Bar-
Rabban;" and Pilate was obliged to release Jesus Bar-
Rabban.

His embarrassment increased.   He feared that too
much indulgence shown to a prisoner, to whom was
given the title of "King of the Jews," might compromise him.   Fanaticism, moreover, compels all powers to make terms with it.   Pilate thought himself
obliged to make some concession; but still hesitating to
shed blood, in order to satisfy men whom he hated,
wished to turn the thing into a jest.   Affecting to laugh
at the pompous title they had given to Jesus, he caused
him to be scourged.[5]   Scourging was the general preliminary of crucifixion.[6]   Perhaps Pilate wished it to
be believed that this sentence had already been pronounced, hoping that the preliminary would suffice.
Then took place (according to all the narratives) a
revolting scene.   The soldiers put a scarlet robe on his
back, a crown formed of branches of thorns upon his
head, and a reed in his hand.   Thus attired, he was led
to the tribunal in front of the people.   The soldiers
defiled before him, striking him in turn, and knelt to

[1]The name of Jesus has disappeared in the greater part of
the manuscripts. This reading has, nevertheless, very great authorities in its favor.
[2]Matt. xxvii. 16.
[3]Cf. St. Jerome. In Matt. xxvii. 16.
[4]Mark xv. 7; Luke xxiii. 19. John (xviii. 40), who makes him
a robber, appears here too much further from the truth than
Mark.
[5]Matt. xxvii. 26; Mark xv. 15; John xix. 1.
[6]Jos., *B. J.,* II. xiv. 9, v. xi. 1, VII. vi. 4; Titus-Livy, XXXIII. 36;
Quintus Curtius, VII. xi. 28.

him, saying, "Hail! King of the Jews."[1]   Others, it is said, spit upon him, and struck his head with the reed. It is difficult to understand how Roman dignity could stoop to acts so shameful.   It is true that Pilate, in the capacity of procurator, had under his command scarcely any but auxiliary troops.[2]   Roman citizens, as the legionaries were, would not have degraded themselves by such conduct.

Did Pilate think by this display that he freed himself from responsibility?   Did he hope to turn aside the blow which threatened Jesus by conceding something to the hatred of the Jews,[3] and by substituting for the tragic denouement a grotesque termination, to make it appear that the affair merited no other issue? If such were his idea, it was unsuccessful.   The tumult increased, and became an open riot.   The cry "Crucify him! crucify him!" resounded from all sides.   The priests becoming increasingly urgent, declared the law in peril if the corrupter were not punished with death.[4] Pilate saw clearly that to save Jesus he would have to put down a terrible disturbance.   He still tried, however, to gain time.   He returned to the judgment-hall, and ascertained from what country Jesus came, with the hope of finding a pretext for declaring his inability to adjudicate.[5]   According to one tradition, he even sent Jesus to Antipas, who, it is said, was then at Jerusalem.[6]   Jesus took no part in these well-meant efforts;

[1] Matt. xxvii. 27, and following; Mark xv. 16, and following; Luke xxiii. 11; John xix. 2, and following.
[2] See *Inscript. Rom. of Algeria,* No. 5, fragm. B.
[3] Luke xxiii. 16, 22.   [4] John xix. 7.
[5] John xix. 9.   Cf. Luke xxiii. 6, and following.
[6] It is probable that this is a first attempt at a "Harmony of the Gospels."   Luke must have had before him a narrative in which the death of Jesus was erroneously attributed to Herod. In order not to sacrifice this version entirely he must have combined the two traditions. What makes this more likely is, that

he maintained, as he had done before Kaïapha, a grave and dignified silence, which astonished Pilate. The cries from without became more and more menacing. The people had already begun to denounce the lack of zeal in the functionary who protected an enemy of Cæsar. The greatest adversaries of the Roman rule were suddenly transformed into loyal subjects of Tiberius, that they might have the right of accusing the too tolerant procurator of treason. "We have no king," said they, "but Cæsar. If thou let this man go, thou art not Cæsar's friend: whosoever maketh himself a king speaketh against Cæsar."[1] The feeble Pilate yielded; he foresaw the report that his enemies would send to Rome, in which they would accuse him of having protected a rival of Tiberius. Once before, in the matter of the votive escutcheons,[2] the Jews had written to the emperor, and had received satisfaction. He feared for his office. By a compliance, which was to deliver his name to the scorn of history, he yielded, throwing, it is said, upon the Jews all the responsibility of what was about to happen. The latter, according to the Christians, fully accepted it, by exclaiming, "His blood be on us and on our children!"[3]

Were these words really uttered? We may doubt it. But they are the expression of a profound historical truth. Considering the attitude which the Romans

he probably had a vague knowledge that Jesus (as John teaches us) appeared before three authorities. In many other cases, Luke seems to have a remote idea of the facts which are peculiar to the narration of John. Moreover, the third Gospel contains in its history of the Crucifixion a series of additions which the author appears to have drawn from a more recent document, and which had evidently been arranged with a special view to edification.

[1]John xix. 12, 15. Cf. Luke xxiii. 2. In order to appreciate the exactitude of the description of this scene in the evangelists, see Philo, *Leg. ad Caium*, § 38.

[2]See *ante*, p. 351.   [3]Matt. xxvii. 24, 25.

had taken in Judea, Pilate could scarcely have acted otherwise. How many sentences of death dictated by religious intolerance have been extorted from the civil power! The king of Spain, who, in order to please a fanatical clergy, delivered hundreds of his subjects to the stake, was more blameable than Pilate, for he represented a more absolute power than that of the Romans at Jerusalem. When the civil power becomes persecuting or meddlesome at the solicitation of the priesthood, it proves its weakness. But let the government that is without sin in this respect throw the first stone at Pilate The "secular arm," behind which clerical cruelty shelters itself, is not the culprit. No one has a right to say that he has a horror of blood when he causes it to be shed by his servants.

It was, then, neither Tiberius nor Pilate who condemned Jesus. It was the old Jewish party; it was the Mosaic Law. According to our modern ideas, there is no transmission of moral demerit from father to son; no one is accountable to human or divine justice except for that which he himself has done. Consequently, every Jew who suffers to-day for the murder of Jesus has a right to complain, for he might have acted as did Simon the Cyrenean; at any rate, he might not have been with those who cried "Crucify him!" But nations, like individuals, have their responsibilities, and if ever crime was the crime of a nation, it was the death of Jesus. This death was "legal" in the sense that it was primarily caused by a law which was the very soul of the nation. The Mosaic law, in its modern, but still in its accepted form, pronounced the penalty of death against all attempts to change the established worship. Now, there is no doubt that Jesus attacked this worship, and aspired to destroy it. The Jews expressed this to Pilate with a truthful simplicity: "We have a law, and by our law he ought to die; because he has made himself the Son of God."[1] The law was detestable, but it was the law of ancient ferocity; and the hero who offered himself in order to abrogate it, had first of all to endure its penalty.

Alas! it has required more than eighteen hundred years for the blood that he shed to bear its fruits. Tortures and death have been inflicted for ages in the name of Jesus, on thinkers as noble as himself. Even at the present time, in countries which call themselves Christian, penalties are pronounced for religious offences. Jesus is not responsible for these errors. He could not foresee that people, with mistaken imaginations, would one day imagine him as a frightful Moloch, greedy of burnt flesh. Christianity has been intolerant, but intolerance is not essentially a Christian fact. It is a Jewish fact in the sense that it was Judaism which first introduced the theory of the absolute in religion, and laid down the principle that every innovator, even if he brings miracles to support his doctrine, ought to be stoned without trial.[2] The pagan world has also had its religious violences. But if it had had this law, how would it have become Christian? The Pentateuch has thus been in the world the first code of religious terrorism. Judaism has given the example of an immutable dogma armed with the sword. If, instead of pursuing the Jews with a blind hatred, Christianity had abolished the régime which killed its founder, how much more consistent would it have been!—how much better would it have deserved of the human race!

[1] John xix. 7.   [2] *Deut.* xiii. 1, and following.

CHAPTER XXV.

DEATH OF JESUS.

ALTHOUGH the real motive for the death of Jesus
was entirely religious, his enemies had succeeded, in
the judgment-hall, in representing him as guilty of
treason against the state; they could not have obtained
from the sceptical Pilate a condemnation simply on the
ground of heterodoxy. Consistently with this idea,
the priests demanded, through the people, the crucifixion of Jesus. This punishment was not Jewish in
its origin; if the condemnation of Jesus had been purely
Mosaic, he would have been stoned.[1]   Crucifixion was
a Roman punishment, reserved for slaves, and for cases
in which it was wished to add to death the aggravation
of ignominy. In applying it to Jesus, they treated him
as they treated highway robbers, brigands, bandits, or
those enemies of inferior rank to whom the Romans
did not grant the honor of death by the sword.[2]   It
was the chimerical "King of the Jews," not the heterodox dogmatist, who was punished. Following out the
same idea, the execution was left to the Romans. We
know that amongst the Romans, the soldiers, their profession being to kill, performed the office of executioners. Jesus was therefore delivered to a cohort of auxil-

[1] Jos., *Ant.*, xx. ix. 1. The Talmud, which represents the condemnation of Jesus as entirely religious, declares, in fact, that he
was stoned; or, at least, that after having been hanged, he was
stoned, as often happened (Mishnah, *Sanhedrim,* vi. 4.)   Talmud of Jerusalem, *Sanhedrim,* xiv. 16. Talm. of Bab., same
treatise, 43 *a*, 67 *a*.
[2] Jos., *Ant.*, xvii. x. 10, xx. vi. 2; *B. J.,* v. xi. 1; Apuleius,
Metam., iii. 9; Suetonius, *Galba,* 9; Lampridius, *Alex. Sev.,* 23.

iary troops, and all the most hateful features of executions introduced by the cruel habits of the new conquerors, were exhibited toward him. It was about noon.[1] They re-clothed him with the garments which they had removed for the farce enacted at the tribunal, and as the cohort had already in reserve two thieves who were to be executed, the three prisoners were taken together, and the procession set out for the place of execution.

The scene of the execution was at a place called Golgotha, situated outside Jerusalem, but near the walls of the city.[2] The name *Golgotha* signifies a *skull;* it corresponds with the French word *Chaumont,* and probably designated a bare hill or rising ground, having the form of a bald skull. The situation of this hill is not precisely known. It was certainly on the north or northwest of the city, in the high, irregular plain which extends between the walls and the two valleys of Kedron and Hinnom,[3] a rather uninteresting region, and made still worse by the objectionable circumstances arising from the neighborhood of a great city. It is difficult to identify Golgotha as the precise place which, since Constantine, has been venerated by entire Christendom.[4] This place is too much in the interior of the

[1] John xix. 14. According to Mark xv. 25, it could scarcely have been eight o'clock in the morning, since that evangelist relates that Jesus was crucified at nine o'clock.

[2] Matt. xxvii. 33; Mark xv. 22; John xix. 20; *Heb.* xiii. 12.

[3] Golgotha, in fact, seems not entirely unconnected with the hill of Gareb and the locality of Goath, mentioned in Jeremiah xxxi. 39. Now, these two places appear to have been at the northwest of the city. I should incline to fix the place where Jesus was crucified near the extreme corner which the existing wall makes toward the west, or perhaps upon the mounds which command the valley of Hinnom, above *Birket-Mamilla.*

[4] The proofs by which it has been attempted to establish that the Holy Sepulchre has been displaced since Constantine are not very strong.

city, and we are led to believe that, in the time of Jesus,
it was comprised within the circuit of the walls.[1]

He who was condemned to the cross, had himself to
carry the instrument of his execution.[2] But Jesus,
physically weaker than his two companions, could not
carry his. The troop met a certain Simon of Cyrene,
who was returning from the country, and the soldiers,
with the off-hand procedure of foreign garrisons,

---

[1] M. de Vogüé has discovered, about 83 yards to the east of the
traditional site of Calvary, a fragment of a Jewish wall analogous to that of Hebron, which, if it belongs to the inclosure of
the time of Jesus, would leave the above-mentioned site outside
the city. The existence of a sepulchral cave (that which is called
"Tomb of Joseph of Arimathea"), under the wall of the cupola
of the Holy Sepulchre, would also lead to the supposition that
this place was outside the walls. Two historical considerations,
one of which is rather strong, may, moreover, be invoked in favor of the tradition. The first is, that it would be singular if
those, who, under Constantine, sought to determine the topography of the Gospels, had not hesitated in the presence of the objection which results from *John* xix. 20, and from *Heb.* xiii. 12. Why,
being free to choose, should they have wantonly exposed themselves to so grave a difficulty? The second consideration is, that
they might have had to guide them, in the time of Constantine,
the remains of an edifice, the temple of Venus on Golgotha,
erected by Adrian. We are, then, at times led to believe that the
work of the devout topographers of the time of Constantine was
earnest and sincere, that they sought for indications, and that,
though they might not refrain from certain pious frauds, they
were guided by analogies. If they had merely followed a vain
caprice, they might have placed Golgotha in a more conspicuous
situation, at the summit of some of the neighboring hills about
Jerusalem, in accordance with the Christian imagination, which
very early thought that the death of Christ had taken place on a
mountain. But the difficulty of the inclosures is very serious.
Let us add, that the erection of a temple of Venus on Golgotha
proves little. Eusebius (*Vita Const.,* iii. 26), Socrates (*H. E.,* i.
17), Sozomen (*H. E.,* ii. 1), St. Jerome (*Epist.* xlix., ad Paul-
in.), say, indeed, that there was a sanctuary of Venus on the
site which they imagined to be that of the holy tomb; but it is
not certain that Adrian had erected it; or that he had erected it
in a place which was in his time called "Golgotha"; or that he
had intended to erect it at the place where Jesus had suffered
death.

[2] Plutarch, *De Sera Num. Vind.,* 19; Artemidorus, *Onirocrit.,*
ii. 56.

forced him to carry the fatal tree. Perhaps they made use of a recognized right of forcing labor, the Romans not being allowed to carry the infamous wood. It seems that Simon was afterward of the Christian community. His two sons, Alexander and Rufus,[1] were well known in it. He related perhaps more than one circumstance of which he had been witness. No disciple was at this moment near to Jesus.[2]

The place of execution was at last reached. According to Jewish custom, the sufferers were offered a strong aromatic wine, an intoxicating drink, which, through a sentiment of pity, was given to the condemned in order to stupefy him.[3] It appears that the ladies of Jerusalem often brought this kind of wine to the unfortunates who were led to execution; when none was presented by them, it was purchased from the public treasury.[4] Jesus, after having touched the edge of the cup with his lips, refused to drink.[5] This mournful consolation of ordinary sufferers did not accord with his exalted nature. He preferred to quit life with perfect clearness of mind, and to await in full consciousness the death he had willed and brought upon himself. He was then divested of his garments,[6] and fastened to the cross. The cross was composed of two beams, tied in the form of the letter **T**.[7] It was

[1] Mark xv. 21.
[2] The circumstance, *Luke* xxiii. 27-31, is one of those in which we are sensible of the work of a pious and loving imagination. The words which are there attributed to Jesus could only have been written after the siege of Jerusalem.
[3] Talm. of Bab., *Sanhedrim,* fol. 43 *a.* Comp. *Prov.* xxi. 6.
[4] Talm. of Bab., *Sanhedrim,* l. c.
[5] Mark xv. 23; Matt. xxvii. 34, falsifies this detail, in order to create a Messianic allusion from Ps. lxix. 20.
[6] Matt. xxvii. 35; Mark xv. 24; John xix. 23. Cf. Artemidorus, *Onirocr.,* ii. 53. [7] Lucian, *Jud. Voc.,* 12. Compare the grotesque crucifix traced at Rome on a wall of Mount Palatine. *Civilta Cattolica,* fasc. clxi. p. 529, and following.

not much elevated, so that the feet of the condemned almost touched the earth. They commenced by fixing it,[1] then they fastened the sufferer to it by driving nails into his hands; the feet were often nailed, though sometimes only bound with cords.[2] A piece of wood was fastened to the upright portion of the cross, toward the middle, and passed between the legs of the condemned, who rested upon it.[3] Without that, the hands would have been torn and the body would have sunk down. At other times, a small horizontal rest was fixed beneath the feet, and sustained them.[4]

Jesus tasted these horrors in all their atrocity. A burning thirst, one of the tortures of crucifixion,[5] devoured him, and he asked to drink. There stood near, a cup of the ordinary drink of the Roman soldiers, a mixture of vinegar and water, called *posca*. The soldiers had to carry with them their *posca* on all their expeditions,[6] of which an execution was considered one. A soldier dipped a sponge in this drink, put it at the end of a reed, and raised it to the lips of Jesus, who sucked it.[7] The two robbers were crucified, one on each side. The executioners, to whom were usually left the small effects (*pannicularia*) of those executed,[8] drew lots for his garments, and, seated at the foot of

[1] Jos., *B. J.*, vii. vi. 4; Cic., *In Verr.*, v. 66; Xenoph. Ephes., *Ephesiaca*, iv. 2.

[2] Luke xxiv. 39; John xx. 25-27; Plautius. *Mostellaria*, ii. i. 13; Lucan., *Phars.*, vi. 543, and following, 547; Justin, *Dial. cum Tryph.*, 97; Tertullian, *Adv. Marcionem*, iii. 19.

[3] Irenæus, *Adv. Nær.*, ii. 24; Justin, *Dial. cum Tryphone*, 91.

[4] See the *graffito* quoted before.

[5] See the Arab text published by Kosegarten, *Chrest. Arab.*, p. 64.

[6] Spartianus, *Life of Adrian*, 10; Vulcatius Gallicanus, *Life of Avidius Cassius*, 5.

[7] Matt. xxvii. 48; Mark xv. 36; Luke xxiii. 36; John xix. 28-30.

[8] Dig., xlvii. xx., *De bonis damnat.*, 6. Adrian limited this custom.

the cross, kept guard over him.[1]   According to one
tradition, Jesus pronounced this sentence, which was in
his heart if not upon his lips: "Father, forgive them,
for they know not what they do."[2]

According to the Roman custom, a writing was attached to the top of the cross, bearing, in three languages, Hebrew, Greek, and Latin, the words: "THE
KING OF THE JEWS." There was something painful
and insulting to the nation in this inscription. The
numerous passers-by who read it were offended. The
priests complained to Pilate that he ought to have
adopted an inscription which would have implied simply that Jesus had called himself King of the Jews.
But Pilate, already tired of the whole affair, refused to
make any change in what had been written.[3]

His disciples had fled. John, nevertheless, declares
himself to have been present, and to have remained
standing at the foot of the cross during the whole
time.[4] It may be affirmed, with more certainty, that
the devoted women of Galilee, who had followed Jesus
to Jerusalem and continued to tend him, did not abandon him. Mary Cleophas, Mary Magdalen, Joanna,
wife of Khouza, Salome, and others, stayed at a certain
distance,[5] and did not lose sight of him.[6] If we must

[1] Matt. xxvii. 36. Cf. Petronius, *Satyr.*, cxi. cxii.
[2] Luke xxiii. 34. In general, the last words attributed to Jesus,
especially such as Luke records, are open to doubt. The desire
to edify or to show the accomplishment of prophecies is percepti-
ble. In these cases, moreover, every one hears in his own way.
The last words of celebrated prisoners, condemned to death, are
always collected in two or three entirely different shapes, by
even the nearest witnesses.
[3] John xix. 19-22.   [4] John xix. 25, and following.
[5] The synoptics are agreed in placing the faithful group "afar
off" the cross. John says, "at the side of," governed by the desire which he has of representing himself as having approached
very near to the cross of Jesus.
[6] Matt. xxvii. 55, 56; Mark xv. 40, 41; Luke xxiii. 49, 55; xxiv.
10; John xix. 25. Cf. Luke xxiii. 27-31.

believe John,[1] Mary, the mother of Jesus, was also at
the foot of the cross, and Jesus seeing his mother and
his beloved disciple together, said to the one, "Behold
thy mother!" and to the other, "Behold thy son!" But
we do not understand how the synoptics, who name the
other women, should have omitted her whose presence
was so striking a feature. Perhaps even the extreme
elevation of the character of Jesus does not render
such personal emotion probable, at the moment when,
solely pre-occupied by his work, he no longer existed
except for humanity.[2]

Apart from this small group of women, whose presence consoled him, Jesus had before him only the spectacle of the baseness or stupidity of humanity. The
passers-by insulted him. He heard around him foolish scoffs, and his greatest cries of pain turned into
hateful jests: "He trusted in God; let him deliver him
now, if he will have him: for he said, I am the Son of
God. He saved others," they said again; "himself he

[1]John xix. 25, and following. Luke, who always adopts a
middle course between the first two synoptics and John, mentions also, but at a distance, "all his acquaintance" (xxiii. 49).
The expression, γνωστοί, may, it is true, mean "kindred."
Luke, nevertheless (ii. 44), distinguishes the γνωστοί from the
συγγενεῖς. Let us add, that the best manuscripts bear οἱ γνωστοὶ
αὐτω, and not οἱ γνωστοὶ αὐτου. In the *Acts* (i. 14), Mary, mother
of Jesus, is also placed in company with the Galilean women;
elsewhere (Gospel, chap. ii. 35), Luke predicts that a sword of
grief will pierce her soul. But this renders his omission of her
at the cross the less explicable.

[2]This is, in my opinion, one of those features in which John
betrays his personality and the desire he has of giving himself
importance. John, after the death of Jesus, appears in fact to
have received the mother of his Master into his house, and to
have adopted her (John xix. 27.) The great consideration which
Mary enjoyed in the early church, doubtless led John to pretend
that Jesus, whose favorite disciple he wished to be regarded, had,
when dying, recommended to his care all that was dearest to
him. The presence of this precious trust near John, insured him
a kind of precedence over the other apostles, and gave his doctrine a high authority.

cannot save.   If he be the king of Israel, let him now come down from the cross, and we will believe him! Ah, thou that destroyest the temple, and buildest it in three days, save thyself."[1]   Some, vaguely acquainted with his apocalyptic ideas, thought they heard him call Elias, and said, "Let us see whether Elias will come to save him."   It appears that the two crucified thieves at his side also insulted him.[2]   The sky was dark;[3] and the earth, as in all the environs of Jerusalem, dry and gloomy.   For a moment, according to certain narratives, his heart failed him; a cloud hid from him the face of his Father; he endured an agony of despair a thousand times more acute than all his torture.   He saw only the ingratitude of men; he perhaps repented suffering for a vile race, and exclaimed: "My God, my God, why hast thou forsaken me?"   But his divine instinct still prevailed.   In the degree that the life of the body became extinguished, his soul became clear, and returned by degrees to its celestial origin.   He regained the idea of his mission; he saw in his death the salvation of the world; he lost sight of the hideous spectacle spread at his feet, and, profoundly united to his Father, he began upon the gibbet the divine life which he was to live in the heart of humanity through infinite ages.

The peculiar atrocity of crucifixion was that one might live three or four days in this horrible state upon the instrument of torture.[4]   The hæmorrhage from the hands quickly stopped, and was not mortal.   The true

[1] Matt. xxvii. 40, and following; Mark xv. 29. and following.
[2] Matt. xxvii. 44; Mark xv. 32.   Luke has here modified the tradition, in accordance with his taste for the conversion of sinners.
[3] Matt. xxvii. 45; Mark xv. 33; Luke xxiii. 44.
[4] Petronius, *Sat.*, cxi., and following; Origen, *In Matt. Comment. series*, 140 Arab text published in Kosegarten, *ob. cit.*, p. 63, and following.

cause of death was the unnatural position of the body, which brought on a frightful disturbance of the circulation, terrible pains of the head and heart, and, at length, rigidity of the limbs.   Those who had a strong constitution only died of hunger.[1]   The idea which suggested this cruel punishment was not directly to kill the condemned by positive injuries, but to expose the slave nailed by the hand of which he had not known how to make good use, and to let him rot on the wood. The delicate organization of Jesus preserved him from this slow agony.   Everything leads to the belief that the instantaneous rupture of a vessel in the heart brought him, at the end of three hours, to a sudden death.   Some moments before yielding up his soul, his voice was still strong.[2]   All at once, he uttered a terrible cry,[3] which some heard as: "Father, into thy hands I commend my spirit!" but which others, more pre-occupied with the accomplishment of prophecies, rendered by the words, "It is finished!"   His head fell upon his breast, and he expired.

Rest now in thy glory, noble initiator.   Thy work is completed; thy divinity is established.   Fear no more to see the edifice of thy efforts crumble through a flaw. Henceforth, beyond the reach of frailty, thou shalt be present, from the height of thy divine peace, in the infinite consequences of thy acts.   At the price of a few hours of suffering, which have not even touched thy great soul, thou hast purchased the most complete immortality.   For thousands of years the world will extol thee.   Banner of our contradictions, thou wilt be the sign around which will be fought the fiercest battles.   A thousand times more living, a thousand times

[1] Eusebius, *Hist. Eccl.*, viii. 8.   [2] Matt. xxvii. 46; Mark xv. 34,
[3] Matt. xxvii. 50; Mark xv. 37; Luke xxiii. 46; John xix. 30.

more loved since thy death than during the days of thy
pilgrimage here below, thou wilt become to such a degree the corner-stone of humanity, that to tear thy
name from this world would be to shake it to its foun-
dations. Between thee and God, men will no longer
distinguish. Complete conqueror of death, take possession of thy kingdom, whither, by the royal road thou
has traced, ages of adorers will follow thee.

CHAPTER XXVI.

JESUS IN THE TOMB

It was about three o'clock in the afternoon, according to our manner of reckoning,[1] when Jesus expired. A Jewish law[2] forbade a corpse suspended on the cross to be left beyond the evening of the day of the execution. It is not probable that in the executions performed by the Romans this rule was observed; but as the next day was the Sabbath, and a Sabbath of peculiar solemnity, the Jews expressed to the Roman authorities[3] their desire that this holy day should not be profaned by such a spectacle.[4] Their request was granted; orders were given to hasten the death of the three condemned ones, and to remove them from the cross. The soldiers executed this order by applying to the two thieves a second punishment much more speedy than that of the cross, the *crurifragium,* or breaking of the legs,[5] the usual punishment of slaves and of prisoners of war. As to Jesus, they found him dead, and did not think it necessary to break his legs. But one of them, to remove all doubt as to the real death of the

[1] *Matt.* xxvii. 46; Mark xv. 37; Luke xxiii. 44. Comp. John xix. 14.

[2] *Deut.* xxi. 22, 23; Josh. viii. 29, x. 26, and following. Cf. Jos., *B. J.,* iv. v. 2; Mishnah, *Sanhedrim,* vi. 5.

[3] John says, "To Pilate"; but that cannot be, for Mark (xv. 44, 45) states that at night Pilate was still ignorant of the death of Jesus.

[4] Compare Philo, *In Flaccum,* § 10.

[5] There is no other example of the *crurifragium* applied after crucifixion. But often, in order to shorten the tortures of the sufferer, a finishing stroke was given him. See the passage from Ibn-Hischâm, translated in the *Zeitschrift für die Kunde des Morgenlandes,* i. p. 99, 100.

third victim, and to complete it, if any breath remained in him, pierced his side with a spear. They thought they saw water and blood flow, which was regarded as a sign of the cessation of life.

John, who professes to have seen it,[1] insists strongly on this circumstance. It is evident, in fact, that doubts arose as to the reality of the death of Jesus. A few hours of suspension on the cross appeared to persons accustomed to see crucifixions entirely insufficient to lead to such a result. They cited many instances of persons crucified, who, removed in time, had been brought to life again by powerful remedies.[2] Origen afterward thought it needful to invoke miracle in order to explain so sudden an end.[3] The same astonishment is found in the narrative of Mark.[4] To speak truly, the best guarantee that the historian possesses upon a point of this nature is the suspicious hatred of the enemies of Jesus. It is doubtful whether the Jews were at that time pre-occupied with the fear that Jesus might pass for resuscitated; but, in any case, they must have made sure that he was really dead. Whatever, at certain periods, may have been the neglect of the ancients in all that belonged to legal proof and the strict conduct of affairs, we cannot but believe that those interested here had taken some precautions in this respect.[5]

According to the Roman custom, the corpse of Jesus ought to have remained suspended in order to become the prey of birds.[6] According to the Jewish law, it

[1] John xix. 31-35.   [2] Herodotus, vii. 194; Jos., *Vita*, 75.
[3] *In Matt. Comment. series*, 140.   [4] Mark xv. 44, 45.
[5] The necessities of Christian controversy afterward led to the exaggeration of these precautions, especially when the Jews had systematically begun to maintain that the body of Jesus had been stolen. Matt. xxvii. 62, and following, xxviii. 11-15.
[6] Horace, *Epistles*, I. xvi. 48; Juvenal, xiv. 77; Lucan., vii. 544; Plautus, *Miles glor.*, II. iv. 19; Artemidorus, *Onir.*, ii. 53; Pliny,

would have been removed in the evening, and deposited
in the place of infamy set apart for the burial of those
who were executed.[1]   If Jesus had had for disciples
only his poor Galileans, timid and without influence,
the latter course would have been adopted.   But we
have seen that, in spite of his small success at Jerusalem, Jesus had gained the sympathy of some important
persons who expected the kingdom of God, and who,
without confessing themselves his disciples, were
strongly attached to him. One of these persons, Joseph,
of the small town of Arimathea (*Ha-ramathaïm*[2]),
went in the evening to ask the body from the procurator.[3] Joseph was a rich and honorable man, a member
of the Sanhedrim. The Roman law, at this period,
commanded, moreover, that the body of the person executed should be delivered to those who claimed it.[4]
Pilate, who was ignorant of the circumstance of the
crurifragium, was astonished that Jesus was so soon
dead, and summoned the centurion who had superin-
tended the execution, in order to know how this was.
Pilate, after having received the assurances of the centurion, granted to Joseph the object of his request.
The body probably had already been removed from the
cross.   They delivered it to Joseph, that he might do
with it as he pleased.

Another secret friend, Nicodemus,[5] whom we have
already seen employing his influence more than once in
favor of Jesus, came forward at this moment.   He ar-

---

xxxvi. 24; Plutarch, *Life of Cleomenes,* 39; Petronius. *Sat.,* cxi.-
cxii.   [1]Mishnah, *Sanhedrim,* vi. 5.
    [2]Probably identical with the ancient Rama of Samuel, in the
tribe of Ephraim.
    [3]Matt. xxvii. 57, and following; Mark xv. 42, and following;
Luke xxiii. 50, and following; John xix. 38, and following.
    [4]Dig. XLVIII. xxiv., *De cadaveribus punitorum.*
    [5]John xix. 39, and following.

rived, bearing ample provision of the materials necessary for embalming.   Joseph and Nicodemus interred
Jesus according to the Jewish custom—that is to say,
they wrapped him in a sheet with myrrh and aloes.
The Galilean women were present,[1] and no doubt ac-
accompanied the scene with piercing cries and tears.

It was late, and all this was done in great haste.
The place had not yet been chosen where the body
would be finally deposited.   The carrying of the body,
moreover, might have been delayed to a late hour, and
have involved a violation of the Sabbath—now the disciples still conscientiously observed the prescriptions of
the Jewish law.   A temporary interment was determined upon.[2]   There was at hand, in the garden, a
tomb recently dug out in the rock, which had never
been used.   It belonged, probably, to one of the believers.[3]   The funeral caves, when they were destined for
a single body, were composed of a small room, at the
bottom of which the place for the body was marked by
a trough or couch let into the wall, and surmounted by
an arch.[4]   As these caves were dug out of the sides of
sloping rocks, they were entered by the floor; the door

[1] Matt. xxvii. 61 ; Mark xv. 47 ; Luke xxiii. 55.
[2] John xix. 41, 42.
[3] One tradition (Matt. xxvii. 60) designates Joseph of Arimathea himself as owner of the cave.
[4] The cave which, at the period of Constantine, was considered
as the tomb of Christ, was of this shape, as may be gathered from
the description of Arculphus (in Mabillon, *Acta SS. Ord. S.
Bened.*, sec. iii., pars ii., p. 504), and from the vague traditions
which still exist at Jerusalem among the Greek clergy on the
state of the rock now concealed by the little chapel of the Holy
Sepulchre.   But the indications by which, under Constantine, it
was sought to identify this tomb with that of Christ, were feeble
or worthless (see especially Sozomen, *H. E.*, ii. 1.)   Even if we
were to admit the position of Golgotha as nearly exact, the Holy
Sepulchre would still have no very reliable character of authenticity.   At all events, the aspect of the places has been totally
modified.

was shut by a stone very difficult to move. Jesus was deposited in the cave, and the stone was rolled to the door, as it was intended to return in order to give him a more complete burial. But the next day being a solemn Sabbath, the labor was postponed till the day following.[1]

The women retired after having carefully noticed how the body was laid. They employed the hours of the evening which remained to them in making new preparations for the embalming. On the Saturday all rested.[2]

On the Sunday morning, the women, Mary Magdalen the first, came very early to the tomb.[3] The stone was displaced from the opening, and the body was no longer in the place where they had laid it. At the same time, the strangest rumors were spread in the Christian community. The cry, "He is risen!" quickly spread amongst the disciples. Love caused it to find ready credence everywhere. What had taken place? In treating of the history of the apostles we shall have to examine this point and to make inquiry into the origin of the legends relative to the resurrection. For the historian, the life of Jesus finishes with his last sigh. But such was the impression he had left in the heart of his disciples and of a few devoted women, that during some weeks more it was as if he were living and consoling them. Had his body been taken away,[4] or did enthusiasm, always credulous, create afterward the group of narratives by which it was sought to establish faith in the resurrection? In the absence of opposing documents this can never be ascer-

[1] Luke xxiii. 56.
[2] Luke xxiii. 54-56.
[3] Matt. xxviii. 1; Mark xvi. 1; Luke xxiv. 1; John xx. 1.
[4] See Matt. xxviii. 15; John xx. 2.

tained. Let us say, however, that the strong imagination of Mary Magdalen[1] played an important part in this circumstance.[2] Divine power of love! Sacred moments in which the passion of one possessed gave to the world a resuscitated God!

[1] She had been possessed by seven demons (Mark xvi. 9; Luke viii. 2.)

[2] This is obvious, especially in the ninth and following verses of chap. xvi. of Mark. These verses form a conclusion of the second Gospel, different from the conclusion at xvi. 1-8, with which many manuscripts terminate. In the fourth Gospel (xx. 1, 2, 11, and following, 18), Mary Magdalen is also the only original witness of the resurrection.

CHAPTER XXVII.

FATE OF THE ENEMIES OF JESUS.

ACCORDING to the calculation we adopt, the death of Jesus happened in the year 33 of our era.[1] It could not, at all events, be either before the year 29, the preaching of John and Jesus having commenced in the year 28,[2] or after the year 35, since in the year 36, and probably before the passover, Pilate and Kaïapha both lost their offices.[3] The death of Jesus appears, moreover, to have had no connection whatever with these two removals.[4] In his retirement, Pilate probably never dreamt for a moment of the forgotten episode, which was to transmit his pitiful renown to the most distant posterity. As to Kaïapha, he was succeeded by Jonathan, his brother-in-law, son of the same Hanan who had played the principal part in the trial of Jesus. The Sadducean family of Hanan retained the pontificate a long time, and more powerful than ever, continued to wage against the disciples and the family of Jesus, the implacable war which they had commenced against the Founder. Christianity, which owed to him the definitive act of its foundation, owed to him also its first

[1] The year 33 corresponds well with one of the data of the problem, namely, that the 14th of Nisan was a Friday. If we reject the year 33, in order to find a year which fulfils the above condition, we must at least go back to the year 29, or go forward to the year 36.

[2] Luke iii. 1.   [3] Jos., *Ant.*, XVIII. iv. 2 and 3.

[4] The contrary assertion of Tertullian and Eusebius arises from a worthless apocryphal writing (See Philo, *Cod. Apocr., N. T.*, p. 813, and following.) The suicide of Pilate (Eusebius, *H. E.*, ii. 7; *Chron.* ad annl. Caii) appears also to be derived from legendary records.

martyrs. Hanan passed for one of the happiest men of his age.[1] He who was truly guilty of the death of Jesus ended his life full of honors and respect, never having doubted for an instant that he had rendered a great service to the nation. His sons continued to reign around the temple, kept down with difficulty by the procurators,[2] ofttimes dispensing with the consent of the latter in order to gratify their haughty and violent instincts.

Antipas and Herodias soon disappeared also from the political scene. Herod Agrippa having been raised to the dignity of king by Caligula, the jealous Herodias swore that she also would be queen. Pressed incessantly by this ambitious woman, who treated him as a coward, because he suffered a superior in his family, Antipas overcame his natural indolence, and went to Rome to solicit the title which his nephew had just obtained (the year 39 of our era). But the affair turned out in the worst possible manner. Injured in the eyes of the emperor by Herod Agrippa, Antipas was removed, and dragged out the rest of his life in exile at Lyons and in Spain. Herodias followed him in his misfortunes.[3] A hundred years, at least, were to elapse before the name of their obscure subject, now become deified, should appear in these remote countries to brand upon their tombs the murder of John the Baptist.

As to the wretched Judas of Kerioth, terrible legends were current about his death. It was maintained that he had bought a field in the neighborhood of Jerusalem with the price of his perfidy. There was, indeed, on the south of Mount Zion, a place named *Hakeldama*

---

[1] Jos., *Ant.*, xx. ix. 1. [2] Jos., *l. c.*
[3] Jos., *Ant.*, xviii. vii. 1, 2; *B. J.*, ii. ix. 6.

(the field of blood[1]). It was supposed that this was
the property acquired by the traitor.[2] According to
one tradition,[3] he killed himself. According to another, he had a fall in his field, in consequence of which
his bowels gushed out.[4] According to others, he died
of a kind of dropsy, accompanied by repulsive circumstances, which were regarded as a punishment from
heaven.[5] The desire of showing in Judas the accomplishment of the menaces which the Psalmist pro-
nounces against the perfidious friend[6] may have given
rise to these legends. Perhaps, in the retirement of
his field of Hakeldama, Judas led a quiet and obscure
life; while his former friends conquered the world, and
spread his infamy abroad. Perhaps, also, the terrible
hatred which was concentrated on his head, drove him
to violent acts, in which were seen the finger of heaven.

The time of the great Christian revenge was, moreover, far distant. The new sect had no part whatever
in the catastrophe which Judaism was soon to undergo.
The synagogue did not understand till much later to
what it exposed itself in practising laws of intolerance.
The empire was certainly still further from suspecting
that its future destroyer was born. During nearly
three hundred years it pursued its path without suspect-

[1] St. Jerome, *De situ et nom loc. hebr.* at the word *Acheldama.*
Eusebius (*ibid.*) says to the north But the Itineraries confirm
the reading of St. Jerome. The tradition which styles the necrop-
olis situated at the foot of the valley of Hinnom *Haceldama,*
dates back, at least, to the time of Constantine.

[2] *Acts* i. 18, 19. Matthew, or rather his interpolator, has here
given a less satisfactory turn to the tradition, in order to connect with it the circumstance of a cemetery for strangers, which
was found near there.   [3] Matt. xxvii. 5.

[4] *Acts. l. c.*: Papias, in Œcumenius, *Enarr. in Act. Apost.,* ii.,
and in Fr. Münter, *Fragm. Patrum Græc.* (Hafniæ, 1788), fasc. i.
p. 17, and following: Theophylactus, in Matt. xxvii. 5.

[5] Papias, in Münter, *l. c.;* Theophylactus, *l. c.*

[6] Psalms lxix. and cix.

ing that at its side principles were growing destined to subject the world to a complete transformation. At once theocratic and democratic, the idea thrown by Jesus into the world was, together with the invasion of the Germans, the most active cause of the dissolution of the empire of the Cæsars. On the one hand, the right of all men to participate in the kingdom of God was proclaimed. On the other, religion was henceforth separated in principle from the state. The rights of conscience, withdrawn from political law, resulted in the constitution of a new power—the "spiritual power." This power has more than once belied its origin. For ages the bishops have been princes, and the Pope has been a king. The pretended empire of souls has shown itself at various times as a frightful tyranny, employing the rack and the stake in order to maintain itself. But the day will come when the separation will bear its fruits, when the domain of things spiritual will cease to be called a "power," that it may be called a "liberty." Sprung from the conscience of a man of the people, formed in the presence of the people, beloved and admired first by the people, Christianity was impressed with an original character which will never be effaced. It was the first triumph of revolution, the victory of the popular idea, the advent of the simple in heart, the inauguration of the beautiful as understood by the people. Jesus thus, in the aristocratic societies of antiquity, opened the breach through which all will pass.

The civil power, in fact, although innocent of the death of Jesus (it only countersigned the sentence, and even in spite of itself), ought to bear a great share of the responsibility. In presiding at the scene of Calvary, the state gave itself a serious blow. A legend full of all kinds of disrespect prevailed, and became universally known—a legend in which the constituted authorities played a hateful part, in which it was the accused that was right, and in which the judges and the guards were leagued against the truth. Seditious in the highest degree, the history of the Passion, spread by a thousand popular images, displayed the Roman eagles as sanctioning the most iniquitous of executions, soldiers executing it, and a prefect commanding it. What a blow for all established powers! They have never entirely recovered from it. How can they assume infallibility in respect to poor men, when they have on their conscience the great mistake of Gethsemane?[1]

[1] This popular sentiment existed in Brittany in the time of my childhood. The gendarme was there regarded, like the Jew elsewhere, with a kind of pious aversion, for it was he who arrested Jesus!

CHAPTER XXVIII.

ESSENTIAL CHARACTER OF THE WORK OF JESUS.

JESUS, it will be seen, limited his action entirely to the Jews. Although his sympathy for those despised by orthodoxy led him to admit pagans into the kingdom of God—although he had resided more than once in a pagan country, and once or twice we surprise him in kindly relations with unbelievers[1]—it may be said that his life was passed entirely in the very restricted world in which he was born. He was never heard of in Greek or Roman countries; his name appears only in profane authors of a hundred years later, and then in an indirect manner, in connection with seditious movements provoked by his doctrine, or persecutions of which his disciples were the object.[2] Even on Judaism, Jesus made no very durable impression. Philo, who died about the year 50, had not the slightest knowledge of him. Josephus, born in the year 37, and writing in the last years of the century, mentions his execution in a few lines,[3] as an event of secondary importance, and in the enumeration of the sects of his time, he omits the Christians altogether.[4] In the *Mishnah,* also, there is no trace of the new school; the passages in the two Gemaras in which the founder of Christianity is named, do not go further back than the fourth or

[1] Matt. viii. 5, and following; Luke vii. 1, and following; John xii. 20, and following. Comp. Jos., *Ant.,* XVIII. iii. 3.

[2] Tacitus, *Ann.,* xv. 45; Suetonius, *Claudius,* 25.

[3] *Ant.,* XVIII. iii. 3. This passage has been altered by a Christian hand.

[4] *Ant.,* XVIII. i.; *B. J.,* II. viii.; *Vita,* 2.

fifth century.[1]   The essential work of Jesus was to create around him a circle of disciples, whom he inspired
with boundless affection, and amongst whom he deposited the germ of his doctrine.   To have made himself beloved, "to the degree that after his death they
ceased not to love him," was the great work of Jesus,
and that which most struck his contemporaries.[2]   His
doctrine was so little dogmatic, that he never thought
of writing it or of causing it to be written.   Men did
not become his disciples by believing this thing or that
thing, but in being attached to his person and in loving
him.   A few sentences collected from memory, and
especially the type of character he set forth, and the
impression it had left, were what remained of him.
Jesus was not a founder of dogmas, or a maker of
creeds; he infused into the world a new spirit.   The
least Christian men were, on the one hand, the doctors
of the Greek Church, who, beginning from the fourth
century, entangled Christianity in a path of puerile
metaphysical discussions, and, on the other, the scho-
lastics of the Latin Middle Ages, who wished to draw
from the Gospel the thousands of articles of a colossal
system.   To follow Jesus in expectation of the kingdom of God, was all that at first was implied by being
Christian.

It will thus be understood how, by an exceptional
destiny, pure Christianity still preserves, after eighteen
centuries, the character of a universal and eternal religion.   It is, in fact, because the religion of Jesus is in

[1] Talm. of Jerusalem, *Sanhedrim*, xiv. 16; *Aboda zara*, ii. 2;
Shabbath, xiv. 4, Talm. of Babylon, *Sanhedrim*, 43 *a*, 67 *a*; *Shabbath*, 104 *b*, 116 *b*. Comp. *Chagiga*, 4 *b*; *Gittin*, 57 *a*, 90 *a*. The two
Gemaras derive the greater part of their data respecting Jesus
from a burlesque and obscene legend, invented by the adversaries of Christianity, and of no historical value.
[2] Jos., *Ant.*, xviii. iii. 3.

some respects the final religion. Produced by a perfectly spontaneous movement of souls, freed at its birth from all dogmatic restraint, having struggled three hundred years for liberty of conscience, Christianity, in spite of its failures, still reaps the results of its glorious origin. To renew itself, it has but to return to the Gospel. The kingdom of God, as we conceive it, differs notably from the supernatural apparition which the first Christians hoped to see appear in the clouds. But the sentiment introduced by Jesus into the world is indeed ours. His perfect idealism is the highest rule of the unblemished and virtuous life. He has created the heaven of pure souls, where is found what we ask for in vain on earth, the perfect nobility of the children of God, absolute purity, the total removal of the stains of the world; in fine, liberty, which society excludes as an impossibility, and which exists in all its amplitude only in the domain of thought. The great Master of those who take refuge in this ideal kingdom of God is still Jesus. He was the first to proclaim the royalty of the mind; the first to say, at least by his actions, "My kingdom is not of this world." The foundation of true religion is indeed his work: after him, all that remains is to develop it and render it fruitful.

"Christianity" has thus become almost a synonym of "religion." All that is done outside of this great and good Christian tradition is barren. Jesus gave religion to humanity, as Socrates gave it philosophy, and Aristotle science. There was philosophy before Socrates and science before Aristotle. Since Socrates and since Aristotle, philosophy and science have made immense progress; but all has been built upon the foundation which they laid. In the same way, before Jesus, religious thought had passed through many revolutions; since Jesus, it has made great conquests: but no one has improved, and no one will improve upon the essential principle Jesus has created; he has fixed forever the idea of pure worship. The religion of Jesus in this sense is not limited. The Church has had its epochs and its phases; it has shut itself up in creeds which are, or will be but temporary: but Jesus has founded the absolute religion, excluding nothing, and determining nothing unless it be the spirit. His creeds are not fixed dogmas, but images susceptible of indefinite interpretations. We should seek in vain for a theological proposition in the Gospel. All confessions of faith are travesties of the idea of Jesus, just as the scholasticism of the Middle Ages, in proclaiming Aristotle the sole master of a completed science, perverted the thought of Aristotle. Aristotle, if he had been present in the debates of the schools, would have repudiated this narrow doctrine; he would have been of the party of progressive science against the routine which shielded itself under his authority; he would have applauded his opponents. In the same way, if Jesus were to return among us, he would recognize as disciples, not those who pretend to enclose him entirely in a few catechismal phrases, but those who labor to carry on his work. The eternal glory, in all great things, is to have laid the first stone. It may be that in the "Physics," and in the "Meteorology" of modern times, we may not discover a word of the treatises of Aristotle which bear these titles; but Aristotle remains no less the founder of natural science. Whatever may be the transformations of dogma, Jesus will ever be the creator of the pure spirit of religion; the Sermon on the Mount will never be surpassed. Whatever revolution takes place will not prevent us attaching ourselves in religion to the grand intellectual and moral line at the head of which shines the name of Jesus. In this sense we are Christians, even when we separate ourselves on almost all points from the Christian tradition which has preceded us.

And this great foundation was indeed the personal work of Jesus. In order to make himself adored to this degree, he must have been adorable. Love is not enkindled except by an object worthy of it, and we should know nothing of Jesus, if it were not for the passion he inspired in those about him, which compels us still to affirm that he was great and pure. The faith, the enthusiasm, the constancy of the first Christian generation is not explicable, except by supposing at the origin of the whole movement, a man of surpassing greatness. At the sight of the marvellous creations of the ages of faith, two impressions equally fatal to good historical criticism arise in the mind. On the one hand we are led to think these creations too impersonal; we attribute to a collective action, that which has often been the work of one powerful will, and of one superior mind. On the other hand, we refuse to see men like ourselves in the authors of those extraordinary movements which have decided the fate of humanity. Let us have a larger idea of the powers which Nature conceals in her bosom. Our civilizations, governed by minute restrictions, cannot give us any idea of the power of man at periods in which the originality of each one had a freer field wherein to develop itself. Let us imagine a recluse dwelling in the mountains near our capitals, coming out from time to time in order to present himself at the palaces of sovereigns, compelling the sentinels to stand aside, and, with an imperious tone, announcing to kings the approach of revolutions of which he had been the promoter. The very idea provokes a smile. Such, however, was Elias; but Elias the Tishbite, in our days, would not be able to pass the gate of the Tuileries. The preaching of Jesus, and his free activity in Galilee, do not deviate less completely from the social conditions to which we are accustomed. Free from our polished conventionalities, exempt from the uniform education which refines us, but which so greatly dwarfs our individuality, these mighty souls carried a surprising energy into action. They appear to us like the giants of an heroic age, which could not have been real. Profound error! Those men were our brothers; they were of our stature, felt and thought as we do. But the breath of God was free in them; with us, it is restrained by the iron bonds of a mean society, and condemned to an irremediable mediocrity.

Let us place, then, the person of Jesus at the highest summit of human greatness. Let us not be misled by exaggerated doubts in the presence of a legend which keeps us always in a superhuman world. The life of Francis d'Assisi is also but a tissue of miracles. Has any one, however, doubted of the existence of Francis d'Assisi, and of the part played by him? Let us say no more that the glory of the foundation of Christianity belongs to the multitude of the first Christians, and not to him whom legend has deified. The inequality of men is much more marked in the East than with us. It is not rare to see arise there, in the midst of a general atmosphere of wickedness, characters whose greatness astonishes us. So far from Jesus having been created by his disciples, he appeared in everything as superior to his disciples. The latter, with the exception of St. Paul and St. John, were men without either invention or genius. St. Paul himself bears no comparison with Jesus, and as to St. John, I shall show hereafter, that the part he played, though very elevated in one sense, was far from being in all respects irreproachable. Hence the immense superiority of the Gospels among the writings of the New Testament. Hence the painful fall we experience in passing from the history of Jesus to that of the apostles. The evangelists themselves, who have bequeathed us the image of Jesus, are so much beneath him of whom they speak, that they constantly disfigure him, from their inability to attain to his height. Their writings are full of errors and misconceptions. We feel in each line a discourse of divine beauty, transcribed by narrators who do not understand it, and who substitute their own ideas for those which they have only half understood. On the whole, the character of Jesus, far from having been embellished by his biographers, has been lowered by them. Criticism, in order to find what he was, needs to discard a series of misconceptions, arising from the inferiority of the disciples. These painted him as they understood him, and often in thinking to raise him, they have in reality lowered him.

I know that our modern ideas have been offended more than once in this legend, conceived by another race, under another sky, and in the midst of other social wants. There are virtues which, in some respects, are more conformable to our taste. The virtuous and gentle Marcus Aurelius, the humble and gentle Spinoza, not having believed in miracles, have been free from some errors that Jesus shared. Spinoza, in his profound obscurity, had an advantage which Jesus did not seek. By our extreme delicacy in the use of means of conviction, by our absolute sincerity and our

disinterested love of the pure idea, we have founded—
all we who have devoted our lives to science—a new
ideal of morality. But the judgment of general history ought not to be restricted to considerations of personal merit. Marcus Aurelius and his noble teachers
have had no permanent influence on the world. Marcus Aurelius left behind him delightful books, an ex-
ecrable son, and a decaying nation. Jesus remains an
inexhaustible principle of moral regeneration for
humanity. Philosophy does not suffice for the multitude. They must have sanctity. An Apollonius of
Tyana, with his miraculous legend, is necessarily more
successful than a Socrates with his cold reason.
"Socrates," it was said, "leaves men on the earth, Apollonius transports them to heaven; Socrates is but a
sage, Apollonius is a god."[1] Religion, so far, has not
existed without a share of asceticism, of piety, and of
the marvellous. When it was wished, after the Antonines, to make a religion of philosophy, it was requisite
to transform the philosophers into saints, to write the
"Edifying Life" of Pythagoras or Plotinus, to attribute
to them a legend, virtues of abstinence, contemplation,
and supernatural powers, without which neither credence nor authority were found in that age.

Preserve us, then, from mutilating history in order
to satisfy our petty susceptibilities! Which of us, pig-
mies as we are, could do what the extravagant Francis
d'Assisi, or the hysterical saint Theresa, has done? Let
medicine have names to express these grand errors of
human nature; let it maintain that genius is a disease
of the brain; let it see, in a certain delicacy of morality, the commencement of consumption; let it class en-

[1] Philostratus, *Life of Apollonius,* i. 2, vii. 11, viii. 7; Unapius,
Lives of the Sophists, pages 454, 500 (edition Didot).

thusiasm and love as nervous accidents — it matters
little.   The terms healthy and diseased are entirely
relative.   Who would not prefer to be diseased like
Pascal, rather than healthy like the common herd?
The narrow ideas which are spread in our times respecting madness, mislead our historical judgments in
the most serious manner, in questions of this kind.   A
state in which a man says things of which he is not
conscious, in which thought is produced without the
summons and control of the will, exposes him to being
confined as a lunatic.   Formerly this was called prophecy and inspiration.   The most beautiful things in the
world are done in a state of fever; every great creation
involves a breach of equilibrium, a violent state of the
being which draws it forth.

We acknowledge, indeed, that Christianity is too
complex to have been the work of a single man.   In
one sense, entire humanity has co-operated therein.
There is no one so shut in, as not to receive some influence from without.   The history of the human mind
is full of strange coincidences, which cause very remote
portions of the human species, without any communication with each other, to arrive at the same time at
almost identical ideas and imaginations.   In the thirteenth century, the Latins, the Greeks, the Syrians, the
Jews, and the Mussulmans, adopted scholasticism, and
very nearly the same scholasticism from York to
Samarcand; in the fourteenth century every one in
Italy, Persia, and India, yielded to the taste for mystical allegory; in the sixteenth, art was developed in a
very similar manner in Italy, at Mount Athos, and at
the court of the Great Moguls, without St. Thomas,
Barhebræus, the Rabbis of Narbonne, or the *Motécallé-
min* of Bagdad, having known each other, without

Dante and Petrarch having seen any *sofi,* without any pupil of the schools of Perouse or of Florence having been at Delhi. We should say there are great moral influences running through the world like epidemics, without distinction of frontier and of race. The interchange of ideas in the human species does not take place only by books or by direct instruction. Jesus was ignorant of the very name of Buddha, of Zoroaster, and of Plato; he had read no Greek book, no Buddhist Sudra; nevertheless, there was in him more than one element, which, without his suspecting it, came from Buddhism, Parseeism, or from the Greek wisdom. All this was done through secret channels and by that kind of sympathy which exists among the various portions of humanity. The great man, on the one hand, receives everything from his age; on the other, he governs his age. To show that the religion founded by Jesus was the natural consequence of that which had gone before, does not diminish its excellence; but only proves that it had a reason for its existence that it was legitimate, that is to say, conformable to the instinct and wants of the heart in a given age.

Is it more just to say that Jesus owes all to Judaism, and that his greatness is only that of the Jewish people? No one is more disposed than myself to place high this unique people, whose particular gift seems to have been to contain in its midst the extremes of good and evil. No doubt, Jesus proceeded from Judaism; but he proceeded from it as Socrates proceeded from the schools of the Sophists, as Luther proceeded from the Middle Ages, as Lamennais from Catholicism, as Rousseau from the eighteenth century. A man is of his age and his race even when he reacts against his age and his race. Far from Jesus having continued Judaism, he represents the rupture with the Jewish spirit. The general direction of Christianity after him does not permit the supposition that his idea in this respect could lead to any misunderstanding. The general march of Christianity has been to remove itself more and more from Judaism. It will become perfect in returning to Jesus, but certainly not in returning to Judaism. The great originality of the founder remains then undiminished; his glory admits no legitimate sharer.

Doubtless, circumstances much aided the success of this marvellous revolution; but circumstances only second that which is just and true. Each branch of the development of humanity has its privileged epoch, in which it attains perfection by a sort of spontaneous instinct, and without effort. No labor of reflection would succeed in producing afterward the masterpieces which Nature creates at those moments by inspired geniuses. That which the golden age of Greece was for arts and literature, the age of Jesus was for religion. Jewish society exhibited the most extraordinary moral and intellectual state which the human species has ever passed through. It was truly one of those divine hours in which the sublime is produced by combinations of a thousand hidden forces, in which great souls find a flood of admiration and sympathy to sustain them. The world, delivered from the very narrow tyranny of small municipal republics, enjoyed great liberty. Roman despotism did not make itself felt in a disastrous manner until much later, and it was, moreover, always less oppressive in those distant provinces than in the centre of the empire. Our petty preventive interferences (far more destructive than death to things of the spirit) did not exist. Jesus, during three

years, could lead a life which, in our societies, would
have brought him twenty times before the magistrates.
Our laws upon the illegal exercise of medicine would
alone have sufficed to cut short his career.   The unbelieving dynasty of the Herods, on the other hand, occupied itself little with religious movements; under the
Asmoneans, Jesus would probably have been arrested
at his first step.   An innovator, in such a state of society, only risked death, and death is a gain to those who
labor for the future.   Imagine Jesus reduced to bear
the burden of his divinity until his sixtieth or seven-
tieth year, losing his celestial fire, wearing out little by
little under the burden of an unparalleled mission!
Everything favors those who have a special destiny;
they become glorious by a sort of invincible impulse
and command of fate.

This sublime person, who each day still presides over
the destiny of the world, we may call divine, not in the
sense that Jesus has absorbed all the divine, or has been
adequate to it (to employ an expression of the school-
men), but in the sense that Jesus is the one who has
caused his fellow-men to make the greatest step toward
the divine.   Mankind in its totality offers an assem-
blage of low beings, selfish, and superior to the animal
only in that its selfishness is more reflective.   From
the midst of this uniform mediocrity, there are pillars
that rise toward the sky, and bear witness to a nobler
destiny.   Jesus is the highest of these pillars which
show to man whence he comes, and whither he ought
to tend.   In him was condensed all that is good and elevated in our nature.   He was not sinless; he has conquered the same passions that we combat; no angel of
God comforted him, except his good conscience; no
Satan tempted him, except that which each one bears

in his heart.   In the same way that many of his great qualities are lost to us, through the fault of his disciples, it is also probable that many of his faults have been concealed.   But never has any one so much as he made the interests of humanity predominate in his life over the littlenesses of self-love.   Unreservedly devoted to his mission, he subordinated everything to it to such a degree that, toward the end of his life, the universe no longer existed for him.   It was by this access of heroic will that he conquered heaven.   There never was a man, Cakya-Mouni perhaps excepted, who has to this degree trampled under foot, family, the joys of this world, and all temporal care.   Jesus only lived for his Father and the divine mission which he believed himself destined to fulfill.

As to us, eternal children, powerless as we are, we who labor without reaping, and who will never see the fruit of that which we have sown, let us bow before these demi-gods.   They were able to do that which we cannot do: to create, to affirm, to act.   Will great originality be born again, or will the world content itself henceforth by following the ways opened by the bold creators of the ancient ages?   We know not.   But whatever may be the unexpected phenomena of the future, Jesus will not be surpassed.   His worship will constantly renew its youth, the tale of his life will cause ceaseless tears, his sufferings will soften the best hearts; all the ages will proclaim that, among the sons of men, there is none born who is greater than Jesus.

[THE END.]

The Best of the World's Best Books
COMPLETE LIST OF TITLES IN
THE MODERN LIBRARY

MISCELLANEOUS

MODERN LIBRARY GIANTS

A series of sturdily bound and handsomely printed, full-sized library editions of books formerly available only in expensive sets. These volumes contain from 600 to 1,400 pages each.

THE MODERN LIBRARY GIANTS REPRESENT A SELECTION OF THE WORLD'S GREATEST BOOKS

MISCELLANEOUS